Moodle 4 E-Learning Course Development

Fifth Edition

The definitive guide to creating great courses in
Moodle 4.0 using instructional design principles

Susan Smith Nash

BIRMINGHAM—MUMBAI

Moodle 4 E-Learning Course Development
Fifth Edition

Group Product Manager: Pavan Ramchandani
Publishing Product Manager: Bhavya Rao
Senior Editor: Aamir Ahmed
Content Development Editor: Feza Shaikh
Technical Editor: Joseph Aloocaran and Shubham Sharma
Copy Editor: Safis Editing
Project Coordinator: Manthan Patel
Proofreader: Safis Editing
Indexer: Tejal Daruwale Soni
Production Designer: Aparna Bhagat
Marketing Coordinator: Anamika Singh and Marylou De Mello

First published: May 2006
Second edition: Jun 2008
Third edition: Jan 2016
Fourth edition: May 2018
Fifth edition: June 2022

Production reference: 2220722

Published by Packt Publishing Ltd.
Livery Place
35 Livery Street
Birmingham
B3 2PB, UK.

ISBN 978-1-80107-903-7

www.packt.com

Dedicated with love and gratitude to my parents

– Susan Smith Nash

Contributors

About the author

Susan Smith Nash has been developing and administering online courses for more than 20 years for both academic and professional training purposes. She earned her Bachelor's of Science, Masters of Art, and Ph.D. at the University of Oklahoma. She has been widely published in the area of instructional design as well as in energy and economic development. Her books for Packt include Moodle E-Learning Course Development, Moodle 3.X Teaching Techniques, and Moodle Course Design Best Practices. Susan's interests include the development and promotion of new technologies and she enjoys studying films from the Golden Age of Mexican cinema, as well as hiking and tennis. Susan lives in Oklahoma, near her son and his family.

About the reviewer

Ian Wild is a solutions architect, software developer, author, and educator with over 25 years of experience working in technology-based roles. He is currently a Principal Technologist for AVEVA, focused on designing and developing solutions to integrate AVEVA's portfolio of cloud-based simulation applications into the AVEVA™ Unified Learning training platform. He has traveled the world working as an eLearning consultant and trainer, helping educators deliver inspiring and engaging online learning. Ian has authored some popular textbooks like Moodle Course Conversion, Moodle Math, and Moodle 3.x Developer's Guide. He was also a technical reviewer on Science Teaching with Moodle, Moodle Multimedia, and Practical XMPP.

Table of Contents

3
Creating Categories and Courses

Part 2: Implementing The Curriculum

4
Managing Resources, Activities, and Conditional Access

5
Adding Resources to Your Moodle Course

6
Adding Assignments, Lessons, Feedback, and Choice

7

Evaluating Students with Quizzes

8

Getting Social with Chats and Forums

9
Collaborating with Wikis and Glossaries

10
Running a Workshop

11
Groups and Cohorts

Part 3: Power Tools for Teachers and Administrators

12
Extending Your Course by Adding Blocks

13
Features for Teachers: Logs, Reports, and Guides

Index

Other Books You May Enjoy

Preface

Moodle 4.0 maintains its flexible, powerful, and easy-to-use platform and adds great new features to enhance the user experience for student success.

This edition addresses the opportunities that come with this major update, Moodle 4.0. You'll learn how to incorporate sound instructional design in the powerful tools in Moodle to achieve your course goals and learning objectives. In doing so, your courses will become effective for instructors, students, course developers, program managers, teaching assistants, and system administrators alike. You'll learn how to plan an effective course with the best mix of resources and engaging assessments that really show what the learner has learned, and also keep them engaged and on track for success. You'll learn how to make sure your students enjoy their collaborations and truly learn from each other. You'll learn how to generate reports and know exactly how the courses are going and what to do to get them back on track. While doing this, you can use Moodle 4.0's new navigation features to help students keep from getting lost. By the end of this book, you will be able to build and deploy your educational program to align with learning objectives and include a full array of course content. You will be able to incorporate "functionality boosters" and accommodate changing needs and goals in our evolving world.

Who this book is for

This book is for novice as well as experienced course developers who would like to incorporate Moodle 4.0's powerful features and make life easier for students, instructors, and administrators. The program also helps with accreditation and deploying across devices to people in diverse situations.

What this book covers

Chapter 1, A Guided Tour of Moodle, explains what Moodle can do and what kind of user experience your students and teachers will have when using Moodle. You will also learn about the Moodle philosophy and how it shapes the user experience. With this information, you'll be ready to decide how to make the best use of Moodle's many features and plan your online learning site.

Chapter 2, Installing Moodle and Configuring Your Site, shows you how to get Moodle up and running for your organization, with an emphasis on cloud-based Moodle. We will help you create the user experience that you want by choosing the right settings for your Moodle installation. By configuring your site to enhance the user experience, you'll enhance their learning experience as well.

Chapter 3, Creating Categories and Courses, explains how to how to create the course, choose the best format for your course considering your course objectives, and enroll students into the course. In addition, we will ensure that the course is well designed and that you are continuously mindful of how learning will take place.

Chapter 4, Managing Resources, Activities, and Conditional Access, provides an overview of the content that goes into your course and explains how to manage it on the course level.

Chapter 5, Adding Resources to Your Moodle Course, shows you how to identify the appropriate resources to add and achieve the course learning objectives, manage the resources, and then use them effectively.

Chapter 6, Adding Assignments, Lessons, Feedback, and Choice, explains how to build course content that provides instructional material while also motivating the learner with engagers and by giving feedback and indicating where they are on the path to the successful achievement of their learning outcomes.

Chapter 7, Evaluating Students with Quizzes, examines Moodle's powerful solution that allows well-designed and well-placed quizzes, and the ability to tie the quizzes in with mastery learning, competency frameworks, certificates, and badges.

Chapter 8, Getting Social with Chats and Forums, teaches you how to add Moodle's communication activities to a course and how to make the best use of them. It includes chats, forums, and other forms of social media.

Chapter 9, Collaborating with Wikis and Glossaries, explains how to develop effective collaborative activities that help achieve learning objectives by adding wikis and glossaries to your course.

Chapter 10, Running a Workshop, shows you how to create a collaborative workshop in Moodle that can include student peer reviews at the heart of the interaction.

Chapter 11, Groups and Cohorts, looks at definitions of groups and cohorts in terms of how they relate to e-learners. We will then discuss the best time and the best way to organize students into groups and cohorts to achieve course learning objectives.

Chapter 12, Extending Your Course by Adding Blocks, describes many of Moodle's blocks, helps you decide which ones will meet your goals, and tells you how to implement them.

Chapter 13, Features for Teachers: Logs, Reports, Guides, covers how to generate and use the many logs, reports, and guides available in Moodle 4.0.

To get the most out of this book

Software/hardware covered in the book	Browser or Operating System support
Moodle 4.0 client	Chrome, Firefox, Safari, Edge
Moodle 4.0 mobile	MobileSafari, Google Chrome
Microsoft Office	Windows, macOS, or Linux

Download the color images

We also provide a PDF file that has color images of the screenshots and diagrams used in this book. You can download it here: `https://packt.link/Hit3O`.

Conventions used

There are a number of text conventions used throughout this book.

`Code in text`: Indicates code words in text, database table names, folder names, filenames, file extensions, pathnames, dummy URLs, user input, and Twitter handles. Here is an example: "You can enter any characters. If you enter @, it will be converted to sequential letters. If you enter #, it will be converted to sequential numbers."

Bold: Indicates a new term, an important word, or words that you see onscreen. For instance, words in menus or dialog boxes appear in **bold**. Here is an example: "Select **Site Administration | Enrolments | Self enrolment. Self enrolment** allows users to choose which courses they want to participate in."

> Tips or important notes
> Appear like this.

Get in touch

Feedback from our readers is always welcome.

General feedback: If you have questions about any aspect of this book, email us at `customercare@packtpub.com` and mention the book title in the subject of your message.

Errata: Although we have taken every care to ensure the accuracy of our content, mistakes do happen. If you have found a mistake in this book, we would be grateful if you would report this to us. Please visit www.packtpub.com/support/errata and fill in the form.

Piracy: If you come across any illegal copies of our works in any form on the internet, we would be grateful if you would provide us with the location address or website name. Please contact us at copyright@packt.com with a link to the material.

If you are interested in becoming an author: If there is a topic that you have expertise in and you are interested in either writing or contributing to a book, please visit authors.packtpub.com.

Share Your Thoughts

Once you've read, we'd love to hear your thoughts! Scan the QR code below to go straight to the Amazon review page for this book and share your feedback.

https://packt.link/r/180107903X

Your review is important to us and the tech community and will help us make sure we're delivering excellent quality content.

Part 1: Getting started

Welcome to Moodle! In this first part of the book, you'll learn about Moodle's philosophy of learning and the way to find and use the unique, open-source Moodle learning management system.

What makes this book unique is that it is much more than just a technical guide for using Moodle. It's a guide that builds in reliable instructional design principles at every step of the way so that you are designing not only courses but an entire learning plan that will help your students succeed and achieve learning objectives and institutional goals.

In addition, you'll be given great guidance as you create a course design plan, and you'll be encouraged to use a course map to make sure that the kinds of resources, assessments, and interactions are aligned with your course goals and that your students will actually learn what they need to learn. You'll also benefit from great suggestions and guidance for encouraging interaction and engagement to help boost course completions and student success.

In this part, we cover the following chapters:

- *Chapter 1, A Guided Tour of Moodle*
- *Chapter 2, Installing Moodle and Configuring Your Site*
- *Chapter 3, Creating Categories and Courses*

1
A Guided Tour of Moodle

With a global pandemic, supply chain issues, and political and economic upheavals resulting in school and work disruptions, the need for online education and training that works in today's world has increased by leaps and bounds. Have online programs kept up? Have the **learning management systems (LMSs)** they use been able to satisfy the thousands of first-time e-learners who may be having to do their work in relative isolation on a phone or tablet, rather than a laptop or desktop system? In many cases, the answer is a resounding "no." Online education experiences have been lambasted for being ineffectual, and educators and training providers openly worry about "lost years" of failure-riddled transitions to e-learning.

What are the main problems? By and large, students and instructors who are new to e-learning and are working remotely do not succeed when learning experiences are complicated, hard to follow, and provided in a single format, such as text only. Almost without exception, they fail when they do not feel they are in touch with anyone, but are adrift and alone, with infrequent, if any, interaction.

Even Moodle, which has emphasized learner interaction, collaboration, and engagement since its inception in 2002, was assailed by detractors. Even though Moodle put out frequent updates, and at the start of 2022 was in version 3.11, it wasn't enough. So, Moodle underwent a massive update with version 4.0, with an emphasis on the user experience. To tackle the issue of getting lost, Moodle makes it easy to navigate. The new design is engaging and new, with refreshed activities keeping students engaged and on track, and instructors informed. Moodle 4.0 has an entirely different user experience and has new features, such as an integrated Dashboard with a built-in Calendar and timeline, which pull in all the deadlines and important dates in an easy, at-a-glance, clickable interface. Many improvements have been made to the activities and resources, and all of them work even better than ever with themes that are more responsive than ever so that they work equally well on tablets, laptops, smartphones, and desktops.

Moodle is designed to be intuitive to use, and its online help is well written. It does a good job of telling you how to use each of its features. What Moodle's help files don't tell you is when and why to use each feature and what effect it will have on the student experience, so that is what this book supplies.

So, with that, we'll get started with a guided tour of Moodle. The goal of this introductory chapter is to give you an overview of the tremendous flexibility and customizability of Moodle, one of the world's most popular and widely used learning platforms. After this chapter, we will learn how to design and develop outcomes-based learning programs that can be used for both training and education, and that follow instructional design principles and accommodate educational psychology to maximize learning.

Moodle is a free, open source LMS that enables you to create powerful, flexible, and engaging online learning experiences. I use the phrase *online learning experiences* instead of *online courses* deliberately. The phrase *online course* often connotes a sequential series of web pages, some images, maybe a few animations, and a quiz put online. There might be some email or bulletin board communication between the teacher and students. However, online learning can be much more engaging than that, especially in a world where we have become more accustomed to incorporating "live" (also called "synchronous") experiences with "on-demand" (also referred to as "asynchronous") content to do as much as possible to replicate the interactions in face-to-face learning. With Moodle 4.0, the user experience is much more streamlined and intuitive than in previous versions, and you can interact more easily using your laptop, tablet, smartphone, or desktop devices. For teachers and administrators, there are more features and options than ever in Moodle 4.0, which opens up more opportunities for you to design a learning experience that results in satisfied students who can demonstrate that they've achieved the course goals.

In this chapter, we will cover the following topics:

- The history of Moodle
- Moodle's philosophy
- A plan to create your learning site
- Step-by-step instructions for using Moodle
- Applying the Module philosophy
- The Moodle experience

In this chapter, you will learn what Moodle can do and what kind of user experience your students and teachers will have when using Moodle. You will also learn about the Moodle philosophy and how it shapes the user experience. With this information, you'll be ready to decide how to make the best use of Moodle's many features and plan your online learning site. First, we will learn about the history of Moodle.

The history of Moodle

As we prepare to embark on our journey, let's take a step back and learn about where Moodle got its name, and how it was developed.

Moodle's name gives you an insight into its approach to e-learning. The official Moodle documentation at `http://docs.moodle.org` states the following:

> *The word Moodle was originally an acronym for Modular Object-Oriented Dynamic Learning Environment, which is mostly useful to programmers and education theorists. It's also a verb that describes the process of lazily meandering through something, doing things as it occurs to you to do them, an enjoyable tinkering that often leads to insight and creativity. As such, it applies both to the way Moodle was developed and to the way a student or teacher might approach studying or teaching an online course. Anyone who uses Moodle is a Moodler.*

The phrase *online learning experience* connotes a more active, engaging role for students and teachers. It connotes, among other things, web pages that can be explored in any order, courses with live chats among students and teachers, forums where users can rate messages on their relevance or insight, online workshops that enable students to evaluate one another's work, impromptu polls that let the teacher evaluate what students think of a course's progress, and directories set aside for teachers to upload and share their files. All these features create an active learning environment, full of different kinds of student-to-student and student-to-teacher interactions. This is the kind of user experience that Moodle excels at and the kind that this book will help you create.

The next section describes **connectivism**, which is the underlying learning philosophy of Moodle, and explains how and why people learn from each other.

Moodle's philosophy of learning

For those of you who are interested, the underlying learning philosophy of Moodle is that of "connectivism." This means that people learn from one another, and Moodle's framework is structured to maximize interactivity with other students and the content itself. When Moodle first debuted, the philosophy usually involved forums, with some potential for real-time chat. However, with the ability to include webinars using BigBlueButton and other add-ins, the possibilities of synchronous (real-time) and asynchronous interactivity have expanded.

One thing to keep in mind as you develop a course that incorporates connectivism as a learning philosophy is that you'll be working with the affective (the emotional) as well as the cognitive domain. This means that you will be engaging the emotions (which is good for motivation). Connectivism also means that you can encourage the sharing of experiences and allow people to build on prior knowledge and experience. Building courses that allow students to scaffold their knowledge with experiential and prior learning can give rise to a very solid approach. Your students will be able to do more with their knowledge, particularly if the course has to do with applied knowledge and skills.

Keep in mind how you will advance the learning objectives as you develop the course. What kinds of students will you have? Will they be in cohorts or be learning individually? How much interaction will be effective? Now, let's learn how to create a plan for your learning site. Even though Moodle was designed for collaborative interaction, it is a very flexible platform and you can design courses for individual self-guided learning as well.

A plan to create your learning site

Whether you are the site creator or a course creator, you can use this book to develop a plan to build your courses and curriculum. As you work your way through each chapter, you will learn how to make decisions that meet your goals for your learning site.

This will help you create the kind of learning experience that you want for your teachers (if you're a site creator) or students (if you're a teacher). You can also use this book as a traditional reference manual, but its main advantages are its step-by-step, project-oriented approach and the guidance it gives you about creating an interactive learning experience.

One of the most exciting new developments with Moodle is that Moodle now has a cloud-based **virtual learning environment** (**VLE**) called **MoodleCloud**. It is free for you to use for 2 weeks if you have fewer than 50 registered users (students, instructors, and so on). You can still customize the course, and you can build in a great deal of flexibility and functionality. It does not have the same number of options as a self-hosted site that you can customize with some of the Moodle partners, but it is straightforward, affordable, and easy to use. MoodleCloud allows you to experiment with designs and also start by building a smaller site or cluster of courses that you intend to grow. It also makes it easy for individuals and organizations to develop new kinds of training, collaboration, and education, and then scale up when needed. Furthermore, MoodleCloud is effective for incorporating webinars offered through its built-in activities, BigBlueButton, or linking to outside webinar providers such as Zoom, GoToMeeting, Google Meet, Teams, and more.

The next section provides an overview of what is contained in each chapter.

Step-by-step instructions for using Moodle

When you create a Moodle learning site, you usually follow a series of defined steps. This book has been arranged to support that process. Each chapter will show you how to get the most out of each step. Each step in this section is listed with a brief description of the chapter that supports that step.

As you work your way through each chapter, your learning site will grow in scope and sophistication. By the time you finish this book, you should have a complete, interactive learning site. As you learn more about what Moodle can do and see your courses taking shape, you may want to change some of the things that you did in the previous chapters. Moodle offers you this flexibility. This book also helps you determine how those changes will cascade throughout your site.

Step 1 – learning about the Moodle experience

Every **LMS** has a paradigm, or model, that shapes the user experience and encourages a certain kind of usage. An LMS may encourage very sequential learning by offering features that enforce a given order on each course. It may discourage student-to-student interaction by offering few features that support it while encouraging solo learning by offering many opportunities for the student to interact with the course material.

In this chapter, you will learn what Moodle can do and what kind of user experience your students and teachers will have when using Moodle. You will also learn about the Moodle philosophy and how it shapes the user experience. With this information, you'll be ready to decide how to make the best use of Moodle's many features and plan your online learning site.

Step 2 – installing Moodle and configuring your site

Chapter 2, Installing Moodle and Configuring Your Site, goes into more depth about how to either install Moodle, customize a solution with a Moodle partner, or use a standard cloud-based installation such as MoodleCloud. This chapter will help you decide on the right hosting service for your needs. It will also help you install and configure Moodle so that it works in the way you would like.

Functionality booster: If you would like to find the latest ways to customize your Moodle installation or add new apps, you can visit the Moodle docs. Here is a link to the Moodle docs for version 4.0: `https://docs.moodle.org/400/en/Main_page`.

Step 3 – creating the framework for your learning site

In Moodle, every course belongs to a category. *Chapter 3, Creating Categories and Courses*, will take you through creating course categories and then creating courses. Just as you chose site-wide settings during installation and configuration, you can choose course-wide settings while creating each course. This chapter will tell you the implications of the various course settings so that you can create the experience that you want for each course. It will also show you how to add teachers and students to the courses.

Step 4 – making decisions about common settings

In Moodle, course material is either a resource or an activity. A resource is an item that the student views, listens to, reads, or downloads. An activity is an item that the student interacts with or that enables the student to interact with the teacher or other students. In *Chapter 4, Managing Resources, Activities, and Conditional Access*, you will learn about the settings that are common to all resources and activities and how to add resources and activities to a course.

Step 5 – adding basic course material

In most online courses, the core material consists of web pages that the students view. These pages can contain text, graphics, movies, sound files, games, exercises – anything that can appear on the **World Wide Web (WWW)** can appear on a Moodle web page. In *Chapter 5, Adding Resources to Your Moodle Course*, you will learn how to add this kind of material, plus find links to other websites, media files, labels, and directories of files. This chapter will also help you determine when to use each of these types of material.

Step 6 – making your courses interactive

In this context, interactive means an interaction between the student and the teacher, or the student and an active web page. Student-to-student interaction is covered in *Chapter 5, Adding Resources to Your Moodle Course*. This chapter covers activities that involve interaction between the student and an active web page, or between the student and the teacher. Interactive course material includes lessons that guide students through a defined path, based on their answers to review questions and the assignments that are uploaded by the student and then graded by the teacher. *Chapter 6, Adding Assignments, Lessons, Feedback, and Choices*, tells you how to create these interactions and how each of them affects the student and teacher experience.

Step 7 – evaluating your students

In *Chapter 7, Evaluating Students with Quizzes*, you'll learn how to evaluate students' knowledge with a quiz. This chapter thoroughly covers creating quiz questions, sharing quiz questions with other courses, adding feedback to questions and quizzes, and more.

Step 8 – making your course social

Social course material enables student-to-student interaction. Moodle enables you to add chats and forums to your courses. These types of interactions will be familiar to many students. *Chapter 8, Getting Social with Chats and Forums*, will show you how to create and manage these social activities.

Step 9 – adding collaborative activities

Moodle enables students to work together to create new material. For example, you can create glossaries that are site-wide and those that are specific to a single course. Students can add to these glossaries. You can also allow students to contribute to and edit a wiki in class.

Moodle also offers a powerful workshop tool, which enables students to view and evaluate each other's work.

Each of these interactions makes the course more interesting but also more complicated for the teacher to manage. The result is a course that encourages the students to contribute, share, and engage. *Chapter 9, Collaborating with Wikis and Glossaries*, and *Chapter 10, Running a Workshop*, will help you rise to the challenge of managing your students' collaborative work.

Step 10 – managing and extending your courses

Chapter 11, Groups and Cohorts, will show you how to use groups to separate the students in a course. You will also learn how to use cohorts, or site-wide groups, to mass enroll students into courses.

Every block adds functionality to your site or your course. *Chapter 12, Extending Your Course by Adding Blocks*, will describe many of Moodle's blocks, help you decide which ones will meet your goals, and tell you how to implement them. You can use blocks to display calendars, enable commenting, enable tagging, show navigation features, and much more.

Step 11 – taking the pulse of your course

Moodle offers several tools to help teachers administer and deliver courses. It keeps detailed access logs that enable teachers to see exactly what content the students access, and when. It also enables teachers to establish custom grading scales, which are available site-wide or for a single course. Student grades can be accessed online and can also be downloaded in a variety of formats (including spreadsheets). Finally, teachers can collaborate in special forums (bulletin boards) reserved just for them. This is what will be covered in *Chapter 13, Features for Teachers: Logs, Reports, and Guides*.

As you put together the course site, you will build in the Moodle philosophy, which incorporates both connectivism ideas about how people learn, as well as social constructionism, both of which stress interactivity.

Applying the Moodle philosophy

Moodle is designed to support a style of learning called **social connectivism**. This style of learning is interactive. The social connectivist philosophy emphasizes collaboration and believes that people learn best when they interact with the learning material, construct new material for others, and interact with other students about the material. The difference between a traditional philosophy and the social connectivist philosophy is the difference between a lecture and a discussion.

Adding resources

Moodle does not require you to use the social connectivist method for your courses. However, it best supports this method. For example, Moodle enables you to add several kinds of resources that students can interact with and use for their foundational instructional material, and then interact with in collaborations, assessments, and more. There are various resources in Moodle 4.0. We will go over the use and function of each one in a later chapter. Please note that Moodle 4.0 features redesigned icons:

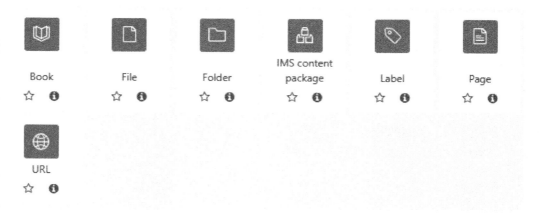

Figure 1.1 – Resources in Moodle 4.0 demonstrating new icons

Let's look at these icons in more detail:

- **Book**: A multi-page resource with chapters and subchapters
- **File**: Digital content that can include supporting files
- **Folder**: Bundles files together
- **IMS content package**: A collection of files packaged according to an agreed-upon standard to be reused in different systems

- **Label**: Information inserted between links to other resources and activities
- **Page**: A web page resource created using the text editor
- **URL**: A web link

Activities

Moodle enables you to add even more kinds of interactive and social course material. This is the course material that a student interacts with by answering questions, entering text, uploading files, and more. The following screenshot shows the various Moodle activities, along with their new icons, which were updated in Moodle 4.0. We will look at these in more detail later in this book. A quick introduction will suffice here:

Figure 1.2 – Activities in Moodle 4.0 demonstrating new icons

Let's look at these icons in more detail:

- **Assignment**: Allows you to upload files to be reviewed by the teacher.
- **BigBlueButton**: A webinar with many features.
- **Chat**: Provides live online chat between students.
- **Choice**: Multiple-choice questions, plus interactive "Did You Know" engagers.
- **Database**: A collection of entries/records.

- **External tool**: Enables you to interact with resources and websites.

- **Feedback**: Custom surveys with multiple question types.

- **Forum**: Asynchronous discussions.

- **Glossary**: Students and/or teachers can contribute terms to site-wide glossaries.

- **H5P**: An HTML5 package containing interactive content launched from within Moodle.

- **Lesson**: A conditional, branching activity.

- **Quiz**: Many different types of questions are provided here, including multiple choice, matching, short answer, and numerical.

- **SCORM package**: A collection of files that are packaged under an agreed standard, focused on learning objects.

- **Survey**: Verified survey instruments that can be used for many different purposes.

- **Wiki**: This is a familiar tool for collaboration with most younger students and many older students.

- **Workshop**: This supports peer review and feedback for the assignments that the students upload.

In addition, some of Moodle's Plugin add-on modules called "**blocks**" add even more types of interaction. For example, a developer has created a block called "**Appointments**," which provides a form for teachers to book 1 on 1 appointments with students. The students can be notified and it can be added to both the teacher's and the student's calendars. Note that the Calendar is also a block. Now, let's learn how to shape the learning experience with Moodle.

The Moodle experience

As Moodle encourages interaction and exploration, your students' learning experience will often be non-linear. Moodle can enforce a specific order upon a course using something called **conditional activities**. Conditional activities can be arranged in a sequence. Your course can contain a mix of conditional and non-linear activities.

In this section, I'll take you on a tour of a Moodle learning site. You will see a student's experience from the time the student arrives at the site, enters a course, and works through some material in the course. You will also see some student-to-student interaction and some functions that are used by the teacher to manage the course.

Working with the demonstration sites to learn and practice

Moodle.org contains two types of demonstration sites where you can start a course from scratch or experiment with courses that are already partially completed and populated. They are both in Moodle 4.0. You can choose your role so that you can experiment with being a student, teacher, manager, administrator, and more. To enter the site and begin, go to `https://moodle.org/demo`:

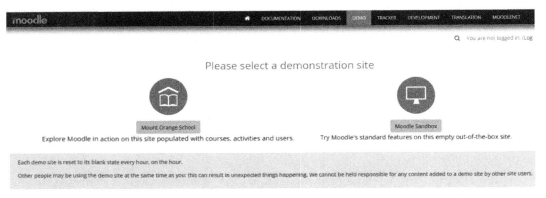

Figure 1.3 – The Moodle demo site has two options: starting from scratch via Moodle Sandbox or partially completed and populated courses via Mount Orange School

> **Tip**
>
> The Sandbox option has more roles and is often easier to use if you want to practice working with plugins. It is located at `https://sandbox.moodledemo.net/`. You will need to log in as an administrator.

The demo site – Mount Orange School

Let's take a look at the way that the site is set up. Notice that there is a menu at the very top of the screen. It provides several menu items, including **Home**, **Dashboard**, **My courses**, and **Site administration**. On the right-hand side, you'll see a column of menu items that says **Main menu**. This is a "block" that has been set up to help students quickly find their way through the course and go to the places that have been set up. This aspect is new in Moodle 4.0:

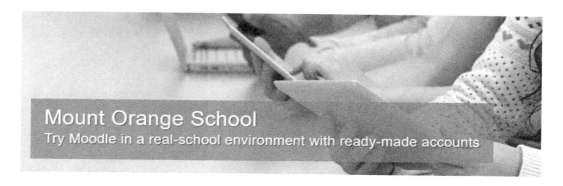

Mount Orange School
Try Moodle in a real-school environment with ready-made accounts
See Moodle in action
This demonstration site gives you the opportunity to explore Moodle in action as a manager, teacher, student, parent or privacy officer. See how students are assessed and learning tracked in a variety of activities with realistic user content.
Choose a role »
About Mount Orange
Mount Orange School provides high quality education for students aged from 8 to 18 years, making full use of the open source learning platform Moodle. The courses are open to guests and showcase Moodle features, highlighting the enhancements each new version brings.
Go to courses »

Figure 1.4 – The Mount Orange School demo, which can be customized

The following is a close-up of the navigation bar at the top of the screen:

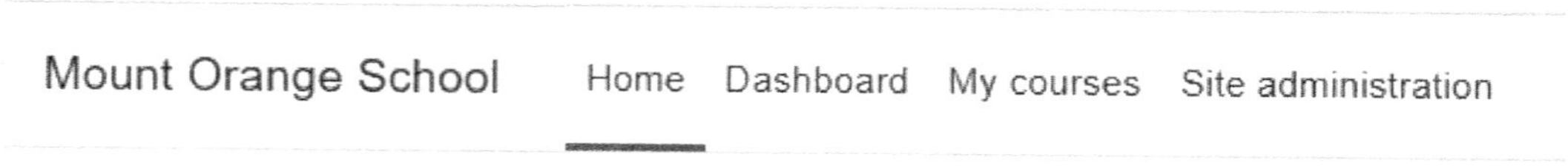
Mount Orange School
Home
Dashboard
My courses
Site administration

Figure 1.5 – A close-up of the navigation bar

Let's review each option:

- **Home**: This is the page you're on now. To edit it, go up to the top right-hand corner and click on the **Edit mode** slider button. Once you've turned that on, you'll see that little pencil icons and gear icons pop up everywhere, ready for you to start editing.
- **Dashboard**: This is a valuable tool that helps students organize their tasks, manage time, and then track the progress of their courses. Any time that you upload a resource or an activity that has a date due, it will appear in the calendar and the timeline.

- **My courses**: This screen lists the courses that you have enrolled in. It is different than the listing of courses on the site's **Home** page, which will list all the courses for the site.

- **Site administration**: This page looks different for different users. For a person with administrator permissions, when you click on the link, a page will open with different categories of configurations. Once you open the **Site administration** page, you'll see a horizontal navigation bar with a list of links. They include the following:

  - **General**: This contains all the general settings and utilities, which range from analytics, competencies, and badges, to licenses and security. The important thing to remember with this list is that all the settings are universal, site-wide settings. You can customize the different courses so that they have independent settings.

  - **Users**: This is where you administer site-wide settings for user accounts, permissions, privacy, and more.

  - **Courses**: This is where you manage and access all the courses and categories on the site, upload new courses, set activity chooser settings, and set up backups.

  - **Grades**: Here, you can set the site-wide settings for grades, grading scales, grade categories, and more. You can also set up site-wide grader reports and grade history.

  - **Plugins**: Moodle 4.0 has a wide array of plugins, which are also activities and controls. If you want your site to do something, chances are, you can find it as a plugin. Keep in mind that plugins can be site-wide or specific to a course or a course category. For an at-a-glance look at the default settings and availability of the different plugins, you can click **Plugins overview**.

  - **Appearance**: This is where you can set the appearance of your site and incorporate themes. The default themes in the demo site are **Boost** and **Classic**.

  - **Server**: Unless you are an administrator, you will have very few reasons to tamper with server settings. However, you may need to look at tasks, email configurations, and web services.

  - **Reports**: This area contains various performance reports for the software and activity of Moodle.

  - **Development**: This area contains links for developers who are creating new code or enhancing and customizing their installation of Moodle. There is a template library that makes it easy to get started. Cookbooks are widely available in Moodle repositories and on GitHub.

Just for fun, let's log in as though we are an administrator for the Moodle Sandbox demo and see what it looks like as we start to configure the site and a course.

Logging in as an administrator on the Sandbox demo site

You've registered as an administrator and have logged in. Now, you can experiment with your first course. Once you've logged in, you'll see that you can switch roles or maintain your role as an administrator. Scroll down and you'll see a link to **My first course**:

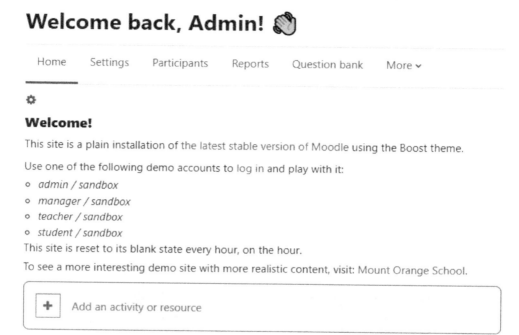

Figure 1.6 – Selecting the role for your demonstration experience

Using moodlecloud.com for cloud-based hosting

Moodle has created a cloud-based version of Moodle, which allows you to set up courses, develop a *sandbox*, and launch courses. It is located at `https://moodlecloud.com/app/en/login`. The pricing depends on the number of users and courses. MoodleCloud is hosted by Moodle and always has the latest version and supports several themes. However, it does not offer all the different themes, and may not be as robust as a solution for those with dedicated servers. I've used it often and I like it. The only downside is that there is sometimes a time lag.

The main menu

Log into MoodleCloud or the Sandbox site. Be sure to switch on **Edit mode** in the top right-hand corner. For the Sandbox demo site, please to go to sandbox.moodledemo. net. Note **Moodle sandbox demo** in the left of the following screenshot. Under that, you'll see a horizontal line of menu items:

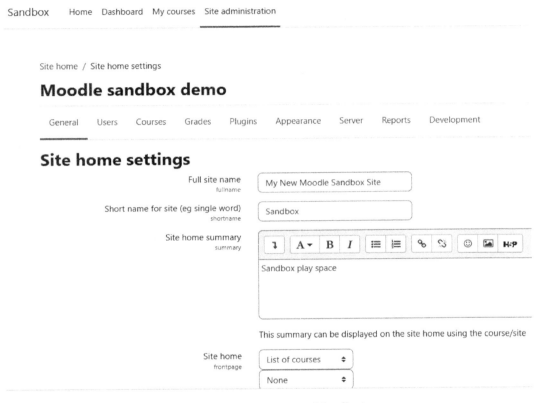

Figure 1.7 – Setting up a new Moodle site

Once you've set up your site, you'll see that there are several menu items on the upper row. They have changed in Moodle 4.0 and make it easier for you to go to the most often-used categories in Moodle. You will see **Home**, **Settings**, **Participants**, **Reports**, **Question Bank**, and **More**:

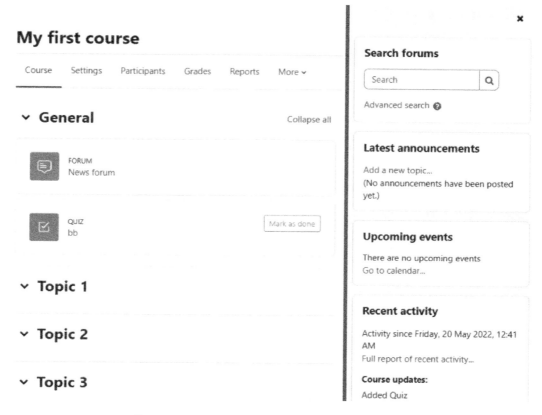

Figure 1.8 – Setting up Moodle 4.0 at the course level

Let's look at these categories in more detail:

- **Home**: This is your site's home page and can be configured to describe the school, list courses, and more.

- **Settings**: This category allows you to set the site's home name, summary, and announcements, as well as adding blocks, such as a Calendar block and a Timeline block.

- **Participants**: Here, you can enroll, unenroll, and manage users. While managing users, you can create groups, groupings, manage permissions, and assign roles.

- **Reports**: Reports have been expanded in Moodle 4.0. You can add competency breakdowns and upload guidelines and rubrics. In addition, you can generate user logs and look at live logs of user activity. You can even create activity reports, track course participation, generate statistics, and set up rules for monitoring events.

- **Question bank**: The fact that the Question Bank appears in the menu of the site's home page is new in Moodle 4.0. It has been set up this way to make it easier for you to develop and manage questions that will then be used for quiz activities. Quizzes of all sorts constitute the heart of many courses, and part of the job of a Moodle site administrator or teacher is to develop, classify, manage, and deploy these questions. We'll learn how to write effective quiz questions, as well as showing you how to work with quizzes and quiz questions, later in this book.

- **More**: This dropdown menu contains three links which relate to your site's content and functionality. The links are: **Content bank**, **Filters**, and **Course reuse**.

Modifying the course and menu items

As always, to be able to edit a course or the menu items, you'll need to go to the top right-hand side of the page and click on **Edit mode**. After that, you can add activities, resources, plugins, and more. We'll go into all of that throughout this book. For now, let's look at how the Moodle experience has been enhanced through Moodle 4.0. Notice that **My courses** still lists your courses, but now, it shows which ones are in progress, and how much of each has been completed:

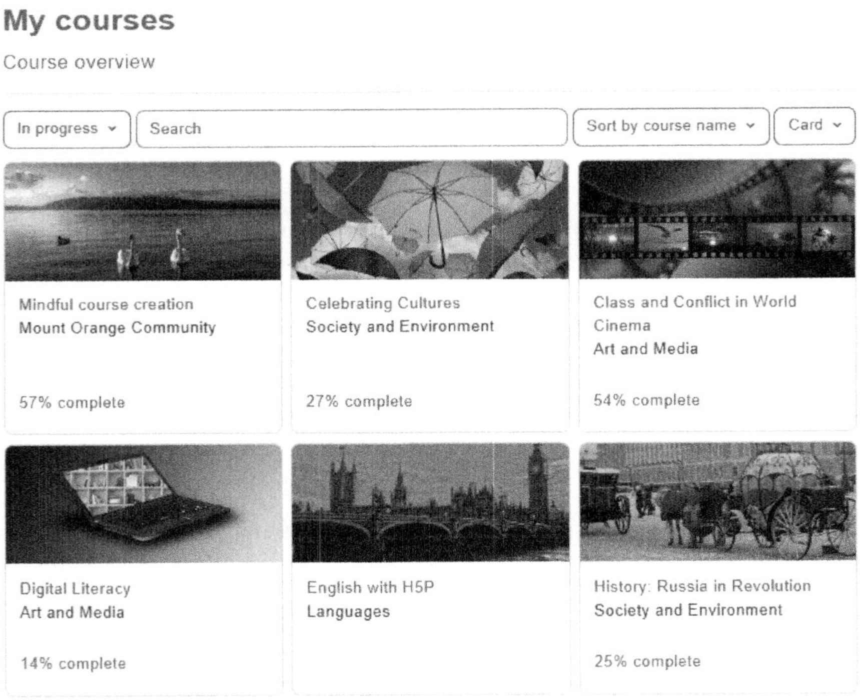

Figure 1.9 – Moodle 4.0's My courses page with a course overview that shows the percentage completed for each course

Then, to further enhance the user experience and enhance time management and develop self-efficacy, Moodle 4.0 has improved the course Timeline, as well as the course Calendar, so that they show the student's deadlines, which can be combined with group members if desired:

Figure 1.10 – Moodle 4.0's updated Timeline and Calendar

Summary

Moodle encourages exploration and interaction among students and teachers. Moodle 4.0's new, redesigned icons, enhanced navigation, and improved user experience have a positive impact on collaboration, interaction, and reflection, resulting in a platform that enhances its core social constructionist pedagogy. As a course designer and teacher, you will have the maximum number of tools at your disposal if you work in this way, which will make your learning experiences as interactive as possible. Creating courses with forums, peer-assessed workshops, surveys, and interactive lessons is more work than creating a course from a series of static web pages. However, it is also more engaging and effective, and you will find it worth the effort to use Moodle's many interactive features. Moodle's design is focused on enhancing learning, and you will enjoy the features that make self-guided and collaborative learning effective.

In this chapter, we learned about the history, development, and underlying philosophy of Moodle. We also learned the basics of how to start designing a site in which you'll build courses, and then include activities and resources in them.

Keep in mind that if you're using the cloud-based VLE version of Moodle, MoodleCloud, you will have built-in options and may not be able to modify the course in the way you could if you had a customized installation from a Moodle partner or a self-hosted installation.

Now, it's time to learn about the basics of Moodle's architecture, and at least read over the installation and configuration information provided in *Chapter 2, Installing Moodle and Configuring Your Site*. Don't be afraid of the technology. If you can master the difficult art of teaching, you can master using Moodle to its full potential.

2
Installing Moodle and Configuring Your Site

In today's world of cloud computing, it is most efficient and economical for organizations to opt into a cloud-based Moodle installation provided by a Moodle partner or `Moodlecloud.com`. Your students will be accessing Moodle from an array of different devices, and Moodle 4.0's brand-new default theme, which is based on Boost, is completely responsive, with new **Site home** options and an easy-to-follow Dashboard. The result is a user experience that helps you stay organized, never miss a deadline, and always know how to get back to the last pages you visited.

In this chapter, we will focus on getting Moodle up and running for your organization, with an emphasis on cloud-based Moodle. We will help you create the user experience that you want by choosing the right settings for your Moodle installation. By configuring your site to enhance the user experience, you'll enhance the user's learning experience as well. In this chapter, you will learn how to configure your Moodle site. Specifically, you will learn how to do the following:

- Configure Moodle.
- Set permissions and select default options.
- Enable site administration, configure permissions, and enroll students.

This chapter will cover the following main topics:

- A brave new Zoom world – planning for blended/hybrid synchronous and asynchronous delivery
- Exploring the site administration menu
- Different languages used in cloud-based Moodle
- Configuring the Dashboard and the **Site home** page

After completion of this chapter, you will be able to get Moodle 4.0 up and running, not only for your organization but also for your personal "sandbox" use. To do so, we focus on cloud-based Moodle, and we review the kinds of considerations you need to keep in mind as you plan for "live" and "on-demand" delivery, and learning that takes place through well-planned interaction, collaboration, and assessment.

Theme and Appearance

Note that in this book I will be using the new Moodle 4.0 theme, as well as the MoodleCloud *Classic* theme. Moodle 4.0 has continued to enhance the user experience, which includes setting up Moodle. Here's a screenshot that uses the Moodle 4.0 Boost theme and shows the new 4.0 Dashboard, with the Timeline at the top, the "at a glance" calendar at the bottom, and **Recently accessed items** on the right:

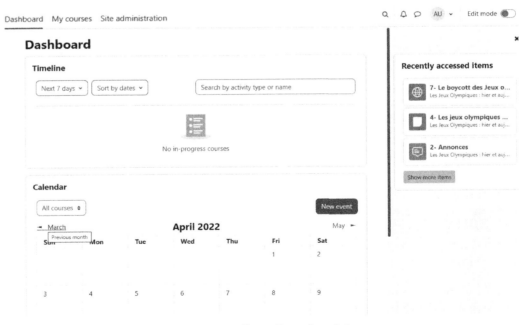

Figure 2.1 – Moodle 4.0 Boost-based theme

Moodle provides very convenient standards, which makes it easy for you to create uniform courses that have an attractive appearance. They can be used for all types of delivery modes that have become popular in today's environment, with institutions often required to offer courses in synchronous, asynchronous, and "blended" delivery modes.

A locally hosted installation

We recommend a cloud-based Moodle installation for most of you because we assume that your primary concern will be to develop and administer online courses that your students, teachers, and administrators will be able to develop and use effectively, even in situations where you have very little lead time.

Nevertheless, there may be situations where you need to install Moodle locally because you would like to save monthly hosting fees, develop a custom solution, or use the installation to experiment.

In some cases, you may wish to install Moodle on a standalone machine. If that is the case, it is recommended that you visit "one-click" installers for Windows and macOS. Keep in mind that they are not suitable for production servers.

The complete install packages that you may wish to use can be found at Moodle.org's Windows download page: `https://download.moodle.org/windows/`. Each is designed for a standalone computer, and they use the XAMPP Apache Friends packages (`https://download.moodle.org/windows/`) and OS X packages. You can download the latest development version of Moodle 4.1, as well as a stable version of Moodle 4.0. You can also download Moodle 3.11.6+. In this book, we are using the stable version of Moodle 4.0.

Moodle is constantly expanding its options, and Moodle 4.0 focuses on giving you choices. You can have a locally installed version, which is a Standard version. You can then expand it by choosing among the 1,982 (of this writing) plugins. Finally, Moodle now has a downloadable app. We will show you where to find each of these options in the next section.

Installing Standard Moodle, enhancing it with plugins, and adding the Moodle app

It is not within the scope of this book to give you detailed instructions on how to install and run Moodle on your own server. However, this section will show you where to go to get the specific instructions and also point out that there are options. You can find all of them on the Moodle downloads page at `https://download.moodle.org/`. Standard Moodle is the base version of Moodle. To be able to add functionality, such as a calendar, you'll need to enhance it with plugins.

Standard Moodle

We'll begin with Standard Moodle. To get started, you will need a web server such as Apache and a database such as MySQL, MariaDB, or PostgreSQL. You'll need to configure PHP because Moodle requires a number of PHP extensions.

For specific installation instructions, please visit Moodle downloads at `https://download.moodle.org/`.

The latest release at the time of writing this book is Moodle 4.0.1. The following screenshot shows the links for downloading packages or downloading Moodle via Git. Please note that the version is updated every week:

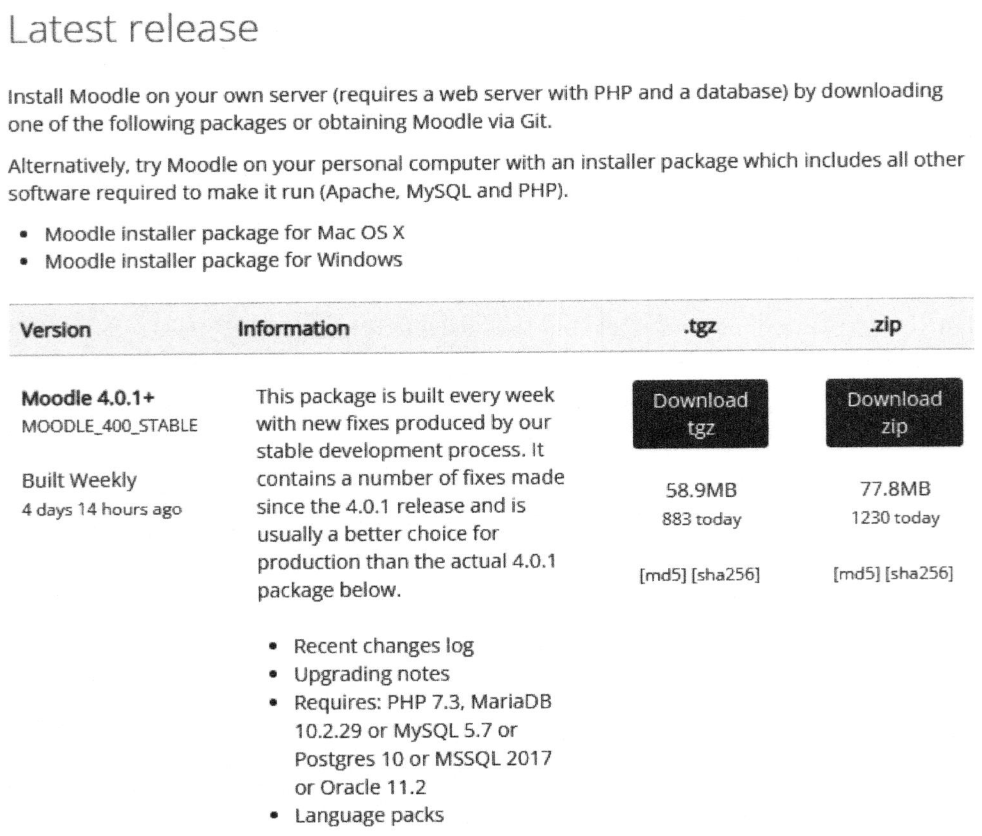

Latest release

Install Moodle on your own server (requires a web server with PHP and a database) by downloading one of the following packages or obtaining Moodle via Git.

Alternatively, try Moodle on your personal computer with an installer package which includes all other software required to make it run (Apache, MySQL and PHP).

- Moodle installer package for Mac OS X
- Moodle installer package for Windows

Version	Information	.tgz	.zip
Moodle 4.0.1+ MOODLE_400_STABLE Built Weekly 4 days 14 hours ago	This package is built every week with new fixes produced by our stable development process. It contains a number of fixes made since the 4.0.1 release and is usually a better choice for production than the actual 4.0.1 package below.	Download tgz 58.9MB 883 today [md5] [sha256]	Download zip 77.8MB 1230 today [md5] [sha256]
	• Recent changes log • Upgrading notes • Requires: PHP 7.3, MariaDB 10.2.29 or MySQL 5.7 or Postgres 10 or MSSQL 2017 or Oracle 11.2 • Language packs		

Figure 2.2 – Moodle's download page

As shown in the preceding screenshot, this page includes links to installer packages and information about the latest version.

After you have successfully installed the latest Standard version of Moodle, you may wish to enhance it with plugins. You can add plugins individually for courses or groups of courses, and you can make the plugins systemwide in the version of Moodle you're hosting on your own server. Here is the link to the location where you can search for plugins: `https://moodle.org/plugins/`. Plugins include activities, themes, and blocks. The following screenshot shows you the redesigned plugin download interface, and the fact that you can search by purpose, popularity, number of downloads, and more:

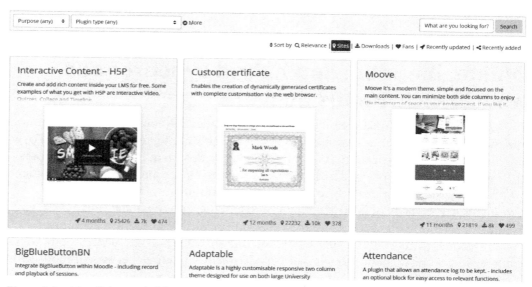

Figure 2.3 – Moodle's searchable page for downloading plugins for an installation on your own server

Moodle Mobile

Moodle Mobile is an app that makes using Moodle on Android devices much easier than always accessing it from the internet.

Specifically, the Moodle app has features that allow you to do the following:

- Browse course content even when offline.
- Find and connect with other people on your courses.
- Receive messages, submissions, and grading notifications.
- Submit assignments from your mobile devices (including uploading files).
- Track course completion progress.
- Complete activities even when offline.

The app is available for Android and can be downloaded from the Google Play Store, or you can download the **Android Package Kit**. The link to the app documentation and also the download is here: `https://download.moodle.org/mobile/`.

The site administrator will need to enable mobile services in the on-premises installation or MoodleCloud.

Now that we have learned how to install Moodle and have reviewed how to enhance Moodle's functionality with plugins, we will look at the best ways to use it in today's world of online, blended, hybrid, synchronous, and asynchronous delivery.

A brave new Zoom world – planning for online, blended, and hybrid synchronous and asynchronous delivery

In 2020, when the global pandemic forced educational institutions to offer courses online, many opted for synchronous solutions in which the bulk of the instruction took place via a web-conferencing application. A learning management system (such as Moodle) was then used as the repository of digital documents, assessments, and grade books. Students who formerly studied exclusively in face-to-face environments now had to navigate the unfamiliar territory of the online classroom and the learning management system. While it was a positive thing to be able to view one's instructor or classmates online via web-conferencing software such as BigBlueButton, Microsoft Teams, or Zoom, web conferencing alone was not enough. The best design brought together synchronous with asynchronous, with collaboration, interaction, and hands-on guided experimentation incorporated into the learning management system.

At the same time, the dramatic shift to synchronous online instruction made it all the more apparent that the experience of web conference-based synchronous instruction and collaborative learning (discussions and team projects in breakout rooms) is dramatically different than the asynchronous experience. Learning is different without a "live" instructor presence, and students cannot see each other in real time. On the positive side, asynchronous is much more flexible because it can be self-paced and materials can be accessed on demand. With Moodle, you have the flexibility to offer synchronous, asynchronous, and blended solutions. For a more in-depth theoretical background and research findings, please refer to the rubrics and findings in *Quality Matters* (`https://www.qualitymatters.org/`) or the UK's *Institute of Education* (`https://eppi.ioe.ac.uk/cms/Default.aspx?tabid=3847`).

As you consider your user experience, take a moment to reflect on how it affects a student's ability to learn. You'll want to keep the learning objectives and outcomes first and foremost in the learner's mind, even as you're setting up your site and thinking about what should be visible to the students. Then, you'll want to ensure that they know what they should be doing next and how this ties to the courses. Informing your decisions is the knowledge of what you'd like the students to accomplish. Specifically, this means you are thinking ahead about how you will clearly map the learning objectives to the course content, activities, and assessment. Mapping the learning objectives can be enhanced using storyboarding. The overall sight should make sense, and your learner should have an idea of how an activity or content will lead to the ability to perform a task and demonstrate skill or mastery.

The following screenshot shows the **Activity** menu and gives you an idea of the range and variety of activities that can be done in both synchronous and asynchronous delivery:

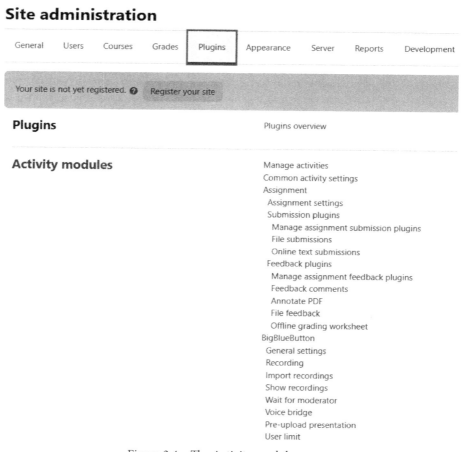

Figure 2.4 – The Activity modules page

These activity modules correspond with both synchronous and asynchronous course design. A blend of synchronous (web conferencing with BigBlueButtonBN, for example) and asynchronous (a forum) can be highly effective.

An easy way to maintain awareness of the user experience is to use the **CORN** mnemonic:

- **C – Clear**: Your outcomes should be clear, as should the process of working through the course. Think of a map and how it guides you to a final destination. A clear map contains just the right amount of information, is not superfluous, and provides help when needed.

- **O – Outcome-focused**: Ensure that you're always tied to the learning outcomes, which are clearly stated at the outset. Then, ensure that each unit or module also contains objectives. Also ensure that you organize your course in a way that provides sufficient scaffolding so that the sequence makes sense.

- **R – Relevant**: Although it can be interesting to include reference blocks, materials, or activities that are not totally related to the course as *enrichment*, keep in mind that you could confuse or derail a student. The material should tie directly to the learning outcomes and help students successfully complete the assessments. Likewise, the assessments need to be relevant and meaningful. If your course contains a synchronous element, make sure that your discussions stay on track and you do not become distracted by tangential topics.

- **N – Needs-based**: Provide the tools your students need to be able to perform their tasks. Make sure that the tools are easy to access and that they enhance the learning experience by giving a student more confidence. Also, ensure that their learning preferences are acknowledged and you're focused on meeting their needs. A prime determinant of user satisfaction is the degree to which a student feels in charge of their own destiny, something that requires them to develop a high degree of self-efficacy and an "I can do it!" attitude. Further, to motivate your students, you'll need to satisfy their needs. They may need a sense of recognition, and so building in rewards and recognition will be part of the way you configure your site.

In this chapter, we're focusing on the settings. Later, we'll go into more depth about how to design and arrange content, activities, and assessments.

In all of these settings, you have choices. Many of the choices in settings that you make will be easy to decide. For example, will you allow your users to select their own time zone? Other choices are not so obvious. You can spend a lot of time trying different settings to see how they affect the user experience. These are the settings that we will focus on in this chapter. The goal is to save you time by showing you the effects that key settings will have on your site.

> **Tip**
>
> If your system administrator or webmaster has installed Moodle for you, you may be tempted to just accept the default configuration and skip this chapter. Don't do that!

Even if you did not install Moodle or are using a cloud-based provider such as MoodleCloud instead of a self-hosted installation, we encourage you to read the configuration sections in this chapter. If you want, work with your system administrator to select the settings that you want. Your administrator can create a site administrator account that you can use for configuring Moodle, or they can select these configuration settings for you.

In the next section, we will describe how to set up Moodle if you're using a cloud-based solution such as MoodleCloud.

Using MoodleCloud

This chapter started with a self-hosted solution. However, what if you're using MoodleCloud, Moodle's cloud-based solution? The good news is that MoodleCloud is extremely customizable, and you will have a great deal of flexibility in the site administration area. There are numerous Moodle hosting providers and partners. However, MoodleCloud is the only one developed and operated by Moodle. Nevertheless, there are a number of Moodle partners, and they offer a wide array of solutions that are often tailored to fit specific needs. Moodle Partners are organizations that have been recognized by Moodle to provide services to schools, institutions, and other organizations that can benefit from Moodle's unique learning management system.

At the time of writing, there are more than 100 Moodle Partners who offer services as experts in Moodle and who can help you configure your site. In many cases, Moodle Partners also offer hosting services with customization. For an up-to-date list, please visit Moodle's list of Certified Moodle Partners: `https://moodle.com/solutions/certified-service-providers`.

MoodleCloud (`https://moodlecloud.com/app/en/login`) is very economical and is a perfect site for teachers, instructional designers, and instructional technologists to develop templates, try out new designs, and pilot an entirely new curriculum or approach. Moodle pricing varies depending on the number of users.

MoodleCloud is cloud-based, as the name indicates, so you do not have to install anything on your computer or a server. You will need the latest versions of your browser (Chrome, Microsoft Edge, Firefox, or Safari). Ensure that cookies are enabled for your site. MoodleCloud has been designed to be very efficient, and it is also responsive, which means that it has been designed to look good on all devices, from laptops to tablets and smartphones.

One advantage of MoodleCloud is that you always have the latest version of Moodle, and when new capabilities emerge, you will be able to use them. For example, you are now able to configure your courses to be compatible with smartphones as well as with tablets, laptops, and computers, for a truly mobile solution.

A potential disadvantage of MoodleCloud is that you do not have the same number of design options because there is a limited number of built-in themes, as opposed to an on-premises solution. Further, MoodleCloud is no longer the most inexpensive version, nor is it free. To learn more, visit MoodleCloud: `https://moodlecloud.com/app/en/login`.

Even though there are a few limitations, MoodleCloud includes features that are valuable to all designers, and you can add a wide array of multimedia resources and activities that include assessment and automatic badge and certificate generation. In the next section, we will learn how to set basic configurations in the site administration menu.

Exploring the site administration menu

After installing Moodle, it is good to set some basic configuration options. Some of these settings determine how the site functions, such as how users are authenticated, what statistics the site keeps, and which modules are turned off and on. Other settings just affect the user experience, such as which languages are available, the color scheme, and what is displayed on the front page and Dashboard. All these settings are available through the **Site administration** menu. The MoodleCloud **Site administration** menu is similar, but it also includes a setting for the mobile application so that your users can easily use their phones or tablets. If your on-premises installation does not include the **Mobile App** menu, ensure that you select a theme that is responsive, which means that it will work on all devices automatically.

The default theme for Moodle demos is Boost, and for MoodleCloud, it's Classic. In this example, we will be using version 4.0.

To access the **Site administration** menu, you must be logged in as an administrative user. Under the **Administration** menu, click on **Site administration** to expand the menu:

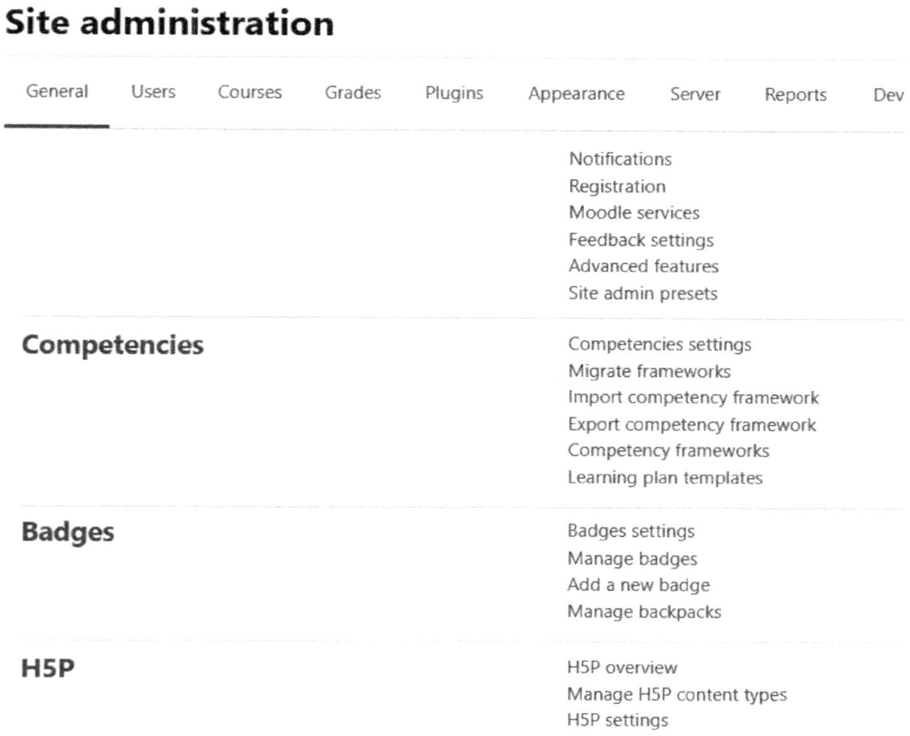

Site administration

General	Users	Courses	Grades	Plugins	Appearance	Server	Reports	Dev

	Notifications
	Registration
	Moodle services
	Feedback settings
	Advanced features
	Site admin presets
Competencies	Competencies settings
	Migrate frameworks
	Import competency framework
	Export competency framework
	Competency frameworks
	Learning plan templates
Badges	Badges settings
	Manage badges
	Add a new badge
	Manage backpacks
H5P	H5P overview
	Manage H5P content types
	H5P settings

Figure 2.5 – The Site administration menu

In this chapter on configuring your site, we'll cover some of the settings under the **Site administration** menu. Other settings will be covered as we build our courses, teach, calculate grades, and update our site.

> **Tip**
>
> The important idea here is that, unlike many other applications, in Moodle, the **Site administration** menu isn't something that you *set and forget*. You return to the configuration settings as your site develops.

Now, let's go through the settings you use to configure your site for the kind of user experience that you want to create.

Configuring authentication methods

Authentication is what happens when a user is logging into your site. When a user is created, an authentication method must be chosen for that user. This can be changed for the user later.

Moodle offers a variety of ways to authenticate users. The following ones should be enabled:

- **MoodleCloud**: Enables authentication for MoodleCloud when using it
- **Email-based self-registration**: Enables a user to create their own account via the **Create new account** button on the login page

You'll find these options under **Administration | Site administration | Plugins | Authentication | Manage authentication**. You can find a brief explanation for each of these options by clicking on **Settings** for a specific option:

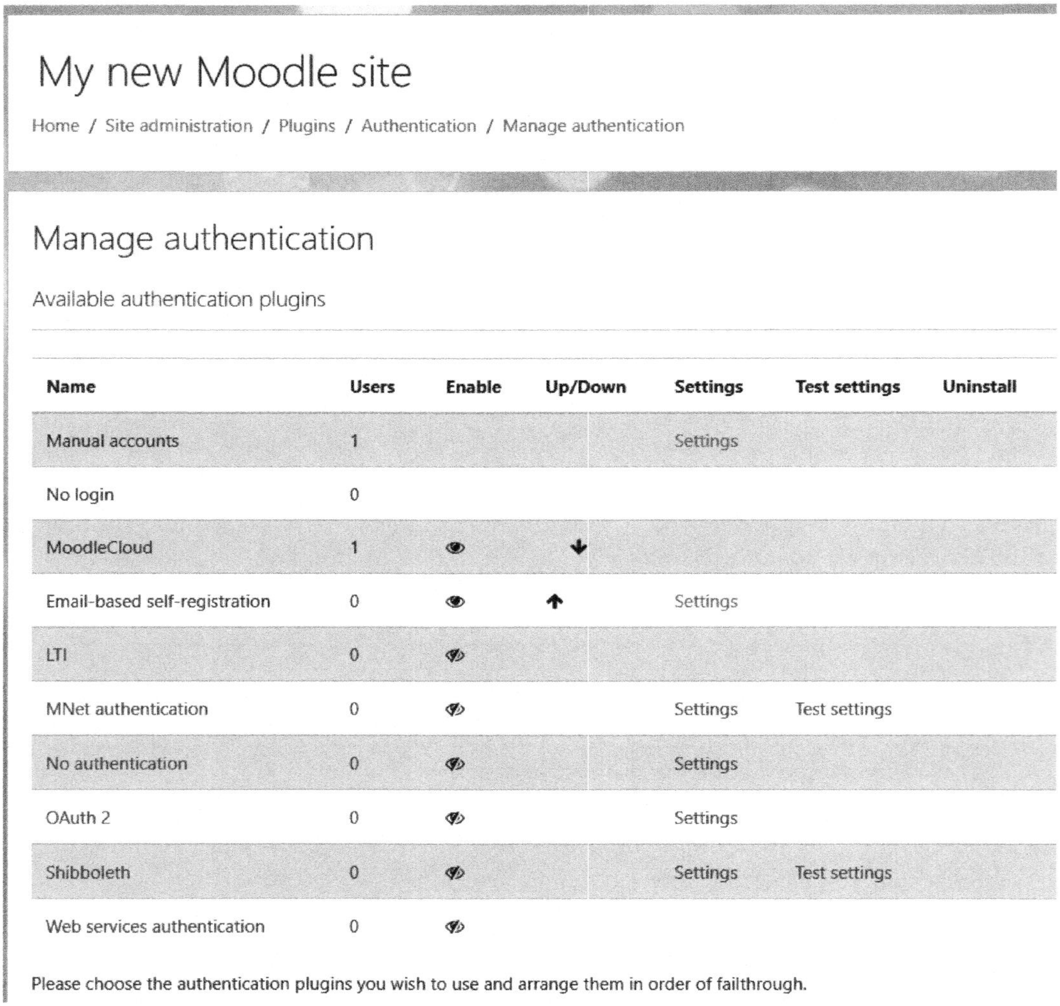

My new Moodle site

Home / Site administration / Plugins / Authentication / Manage authentication

Manage authentication

Available authentication plugins

Name	Users	Enable	Up/Down	Settings	Test settings	Uninstall
Manual accounts	1			Settings		
No login	0					
MoodleCloud	1	👁	↓			
Email-based self-registration	0	👁	↑	Settings		
LTI	0	👁̸				
MNet authentication	0	👁̸		Settings	Test settings	
No authentication	0	👁̸		Settings		
OAuth 2	0	👁̸		Settings		
Shibboleth	0	👁̸		Settings	Test settings	
Web services authentication	0	👁̸				

Please choose the authentication plugins you wish to use and arrange them in order of failthrough.

Figure 2.6 – The Manage authentication menu

In the next section, we will talk about how to create new users.

Manually creating a new user

To create a new user, follow these steps:

1. Log in with your administrator account.
2. Go to the left panel and click **Site administration**.
3. Click the **Users** tab.
4. Click **Add a new user**.
5. Add the user details.
6. Click **Create user**.

The following screenshot shows the dialog for adding a user, which requires the administrator to assign a username, password, authentication method, what user information should be displayed, and MoodleNet profile:

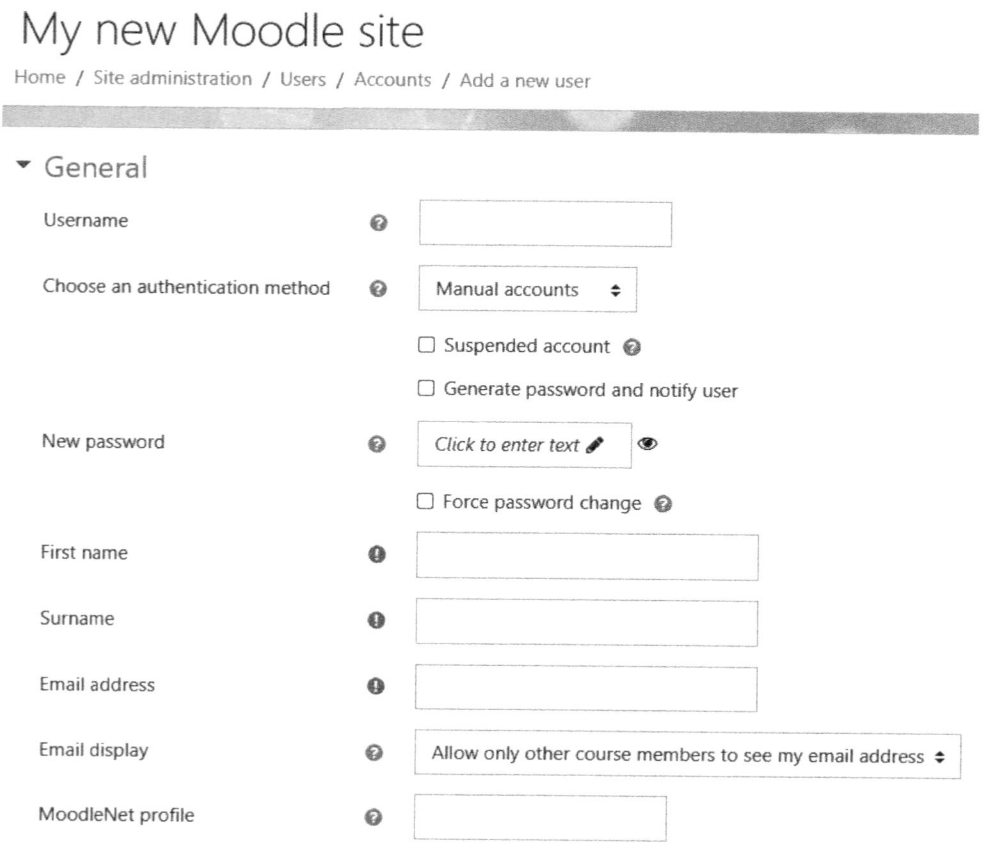

Figure 2.7 – The dialog for adding a user

Suspending a user's account

You may need to suspend a user's account if they have not paid their tuition. The result of this procedure is that the user's authentication method is changed to `no login`:

1. From the **Administration** menu on the left of the page, click on **Site administration | Users | Accounts | Browse list of users**. The **Users** page will be displayed. On this page, search for the user.

2. In the **New filter** area, enter all or part of the user's name.

3. Click on the **Add filter** button. The user will appear in the list at the bottom of the page.

4. Next to the user's name, you will see an "eye" icon. Mouse over it to activate the "suspend user" command, then click on it. When activated, a line will go through the eye icon indicating it is not visible. Once the eye has a line through it, the user's account has been suspended.

Figure 2.8 – Users and accounts

User roles

There are a number of user roles. Moodle allows you to enable and also configure them.

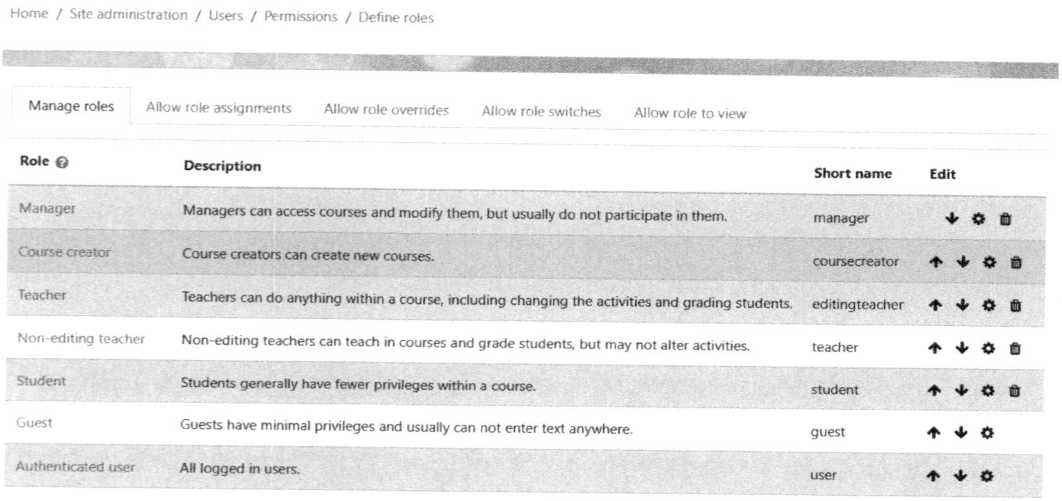

Home / Site administration / Users / Permissions / Define roles

Manage roles	Allow role assignments	Allow role overrides	Allow role switches	Allow role to view

Role	Description	Short name	Edit
Manager	Managers can access courses and modify them, but usually do not participate in them.	manager	↓ ⚙ 🗑
Course creator	Course creators can create new courses.	coursecreator	↑ ↓ ⚙ 🗑
Teacher	Teachers can do anything within a course, including changing the activities and grading students.	editingteacher	↑ ↓ ⚙ 🗑
Non-editing teacher	Non-editing teachers can teach in courses and grade students, but may not alter activities.	teacher	↑ ↓ ⚙ 🗑
Student	Students generally have fewer privileges within a course.	student	↑ ↓ ⚙ 🗑
Guest	Guests have minimal privileges and usually can not enter text anywhere.	guest	↑ ↓ ⚙
Authenticated user	All logged in users.	user	↑ ↓ ⚙

Figure 2.9 – User role configuration

Moodle makes adding a new user fairly flexible. You can give the user a username that corresponds to a unique ID for the institution, such as the user's email address, and you can also set up authentication methods, a password, and a unique profile. It is a good idea to set up username protocols and also authentication methods in a way that is uniform across all courses and programs in the institution.

Here are the standard roles in Moodle:

- **Site administrator**: Has the ability to do everything on the site.
- **Manager**: An administrator but with fewer permissions.
- **Course creator**: Can create courses.
- **Teacher**: Can manage and add content to courses.
- **Non-editing teacher**: Can grade student work and post.
- **Student**: Can access and participate in courses.
- **Guest**: Can observe courses but not participate.
- **Authenticated user**: All logged-in users have this role.

Your Moodle site has a special user category called **Guest**. It is a practical designation because it allows people to enter your course for a number of different purposes. This user can be granted access to courses, without requiring them to be enrolled. Essentially, you are allowing anonymous users to access your site and/or course.

In the following screenshot, the "**Guest**" button indicates that guest access has been enabled for this site. If you disable guest access, this button does not appear:

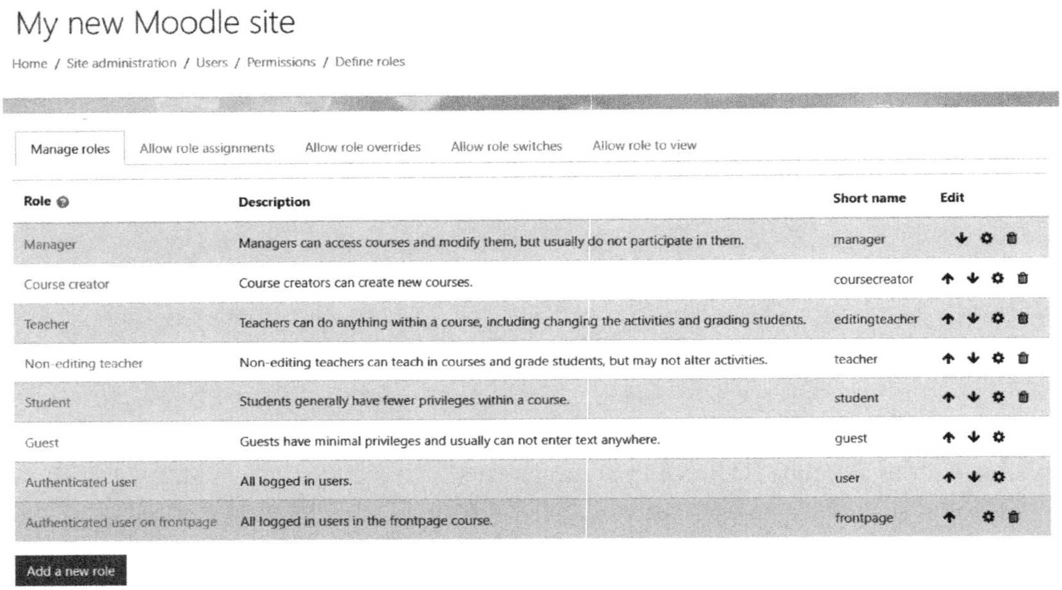

My new Moodle site

Home / Site administration / Users / Permissions / Define roles

Manage roles	Allow role assignments	Allow role overrides	Allow role switches	Allow role to view

Role ❓	Description	Short name	Edit
Manager	Managers can access courses and modify them, but usually do not participate in them.	manager	↓ ⚙ 🗑
Course creator	Course creators can create new courses.	coursecreator	↑ ↓ ⚙ 🗑
Teacher	Teachers can do anything within a course, including changing the activities and grading students.	editingteacher	↑ ↓ ⚙ 🗑
Non-editing teacher	Non-editing teachers can teach in courses and grade students, but may not alter activities.	teacher	↑ ↓ ⚙ 🗑
Student	Students generally have fewer privileges within a course.	student	↑ ↓ ⚙ 🗑
Guest	Guests have minimal privileges and usually can not enter text anywhere.	guest	↑ ↓ ⚙
Authenticated user	All logged in users.	user	↑ ↓ ⚙
Authenticated user on frontpage	All logged in users in the frontpage course.	frontpage	↑ ⚙ 🗑

Add a new role

Figure 2.10 – On the permissions screen, enabling login as a guest

Who Is This Guest?

Who is your guest visitor? Although you cannot identify a guest by name, you will usually know who the guest is because you will give access for special short-term purposes. It is a good idea to avoid having too many guests. Guest spots should be reserved for special purposes. Remember that in the logs showing guest activities, you are looking at the activities performed by every visitor who used the guest account.

The **Permissions** page for guest access allows you to set the role:

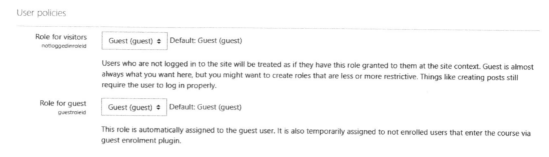

Figure 2.11 – Setting permissions for guest access

Now that you have added users, they can be enrolled in courses.

Enrollment methods

In Moodle, enrollment is referred to as "enrolment." It's a way to indicate the role of users so that they can participate in different levels in the course. The process is completed via a plugin, and there are several options. To access all of them, please go to **Site Administration | Plugins | Enrolments.**

Manual enrolments should be enabled sitewide to let students get added manually. To configure preferences, please go to **Site Administration | Plugins | Enrolments | Manual enrolments**

Guest access can be useful for course observers who will need access but are not actually enrolled as users. To configure **Guest access**, go to **Site Administration | Plugins | Enrolments | Guest access.**

Cohort sync is useful if you are using cohorts. You can access this at **Site Administration | Plugins | Enrolments | Cohort sync**

Self enrolment is helpful if you want users to be able to enroll themselves. Head to **Site Administration | Plugins | Enrolments | Self enrolment**

Manage enrol plugins allows the administrator to enable all the plugins described above, and many other plugins too. Going into the details of enrollment plugins (called "enrol plugins") is outside the scope of this book, but it is useful to see that **Enrolment on payment** and **PayPal** are options. Once enabled (by clicking on the eye icon), one can change the settings by clicking **Settings.** You can do this by navigating to **Site Administration | Plugins | Enrolments | Manage enrol plugins.**

Manage enrol plugins

Available course enrolment plugins

Name	Instances / enrolments	Version	Enable	Up/Down	Settings
Manual enrolments	3 / 104	2022041900	👁	↓	Settings
Guest access	3 / 0	2022041900	👁	↑ ↓	Settings
Self enrolment	3 / 0	2022041900	👁	↑ ↓	Settings
Cohort sync	0 / 0	2022041900	👁	↑ ↓	Settings
PayPal	0 / 0	2022041900	👁	↑ ↓	Settings
Enrolment on payment	0 / 0	2022041900	👁	↑	Settings

Figure 2.12- List of enabled enrolment methods visible through "Manage enrol plugins"

Self enrolment

This allows users to enroll themselves in courses. As with guest access, you must enable this method under **Site administration** for your entire site and also activate it for a specific course.

On the **Settings** page for **Self enrolment**, you can choose to require an enrollment key:

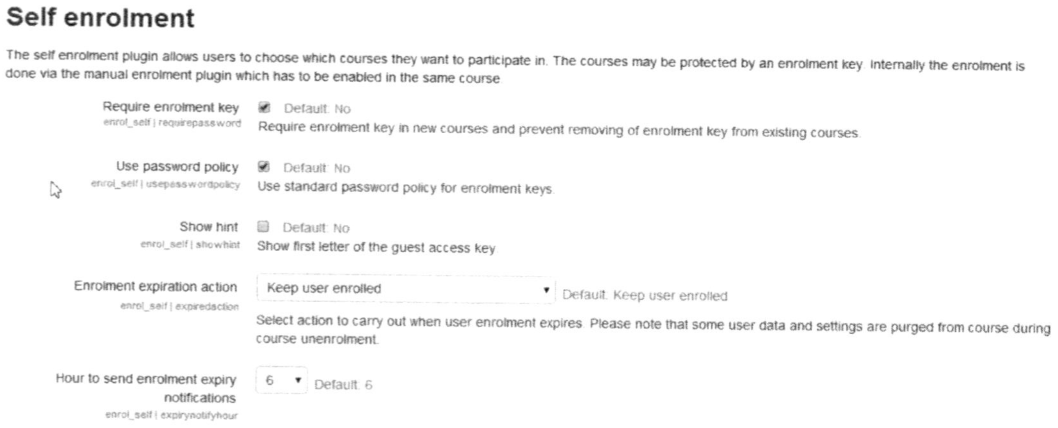

Self enrolment

The self enrolment plugin allows users to choose which courses they want to participate in. The courses may be protected by an enrolment key. Internally the enrolment is done via the manual enrolment plugin which has to be enabled in the same course.

Require enrolment key enrol_self | requirepassword	☑ Default: No Require enrolment key in new courses and prevent removing of enrolment key from existing courses.
Use password policy enrol_self | usepasswordpolicy	☑ Default: No Use standard password policy for enrolment keys.
Show hint enrol_self | showhint	☐ Default: No Show first letter of the guest access key
Enrolment expiration action enrol_self | expiredaction	Keep user enrolled ▼ Default: Keep user enrolled Select action to carry out when user enrolment expires. Please note that some user data and settings are purged from course during course unenrolment.
Hour to send enrolment expiry notifications enrol_self | expirynotifyhour	6 ▼ Default: 6

Figure 2.13 – The Self enrolment screen with customizable features for new users

For the self-enrolment option, start with **Plugins**, and then open **Site administration** - **Plugins** -> **Enrolments – Self enrolment**.

The **enrollment key** is a code that the user must enter when enrolling in a course. You can manage enrolment keys by scrolling down and finding the part of the menu labeled **Enrolment instance defaults**. Once the user is enrolled, the enrollment key is no longer needed. Now that we have enrolled our students, we can move on to other key settings that will affect the functioning of the site. In the next section, we will learn how to configure the front page and default dashboard.

> Tip
> The enrollment key ensures that only those to whom you give the key can enter your course. You may wish to add two-factor identification to avoid people passing the key on to others.

Configuring the front page and the Default Dashboard

In Moodle 4.0, the Dashboard has been updated and streamlined to make it easier to configure and use, and it makes working in Moodle easier and more enjoyable. The **Default Dashboard** page contains a Timeline, which consists of activities that have been assigned a due date, and thus can appear on a calendar. Note that, by default, only activities taking place in the upcoming 7 days will show up. There is also the option to sort by dates and also to search by activity type or name. The calendar allows you to look at all the courses at once or just one at a time to be able to plan and stay up to date with assignments and other activities.

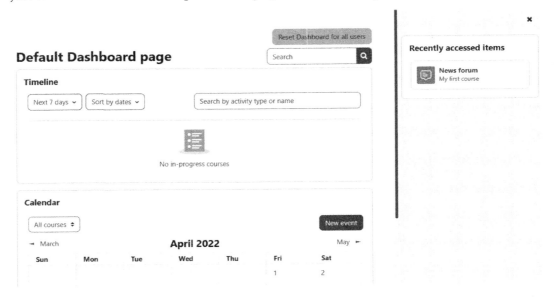

Figure 2.14 – Customizing the Default Dashboard page

One new feature of Moodle 4.0 is the **Recently accessed items** feature in the right-hand column. The purpose of the feature is to give you a "breadcrumb trail" to easily return to the items last accessed quickly and efficiently, without having to return to the main menu and click through all the screens. This feature is one of the most useful of the Moodle 4.0 user experience improvements, as it improves navigability.

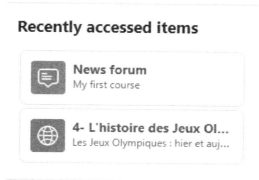

Figure 2.15 – Recently accessed items on the Default Dashboard page

Keep in mind that students will probably not see your site front page unless you've made the default start page your **Site home** page. If you do make the site home page your start page, you can use the **Site home** drop-down menus, which allow you to modify what appears on the front page.

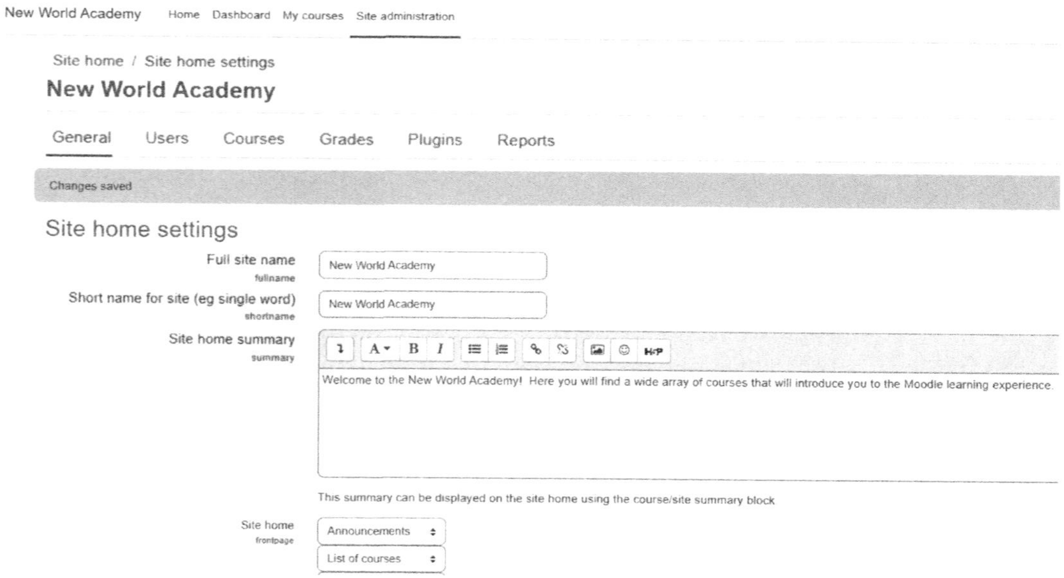

Figure 2.16 – Customizing the configuration of your Site home page (the front page)

Early in the process of building your site, you can make some decisions about the look and functioning of your Site home page. This section deals with the settings that make sense to select when you're first building your site. However, some configuration settings on the Site home page won't make sense until you've created some courses and seen how Moodle works.

The front page settings page

In Moodle 4.0, the front page is now referred to as Site home. Thus, the settings for the front page of your site are found under **Site administration** | **Site home** | **Site home settings**.

The full site name

The full site name appears at the top of the Site home page, in the browser's title bar, and also on the page tab when browsing with tabs.

You can create a summary of the site. Enter your summary in the **Site home summary** box, and it will appear on your Site home page (the front page). On MoodleCloud, you will not see this. You'll need to manually set your front page. The instructions can be found here: `https://docs.moodle.org/400/en/Change_your_front_page`. You may wish to include your institution's mission statement here as well:

Figure 2.17 – Adding a summary of your site that will appear to users

This summary appears in the left or right column of your site's front page. As you write your course descriptions and keywords, consider how you want to connect to specific social media sites. That will help you determine the terms and links to include.

Summary

Moodle 4.0 makes it easier for students, teachers, and administrators to navigate the platform by adding new navigation options and placing an activity history on the side of the Dashboard. Individuals and organizations that want to install a Standard version on their own servers can still do so, and they can enhance the global functionality with plugins. We also discussed Moodle Mobile, which is an app for Android users that enables them to access and use Moodle even when offline. In this chapter, we learned how to get started with Moodle, beginning with configuration and then selecting the available roles for users. We discussed the Dashboard's new features and also how Moodle 4.0 has enhanced the user experience. We covered the settings that, from experience, you are most likely to change. Many of these settings affect the behavior of the entire site. You don't need to get these choices perfect the first time because you can return to these settings and edit them at will. As you proceed with building your site, you will probably want to experiment with some of them. You will find that Moodle 4.0 is more customizable than ever.

In the next chapter, we will create courses and categories for our Moodle site.

3
Creating Categories and Courses

This chapter shows you how to create a new blank course. In this chapter, you will see how to create the course, choose the best format for your course considering your course objectives, and enroll students in the course. In addition, we will ensure that the course is well designed and that you are continuously aware of how learning will take place.

Moodle 4.0 offers major **user experience** (**UX**) improvements, and they are evident from the moment you start creating courses. First, there are navigation improvements that allow you to see your courses at a glance, navigate back to the last place you visited, and see all your courses at a glance in an improved Dashboard that merges calendars and timelines from all courses. You will also learn how to create course categories and use those categories to organize your course catalog. In keeping with current methods of instruction, which often involve Zoom, Teams, BigBlueButton, and other web conferencing software, you can also make it clear which courses are fully online or which have a blended delivery, with both synchronous and asynchronous elements. They should align with your institution's mission and vision so that you maintain a coherent presence. You will also be able to use the results for marketing and promoting your programs and your institution.

This chapter will cover the following main topics:

- Planning based on your institution's mission and vision

- Accreditation considerations

- Creating courses

- Enrolling teachers and students

By the end of this chapter, you will be able to set up blank courses and then group them into categories for your new course in Moodle 4.0.

Planning based on your institution's mission and vision

Many learning organizations offer similar courses, yet their students feed back remarkably different experiences and outcomes. How can that be, if the content is identical? The reality is that your course content is just a part of the learning equation because it's all about the learning, not the teaching. A large component has to do with how the content is framed, contextualized, and then applied. Each ties into the primary mission and vision of your organization.

As your organization decides what it wants to be in the world and how it wants to make an impact, it must devise its primary mission – that is, the *how we will do it* component to the overarching *what our ideal world looks like* question. If you think this sounds a bit utopian, you are right. It is. The best learning organizations want to create a better world, even if that utopia will never actually exist in the real world, and to get there, they need to determine action steps, which translate to a mission implemented by strategy and tactics that can be implemented as follows:

- **Framework**: Think of the framework as the pillars that hold up your mission and vision. Define them. Then, as you do, they will help you create structures and categories of your organization's offerings.

- **Contexts**: Who do you identify as your main student body? What is your main target? Who are your learners? Where are they? What are their main strengths, abilities, and cultural backgrounds? You will need to define your audience as well as your instructors if you want to have an effective learning organization. You'll also need to have a sense of your learners, the learning environment, and the limiting/enabling technologies in order to sequence your courses and ensure that they are at the correct level and presented in the right order.

- **Application**: Engaged students are the ones who are actively working with the content. They are the ones who are focused on being able to do more than simply memorize facts, answer questions, and then forget it all. Application involves invoking experiential learning and connecting to real-world situations and problems. So, as you create your courses and classify them, be sure to think about how it will be possible for your learners to put learning blocks together across a curriculum and prepare themselves to be completely autonomous.

You may think that frameworks, contexts, and application are too much to think about right now. After all, aren't you just putting together a list of courses? Yes and no. The list cannot be properly categorized if you do not know its ultimate purpose, its level, and what you want your students to do with the knowledge. This is particularly the case as you start thinking about ways to build on knowledge and have your students develop knowledge that will have real-world implications.

Further, the way you put together your list of courses will help you as you prepare your organization for its accreditation reviews. As you will see in the next section, the way you set up your presence in Moodle will have a significant impact on how you are viewed in accreditation and certification reviews.

Accreditation considerations – organization and alignment

In order to maintain accreditation, colleges and universities must undergo periodic reviews. With the proliferation of online courses, it is more important than ever to clearly map out an overall curriculum and course goals, and ensure that courses align with the institutional mission and vision, along with long-term goals and objectives. Further, with the need to be flexible with synchronous and asynchronous course delivery, it is important to demonstrate that you are including faculty training. Most accredited organizations that offer online instruction require instructors to take and successfully complete, at the very minimum, a course in the subject. They may also take courses covering the basics of instructional design and student motivation.

One of the best strategies for demonstrating that your courses and curriculum have been designed with a plan in mind and that they adhere to a mission is to create categories and subcategories that then appear on your Moodle site. If you use personalized learning that allows students to advance to higher levels of learning once they have demonstrated mastery of concepts or skills, this is a time to map out competency frameworks. Basically, each learning objective aligns with an assessment, and when the assessment is completed with a passing score, that competency has been satisfied, and the student can move on to the next section.

Every Moodle course must be assigned to at least one course category. The categories should correspond to your institution's course catalog, the document that you prepare for your self-review study, and then later, the document you submit to the accreditation team. This is an excellent example of how Moodle's organization can help you achieve consistency in all the places where you display courses, ranging from the course catalog to the strategic planning documents. Moodle can function as your foundation.

Choosing the best option for your front page or dashboard

When you are deciding which option to use for your front page, try to put yourself into your student's situation:

What your students are looking for	Consider using the following
A specific course by name	An uncategorized list of courses, displayed alphabetically.
A specific type of course, but they are unsure of the name	A combo list or category list so that the student sees the types of courses offered.
Either specific courses by name, or types of courses	A combo list. Add a note to the front page that informs the student they can search for courses by name (refer to the *Add instructions to your front page with labels* section in *Chapter 5, Resources, Activities, and Conditional Access*).
If users are not sure what they are looking for	An uncategorized list of courses, if you have only a few courses. You can use the course description to sell each course. If your list of courses is too long for the front page, you'll need to use a category list and include information on the front page to convince visitors to explore the categories (refer to the *Add instructions to your front page with labels* section in *Chapter 5, Resources, Activities, and Conditional Access*).

Figure 3.1 – The Dashboard options

Now that we have discussed how each option can affect how your student sees and uses the site, let's create course categories. As you are planning, be sure to create a list of the categories and courses.

Creating course categories

You must be a site administrator to create, edit, and delete course categories. Throughout this chapter, we are assuming that you are a course administrator or manager. Perform the following steps to create course categories:

1. If you're not logged in as the administrative user, log in now. Use the **Login** link at the upper-right corner of the page.

2. You should be looking at the home page of your new Moodle site.

3. From the **Administration** menu on the left of the page, click on **Site administration | Courses | Manage courses and categories**. This displays the **Course categories** page. On this page, you create new categories and courses. Here, you can also arrange the order in which the categories are displayed on the front page.

4. Click on the **Create a new category** link. The **Add new category page** is displayed.

5. Select where in the hierarchy of categories this one will be. In the following example of a new category, **Entrepreneurship**, we will go into the Parent category, which is the top level:

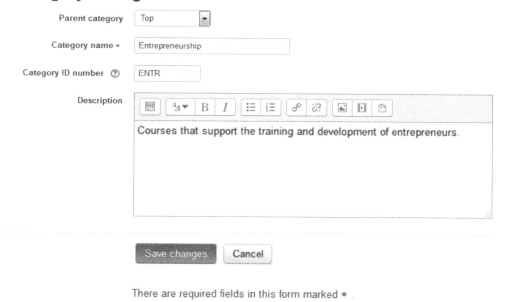

Figure 3.2 – Editing category settings

6. In the **Category name** field, enter a name for the category. Your users will see this in the category list.

7. In the **Description** field, enter a description for the category. If you configure your front page to show a list of categories, the user will see this description upon selecting a particular category. Enter some information in order to help your users decide whether this is the category they need.

The category description can have the same features as any Moodle web page. For example, you can add a graphic to the category description, as shown in the following screenshot:

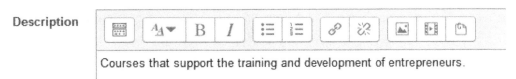

Figure 3.3 – Adding the category description

In *Chapter 4, Managing Resources, Activities, and Conditional Access*, we will show you how to use Moodle's web page editor. This is the same editor that you saw in the preceding screenshot.

8. Click on the **Create category** button. Moodle creates the category and redirects you to the **Manage courses and categories** screen.

Rearranging course categories

You must be a site administrator to rearrange course categories. The order in which you put them on this page is the order in which your users will see them listed.

If you're not logged in as a site administrator, log in now. Use the **Login** button at the upper-right corner of the page. Here are the steps to follow:

1. You should be looking at the home page of your new Moodle site.

2. From the **Administration** menu on the left of the page, click on **Site administration | Courses | Manage courses and categories**. This displays the **Course categories** page.

To move a category up or down in the list, click on the arrow button next to the category:

Figure 3.4 – Moving course categories up or down

3. To convert a category into a subcategory, select the category and then use the **Move selected categories to** drop-down list:

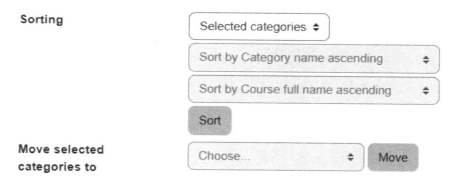

Figure 3.5 – Converting a category to a subcategory

4. You do not need to save your changes. The changes you make on this page are automatically saved as you click on the corresponding buttons.

Now that you have learned how to create categories, you'll now move on to creating the courses that you'll use to populate the categories. You will also learn how to classify the courses, create descriptions, and develop them so that they are both easy to find and place in different parts of your Moodle site.

Displaying courses and categories on your dashboard and front page

The Dashboard gives you a place to bring together all the items you will access often, and it keeps you from having to navigate through many links. For example, you can see **Learning plans**, **Recently accessed courses**, **Online users**, **Recently accessed items**, and a Timeline, all on one screen, as demonstrated in the following screenshot:

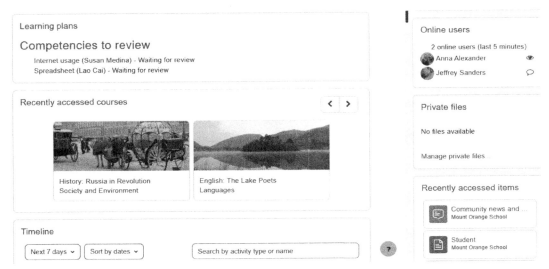

Figure 3.6 – A combo list for the Dashboard of your new site

If you have a large number of categories and courses, or they are complex, a combo list might be too long for your front page. In that case, you can display just the course categories. Then, the user would select a category and see the courses under that category, as they show up as drop-down menus or a simple list.

You have the option to create new categories and also to organize them so that they appear in the order that you would like. Keep in mind that these categories will appear in a block on the left. You can also edit the names of the courses if they are too long for the space.

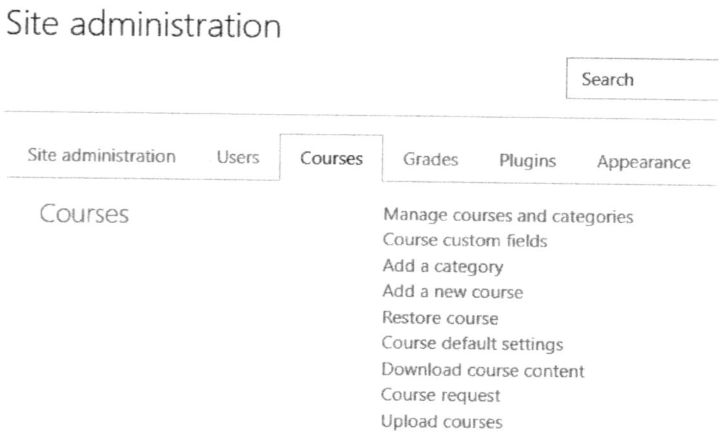

Site administration

Search

Site administration   Users   Courses   Grades   Plugins   Appearance

Courses

Manage courses and categories
Course custom fields
Add a category
Add a new course
Restore course
Course default settings
Download course content
Course request
Upload courses

Figure 3.7 – Selecting the Manage courses and categories option

To set up a new course category, you will complete the fields. You may wish to include your course under an existing category or start a new one without a parent category, as illustrated in the following screenshot:

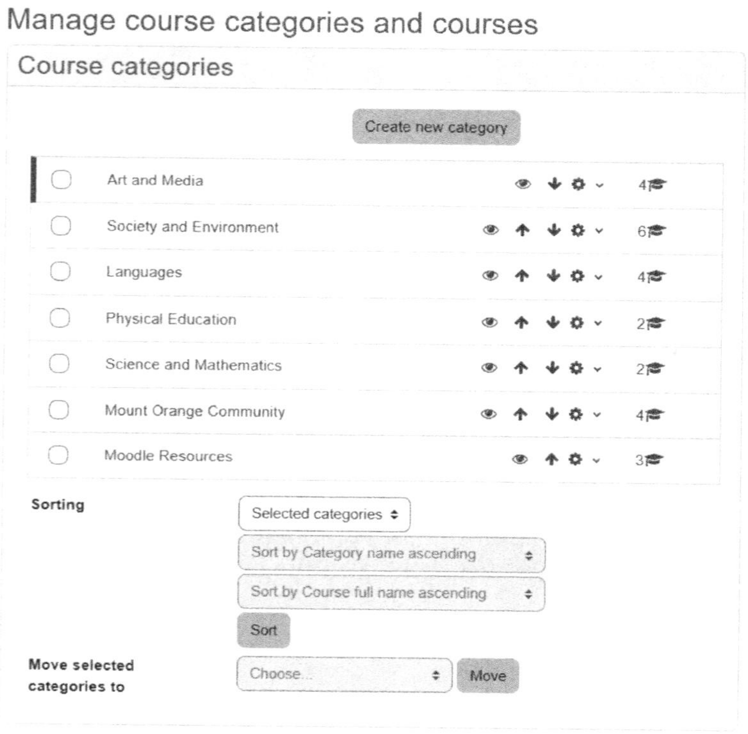

Manage course categories and courses

Course categories

Create new category

○ Art and Media	👁 ⬇ ⚙ ˅	4🎓
○ Society and Environment	👁 ⬆ ⬇ ⚙ ˅	6🎓
○ Languages	👁 ⬆ ⬇ ⚙ ˅	4🎓
○ Physical Education	👁 ⬆ ⬇ ⚙ ˅	2🎓
○ Science and Mathematics	👁 ⬆ ⬇ ⚙ ˅	2🎓
○ Mount Orange Community	👁 ⬆ ⬇ ⚙ ˅	4🎓
○ Moodle Resources	👁 ⬆ ⚙ ˅	3🎓

Sorting

Selected categories ⇕

Sort by Category name ascending ⇕

Sort by Course full name ascending ⇕

Sort

Move selected categories to

Choose... ⇕   Move

Figure 3.8 – Creating and managing course categories

Note that when you open the **Course and category management** page, you have the opportunity to customize the category itself. You can edit the category, add a description (through **Edit**), assign roles, create permissions, create cohorts of students who are enrolled in Moodle, and create filters. You can also upload a learning plan template and a competency framework. There are many competency frameworks available through the **Plugins** library, or you can develop your own:

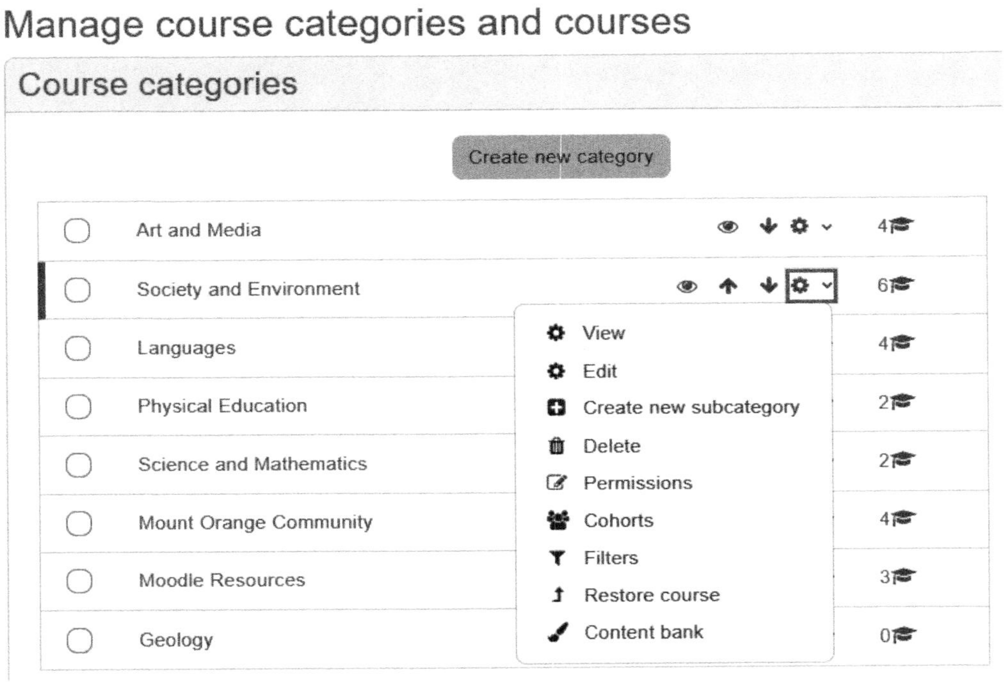

Manage course categories and courses

Course categories

Create new category

○ Art and Media	👁 ↓ ⚙ ⌄	4🎓
○ Society and Environment	👁 ↑ ↓ ⚙ ⌄	6🎓
○ Languages	⚙ View	4🎓
○ Physical Education	⚙ Edit ➕ Create new subcategory	2🎓
○ Science and Mathematics	🗑 Delete ☑ Permissions	2🎓
○ Mount Orange Community	👥 Cohorts	4🎓
○ Moodle Resources	▼ Filters ↑ Restore course	3🎓
○ Geology	✏ Content bank	0🎓

Figure 3.9 – Selecting menu items to modify categories

There are several ways to display categories on your home page (the front page) of your Moodle site. Note that some people refer to the front page as the home page (as per Moodle docs), while others may refer to it as the course Dashboard. To begin, look at the left side of your Dashboard, where you will see a menu:

1. Click on **Site administration** and then on **Plugins**. Blocks are under **Plugins**, so be sure to navigate to **Blocks** after clicking on **Plugins**.

Blocks

Manage blocks
Accessibility review
Activity results
Course overview
Courses
Online users
Recently accessed courses
Section links
Starred courses
Text

Figure 3.10 – The Blocks page

To include the course category in the recently accessed block items to make navigation easier, click **Recently accessed courses** and then click the checkbox next to **Default: Yes**. Then, click **Save Changes**.

2. You can also make sure that the Dashboard contains the course category, summary, card, and list by clicking **Course overview** from the menu in the **Blocks** section shown in *Figure 3.9*, and then checking the following options:

Course overview

Appearance

Display categories block_myoverview | displaycategories	☑ Default: Yes
	Display the course category on dashboard course items including cards, list items and summary items.
Available layouts block_myoverview | layouts	☑ Card
	☑ List
	☑ Summary
	Default: Card, List, Summary
	Course overview layouts which are available for selection by users. If none are selected, the card layout will be used.

Figure 3.11 – Configuring what will appear on the Dashboard

3. Once you have created a **Courses** block, the block will appear as a menu in the upper-right-hand corner in the Classic theme. Once you have your **Courses** block, you can then add items to it from the right-hand menu, as demonstrated in the following screenshot:

Figure 3.12 – Adding a block from your course

The list that shows both course categories and the courses is called the **combo list**. You can configure the courses block to make it visible on the left or right of the screen in the Classic theme, as shown here:

Figure 3.13 – Displaying recently accessed courses on the Dashboard in version 4.0

Functionality booster

As you create categories and subcategories, consider creating two new categories – asynchronous courses, and blended synchronous and asynchronous courses. If you do not want to have these categories show up on the front page, you can hide those subcategories by going to **Site administration | Front page | Front page settings | Maximum Category Depth**.

Displaying an uncategorized list of courses on your front page

Another option for showing courses on the front page is as an uncategorized list. This is a good option if your site has only a few courses or you are trying to establish a new brand or certificate program that contains an unusual combination of courses. If you include an uncategorized list, you may wish to describe the reasons for offering the courses, and tie them to your program's overall vision.

Keep in mind that your categories can be aligned with topics, subjects, fields of study, or even delivery mode. You can have 100% asynchronous, blended synchronous and asynchronous, or blended face-to-face and asynchronous. Some institutions have classified categories as online courses (100% asynchronous), blended courses (asynchronous, plus Zoom), and "live" web courses (synchronous delivery).

The site in the following screenshot shows a simple list of courses with the course descriptions:

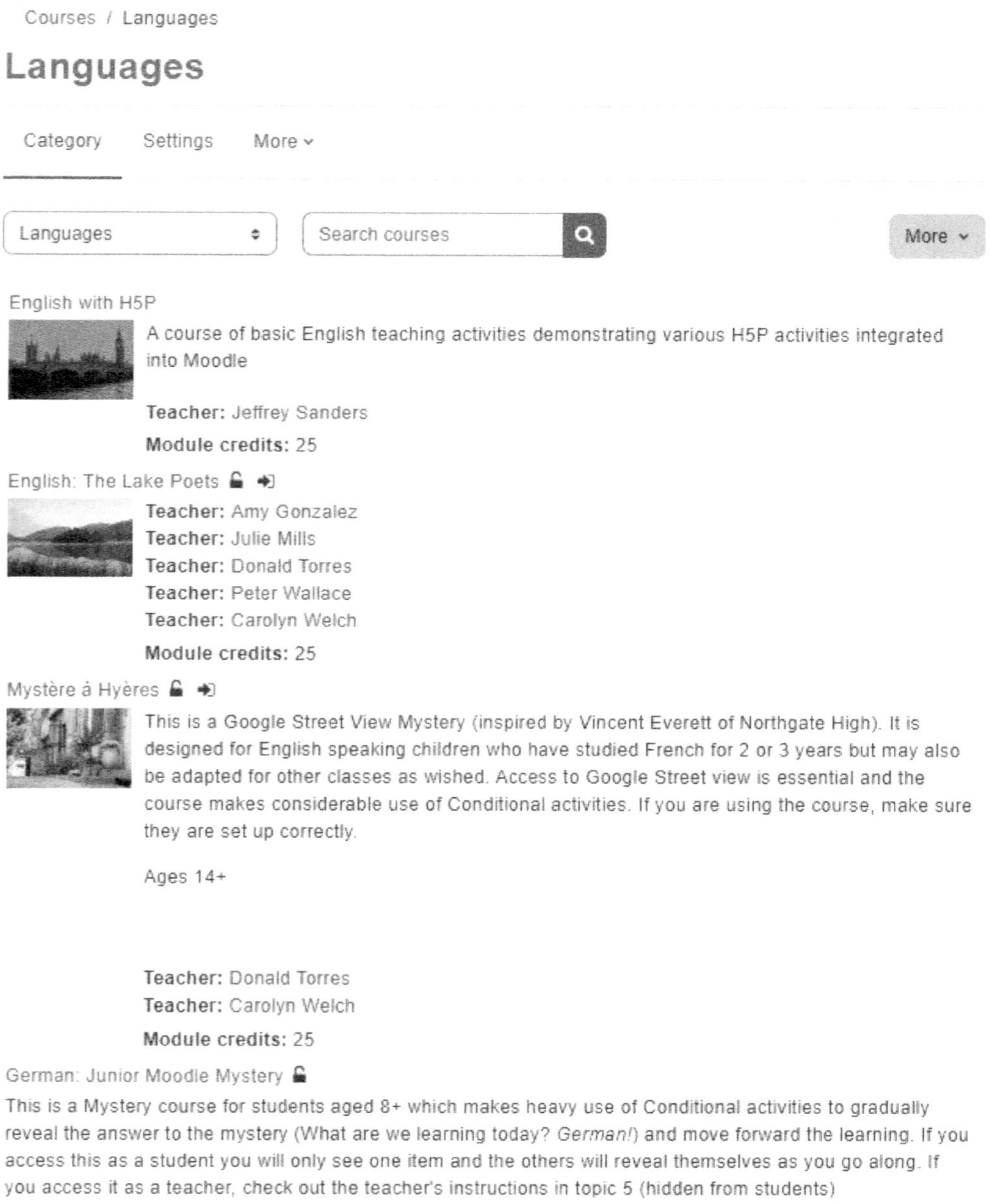

Courses / Languages

Languages

Category   Settings   More ∨

| Languages ⬍ | Search courses 🔍 | | More ∨ |

English with H5P

A course of basic English teaching activities demonstrating various H5P activities integrated into Moodle

Teacher: Jeffrey Sanders

Module credits: 25

English: The Lake Poets 🔒 ➔]

Teacher: Amy Gonzalez
Teacher: Julie Mills
Teacher: Donald Torres
Teacher: Peter Wallace
Teacher: Carolyn Welch

Module credits: 25

Mystère à Hyères 🔒 ➔]

This is a Google Street View Mystery (inspired by Vincent Everett of Northgate High). It is designed for English speaking children who have studied French for 2 or 3 years but may also be adapted for other classes as wished. Access to Google Street view is essential and the course makes considerable use of Conditional activities. If you are using the course, make sure they are set up correctly.

Ages 14+

Teacher: Donald Torres
Teacher: Carolyn Welch

Module credits: 25

German: Junior Moodle Mystery 🔒

This is a Mystery course for students aged 8+ which makes heavy use of Conditional activities to gradually reveal the answer to the mystery (What are we learning today? *German!*) and move forward the learning. If you access this as a student you will only see one item and the others will reveal themselves as you go along. If you access it as a teacher, check out the teacher's instructions in topic 5 (hidden from students)

Figure 3.14 – Displaying the available courses with descriptions

In this section, we learned about the ways to set up site-wide categories and course classifications so that when we create courses, we can organize them well. Now, we will learn how to create courses.

Creating courses

As stated earlier, every course belongs to a category. Don't worry if you mistakenly put a course into the wrong category.

Creating a course and filling it with content are two different functions. In this section, we will talk about creating a blank course, with no content. In the later chapters, we will learn how to add material to a course.

To create a course, a user must have the site-wide role of the site administrator or manager. To add material to a course, a user must be a site administrator, course creator, manager, or teacher (usually, the teacher adds material). The following tables show what the different roles can do.

Moodle site roles:

	View and edit personal profile	Manually add, edit, and disable users	Add and delete courses	Add blocks	Course administrator rights in all courses	Change theme, banner, and so on
Site administrator	x	x	x	x	x	x
Course creator	x	x	x	x		
Authenticated user	x					

Figure 3.15 – Moodle site roles

Moodle course roles:

Access to individual courses	View courseware	Participate in activities	View personal records	View student records	Add and edit courseware	Edit course settings	Set course roles
Course administrator	x	x	x	x	X	X	x
Teacher	x	x	x	x	X		

Access to individual courses	View courseware	Participate in activities	View personal records	View student records	Add and edit courseware	Edit course settings	Set course roles
Non-editing teacher	x	x	x	x			
Student	x	x	x				
Guest with read-only access	x						

Figure 3.16 – Moodle course roles

In this section, we have learned about site-wide roles and course-specific roles. Next, we will look at creating a new blank course.

Creating a new blank course

When you create a blank course, most of your choices and settings will be done on the settings page for the course. The Moodle **Help** icons on this page do a good job of explaining the purpose of each setting. However, the directions do not specify the implications of the choices you make on this page.

In the instructions given next, I've added some commentary content to help you determine how your choices will affect the operation of your course and how the student/teacher is affected by those choices. My goal is to help you make the right choices in order to create the teacher/student experience you want.

The result of this procedure is a new course, ready for course material to be added. To create a new blank course, follow these steps:

1. Log in to the site as a site administrator, manager, or course creator.
2. Select **Site Administration | Courses | Manage courses and categories**.
3. Click on the **Create new course** link. The **Edit course settings** page is displayed.
4. From the drop-down list at the top of the page, select a category for the course. You can use the drop-down list to change the category at any time. The list shows both visible and hidden categories.

   As your site grows and you add more categories, you might want to reorganize your site. However, if a student logs in while you are in the middle of creating categories and moving courses, they might be confused. You can speed up the reorganization time by hiding your categories as you create them. This lets you take your time while thinking about what categories to use. Then, move the courses into the categories.

   Each course will disappear until you finally reveal the new categories.

5. Enter a full name and a short name for the course.

6. The full name of the course appears at the top of the page when viewing the course, and also in the course listings. The short name appears in the breadcrumb, or navigation bar, at the top of the page. In the following example, the full name is `The Happy Little Trees of Bob Ross: Pop Art and Kitsch`, and the short name is `BobRossPopArt`.

7. You can add the course summary in **Description**.

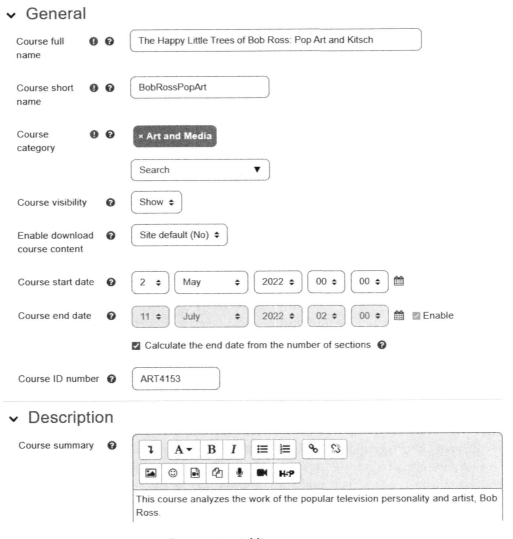

Figure 3.17 – Adding a new course

The full name also appears in the page's title and metadata, which influences how it appears in the search engines. The metadata may not be too important for some course creators, but for those who are marketing the courses and want them to appear in search results, it is important. The following is the HTML code, generated by Moodle, for the preceding example:

```
<head>
<title>Course: The Happy Little Trees of Bob Ross: Pop
Art and Kitsch </title>
<link rel="shortcut icon" href="http://localhost/moodle/
theme/image.php/standard/theme/1359480837/fav icon" />
<meta http-equiv="Content-Type" content="text/html;
charset=utf-8" />
<meta name="keywords" content="moodle, The Happy Little
Trees of Bob Ross: Pop Art and Kitsch " />
```

Note the full course name in the `<title>` and `<meta>` tags. Many search engines give a lot of weight to the `title` tag. If your Moodle system is open to search engines, choose your course title with this in mind.

8. Enter a course ID number. *Chapter 2, Installing Moodle and Configuring Your Site,* talked about using an external database for enrollment information. If you are using an external database to enroll students, the ID number that you enter into this field must match the ID number of the course in the external database. If you're not using an external database for enrollment information, you can leave this field blank.

9. Enter a course summary. If you choose to display a list of courses on the front page, the course summaries are displayed with the names of the courses, as shown in the following screenshot:

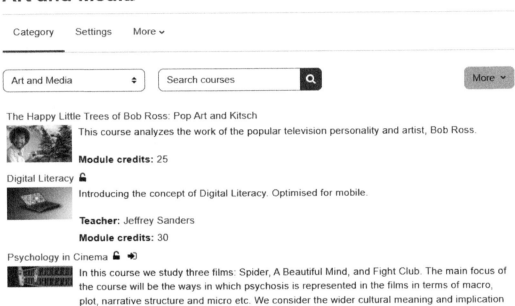

Figure 3.18 – Displaying course summaries

You can add a description of the course through the course summary. It appears in the text box in the **Description** section, next to **Course summary**, as shown below. You can format it in many ways, including selecting a special font, using bold-face, italics, and even including multimedia content:

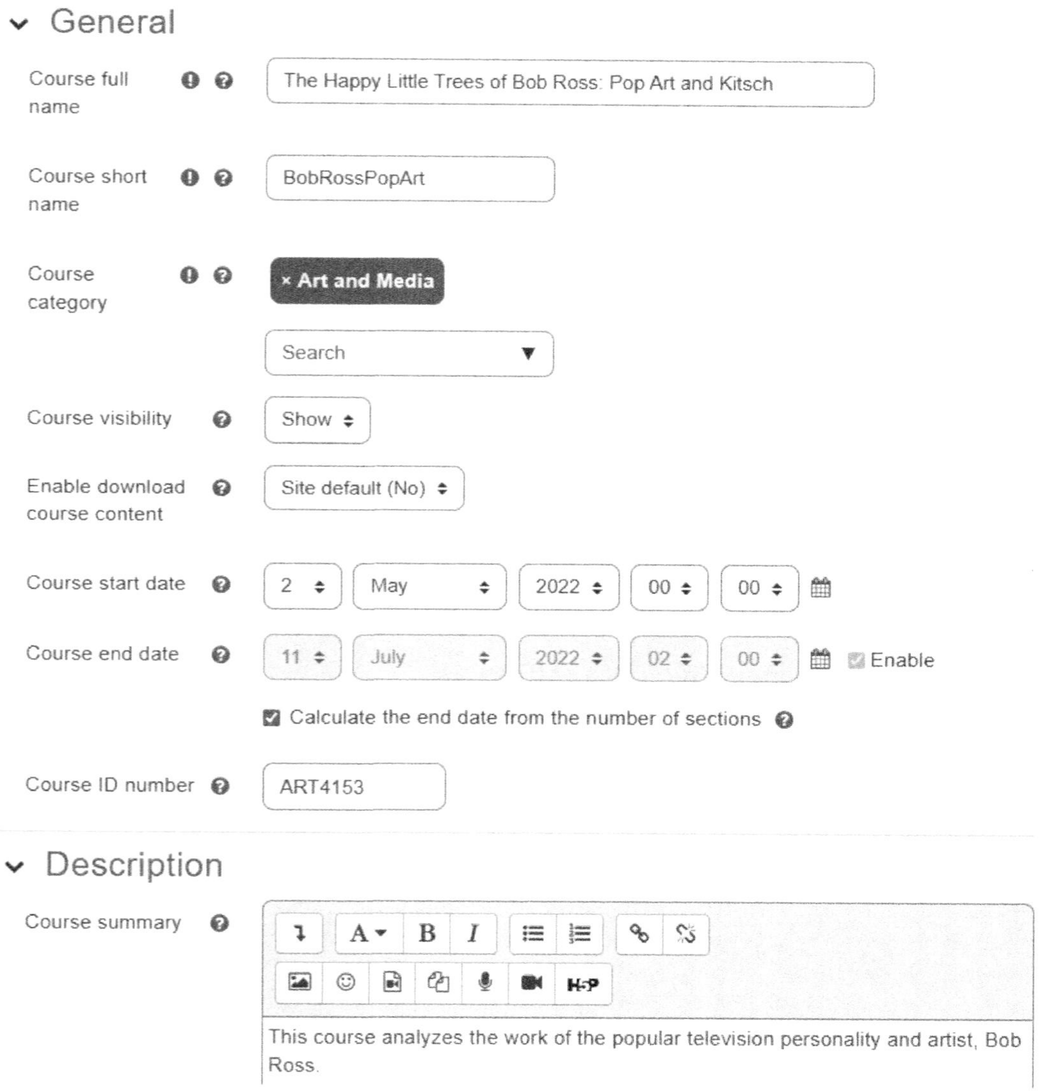

∨ General

Course full name	❶ ❷	The Happy Little Trees of Bob Ross: Pop Art and Kitsch
Course short name	❶ ❷	BobRossPopArt
Course category	❶ ❷	× **Art and Media**
		Search ▼
Course visibility	❷	Show ⬍
Enable download course content	❷	Site default (No) ⬍
Course start date	❷	2 ⬍ May ⬍ 2022 ⬍ 00 ⬍ 00 ⬍ 📅
Course end date	❷	11 ⬍ July ⬍ 2022 ⬍ 02 ⬍ 00 ⬍ 📅 ☑ Enable
		☑ Calculate the end date from the number of sections ❷
Course ID number	❷	ART4153

∨ Description

Course summary	❷	⌄ A▾ B I ≔ ≔ % ⅏
		🖼 ☺ 📄 🗗 🎤 🎥 H-P
		This course analyzes the work of the popular television personality and artist, Bob Ross.

Figure 3.19 – Formatting the course summary

10. If you allow visitors to see your front page without logging in, they will probably read your course summaries before enrolling. Consider the summary to be a résumé of the course. Your course summaries need to be informative and work as a sales tool. They should offer enough information to help your visitors decide whether they want to enroll and should describe the courses in their best light. The summary can include learning objectives and the duration of the course.

11. Select a format for the course. Among your choices are the following:

Course format
Format
Topics format
Single activity format
Social format
Topics format
Weekly format
Number of sections
Hidden sections
Hidden sections are shown as not available
Course layout
Show all sections on one page

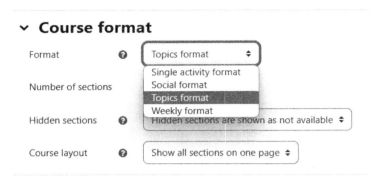

Figure 3.20 – Selecting the course format

- **Topics**: The Topics format is the most intuitive format to use for a course. As it displays each part of the course as a numbered topic, this format encourages most students to proceed through the course sequentially. However, by default, Moodle does not enforce this sequence, so students are free to jump back and forth in the course.

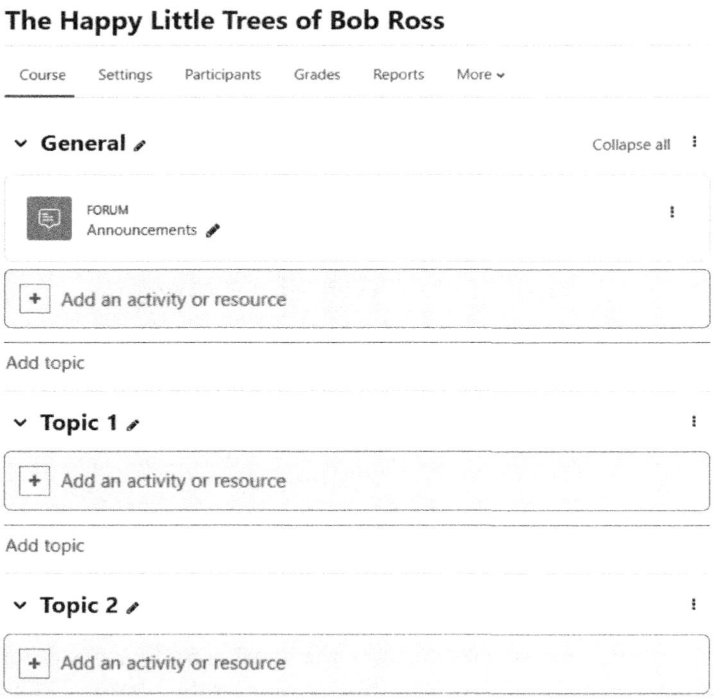

The Happy Little Trees of Bob Ross
Course
Settings
Participants
Grades
Reports
More
General
Collapse all
FORUM
Announcements
Add an activity or resource
Add topic
Topic 1
Add an activity or resource
Add topic
Topic 2
Add an activity or resource

Figure 3.21 – The topics format

- **Weekly**: Unless this is changed by the site administrator, this is the default format for a new course.

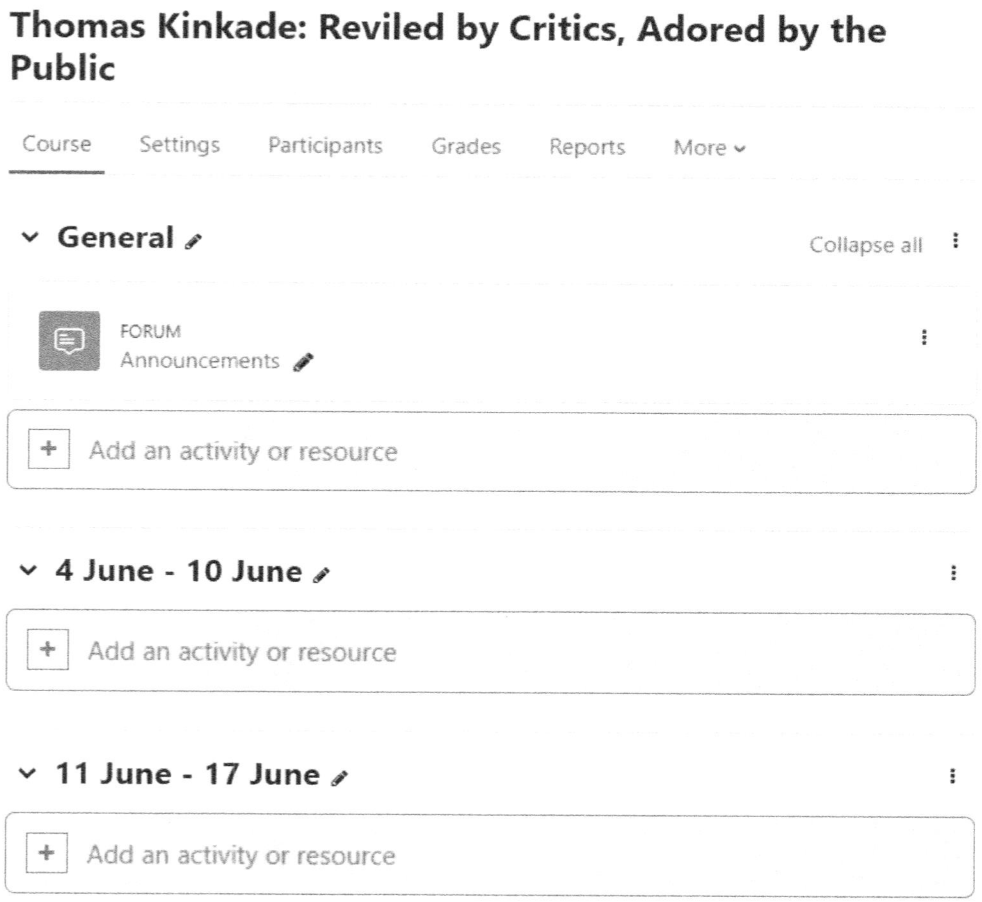

Thomas Kinkade: Reviled by Critics, Adored by the Public

Course   Settings   Participants   Grades   Reports   More ⌄

⌄ **General** ✎   Collapse all   ⋮

    FORUM
    Announcements ✎   ⋮

    [+] Add an activity or resource

⌄ **4 June - 10 June** ✎   ⋮

    [+] Add an activity or resource

⌄ **11 June - 17 June** ✎   ⋮

    [+] Add an activity or resource

Figure 3.22 – The weekly format

- **Social**:The **Social** format turns the entire course into one discussion forum. Discussion topics are displayed on the home page of the course. Replies to a topic are added and read by clicking on **Add discussion topic**. The **Social** format is very different from a traditional, sequential course. It lacks the ability to add activities and resources in the main course area, which you find in the **Topic** and **Weekly** formats. However, because the **Social** format turns the entire course into a discussion forum, it offers you the chance to put a discussion forum right into the course listings. Then, you can have a discussion appear in the course listing on the front page of your site.

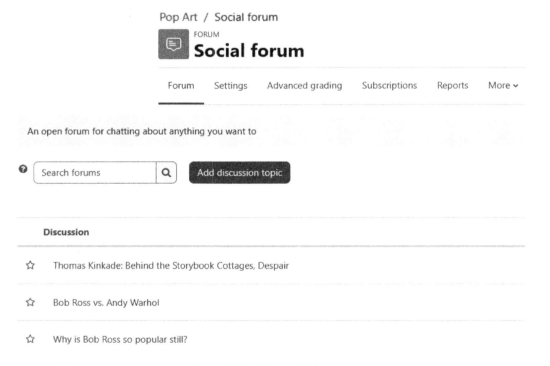

Figure 3.23 – The social format

- **Single Activity**: The Single Activity format looks like the **Social** format and usually centers around a discussion thread or forum.

> **When Should I Use the Sharable Content Object Reference Model (SCORM) Format?**
>
> If you want to use a SCORM package as a part of your course, use the **Topics** or **Weekly** format. Then, you can add the SCORM package as an activity in the course.

In the previous section, we learned how to set up and format a new course. Now, we can fine-tune the structure of the course by selecting the way the content modules are organized. The modules are labeled as weeks or topics, and you can adjust how many you have. In the following steps, you will learn how to configure your modules.

Before you start, it is a good idea to outline your course structure so that they align with your course goals. Course planning is vital in order to achieve your course objectives. So, to get started, you'll need to take a look at your learning objectives and then map them across the course. To do so, each module will relate to at least one learning objective. Each module will contain course content and activities, which we will cover in later chapters.

	Week 1	Week 2	Week 3	Week 4
Learning Objective 1	x			x
Learning Objective 2	x	x		
Learning Objective 3		x	x	
Learning Objective 4		x	x	x
Learning Objective 5			x	x

For now, make sure that your modules align with your organization's timelines and academic structure. For example, if you use a semester structure, you may wish to use the weekly format. Then, you can make sure to distribute the work (instructional materials, assessments, and activities) in a way that makes sure you cover the content comprehensively.

A course map can simply be a spreadsheet in which you list the learning objectives and then align them with the modules and the content.

Here is how to format your modules:

1. Select the number of weeks/topics in the course window. If you selected the **Topics** or **Weekly** format for your course, you must specify how many topics or weeks your course will have. You can change the number of weeks or topics in a course whenever you want. If you increase the number, blank weeks/topics are added. If you decrease the number, weeks/topics are deleted, or so it seems. One of Moodle's quirks is that when you decrease the number of sections in a course, the topics that are dropped are not really deleted; they're just not displayed to the students. If you increase the number of topics, those hidden topics will again be displayed to the students with their content intact. Also, teachers who are in editing mode will see the dropped topics as grayed out, in a section called **Orphan**. The teacher can still access and edit those orphaned topics.

2. Note that this is different from hiding weeks/topics from students. When you hide topics or weeks, students can't see them, but the teacher can. When a section disappears because the number of weeks/topics in the course is reduced, it is unseen to everyone, even the teacher. The only way to bring it back is to increase the number of weeks/topics.

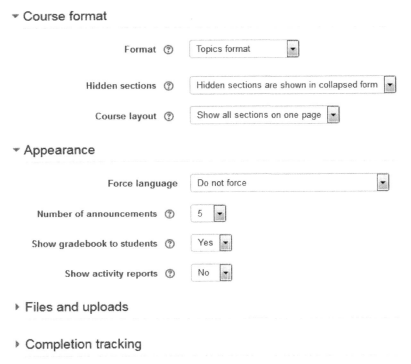

Figure 3.24 – Configuring the course format

- For a **Weekly** course, this field sets the starting date shown. It has no effect on the display of **Topic** or **Social** courses. Students can enter a course as soon as you display it; the course start date does not shut off or hide a course until the start date. The only other effect of this field is that logs for the course activity begin on this date.

- If you want to limit the dates on which a course is available for the students to enroll, look under **Course administration | Enrolled users | Enrolment methods**. Enable the **Self enrolment** enrollment method. Then, in the settings for **Self enrolment**, set the enrolment duration.

- If you want to test a course without creating user records, enter a date in the future for **Enrolment duration**. As you test the course, your activity will not be included in the logs. The same applies to administrators and teachers.

3. Select how the course will display hidden sections. You can keep a section that you're working on hidden and then reveal it when you're finished. If you want to modify an existing section, you can create a hidden duplicate of the section, work on it, and with a few clicks in a few seconds, hide the old section and reveal the new one. For example, if you are keeping sections hidden to keep your students together, be sure to add a signpost at the end of each one that tells them there is more to come. For example, you could congratulate them for successfully completing the module and that more will be available, as per the schedule or syllabus.

> **Tip**
>
> You can move resources between sections in a course. This makes a hidden section a convenient place to hold the resources that you might want to use later or that you want to archive. For example, if you find a site on the web that you might want to use in your course later but you're not sure, you can create a link to the site in a hidden section. If you eventually decide that you want to use the site, you can just move that link from the hidden section to one of the sections in the use-later pile.

4. Specify how many news items to show in the **Announcements** block. The maximum number of news items that the block will show is 10.

5. If **Show gradebook to students** is set to **Yes**, a student can view a list of all their grades for the course by clicking on the **Grades | Grade item settings** link in the **Site administration** block, as shown in the following screenshot:

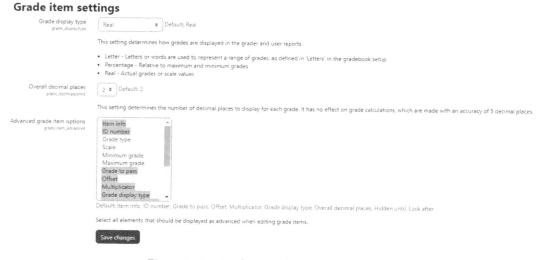

Figure 3.25 – Configuring the grade item settings

If the course allows **Guest access**, the guests will not be able to earn grades. So, if your site has a free sample course and you want people to see how Moodle displays their grades, you might want to encourage people to register for that free sample.

The setting for the maximum upload size limits the size of a file that a student can upload to this course. There is also a site-wide limit set under **Site Administration | Security | Site policies**. The smaller of the two settings – site-wide or course-wide – takes precedence here.

Figure 3.26 – Selecting the maximum upload size

The color and icons that Moodle uses are determined by its theme. Usually, you would use the same theme throughout your site. In the screenshot below, you can see the choice of either Boost or Classic theme.

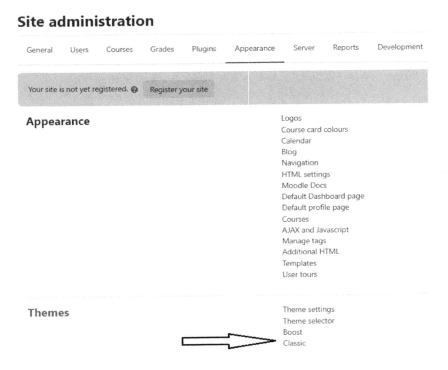

Figure 3.27 – Selecting the theme

> **Tip**
>
> A theme can do more than just provide a pleasant color scheme. For example, you can assign courses a distinctive theme for each teacher or assign the same theme to all the courses in a category. Themes are selected by the site administrator in the **Site administration** menu. For more about themes, check out the official Moodle site at `https://moodle.org/`.

6. Select **Group mode**.

    Later in the book, you will learn how to separate the students in a course into groups. This setting determines how the individual activities in the course react to the presence of groups in the course. If you do not use groups in the course, this setting has no effect.

    When set to **No**, all students in the course are considered to be in one big group. When set to **Separate**, students in a group cannot see the names of any other groups – that is, the work done by different groups is kept separate. When set to **Visible**, students in different groups can see each other.

    You can change this setting for individual activities. For example, suppose you want to run groups through a course separately. However, you have one project where you want all the students, in all the groups, to be able to see each other's work. You can choose **Separate** for the course and, for that one project, override the setting with **Visible**. Now, only for that one project, each group can see the other group's work.

> **Functionality Booster – If It's a Hybrid Course, Clearly Indicate Web Conferencing**
>
> Make sure that your groups have access to the web-conferencing links. If you are using BigBlueButton, the controls are easily accessible through Moodle. However, if you're using Teams or Zoom, you'll need to make sure that you provide the links and access information in a clear place. If you use groups, be sure that the web-conferencing information is clearly available and updated so that a student can access the web conference while in Moodle, or directly.

7. Normally, the group mode of a course can be overridden for each activity. When a course creator adds an activity, a teacher can choose a different group mode than the default one set for the course. However, when **Force group mode** is set to **Yes**, all activities are forced to have the same group mode as the course.

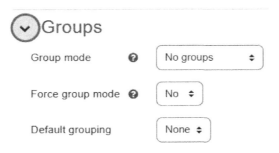

Figure 3.28 – Configuring group mode

8. The default grouping for the course determines how groups are filtered in the gradebook. This setting has no effect unless you are using groupings. A grouping is a group of groups. It can consist of one or more groups from the course. All groups can then be managed as a single group.

9. While you're working on a course, you may want to set **Course visibility** to **Hide**. This will completely hide your course from the students' view. Teachers and administrators can still see the course, so you can collaborate on the course content with them.

Figure 3.29 – Making the course visible or not

10. Select a setting for **Force language**. Selecting **Do not force** enables a student to select any language on the pull-down list of languages.

    Remember that the languages on the pull-down list are limited by the setting you choose under **Site administration | Language | Language settings | Display language menu and Languages on language menu**. Also, you must have the language pack installed for any language that you want to use. Also, remember that only the standard Moodle menus and messages are translated automatically when a student selects a different language.

11. If you want to use different terms for the roles in your course, you can use **Role renaming**. Moodle inserts your term for a teacher or student into its standard messages. You can substitute the term `teacher` with `instructor`, `leader`, or `facilitator`. For students, you can use terms such as `participant` or `member`.

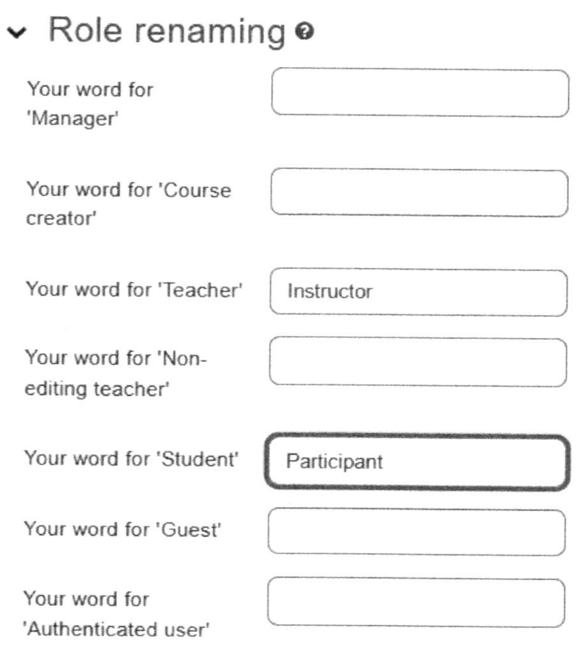

∨ Role renaming ❷

Your word for 'Manager'

Your word for 'Course creator'

Your word for 'Teacher'   Instructor

Your word for 'Non-editing teacher'

Your word for 'Student'   Participant

Your word for 'Guest'

Your word for 'Authenticated user'

Figure 3.30 – Renaming roles

12. You can add meta tags to help the course become more searchable.

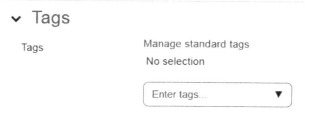

∨ Tags

Tags   Manage standard tags
              No selection

              Enter tags...   ▼

Figure 3.31 – Adding meta tags

13. Course custom fields allow you to assign the number of credits.To find the course custom fields, you need to go back to the **Site administration** page, then click on Courses. You will then see **Course custom fields** in the list of options after **Manage courses and categories**.

Figure 3.32 – Determining the number of credits

14. Finally, at the bottom of the page, click on the **Save changes** button.

Congratulations! You now have a new blank course. You're ready to start configuring and filling it with great material. In the next section, you will learn how to enroll students in the course and assign roles, giving them customized levels of access and permissions.

Enrolling teachers and students

Who will teach your course? Also, how will students be enrolled? The settings that you choose for your course enrollment will determine that. In this section, will learn how to enroll teachers and students in Moodle.

Assigning teachers

After a site administrator, manager, or a course creator has created a blank course, they can assign a teacher to build the course.

To assign a teacher to a course, carry out these steps:

1. Enter the course as an administrator or manager.

2. From within the course, select **My Courses | Participants | Enrolled users**.

3. In the upper-left corner of the page, click on the **Enrol users** button. The **Enrolled users** window is displayed, as shown in the following screenshot:

Figure 3.33 – Enrolling users

4. To find a user, enter any part of the user's name into the search field and then press *Enter* or *Return* on your keyboard:

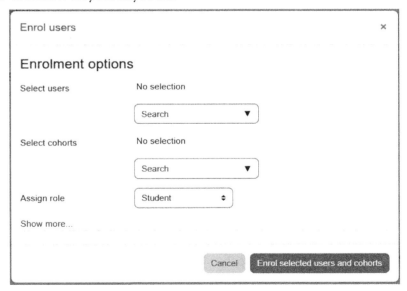

Figure 3.34 – Finding enrolled users

5.   From the **Assign role** drop-down list, select **Teacher**.

6.   Next to the user's name, click on the **Enrol** button. The display of that user's name will change to indicate that they are enrolled.

7.   When you have finished enrolling users, click on the close box for this window. On returning to the **Enrolled users** page, you will see the user added to the list of enrolled users.

How to set enrollment methods

A teacher can enable, disable, and arrange only the interactive enrollment methods. Interactive enrollment happens when a user tries to enroll in a course. The user must do something to be enrolled, such as select a course and confirm that they want to enroll, or pay for a course. Non-interactive enrollment methods are checked when a user tries to log in to a course – for example, an external database or Lightweight Directory Access Protocol (LDAP) server. Only a site administrator can enable or disable a login-time enrollment method. These are managed not at the course level but the site level. For in-depth guidance about enrollment methods, visit Moodle Docs `https://docs.` `moodle.org/400/en/Main_page`.

However, you may need to customize the methods for a specific course. So, for each course, you can enable or disable any or all of these enrolment methods. The following steps will guide you:

1.   Enter the course as a site administrator or teacher.

2.   Select **Site Administration | Plugins | Enrolments | Self enrolment**. The **Self enrolment** page allows users to choose which courses they want to participate in, as shown in the following screenshot:

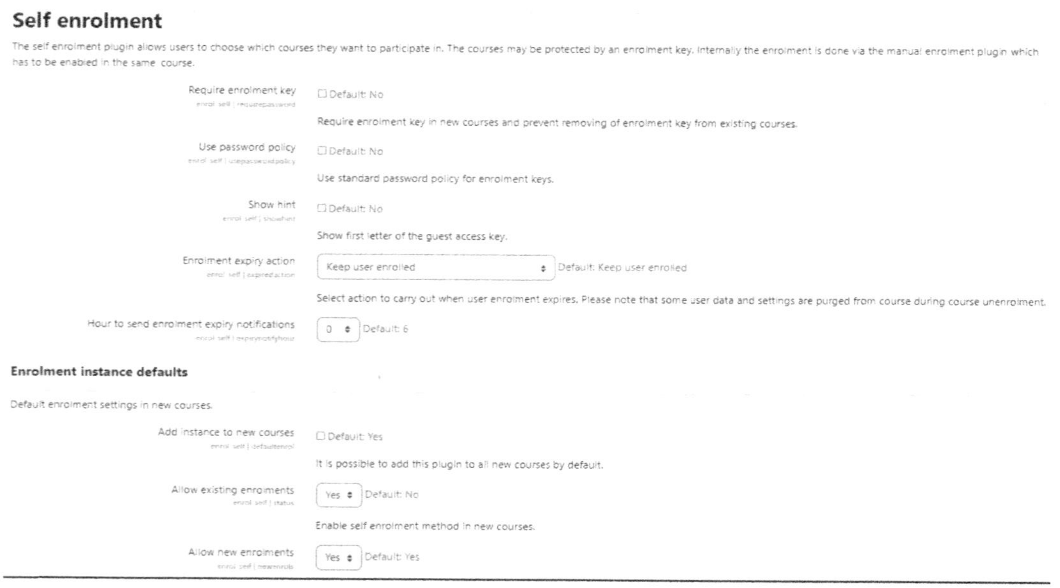

Self enrolment

The self enrolment plugin allows users to choose which courses they want to participate in. The courses may be protected by an enrolment key. Internally the enrolment is done via the manual enrolment plugin which has to be enabled in the same course.

Require enrolment key enrol_self | requirepassword	☐ Default: No
	Require enrolment key in new courses and prevent removing of enrolment key from existing courses.
Use password policy enrol_self | usepasswordpolicy	☐ Default: No
	Use standard password policy for enrolment keys.
Show hint enrol_self | showhint	☐ Default: No
	Show first letter of the guest access key.
Enrolment expiry action enrol_self | expiredaction	[Keep user enrolled ⬍] Default: Keep user enrolled
	Select action to carry out when user enrolment expires. Please note that some user data and settings are purged from course during course unenrolment.
Hour to send enrolment expiry notifications enrol_self | expirynotifyhour	[0 ⬍] Default: 6

Enrolment instance defaults

Default enrolment settings in new courses.

Add instance to new courses enrol_self | defaultenrol	☐ Default: Yes
	It is possible to add this plugin to all new courses by default.
Allow existing enrolments enrol_self | status	[Yes ⬍] Default: No
	Enable self enrolment method in new courses.
Allow new enrolments enrol_self | newenrols	[Yes ⬍] Default: Yes

Figure 3.35 – Displaying the self enrolment methods

3. To enable or disable an enrollment method for a course, click on the eye icon. When it is open, the enrollment method can be used for that particular course. When the eye is closed, that enrollment method is not available for that course.

4. Place the enrollment methods in the order in which you want this course to use them. Do this by clicking on the up and down arrows next to each enrollment method.

Many enrollment methods have a separate page for settings where you can configure the method, as follows:

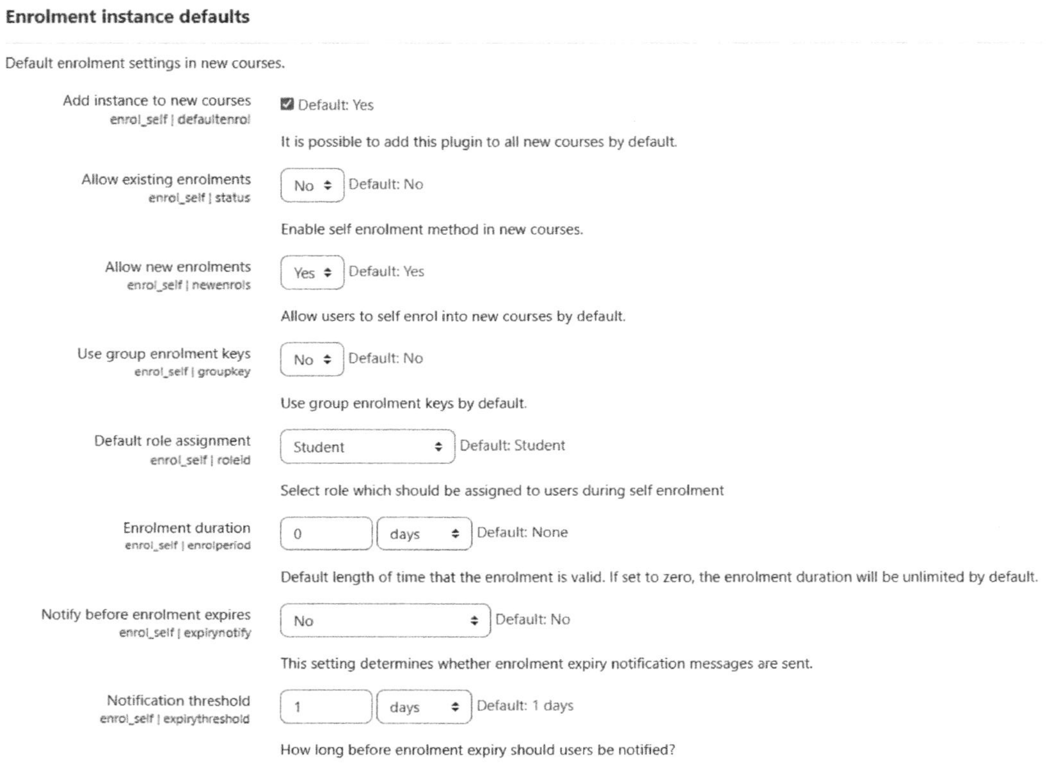

Enrolment instance defaults

Default enrolment settings in new courses.

Add instance to new courses enrol_self | defaultenrol	☑ Default: Yes It is possible to add this plugin to all new courses by default.
Allow existing enrolments enrol_self | status	No ⬍ Default: No Enable self enrolment method in new courses.
Allow new enrolments enrol_self | newenrols	Yes ⬍ Default: Yes Allow users to self enrol into new courses by default.
Use group enrolment keys enrol_self | groupkey	No ⬍ Default: No Use group enrolment keys by default.
Default role assignment enrol_self | roleid	Student ⬍ Default: Student Select role which should be assigned to users during self enrolment
Enrolment duration enrol_self | enrolperiod	0 days ⬍ Default: None Default length of time that the enrolment is valid. If set to zero, the enrolment duration will be unlimited by default.
Notify before enrolment expires enrol_self | expirynotify	No ⬍ Default: No This setting determines whether enrolment expiry notification messages are sent.
Notification threshold enrol_self | expirythreshold	1 days ⬍ Default: 1 days How long before enrolment expiry should users be notified?

Figure 3.36 – Configuring self-enrollment options

If you enable an enrollment method, you should at least look at the settings page for that method and determine whether you need to change any of the settings.

Summary

In this chapter, we learned how to start the process of building courses. We started by identifying how to work with categories and then configure courses in several different ways.

Moodle 4.0 includes a number of enhancements to give administrators more flexibility in how to display information in the Dashboard and on the **Site home** page, which greatly enhances the UX. The new options and flexibility mean that an administrator has more options, which in turn means more complexity in configuring the site and courses.

In this chapter, we covered how to customize the appearance of your courses so that it matches the needs of our learners and use Moodle as a powerful tool for creating the documentation necessary for accreditation reviews.

We also discussed the importance of including links to web conferencing in the case of synchronous and hybrid synchronous/asynchronous courses.

In general, make your best guesses when you first create a course, and don't let uncertainties about any of these settings stop you. As you add static, interactive, and social materials in the upcoming chapters, you can revisit the course structure and settings in this chapter and change them, as needed. In the next chapter, we will learn about resources in Moodle and how to use them.

Part 2: Implementing The Curriculum

In this book, you learn much more than simply how to set up resources and activities. You learn how to select the resources and activities that are the best fit for your course goals, the unique needs of the learners, and a unique blend of on-demand, "live," or blended delivery.

At each step, we use solid instructional design principles to guide along the way and create an ideal blend of interaction, engaging course content, and activities to help students review their knowledge and then demonstrate their knowledge and skills.

After you have completed Part 2, you will be able to use your course design plan to build courses that incorporate Moodle's activities and resources as well as the new functionality of Moodle 4.0. You will be able to use the flexibility of Moodle to incorporate content that engages students, accommodates all kinds of learners, and allows multiple methods of delivery. You'll also be able to add activities that keep your students engaged and on tasks. In addition, you'll find ways for students to interact with each other and collaborate. Finally, you'll be able to develop a wide array of assessments that help assure that students can demonstrate achievement of learning objectives and course goals.

In this part, we cover the following chapters:

4
Managing Resources, Activities, and Conditional Access

Living in a world where synchronous web conference delivery is a major part of content delivery means that your on-demand resources and activities need to be easily accessed, clearly mapped to course objectives, and incorporated into a web conference if needed. Further, as you develop your courses and curriculum in Moodle, it is important to plan well so that there is a level of consistency in an organization and presentation. Not only will you standardize your curriculum – you will also standardize your courses. Although it's easy to think that the flashiest content or assessment should be showcased, the reality is that you should keep your attention focused on the course learning objectives. All your content and assessments should map directly to the learning objectives. This chapter does not focus on specific resources or activities; that content is covered in later chapters. Our goal for this chapter is to provide an overview of the content that goes into your course and how to manage it at the course level. We'll introduce resources and activities but will not go into detail about each one until later chapters. Right now, the goal is to be able to see the big picture in order to plan your courses.

Before we begin, keep in mind that Moodle 4.0 has redesigned icons for the resources and activities, which makes it easier to incorporate scaffolding so that students can move forward through a course in a way that builds on the knowledge they're gaining, giving them a chance to apply it in a way that is more likely to result in success.

The goal of this chapter is to show you how to add content that provides instruction and assessment. You will also learn how to control students' access to resources, activities, and assessments.

The following topics will be covered in this chapter:

- Getting content ready
- Mapping your approach
- Identifying course goals and learning objectives
- Common settings
- Universal design for learning
- Adding a resource or activity
- Entering a name and description
- Showing and hiding a resource
- Setting the availability of a resource
- Rearranging items on the course home page

By the end of the chapter, you'll be able to list the types of resources and activities that Moodle offers and identify uses for them. You will be able to put together lessons with a wide variety of content and be able to align them to learning objectives. You'll also be able to use the resources and activities to engage your learners and keep them focused and energized about learning.

Course material – resources and activities

In Moodle, course material is either a resource or an activity. A **resource** denotes instructional material in the form of digital files used by students. They can be viewed, read, listened to, or saved. They can include web pages, links, files, graphics, videos, audio, and embedded social media.

An **activity** can include interactive applications, including polls, quizzes, assignments, tests, discussion forums, and wikis. They all involve interaction, either independently or with other students. Keep in mind that activities are interactive, while resources are not. Learners actively engage with activities, while resources can be passive.

Activities can be assessments, and thus can be graded. Keep in mind that if you are developing a course curriculum for a certificate or degree program, you will need to ensure that they are presented in a consistent manner. You may wish to create a set of guidelines in a **Course Design Document** (**CDD**), which you can share with all the instructors and instructional designers/technologists that are involved in creating courses or materials for it. The CDD can translate to a template, customized for all the courses and the curriculum. Your CDD can include your course map, which links the resources and activities to their corresponding learning objective.

Now that we have introduced the resources and activities, and we've discussed the importance of using a planning document such as a Course Design Document (CDD), we will review the steps to follow while getting your content ready for use in the course.

Getting content ready

It is a good idea to create a list of the resources that you will use and incorporate them in your course outline and a spreadsheet. You may wish to create a plan in the form of a storyboard, especially if you have a clear sequence of content and plan to incorporate different types of media. Your resources and activities are learning objects, which means that you can upload or link to them as objects and place them where it is most convenient. If any of your resources require plugins, make sure that they are installed.

Mapping your approach

Mapping your course materials (resources and assessments) to your learning objectives will help you avoid creating a course that confuses students, and it will help them achieve their learning goals.

The best sequence for mapping is to follow a simple workflow, depicted as follows:

1. Identify your learning objectives.
2. Create a course sequence (chapters or units).
3. Write the specific learning goals for each chapter or unit, and tie them to your main learning objectives.
4. For each unit or chapter, you'll have the following:

    * Chapter learning objectives

    * Course content (directly tied to learning goals)

    * Activities (should be measurable and tied directly to your learning objectives)

One popular way to create a course map is to develop a spreadsheet that creates an "at a glance" planning guide. Here is a very simple example of an initial course map. We will build it out further a bit later and use it as the foundation for the CDD:

Modules	Learning Objective 1	Learning Objective 2	Learning Objective 3	Learning Objective 4
Module 1	X			
Resources 1 (list the resources specifically for each module)	X			
Assessment 1 (list the activities specifically for each module)	X			
Module 2	X	X		
Resources 2		X		
Assessment 2		X		
Module 3			X	
Resources 3		X	X	
Assessment 3			X	
Module 4			X	X
Resources 4	X		X	X
Assessment 4			X	X

Once you have mapped your course materials to your learning objectives, you can move ahead to developing a course design plan, which can be in the form of a template-type document. Some people find a storyboard approach to be most convenient; others prefer to maintain a course map.

Identifying course goals and learning objectives

The learning objectives for a course correspond to the measurable performance that you would like your students to be able to accomplish by the end of the course. Course goals and learning objectives are often used interchangeably, although technically speaking, they should not be. Learning outcomes are statements that describe the knowledge or skills students should acquire by the end of a particular assignment, class, course, or program, helping students understand why that knowledge and those skills will be useful to them.

Learning objectives are similar to goal statements, but they are more specific and often relate to Bloom's taxonomy. They describe what students will be able to do by the end of a learning activity, using verbs that relate to cognitive levels:

- They are specific and measurable.

- They are student-centric.

- The verbs correlate to a hierarchy of cognitive skills, such as Bloom's taxonomy.

The best way to approach this is to develop a CDD that serves as a template and a checklist for the things to include in each course, as well as the offline/paper format. The CDD is organized around the overall learning goals and then the more specific learning objectives, which are then aligned with the course instructional materials and assessments.

As you develop your template (the CDD), you'll need to ask a few questions. How do you actually frame learning objectives on the course and at the unit level? How do you ensure that you frame them so that they're measurable and also at the correct cognitive level?

Bloom's taxonomy is the standard used for writing learning objectives, particularly in the cognitive domain. Bloom's taxonomy is used to classify educational learning objectives into levels of complexity and specificity. First developed in 1948 by Benjamin Bloom and later modified, the tool provides a framework for selecting the verbs used in describing outcomes and then mapping them to activities.

As one can see in the following diagram, in Bloom's taxonomy, the lowest rung of the ladder is the least complex, and it ascends to finally achieve the highest level of complexity:

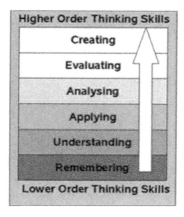

Figure 4.1 – A representation of Bloom's taxonomy

The value of using Bloom's taxonomy for developing a course as well as an instructional strategy is that it assures both clarity and consistency in design.

Further, by using Bloom's taxonomy, you can ensure that students follow a sequence, from less complex to more complex, and properly scaffold the learning so that concepts and skills build on each other at levels of increasing complexity and difficulty.

Now that you have mapped your course and have identified the learning objectives, you are ready to learn how to add and manage resources and activities in your course.

The map – CDD

We've mentioned planning and mapping the course. Now, we will go into more detail. If you are working in schools, it is likely that you are already required to develop a plan and follow the format established in your school. However, if you are in charge of corporate training, you may not be required to produce planning documents. Nevertheless, it is an excellent idea, especially if you require your employees to complete training in order to comply with regulations.

Let's return to the concept of a map for your course. This is known as the **Course Design Document (CDD)**. It is also often called the **Instructional Design Document**. It is a document that contains the basic organization, structure, formatting, and style elements to make sure that all the units are uniform and consistent. It also incorporates the instructional strategy, which will describe when and where to incorporate activities and items intended to engage the learner, connect to course learning objectives, practice for mastery, and retain knowledge.

You'll use the CDD as a guide for developing courses in your organization, allowing you to make sure that they are consistent. Here is an example of the items to include:

1. The main learning goal of the course
2. Learning objectives for the course (not more than seven or eight)
3. Information about who should take this course
4. A unit learning objective
5. A unit engager ("Did you know?" questions)
6. Unit instructional content (readings, videos, audio lectures, and graphics)
7. Learning activities – types and so on
8. Unit assessment(s) – types and so on
9. A template with formatting

The CDD will help you not only in the design of courses but also in working for accreditation visits. The CDD can take the form of a spreadsheet that builds on the course map. In the following table, you can see the design of the first module, which has more elements to make the course effective and engaging. This example only contains **Module 1** because all the other modules would contain the same elements. Note that I've covered a scenario where some of the content and activities in a module can actually satisfy more than one learning objective:

CDD FOR THE FIRST MODULE IN THE COURSE

Modules	Learning Objective 1	Learning Objective 2	Learning Objective 3	Learning Objective 4
Module 1 – title	X			
An introduction to the module announcement guide				
Map, diagram, or graphic 1	X		X	
Interactive engager 1 – Did you know? or a test of knowledge	X			
Resources 1 (list the resources specifically for each module) – include video, a transcript, and audio only	X	X		
Collaborative resources 1 – a discussion forum, wiki, and so on.	X			
Assessment 1 (list the activities specifically for each module, including practice assessments)	X			
Wrap-up for the module – a summary announcement	X			
A post-module survey (satisfaction, and so on)	X			

Your CDD can be a part of your self-review, in which you discuss all the different elements of the course content preparation and implementation and explain your strategy for keeping things consistent.

A universal design for learning

As you start to develop your course material, use Universal Design for Learning as a guideline to make sure that your learners have access, regardless of any physical or cognitive limitations. **Universal Design for Learning (UDL)** seeks to make learning possible for all learners, and it utilizes three different core areas – emotions, cognition, and physicality. Here is a link to the website: `https://udlguidelines.cast.org/`.

Using UDL will help you appeal to all kinds of learning styles, and learners who have audio, visual, or kinesthetic learning preferences will be accommodated. The three main areas of UDL are engagement, representation, and action and expression.

Further, UDL seeks to make sure that multiple ways of presenting material are incorporated so that someone who may have low mobility, low vision, low hearing, or cognitive challenges is able to participate:

The goal of Universal Design for Learning is to make sure that multiple means are used to achieve the following: Engagement, Representation, and Action and Expression. We will describe each one now:

- **Engagement**: UDL asks course designers to make sure that there are multiple means of engagement. UDL provides a number of different strategies to recruit interest and then, once interest has been gained, sustain effort and persistence. Finally, UDL provides strategies to develop a course that automatically builds self-regulation. For example, you might take a building block approach and break up large tasks into smaller activities so that students can make progress in bite-sized chunks along the way and then get rewarded for it.

- **Representation**: UDL provides strategies for designing a course that has materials that can be accessed in many different ways and use different senses. For example, if you have an audio recording, make sure to include a text transcript. Likewise, if you have a text, make sure that it can be converted to speech through an app. Make sure that when you develop your course, you include glossaries for specialized vocabulary and symbols and that your presentations are clear. Make sure you can promote understanding across languages, perhaps by including a translation function. Finally, be sure to use a scaffolding approach and facilitate comprehension by providing background knowledge, making it easy for a learner to see the big ideas. You can use resources for this such as content files, and you can also incorporate "check your knowledge" interactive activities.

- **Action and expression**: UDL asks you to think about what your learners will do when they encounter content or activities. How can you make sure that they can navigate easily and accomplish the task, even if they lack physical mobility? Also, what if they have low vision or low hearing? How will you make sure they have access and that you can make accommodations? Make sure that you build in assistive technologies where possible, and provide links to obtain them. Expression and communication are important for UDL, and make sure that you accommodate diversity and different cultural ways of understanding content. Use multiple media for communication, and as you ascend the levels of difficulty with Bloom's taxonomy, design the course so it ascends gradually rather than jumping around between levels of difficulty. Finally, help your learners succeed by building in goal-setting activities. You can include checklists or a clear set of guidelines. You can build in a framework for periodic announcements that help keep students on track. You can build in a template for instructors to fill in to help provide supportive tasks, such as guides to searching databases in the online library, or quick tips for designing discussion prompts that encourage students to share their lived experiences so that the virtual classroom is a place of community and supportive attitudes.

As you start to think about the course material, get to know who your learners will be. What are their backgrounds? Are they busy working adults? Are they part of a specific cohort from a degree program, certificate, or corporate training group? What do they plan to do with the knowledge once they have it?

As we move forward with our course map and our UDL strategy, let's familiarize ourselves with settings.

Settings that are common to all resources and activities

Once you have mapped out your course and made a list of the resources and activities that you'd like to add, you're ready to start taking a look at settings.

For all the different kinds of resources and activities, the first few clicks for adding them are the same. Also, there are some common settings that you will need to choose for all the resources and activities that you add. The following sections will explore these common settings in detail.

Adding a resource or activity

Here's the way to get started as you add a resource or activity. This applies to all resources and activities that you may wish to add.

Start by logging in as an administrator, course creator, manager, or teacher. Then, click on **Turn editing on**, which is found in the upper-right corner of the homepage or the **Administration** menu.

Here are the steps to add a resource or activity:

1. In a topic or week where you want to add the resource, click on **Add an activity or resource**. Go ahead and create placeholder activities or resources. You can move them around the course later.

2. To select the kind of resource or activity that you want to add, click on the kind of resource or activity in the **Add an activity or resource** dialog.

3. Click on the **Add** button.

4. Next, you can add more details that are particular to each resource or activity:

Figure 4.2 – Add an activity or a resource

Entering the name and description

For every resource or activity that you add, you must enter a name and description. You will also choose whether and when the description is displayed. As these fields are common to every resource or activity that you add, let's cover them under the respective sections.

Here is what you will see when you click on **Add an activity or resource**. If you are familiar with earlier versions of Moodle, you will see immediately that the menu displays icons instead of a list of names. It also includes **i** links that take you to an informational description of the resource or activity, along with helpful tips on effective ways to use them. Moodle 4.0 has updated and modernized the icons so that they are easy to recognize and use with all kinds of devices.

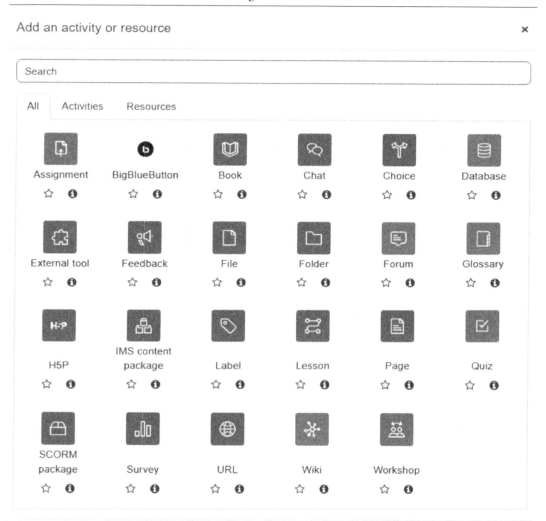

Figure 4.3 – A screenshot of the Add an activity or resource screen where you select
the kind of activity or resource you need to add

To give a name and description to a resource or an activity, do the following to add a page:

1. Enter a name in the **Name** block:

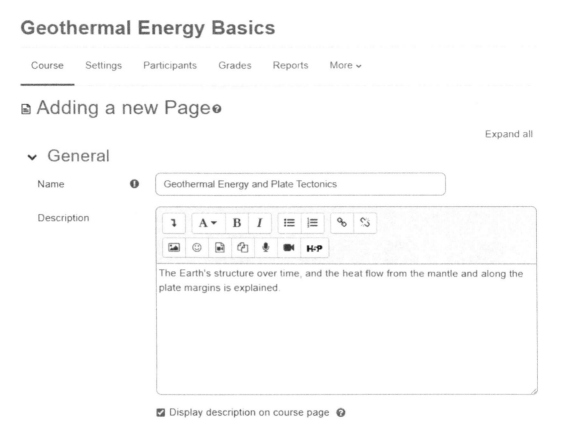

Figure 4.4 – How to update a page

When you are done with editing and saving the resource or activity, this name will appear as a link on the course page.

2.   Enter a description in the **Description** block:

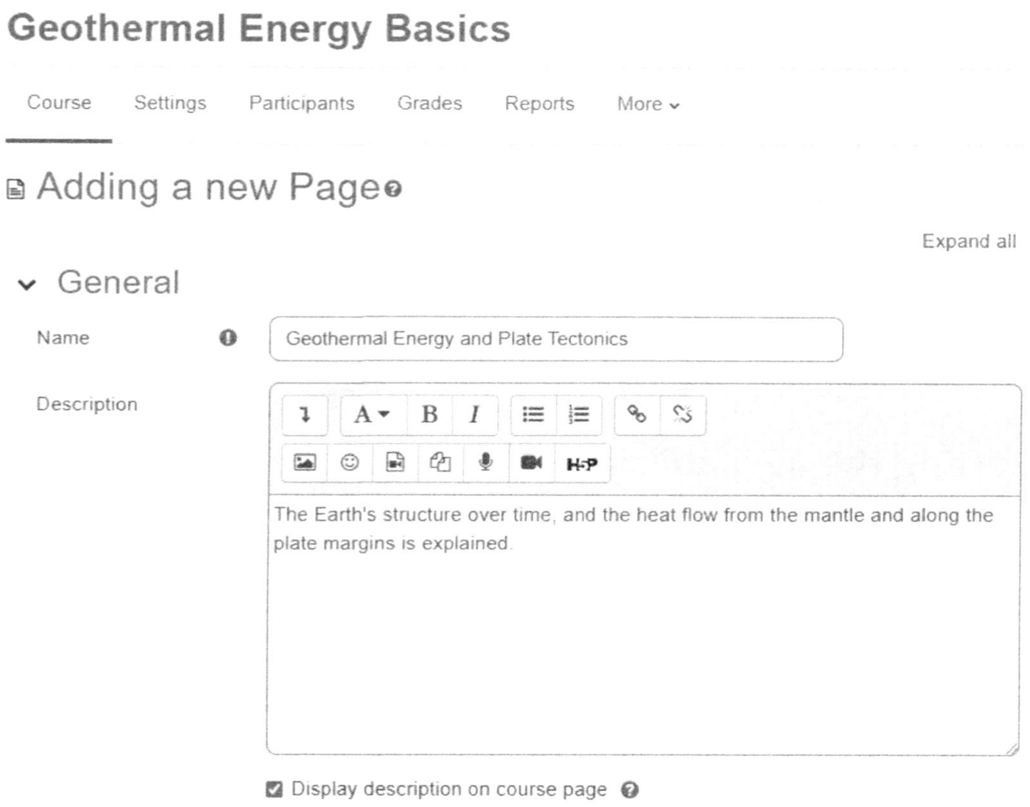

Geothermal Energy Basics

Course   Settings   Participants   Grades   Reports   More ∨

🗎 Adding a new Page❷

Expand all

∨ General

Name   ❶ | Geothermal Energy and Plate Tectonics |

Description

The Earth's structure over time, and the heat flow from the mantle and along the plate margins is explained.

☑ Display description on course page ❷

Figure 4.5 – The screen in Moodle that shows how to enter a description in a Description block

The item's description can appear on the course home page and also when the item appears in a list of resources for your course.

Showing and hiding a resource or an activity

When you add a resource or an activity to a course, you can make the item invisible to students until you are ready for them to see it. For example, you might want to keep a web page hidden until you have finished writing it. Alternatively, you might want to reveal a series of activities as the class completes them, as a group.

When you hide an item, it is still visible to a teacher, course manager, and site administrator. It is hidden only from students and visitors.

To show or hide an item, click on the eye icon next to it.

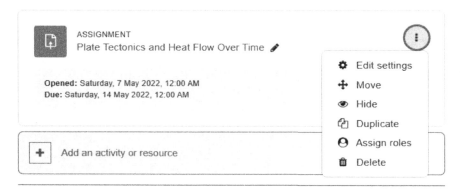

Figure 4.6 – Showing and hiding items

Setting the availability of a resource or an activity

Every resource or activity that you add will have **Common module** settings. If conditional access and/or completion tracking is enabled for the site, **Restrict access** settings are also added. As each item comes with these settings, we'll go through them once in the following sections.

Using the visibility setting to show or hide a resource

Under **Common module settings**, which are the settings you'll see when configuring any resource or activity, the visibility setting determines whether the resource or activity is visible to students, as shown here:

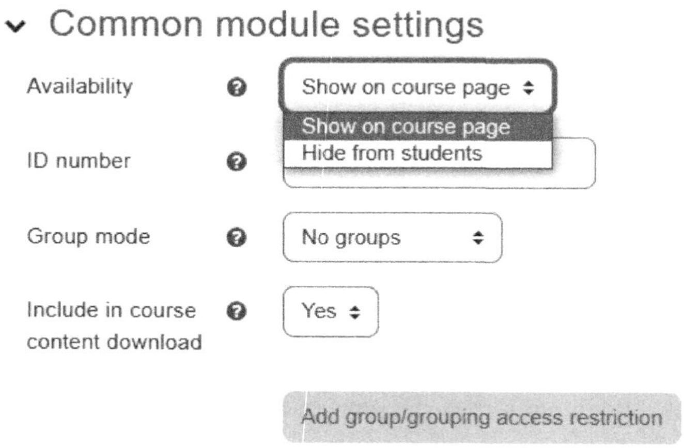

Figure 4.7 – How to add common module settings

Teachers and site administrators can *always* see the item. Setting this to **Hide from students** will, as expected, hide the item from students. Teachers can hide some resources and activities at the beginning of a course and reveal them as the course progresses. Alternatively, you can keep an item hidden while you're developing it and reveal it only when it's complete. This ties in with the **Show** and **Hide** setting on the course's main page. To determine whether it is visible or hidden to students, take a look at the eye icon. If the eye icon has a line through it, it is not visible.

The gradebook

You can collect and track grades using the course gradebook. The gradebook brings together the results of assessments that you have set up in your course. Keep in mind that the gradebook displays as a spreadsheet that contains rows for the course, the category, and then columns for each graded activity.

Let's take a look at the course display. Along the top of the report are rows that correspond to **Assignments**, **Quizzes**, and **Lessons**. Then, each row will have columns that align to each specific graded activity.

You can display the categories in different ways:

- Grades only (without the total column)
- Collapsed (the category total column only)
- Full view (the totals column for each category)

Keep in mind that you can hide columns or individual grades. It depends on what level of detail you need in order to keep track of your course and what kind of information you need in order to create reports for your organization.

The following screenshot shows the options you have to customize the gradebook and how it is displayed. Moodle 4.0 gives you more options than ever before, and it also makes it easier to go to a single place for all the gradebook and grade settings. Note that the appearance is laid out in a way that is intuitive so that even if you forget what each option means, you can click on the pull-down menu and discover your options.

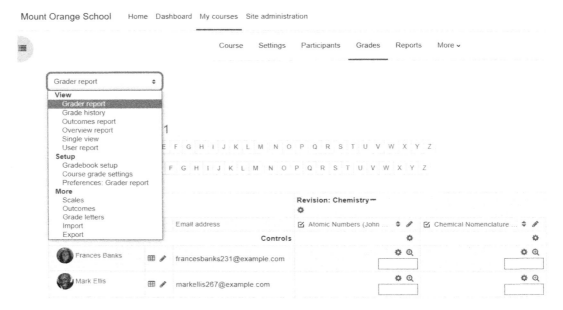

Figure 4.8 – How to modify the way that the gradebook and grader reports are calculated and displayed

Rearrange/move items on the course home page

After you've created resources and activities, you may need to change the order in which they appear to students. It's easy to do so because you can easily rearrange and move items on the home page so that they appear in a way that is most convenient for them (and the instructors).

As you build your course, you will be adding resources and activities to the course page. Moodle enables you to easily reposition these items. It's so easy to reposition them that I recommend not even worrying about getting them in the right place as you create them. Just go ahead and create, and you can rearrange them later.

Rearranging items on the course page can be done like this:

1. Log in to your course as a teacher or site administrator.

2. At the upper-right corner of the page, if you see a button that reads **Turn editing on**, click on the button. If it reads **Turn editing off**, you do not need to click on this button.

3. Next to the item that you want to move, place the mouse pointer over the crosshairs icon.

4. Drag the item to where you want it on the course page and drop it.

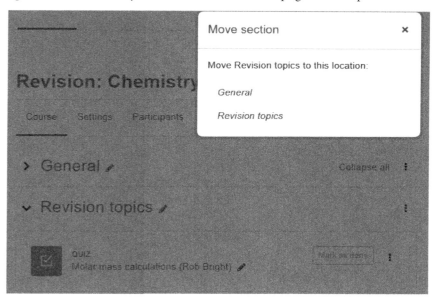

Figure 4.9 – How to move sections

Restricting access

The **Restrict access** setting enables you to set conditions that control whether a student can see this resource. You can use four kinds of conditions – dates, grades, user profiles, and customized fields. Restricting access can be a good way to ensure that students progress through the course in a way that builds on the knowledge they're gaining, and thus sets up effective scaffolding. We will examine more specific examples later, but it is a good idea for you to have an idea of this functionality now.

Also, keep in mind that we're talking about access to a resource in a course and not the course itself. In the following screenshot, we can see the restrictions and conditions for access to a resource:

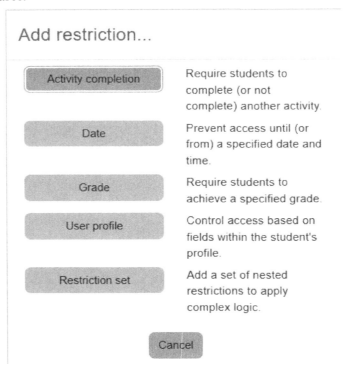

Figure 4.10 – Adding restrictions and conditions for access to a resource

In the following screenshot, the user is adding a date restriction to a resource. When might you want to restrict access? Restricting access is often a good idea if you want students or team members to make sure that they progress through a course in a synchronized way so that they are communicating clearly. It is also important if you want to motivate students by requiring them to achieve a minimum passing score on an assessment in order to progress. When an activity or resource is not yet open to a user, you can prevent users from seeing it on the course home page. The following example shows the eye icon next to the access condition. If the eye icon is open, then the student sees the activity/resource listed on the course home page even before the user has access. The activity/resource will be displayed in gray type. If the eye icon is closed, the item will be hidden from the user until the user has access:

⌄ **Restrict access**

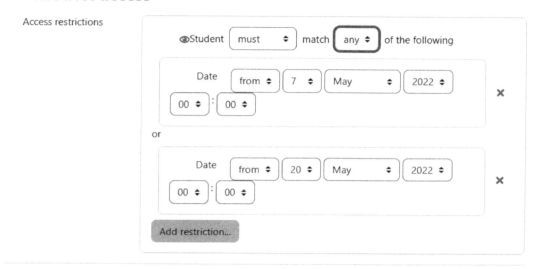

Figure 4.11 – A user adding a date restriction

Adding a **from** restriction makes the resource available on that date and time onward. If you do not add a **from** restriction, the resource becomes available immediately.

Adding an **until** restriction sets a date and time when the resource becomes unavailable. If you do not add a **from** restriction, the resource defaults to the time you establish the first date, and thus is closed immediately.

If your students report that they can't see an activity or resource, be sure to go back and check your settings. It's possible that you've not given them access.

The **Grade** condition setting enables you to specify the grade that a student must achieve in another activity in this course before being able to access the item.

In the following screenshot, you can see that the item will become available to the student only after the student scores at least 70 percent in the course. You may wish to refer back to *Chapter 2, Installing Moodle and Configuring Your Site*, for more details. Note that the course has established a start date and last available date.

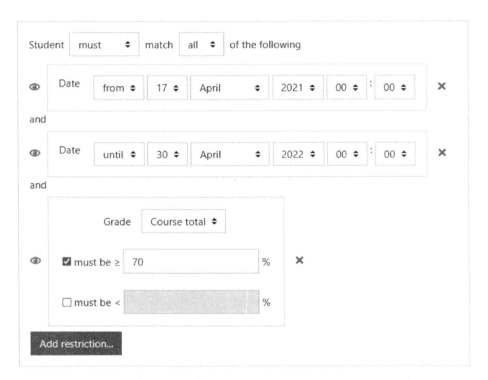

Figure 4.12 – How to configure it so that it is necessary to earn 70 percent in order to progress

Creating the activity completion settings

Depending on the type of activity, it is necessary to set the conditions and the completion requirements:

1. Select an activity or resource.

2. Under the **Administration** menu for the activity or resource, select **Edit settings**. In the following example, we are working with a forum in the course.

3. The **Settings** page is displayed. Scroll down to the section that is labeled **Activity completion**.

4. The **Completion tracking** field determines how this activity or resource gets marked as complete.

Either the student deliberately marks it as complete (**Students can manually mark the activity as completed**) or the student does something and then the activity is automatically marked as complete (**Show activity as complete when conditions are met**). Don't worry about which activities at this point. Just keep in mind that Moodle has a wide array of activities, which we will explore in more detail in future chapters.

If you choose to have the student manually mark the activity or resource as complete, the student will mark it as complete from the home page of the course.

If you choose to have the activity or resource automatically marked as complete, choose the following conditions that cause it to be so:

1. If you selected **Show activity as complete when conditions are met**, you must select the conditions that will cause the activity or resource to be marked as complete.

    If this is a resource, the student cannot earn a grade for it. Only **Student must view this activity to complete it** will be available.

    If this is an activity, both **Student must view this activity to complete it** and **Student must receive a grade to complete this activity** will be available.

2. At some point, you might want to run a report. You will learn how to run reports later in the chapters but to familiarize you with some of the capabilities early on, we're mentioning them here. For example, you may want to run the **activity completion report**. If you think you will want to use that report, then enable the setting for the expected completion date. This does not display the expected completion date to the student. You are not setting a due date with this setting. Only the teacher will see this date in the activity completion report. If you want to tell the student to complete this activity or resource by a specific date, you will need to use some other method to do so.

3. Once you have finished setting the completion conditions, either save the activity or resource, or continue modifying the other settings on the **Settings** page and then save.

Creating the activities or resources that will be restricted

Now that you have created the activities that need to be completed and set their completion conditions, you are ready to create an activity that will be restricted.

As stated earlier, the later chapters show you how to create resources and activities. Once you've created the resource or activity that will be restricted, proceed to the next set of instructions. To do so, you can refer back to the course map and the CDD, as shown earlier in the chapter.

Setting the competency conditions

Finally, in the resource or activity that we are trying to restrict, let's choose when it becomes available, as follows:

1. Select an activity or resource.

2. Under the **Administration** menu for the activity or resource, select **Edit settings**.

3. The **Settings** page is displayed. Scroll down to the section that is labeled **Competencies**.

4. For the **Activity completion condition** field, select the activity or resource that must be completed.

5. Select the **Send for review** condition.

6. You can add more completion conditions by clicking on the **Upon activity completion** button.

7. Either save the activity or resource, or continue modifying the other settings on the **Settings** page.

The following screenshot is an example of a course that has many activities, and the instructor wants the students to follow a specific sequence and not jump around.

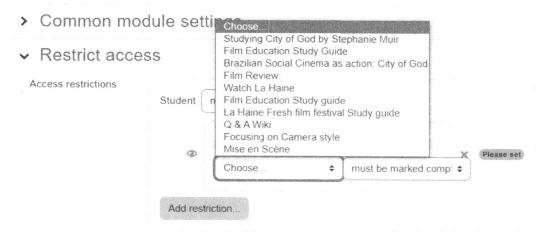

Figure 4.13 – Requiring students to complete activities before gaining access to a section that has restricted access

This setting is especially useful for quizzes. You can ensure that students review the material they need before taking a quiz and that they know what is required before the quiz becomes available. This is a good place to stop and reflect on how to enhance students' abilities to learn and retain knowledge.

> **Tip**
> You can also drag and drop entire topics. You'll know that you can do this if you see a crosshairs icon next to a topic. Just drag the crosshairs icon and drop it where you want the topic to go.

One of the most effective ways to ensure that your students move seamlessly through a course and that they're ready for the next level is to tie forward progress to the successful completion of a section, unit, or module. Be sure to keep the overall course design in mind, and also to make sure that the activities and resources are in ascending levels as per Bloom's taxonomy. Also, as you're creating your course flow, make sure you refer to the course map and the CDD.

Summary

In this chapter, you learned how to plan your courses so that you can map resources and activities to course learning objectives. You learned how the CDD can serve as a blueprint for course development and form the cornerstone and cognitive foundation of an instructional strategy. The chapter also covered the difference between resources and activities and the basics of adding them to a course. You also went through settings that are common to the different kinds of resources and activities.

Moodle 4.0's redesigned **Resources** and **Activities** icons are quickly identifiable and help users quickly recognize an activity or resource, appearing in the user's timeline for easy navigation.

In the next few chapters, you will learn about specific settings for specific resources and activities and how to make the best use of them. While you're learning how to work with those items, you can refer back to this chapter for a reminder on how to use common settings.

5
Adding Resources to Your Moodle Course

Resources are the instructional materials that students use to achieve the learning and performative outcomes of a course. In a world where face-to-face instruction is often severely curtailed, and synchronous web conferencing and asynchronous deliveries are often blended, readings, videos, maps, podcasts, and other kinds of documents are the key building blocks that are used in each course. Moodle gives you a way to organize the materials so that they flow in accordance with your course plan, and you can make the resources available in a way that makes sense, given your learning goals. The flexibility that Moodle offers has become increasingly important in today's environment of blended synchronous and asynchronous learning. This chapter will teach you how to add those resources to a course, as well as how to make the best use of them. We will also discuss how to select, sequence, and deploy the resources so that they contribute to student success in achieving outcomes.

In this chapter, we will cover the following topics:

- Tying resources to course outcomes
- Adding different kinds of resources
- Adding URLs and embedded resources
- Adding pages

- Adding files for your students to download
- Adding media – video and audio
- Organizing the resources

By the end of this chapter, you will be able to identify the appropriate resources to add and achieve the course learning objectives, manage the resources, and then use them effectively.

Tying resources to course outcomes

This is the time to review your course plan, which will involve the course map and **Course Design Document (CDD)**, which we discussed in *Chapter 3, Creating Categories and Courses*. As you may recall, the course map and CDD constitute a storyboard and learning outcomes. In Moodle, "resources" refer to the content that you'll include in the course. The interactive assessments and engagers are referred to as "activities," but we'll cover that in *Chapter 6, Adding Assignments, Lessons, Feedback, and Choice*. For now, let's consider the best way to develop the course materials that will best align with the course goals.

It is great to have lots of resources, especially those that align with all kinds of learners in the course. However, unless they are organized well, and they tie clearly to course outcomes, you'll generate frustration instead of confidence.

Planning and organization are the keys to success in selecting, sequencing, and deploying your resources. Always tie them first to the learning outcomes, and then ensure that they are grouped in ascending order of complexity so that you're building a strong foundation and then scaffolding it at higher levels.

So, the first step should always be to list the course outcomes and then create an outline of your course in which you start to identify the resources you'll need:

1. List course outcomes.
2. Review your course outline.
3. Identify the resources you'll need.
4. Map the resources to your outcomes and identify any gaps that may exist.
5. Develop your storyboard or CDD to place the materials in sequence.

The following is a planning grid or framework that you can use to keep track of your resources and make sure there are no gaps when it comes to your learning objectives and the Bloom's taxonomy levels. Keep in mind that the following table is simply a framework and that the entries I've incorporated are simply to help you get started. To make it easier to conceptualize, I'm using the example of a course called *English 1102: Writing about Literature*:

Learning Objective	Course Module	Bloom's Taxonomy Level	Readings (with the ability to use speech-to-text assistive technologies)	Graphics (with alt-tags that describe what is happening in the graphics)	Audio or Video (with a closed captioning option for hearing-impaired learners, as well as transcripts)
Define literary genres.	1	Remember	Definitions of literary genres. The file is in the course. List the filename and location (repository, URL, and so on)	Include a thumbnail, along with the filename and location. You may include a thumbnail of a painting of Lady Macbeth and tag it as "Drama."	Be sure to include audio files of the definitions of genres. Include the filename and location. Indicate the transcript's filename and location.
Explain how and why Richard III is an anti-hero.	2	Understand	A video that explains how and why Richard III is an anti-hero, along with Lady Macbeth, Macbeth, and others.	Include a thumbnail of Richard III, perhaps of the car park in England where they found his body and were able to analyze his twisted spine.	Make sure you have transcripts for any videos, as well as also a speech-to-text accommodation for the hearing-impaired.
Write a blank verse poem in the style of John Ashbery.	3	Apply	John Ashbery's "The Instruction Manual" in text, audio, and a video.	Find a graphic that evokes the mood of the poem "The Instruction Manual."	A link to "The Instruction Manual" at the Poetry Foundation, and also include a reading of it.

Learning Objective	Course Module	Bloom's Taxonomy Level	Readings (with the ability to use speech-to-text assistive technologies)	Graphics (with alt-tags that describe what is happening in the graphics)	Audio or Video (with a closed captioning option for hearing-impaired learners, as well as transcripts)
Analyze the structure and use of repeated elements in Zora Neale Hurston's short story "Sweat."	4	Analyze	Zora Neale Hurston's short story "Sweat," which includes text, audio, and a video with tags.	Create a collage of a wicker basket holding laundry, a rattlesnake, a high-heeled shoe, a leather whip, and a bar of soap.	Provide the text, plus an audio file of a reading of the story.
Critique the way that Jamaica Kincaid builds a story based on a collage of phrases and sayings.	5	Evaluate	"Girl" by Jamaica Kincaid, which would include the text of the story, plus an audio recording.	Include a photo or painting of a female teenager from Antigua in the Caribbean.	Provide the text, plus an audio file of a reading of the story.
Design a booklet with commentary featuring the geological poems of Emily Dickinson.	6	Create	The poems of Emily Dickinson, including references to geology. Include text and audio recordings. Also, include an article about Emily Dickinson and the state of geological science in the mid-19th century.	Include a painting from the Hudson River School artists painting New England landscapes.	Provide the text, plus an audio file of a reading of the poems. Also, include links to the Hudson River School artists and a few articles on the state of the science of geology in the mid-19th century. All should be in a form that can be used with text-to-speech apps.

Figure 5.1 – Course map (planning grid)

It is also a good idea to tie course resources to delivery methods (synchronous, asynchronous, blended pedagogy, and so on) so that you can optimize the way that they are deployed. For example, a 90-minute video might be appropriate for asynchronous or *on-demand* courses, but not for a synchronous course, where *live* interaction is where most of the learning takes place.

Now that you've learned how to connect your resources to learning outcomes, you'll learn how to add the resources to your course so that you can use them effectively.

Adding different kinds of resources

The following table lists the types of resources that are available in Moodle. Resources can be added from the **Add an activity or resource** drop-down menu. Using this menu, you can add the following resources:

Resource	Description	Advantages	Disadvantages
Book	A book is a series of web pages, organized into chapters. A book can consist of one or more chapters. This is a good option for presenting a series of web pages that you want the student to read in order. It keeps things neat and clean so that your students do not have to wade around in a chaotic jumble of content.	The material is presented in a set sequence that clarifies the timing and the order to engage with the content. The presentation is clear and clean.	There is little or no flexibility to change the order of the chapters once they have been set. Also, it is not possible to break down subchapters.
File	Moodle can serve a single file to your student. If Moodle's built-in media player can play the file, you can configure it to automatically embed. Alternatively, you can configure the file so that it downloads to the student's computer and lets the student's computer determine how to open and display it. You can place file instances within the folder of a chapter, which makes it easy for the student to know which resources correspond to particular sections of the course.	It is easy to rearrange and reorder the files. Letting students download files makes it possible for them to access the content, even if they do not have internet access.	Files can be small, and rearranging them can be time-consuming if you want to rearrange a number of them. Also, it is necessary to ensure that the student has a way to open the file, especially if it is in a non-standard format.

Resource	Description	Advantages	Disadvantages
Folder	A folder is a collection of files that you have added to the course. For example, you can have a folder for each topic in a course, where you give the student all the files needed to complete the exercises for that topic. Alternatively, a folder can be for a specific activity, especially if there is a project that needs to be completed and the instructions, guidelines, and examples are within that set.	Folders are wonderful "one-stop-shop" places where students can easily find the content they need.	Once a file is within a folder, the title of the file is not visible until the folder is opened. It can be hard to find individual files.
Label	A label is a text, graphic, or media file that you put on the home page of a course. Almost anything that you can put onto a web page, you can put onto the home page of your course. You usually use a label to describe or label the content around it. You can use labels as signposts to help learners organize information into categories.	Labels are wonderful navigational tools and they help students know where to go.	If you do not use labels that correspond to the objectives, modules, or chapters (or books), it can be very confusing for the student. Furthermore, labels can make the course page too long.
Page	A Moodle page is a web page that you create using Moodle's web page editor. A page is effective in organizing content around a specific topic. On the page, you can include links, folders, and files, and you can also create text content. A page can have the appearance of a digital textbook.	Pages can incorporate a great deal of information in one place. They are portable, which is to say that you can insert them wherever you'd like into one or more courses.	Pages can take some time to build and can also get lost if they're not linked into the course well.
URL	A URL is a link to another place on the web. Usually, you link to a page or file that exists outside of Moodle. However, you can link to a place inside your own Moodle site.	Using links is a great way to save storage space and time. The link's tags and descriptions can often be incorporated into your description.	Web pages can change and your link may go dead without your realizing it, and as it does so, you lose the content you were depending on for your course.

Resource	Description	Advantages	Disadvantages
Lesson	Although classified as an activity, a lesson can be considered a resource or an activity. It's a bundled set of pages or instructional activities that are designed as pathways to learning. They should align with your storyboard or CDD and fit into the overall learning plan to tie to learning objectives.	A lesson is a great way to bundle a module and make sure that students follow a sequence of content and activities and that they stay engaged with a blend of content, interactive activities, and mini-assessments.	Lessons can take time to build, and to be effective, they should be planned very carefully. Some of the content may become stale and it may be necessary to go in and update that content or activities. You must keep very well organized to keep track of the individual components in the lesson and their versions.
H5P	H5P stands for HTML5 Package, and it is the latest specification of the HTML markup language web framework, which accommodates interactive, self-playing content such as presentations, videos, questions, games, quizzes, and more. H5P packages are often acquired externally and can be uploaded to the Moodle site. Quiz activities are auto-graded and the grades go into the gradebook.	HTML5 packages are often professionally done and are available from educational material providers. The auto-grading aspect is very convenient. The materials are of high quality and are engaging. HTML5 templates are often responsive, so they look good and work on different devices and in different browsers (ideally).	HTML5 can be expensive, and since it often comes as a package, you can't customize or modify specific parts of the packages. Like Java, CSS, JavaScript, and other older languages, HTML5 will eventually become obsolete. It also may be vulnerable to security issues.

Resource	Description	Advantages	Disadvantages
 SCORM package	A SCORM package consists of bundled learning objects that can be zipped and added to a course. The learning objects are often pages, and the SCORM package contains a table of contents, consisting of the course content and quizzes, which, when graded, are recorded in the gradebook.	SCORM packages are often used for presenting content, including multimedia and animation. They can also include assessments. Many institutions require content that is uploaded to be SCORM-compliant. SCORM was first developed by the US government, and thus has a high rate of adoption.	SCORM packages can contain animation and multimedia in old formats that will no longer play, or that require external drivers. You must be aware of this when evaluating pre-packaged SCORM bundles.

Figure 5.2 – Different kinds of resources

Having a selection of resources that comprise your instructional materials and connect to the learning objectives will help you have a successful course, as well as helping your students have a very positive user experience. Now that you know what is possible, you will learn how to link to them and embed them for maximum functionality.

Adding URLs and embedded resources

On your Moodle site, you can show content from anywhere on the web using a link. You add this link to your course's home page. When the student clicks on the link, the linked item is displayed.

When using content from outside sites, you need to consider the legality and reliability of using the link. Is it legal to display the material within a window on your Moodle site? Will the material still be there when your course is running? When in doubt, link to the resource. Take a moment to review the Creative Commons license, as well as resources that are available for educational use under FAIR guidelines: `https://creativecommons.org/licenses/`.

Display options – Embed, Open, and In pop-up

You can choose how the page is displayed; there are three options:

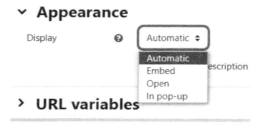

Figure 5.3 – Configuring the appearance of the URL or embedded resource

You can **embed** the linked page into a Moodle page. Your students will see the **Navigation** bar; any blocks that you have added to the course and navigation links will be shown across the top of the page, just like when they view any other page in Moodle. The center of the page will be occupied by the linked page.

Open will take the student off your site and open the linked page in the window that was occupied by Moodle.

Finally, **In pop-up** will launch a new window on top of the Moodle page, containing the linked page:

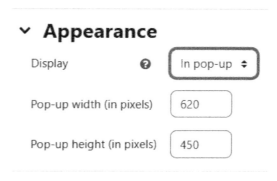

Figure 5.4 – Configuring the resource to create a pop-up window

We will look at these options in detail in the following sections.

Embed

To embed a page or a player, you will need to copy and paste the **embed** HTML code when you select a resource to include. You will see the options, and when the window for embed opens, you can simply paste the code into the box.

Open

When the user clicks on the link to the resource on the course home page, Moodle displays the page, along with the description of the link and a link to the outside page:

Figure 5.5 – An example of how an embedded page is displayed within Moodle

Clicking on the link activates the player, which is now embedded in your page. The learner can now view the resource while staying in Moodle (in this case, a YouTube video). However, sometimes, the video might be too tiny for the detail, and the learner would like to watch it in full screen. In that case, they would click on the *enlarge* square, which will take the learner outside Moodle and directly to the YouTube video:

Figure 5.6 – Clicking the bracketed square in the embedded YouTube
view will expand the view to full page

In pop-up

When the learner clicks on the link to the resource on the course home page, Moodle displays the page with the description of the link and a link to the external page:

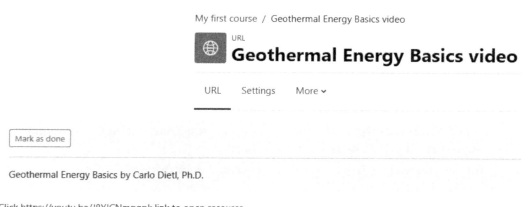

Figure 5.7 – The link to the resource that's been set to pop-up mode

Clicking on the link opens a pop-up window containing the external page. It is displayed on top of the window that's displaying your Moodle site:

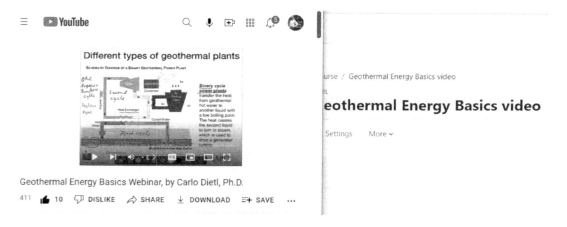

Figure 5.8 – In pop-up mode

Clicking a link when you're using **In pop-up** mode will open the page of an external website on top of the window.

The following section contains instructions for creating a link on your course home page, and for using these options.

Adding links

To add a link to a resource on the web, follow these steps:

1. In the topic or the week where you want to add the resource, click **Add an activity or resource**. If you're not sure where you want to add the link, just make your best guess. You can move it around the course later.

2. The **Add an activity or resource** dialog box will be displayed. Click on the radio button next to **URL**.

3. Click on the **Add** button.

4. Enter a **Name** and **Description** for the link. To learn more about how the name and description affect the learner experience, please refer to *Chapter 4, Managing Resources, Activities, and Conditional Access.*

5. In the **External URL** field, enter the web address for this link.

6. Under **Appearance**, from the **Display** drop-down menu, select the method that you want Moodle to use when displaying the linked page – that is, **Embed**, **Open**, or **In pop-up**. Choosing **Automatic** will make Moodle choose the best method for displaying the linked page.

   For more information about these display options, check out the *Display options – Embed, Open, and In pop-up* section, explained previously.

   The **Display URL description** checkbox will affect the display of the page, but only if **Embed** is chosen as the display method. If selected, the **Description** details will be displayed below the embedded page.

7. Under **Appearance**, you can set the size of the pop-up window. If you don't select **In pop-up** as the display method, these fields will have no effect.

8. Under **Parameters**, you can add parameters to the link. In a web link, a parameter will add information about the course or a student to the link.

9. **Common Module Settings**, the **ID number** field, and the **Restrict Availability** settings were covered in *Chapter 4, Managing Resources, Activities, and Conditional Access.*

10. Click on one of the **Save** buttons at the bottom of the page to save your work.

In addition to URLs and embedded pages from outside websites, it is possible to add additional pages to the course. In the next section, you will learn how to add pages and then add content to them.

Adding pages

Moodle enables you to compose a web page and add it to your course. The page that you add will be created and stored on your Moodle site. Be very strategic when adding Moodle pages. If you are not careful, you'll create confusion. Here are the best ways to use pages:

- **Add content that ties to the course outline**: You may have short narratives or an entire chapter. Creating pages rather than a file allows you to also include links and for the navigation to flow very smoothly so that your students stay within Moodle at all times.

- **Add portal pages with introductions, plus links, files, and books**: You may wish to have a long introduction to your content for a specific unit or chapter of your course. You can create a page, add your introduction (including graphics and text), and then have an organized set of links, files, folders, and even books.

When you add a page to your course, Moodle displays a text editor. Using this editor, you can put almost anything onto the Moodle web page that a normal web page can contain.

A link to the page that you create will appear on the course's home page.

If you can use a basic word processor, you can use most of the web page editor's features. A full discussion of the editor's features is beyond the scope of this section. Instead, we will examine a few of the key features that are available in Moodle's editor. Please note that you can include math and chemical symbols, as well as HTML.

Adding a page to your course

To add a page to your course, follow these steps:

1. In the topic or the week where you want to add the resource, click on **Add an activity or resource**. If you're not sure where you want to add the link, just make your best guess. You can move it around the course later.

2. The **Add an activity or resource** dialog box will be displayed. Click on the radio button next to **Page**.

3. Click on the **Add** button.

4. Moodle will display the **Settings** page for this resource.

5. Enter a **Name** and **Description** for the page. The name will become the link to this page and will appear in the section that you added it to on the course's home page.

If you select the **Display description on course page** checkbox, the description will appear on the course's home page. You can use this feature to tell the student what to expect when they view the page and tell them its purpose:

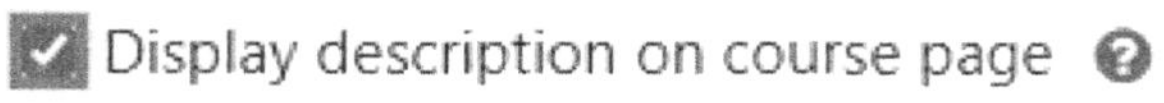

☑ Display description on course page ❓

Figure 5.9 – Selecting the checkbox to display the description on the course page

To learn more about how the name and description affect the user experience, please refer to *Chapter 4, Managing Resources, Activities, and Conditional Access*.

On the **Settings** page, you can compose the web page. Scroll down to the **Content** section; you will see a text editor for composing the page and for editing the page's content:

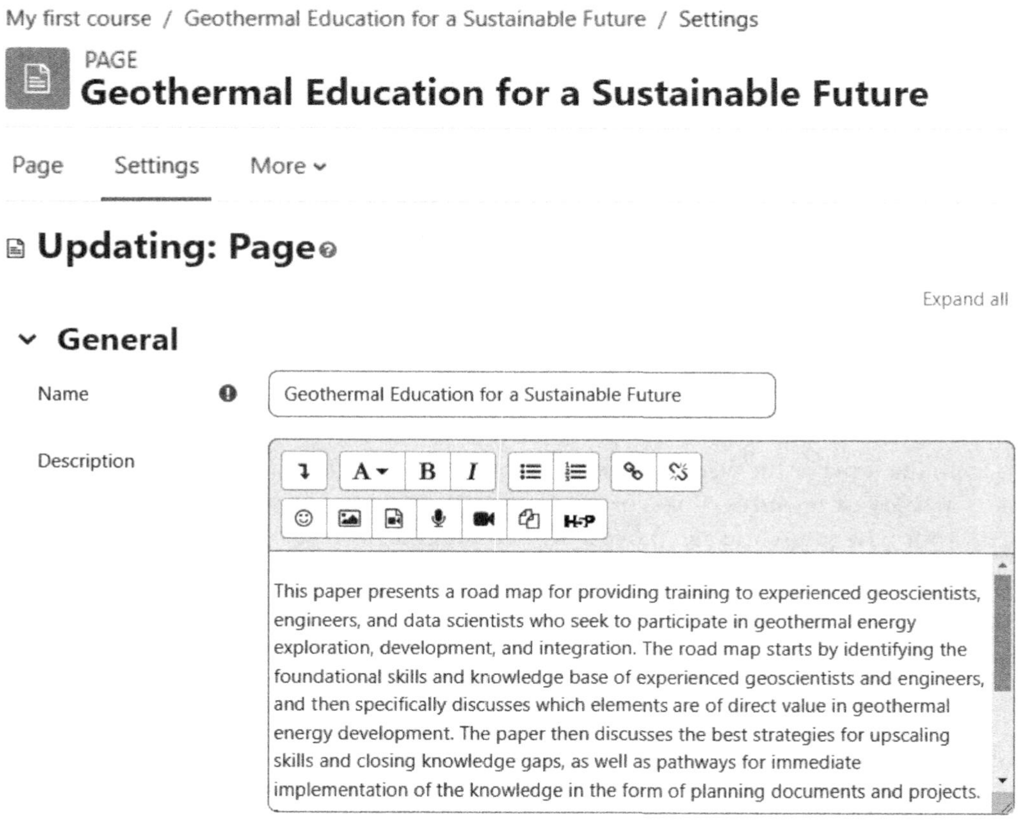

My first course / Geothermal Education for a Sustainable Future / Settings

PAGE
Geothermal Education for a Sustainable Future

Page   Settings   More ⌄

📄 Updating: Page❓

Expand all

⌄ General

Name   ❗   Geothermal Education for a Sustainable Future

Description

| ⤵ | A ⌄ | B | I | ☰ | ☰ | % | ⚒ |

| ☺ | 🖼 | 🖼 | 🎤 | 🎬 | 🗂 | H5P |

This paper presents a road map for providing training to experienced geoscientists, engineers, and data scientists who seek to participate in geothermal energy exploration, development, and integration. The road map starts by identifying the foundational skills and knowledge base of experienced geoscientists and engineers, and then specifically discusses which elements are of direct value in geothermal energy development. The paper then discusses the best strategies for upscaling skills and closing knowledge gaps, as well as pathways for immediate implementation of the knowledge in the form of planning documents and projects.

Figure 5.10 – The text editor in the Settings page, which allows you to compose the new page

Adding images

When you select an image to add to a Moodle page, you can choose images from those that you have already uploaded in Moodle, or you can upload a new image. Uploading huge image files can take up space and slow down page load times. It is a good idea to optimize your images.

A less obvious feature is the ability to link to a picture that is hosted on another website. If you are using pictures hosted on another website, you can add the link, but be aware that link addresses change often. Also, be sure to give credit.

Inserting an image file

This procedure is for inserting an image file that you have archived on your computer or an external hard drive or flash drive. In this example, the user has a diagram that they want to insert into the page, as follows:

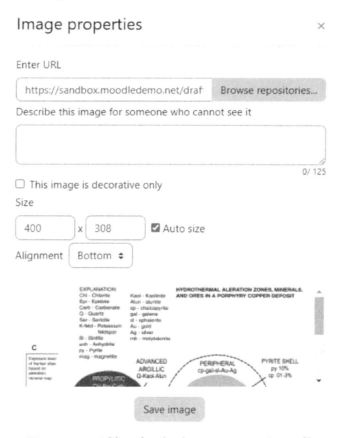

Figure 5.11 – Adding details when inserting an image file

To insert an image file, follow these steps:

1. On the Moodle page, click to place the insertion point where you want the image to appear.

2. Click on the **Choose File** icon, as shown here:

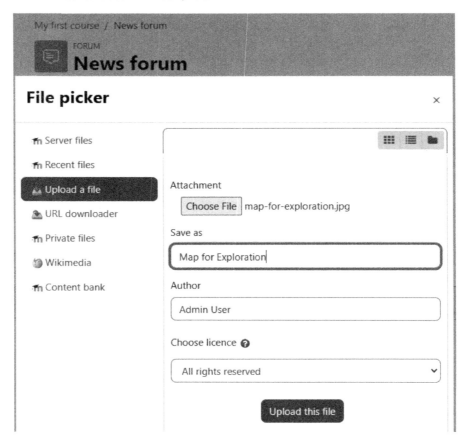

Figure 5.12 – Inserting an image in a news forum by clicking on the Insert Image icon

3. The **Insert/Edit image** window will appear. In this window, click on the **Find or upload an image** button.

4. The **File picker** window will be displayed. In this window, click on the **Upload a file** link.

5. Click on the **Choose File** button.

6. Locate the file on your computer and select it.

7. Click on the **Open** or **OK** button.

8. In the **Save as...** field, give the file a user-friendly name. You can use special characters and spaces.

9. The **Author** field is automatically filled in with your name. If someone else is the owner of this file, enter their name here.

10. From the drop-down list, choose a **license** for this file. This allows you to inform other Moodle teachers who want to use this file about what they can legally do with the file.

11. Click on the **Upload this file** button. The file will be uploaded to your Moodle system and you will be returned to the **Insert/edit image** window.

12. It is good practice to fill in the **Image description** field. This is used by visually impaired users who can't see the image and by search engines to index the image.

13. If needed, fill out the fields under **Appearance**. You may want to resize the picture since Moodle will, by default, display the picture at its original size.

14. Click on the **Insert** button. The picture will be inserted into the page.

Pasting text

Many times, we prefer to write text in our favorite word processor instead of writing it in Moodle, or we find text that we can legally copy and paste into Moodle. Moodle's text editor allows you to do this.

However, ensure that you keep in mind that Microsoft Word's various versions can do strange things to formatting. You may wish to strip out all the macros that create very clean text. You can use Notepad, or even Notepad++ (`https://notepad-plus-plus.org`). Once you've stripped out Microsoft's macros, you'll have to go back in and format (bold, underline, and so on), and you'll have to make your URLs live.

To paste text into a page, you can just use the keyboard shortcut. Try using *Ctrl + V* for Windows PCs and *Command + V* for Mac. If you use this method, the format of the text will be preserved.

Stripping out the formatting when pasting text from Microsoft Word

When you paste text from a Microsoft Word document onto a web page, it usually includes a lot of non-standard HTML code. The same thing occurs with other word processing programs, such as Google Docs. This code doesn't work well in all browsers and it makes it more difficult to edit the HTML code on your page. Many advanced web page editors can clean up Word HTML code. Keep in mind that the editor cleans up any code that could be dangerous and create vulnerabilities that could be exploited by hackers. So, don't be surprised if your text looks different than you had expected.

Moodle's web page editor can also clean up Word HTML code. You can also use Moodle's editor function to include math and chemical symbols.

When pasting text that was copied from Word, use the **Clear Formatting** icon. This will strip out most of Word's non-standard HTML code:

Geothermal Energy Basics / Education for a Sustainable Future

Figure 5.13 – The Clear Formatting icon

To strip out extraneous coding from Microsoft Word, Google Docs, or another program, click on the **Clear Formatting** icon.

Accessibility checker – do you need to add headings for assistive technologies?

To determine whether or not you need to add more headings to your text so that people who rely on assistive technologies can access the content, click on the button with a person with their arms out, as highlighted in the following screenshot. Doing so will help you align with *Universal Design for Learning* principles:

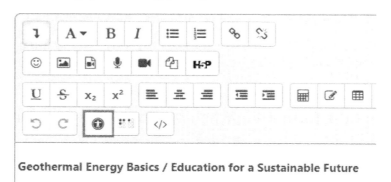

Geothermal Energy Basics / Education for a Sustainable Future

Figure 5.14 – The Assistive Technologies icon

To make sure your text is accessible for assistive technologies, click the **Clear Formatting** icon.

Composing in an HTML editor and uploading to Moodle

There are a few disadvantages of relying on Moodle to strip out Microsoft Word macros. First, the spacing is rarely exactly right, and to correct it takes quite a bit of time. However, it may not be possible to be online all that time, so you may wish to work offline and not in Moodle. So, you may want to compose your web page in an HTML editor such as **Adobe Dreamweaver** or even the free web-based HTML editor **SeaMonkey**. This is especially true if you want to take advantage of these editors' ability to insert advanced features into your web page. How, then, do you get that page into your Moodle course? You can copy and paste the HTML code from your web page editor into the Moodle page editing window. To do this, you must do the following:

1. Select the HTML view in your web page editor. For example, in Dreamweaver, you would select **View | Code**, and on the front page, you would select **View | Reveal Codes**:

Figure 5.15 – The HTML icon

To reveal the HTML code in Moodle and edit it, click the **HTML** icon.

2. Select the HTML code in your web page between the two body tags – that is, drag from just after the `<body>` tag near the top, to just before the `</body>` tag at the end. Copy the code with **Edit | Copy** or by pressing *Ctrl + C*. Then, do the following:

    I.   Switch over to Moodle and create the new web page.

    II.   Show the HTML code by clicking on the icon.

    III. Paste the code by pressing *Ctrl + V.*

A second method is to publish your web page someplace outside of Moodle and create a link to it from your course. Linking to your website is a good idea because when you paste text into the editor, Moodle will remove anything that it identifies as "dangerous."

Learning more about HTML

To learn more about HTML code, you can start with the organization responsible for defining the standards. The *World Wide Web Consortium* maintains the complete standards for HTML online at `https://www.w3.org/standards`. It maintains a basic tutorial at `https://www.w3schools.com/html/html_intro.asp`. Everything that's covered in this basic guide can be done using the editor in Moodle in its normal mode. The advanced HTML guide at `http://www.w3.org/MarkUp/Guide/Advanced.html` covers some features that you would need to go into the HTML view to add, such as defining clickable regions within images and using rollovers.

In addition to adding pages that contain content, it is possible to add files for students to download. Please note that Moodle often has a limited amount of space for hosting content on Moodle (either on-premises or in the cloud). So, you may consider having students download files from a cloud-based file-sharing site such as OneDrive, Dropbox, or Google Drive.

In the next section, you will learn how to add files for students to download, as well as how to make sure that they can both download and open them so that they can use them.

Adding files for your students to download

You can add files to a course so that your students can download them onto their personal computers. Some examples of files you may want students to have are forms to fill out, readings to complete before class, and word processing files to edit.

When a student selects a file from the course

When a student selects a file from your course, the student's computer will attempt to open that file. Moodle will only pass the file to the student's computer. For example, if it's a PDF file, your student's computer will probably try to use Adobe Reader or the Preview app to open the file. If it's a word processing file, your student's computer will attempt to use Word or some other word processor to open it. If your student's computer doesn't have a program that can open that type of file, it will probably prompt the student to save the file. In the case of a graphic or a sound file, their computer will use whatever resident application's most convenient. It is usually not the ideal one.

You can override this behavior with a setting called **Force download**. When you choose that setting, your student's computer will not try to open the file. Instead, it will download the file and prompt the student to save it.

If you want the student to use the file immediately upon accessing the file, just go with the default behavior. If you want the student to save the file for future use, select the **Force download** setting.

You will see this setting in the next section, when we look at the instructions for adding files to your course.

File repositories

Every file that you upload into a Moodle course is stored in a Moodle repository. Before we add files to our course, we need to understand how repositories work and how to choose the right kind for our course.

Types of repositories

A repository is a storage area that Moodle can access. The repository doesn't need to be on your server – it just needs to be accessible to your Moodle system. For more information about how to increase functionality and customize Moodle, you may wish to read a book on Moodle administration Moodle 3 Administration, `https://www.packtpub.com/product/moodle-3-administration-third-edition/9781783289714`

Repositories need to be enabled by the site administrator, under **Site administration | Plugins | Repository | Manage repositories**. Here are some examples of file repositories:

Type of Repository	When To Use
Server files	You want to reuse a file that you uploaded into another course. For example, you may want to reuse a graphic that you added to a page in another course or a document that you added to another course.
Upload a file	The file that you want to add to your course resides on your computer, and you want to use it in the current course. The file must be no larger than the upload limit for your Moodle system.
Filesystem	The file that you want to use has been uploaded to the Moodle data directory. You usually do this when the file is too big to upload directly into Moodle or when you need to upload a lot of files all at once.

Type of Repository	When To Use
OneDrive, Dropbox, Google Docs, Amazon Web Services	You want to use a service outside of Moodle to store your files. If you're using an inexpensive, shared hosting service for Moodle, you may get more storage space and better upload/download speed using a third party to store your large course files.
Flickr, Google Photos, Web Albums	You want to use photos that are part of an online album.

Figure 5.16 – When to use different types of repositories

Now that we have reviewed the different types of repositories, let's discuss when and how to use them.

Using file-sharing services to collaborate

When you use a file repository such as Dropbox, Google Drive, or OneDrive, you are storing your files outside of Moodle. This is a great way to collaborate. It is a good idea to use file-sharing services as well when collaborations continue beyond the time and scope of the course.

Using repositories to overcome Moodle's limit on file sizes

There is a limit to the size of a file that can be uploaded into your Moodle system. This limit changes for different Moodle sites. If you are using MoodleCloud, then there are even more compelling reasons to use repositories. Here, you can create a master document with links to the content that lives outside your course.

Three settings limit the size of a file that can be uploaded into Moodle. Two of those settings are on your web server. The administrator for your web server will need to change them. If you are using a shared hosting service, you may not be able to change these settings. The third setting is in Moodle; it can be changed by the system administrator.

The size limit for uploaded files is the smallest of these three settings.

In Moodle, under **Site administration | Courses | Course default settings**, look for the **Maximum upload size** setting. The maximum size available under that setting is taken from the php.ini file. You can set a lower limit than this but not a higher limit. For this, please check with your site administrator or check out Packt's book, *Moodle Administration*, at https://www.packtpub.com/product/moodle-4-administration-fourth-edition/9781801816724.

When you upload a file into Moodle, it will be placed in a file repository. By default, it will appear in the **Server Files** repository. If the **Recent Files** repository is enabled, the file may also appear there. If the file is too large, Moodle will not allow it to upload.

Functionality Booster

In today's environment of hybrid synchronous and asynchronous delivery, Moodle can be a lifesaver. If you are using BigBlueButton or another web-conferencing platform, you can make resources immediately available by posting them in **Resources** within Moodle, and also by including a link in the chat room of Zoom.

You may also record a Zoom meeting. Later, you can download the version of the .mp4 video file that you prefer. You can also download the transcript. Once you've downloaded it, you can upload the .mp4 video file to the video hosting service you prefer, which could be YouTube, Vimeo, or another service.

The transcript of the audio can be a vital tool, particularly for those who may be hearing-impaired or whose first language may not be English (or the language of the webinar). Having an audio transcript available helps you adhere to the principles of Universal Design. Keep in mind that you may need to do a bit of copy-editing.

Once you've added descriptions and transcripts of media, you can add the media itself. You will learn how to do so in the next session.

Adding media – video and audio

If you want to add video or audio to your course, you have three choices:

- First, you can add it as a resource or file. If you do that, when the student selects the file, one of two things will happen: either the media file will be downloaded to the student's computer and played by the software on their computer, or Moodle will try to play that file with its built-in media player. If multimedia plugins are enabled under **Site administration | Plugins**, Moodle will try to play the file in its built-in media player. If multimedia plugins are not enabled, the file will be played using whatever media player is on the student's computer. HTML5 was designed to make it easy to play media of all kinds from all kinds of devices (phones, tablets, and laptops) and all browsers. Moodle accommodates HTML5.

- Second, you can embed the media on a Moodle page (please refer to the *Adding pages* section). This will cause the media to be played on the web page.

- Third, you can copy and embed code into the HTML of your page in Moodle. You will see a small screenshot containing the URL and a **Play** icon. The player looks like it is in Moodle, but it's being played from the host (YouTube, Vimeo, and so on). You can also add entire packages containing multimedia by uploading a SCORM package or HTML5 via the H5P functionality.

Adding video or audio to a page

This procedure will add video, audio, or an applet to a Moodle page. You must own the file that you are adding – that is, the file is on your computer and not on another website. If the file that you want to appear is on another website, see you will need to embed the media rather than uploading it.

1. On the Moodle page, click to place the insertion point where you want the media to appear.

2. Click on the **Insert Moodle media** icon:

Figure 5.17 – To incorporate media, click on the Insert Moodle media icon

3. A pop-up window will appear. In this window, click on the **Insert media** button. You will have a chance to insert a **link, video, or audio**. In each, you have the option to upload from a URL, which is what I'm doing here. If you do not want to do that, you can click on **Browse repositories...** and go to the file picker:

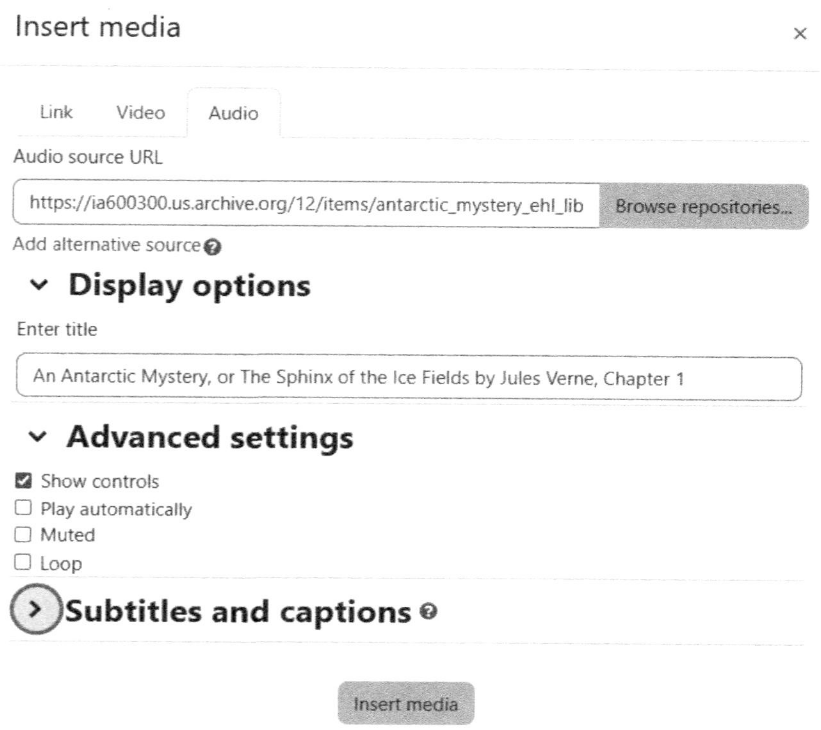

Insert media   ×

Link   Video   Audio

Audio source URL

https://ia600300.us.archive.org/12/items/antarctic_mystery_ehl_lib   Browse repositories...

Add alternative source ❓

∨ **Display options**

Enter title

An Antarctic Mystery, or The Sphinx of the Ice Fields by Jules Verne, Chapter 1

∨ **Advanced settings**

☑ Show controls
☐ Play automatically
☐ Muted
☐ Loop

❯ **Subtitles and captions** ❓

Insert media

Figure 5.18 – Configuring the view of inserted media resources

4. If your media is on your server, you can upload it from the file picker menu. The
    File picker window will be displayed. In the *File repositories* section, you learned
    how to add a file from a repository. In this example, we'll upload the file from your
    computer. Click on the **Upload a file** link:

File picker

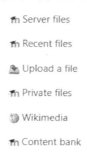

🏠 Server files

🏠 Recent files

🖼 Upload a file

🏠 Private files

🌐 Wikimedia

🏠 Content bank

Figure 5.19 – To add a file from a repository, click on the Upload a file icon

5. Click on the **Choose File** button.

6. Locate the file on your computer and select it.

7. Click on the **Open** or **OK** button.

8. Optionally, give the file a name that you want it to have in Moodle. This is in the **Save as** field.

9. By default, the **Author** field contains your name. If someone else created this file, give them proper credit by entering their name as the author.

10. The **Choose license** drop-down list allows you to select a license so that other teachers know what kind of copyright the file has:

Figure 5.20 – Selecting copyright or licensing options

11. Click on the **Upload this file** button; the file will be uploaded to your Moodle system.

12. If needed, fill out the fields under **Appearance**. You may want to resize the picture since Moodle will display the media at its original size by default.

13. Click on the **Insert** button. The media will be inserted into the page.

If you are inserting a podcast, you may not be able to insert only the .mp3 file. In the case of a podcast, you'll need to embed the HTML code. The following is an example of SoundCloud:

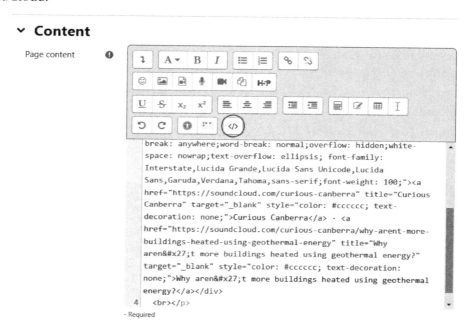

Figure 5.21 – As you edit the media description, you may not see the media

Once you've saved the pasted embed code, the podcast player will show up, and it will include any graphics that are in the podcast as well:

Figure 5.22 – Media player with description

The media player and the description will both appear in the window once you save the description.

To embed a video on a page, follow these steps:

1. Find the media that you want to link to. For example, you may find a video on several different sites. Here are a few: `https://vimeo.com/`, `https://youtube.com`, and `https://www.ted.com/talks`.

2. Check the license for the material to ensure that you have the right to use it as you intend.

3. Somewhere on the page, you will see a button or link that will give you the HTML code to embed the video, either by copying and pasting the URL or the entire embed code block:

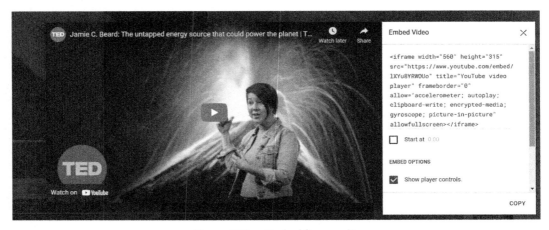

Figure 5.23 – Embedding media

To embed media, click on the **Share** link, then copy and paste the HTML code, either for the link or the full embed code block.

4. Copy the code for embedding the video.

5. Switch back to Moodle, where you are editing the page.

6. On the Moodle page, click to place the insertion point where you want the media to appear.

7. Click on the **Edit HTML source** icon. You can add text and more items if you want. Note that Moodle 4.0's HTML editor is very easy to use and automatically positions the media in the middle of the page:

Figure 5.24 – The embedded media automatically centers in the middle of the Moodle page

Functionality Booster

In a hybrid course that has synchronous webcasting (Zoom, for example), you may find that people are not as engaged as you may wish. Some people like to combat audience apathy by including periodic polls or opinion questions in **Chat**. This is a good idea, and you can save the responses as a historical reference and an engager.

If you want to be able to save the polls and opinion questions, you can build them as a choice question in Moodle and then simply link to them in the **Chat** section of Zoom. I suggest that students keep two windows open: one with the Zoom meeting and the other with Moodle, where they can participate in **Choice**. By incorporating Choice into Moodle, webinar attendees who watch the recording can still participate in the poll or opinion question.

Once you have added items such as media to your course, you can add labels to the items that you've added to make it easier for students to identify them. To make it even easier to navigate and to improve the user experience, let's learn how to move material around on the course page.

Using labels to further organize your course

The main tools for organizing a course in Moodle are sections and labels. In this section, we'll learn how to use them and how to move material around on the course page.

Naming your topics

In a course that uses the topics format, your topics are automatically named and numbered, as shown in the following screenshot:

Figure 5.25 – Adding a label to help further indicate what the topic is about

You can move the label so that it appears immediately under the topic:

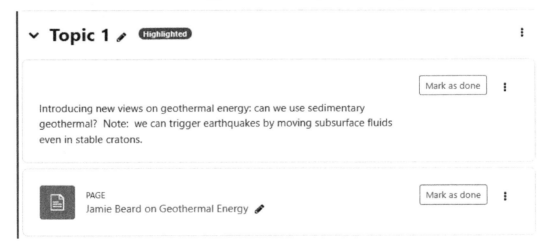

Figure 5.26 – Moving the label's position

You may wish to add graphics for engagement to the label. You can do so by opening the label and modifying it. In this case, I clicked on the **Insert media** icon, then clicked on **Repositories**. I selected **Wikimedia** from the **File picker** window and then entered `geothermal energy New Zealand` as my search term. Success! I have quite a few to choose from:

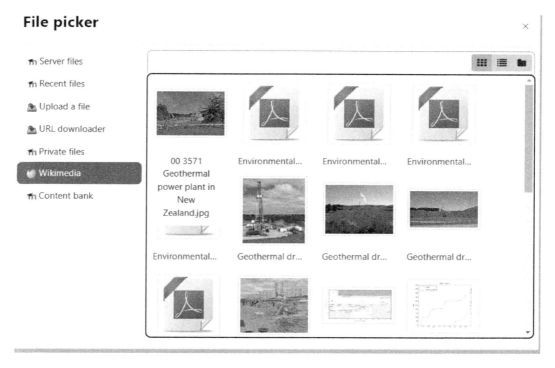

Figure 5.27 – Wikimedia label and images

You can add graphics that illustrate your topic by adding a label and then selecting from Wikimedia or other sources.

The result is very attractive and engaging. The label looks like it is a part of the topic, and it gives you a chance to add items that will engage the learners:

Introducing new views on geothermal energy: can we use sedimentary geothermal? Note: we can trigger earthquakes by moving subsurface fluids even in stable cratons.

Figure 5.28 – Using the label to describe the graphic

After making all the necessary changes to the label, you may want to modify your topic's name. To add a name and description to a **Topic**, follow these steps:

1. Log in to your course as a teacher or a site administrator.
2. In the top-right corner of the page, if you see a button called **Turn editing on**, click on it. If it's called **Turn editing off**, you do not need to click on this button.

3. Next to the topic's number, click on the **Edit summary** button:

Figure 5.29 – To edit the summary, click on the Edit Summary icon

4. The **Summary** page for your **topic** will be displayed. You must uncheck the **Use default section name** checkbox. If there is a checkbox in this field, you cannot edit the name or description of the topic.

5. In the **Section name** field, enter the name of your **topic**.

6. In the **Summary** field, enter a description. This is a full-featured web page editor, so you can enter text, graphics, and media:

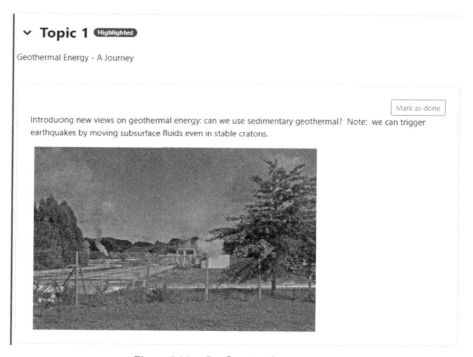

Figure 5.30 – Configuring the summary

7. Save your work. You will be returned to the course home page. The name and summary of the topic will be displayed.

Rearranging/moving items on the course home page

As you build your course, you will be adding resources and activities to the course page. Moodle allows you to easily reposition these items. It's so easy to reposition them that I recommend that you don't even worry about getting them in the right place as you are creating them. Just forge ahead and create – you can rearrange later.

Rearranging items on the course page can be done like so:

1. Log in to your course as a teacher or a site administrator.
2. In the top-right corner of the page, if you see a button called **Turn editing on**, click on it. If it's called **Turn editing off**, you do not need to click on this button.
3. Next to the item that you want to move, place your mouse pointer over the **Crosshairs** icon
4. Drag the item to where you want it on the course page and drop it.

"Instant course" with videos in the public domain – a good idea?

In the last few years, the number of educational videos has proliferated, and they are often of very high quality. For example, the **United States Department of Agriculture (USDA)** has made a number of their food inspection training videos available on their website: `https://www.fsis.usda.gov/inspection/inspection-training-videos/regulatory-education-video-seminars`. If you are a school that offers vocational training, you're probably thrilled that such high-quality resources exist and that they are free to use for educational purposes.

It may be tempting to simply upload the videos into separate modules. You say to yourself, "Yippee! Instant course!" and you tell yourself it's all good. After all, the videos contain instructions. But is such an approach legitimate? Is it a full course? The short answer is "no." Even if the video has learning objectives within it, you still need to frame the instructional video within an instructional strategy.

So, if you are lucky enough to find resources in the public domain that perfectly align with your goals, you'll still need to create a course map and a CDD that include the elements we discussed earlier in this chapter.

Summary

In this chapter, we looked at the resources that are available in Moodle. They are non-interactive course materials (books, pages, URLs, files, and labels) that form the core of most online courses.

Adding static material first gives you a chance to think about how the material will be discussed and used. Later, you can add more dynamic resources, and make connections to the course objectives and the assessments. The intent of Moodle 4.0 is to enhance your learning experience, as well as giving you more opportunities to deploy resources in ways that trigger thoughts and connections to the learning objectives and course goals, and help you demonstrate mastery.

What we emphasized in this chapter was the importance of selecting, sequencing, and deploying resources so that they always advance the goals of the course and help students meet their learning objectives. We also discussed how to incorporate current practices that include blended asynchronous/synchronous delivery, particularly when there is a desire to include webinars, which are then recorded (with transcripts).

Organizing your resources for students so that they know which chapter or unit they correspond to can help instill a sense of confidence and an "I can do it!" attitude in them. We also provided functionality tips for strategies to boost student engagement for blended synchronous and asynchronous courses.

In the next chapter, you will learn how to add some interactive material. Instead of just reading and viewing material that you post, the student will produce work and interact with their teacher and peers online.

6
Adding Assignments, Lessons, Feedback, and Choice

Course activities enable learners to interact with the instructor, the learning system, or each other. They also allow learners to develop confidence by being rewarded with a badge or certificate when they complete the activities. Above all, course activities should connect to the learning objectives of the course and correspond to the appropriate level of knowledge in the cognitive domain, as indicated in Bloom's Taxonomy, which we reviewed in *Chapter 4, Managing Resources, Activities, and Conditional Access*. Your instructional strategy will be very effective if you ensure that every step of your course planning integrates the learning objectives with the appropriate level of content and activities, as well as that each step has measurable outcomes. Your institution may have to undergo periodic reviews of its curriculum, instructional strategy, instructional delivery system (learning management system), materials, and assessments to maintain its accreditation or certification status. In addition to developing effective course content and assessments, this chapter will help you engage learners and allow them to persist in their studies to achieve their learning goals.

In the previous chapter, we learned how to add resources, or static course material, such as web pages, links, and media. We saw that all activities are added from the **Add an activity or resource** menu after we select the **Turn editing on** option. In this chapter, we'll provide an overview of all the activities, and then take a closer look at **assignments**, **lessons**, **feedback**, and **choices**. We are starting with those activities because they often form the foundation of courses.

In addition, we will review how Bloom's Taxonomy helps you align your learning objectives with measurable assessments, as well as how to apply this knowledge for institutional accreditation and licensing requirements.

The following topics will be covered in this chapter:

- Instructional strategies
- Learning objectives
- Competency and mastery learning definitions
- Definitions
- Understanding assignments
- Setting up lessons
- Developing Feedback Modules
- Exploring Choice

As we go through this chapter, we will learn how to add several kinds of interactive course material: assignments, lessons, choices, and feedback. We will also discuss how to organize the content to build micro-competencies, and then to affirm micro-learning milestones and generate certificates (which are installed separately) and badges.

By the end of this chapter, you'll be able to build course content that provides instructional material, while also motivating the learner with engagers by giving feedback and indicating where they are on the path to achieving the learning outcomes. You'll also be able to develop badges and certificates that encourage learners to persist and complete the course.

Instructional strategy

We discussed instructional strategies earlier in this book, and we did so in a global sense. Now, we will look at how the instructional strategy plays itself out as you start applying the principles and having students do things (activities).

Your instructional strategy involves mapping out how you'll achieve learning outcomes by strategically placing instructional material, engagers, lessons, assessments, feedback, and shareable evidence of mastery, such as certificates and badges. Another way to think of it is that your instructional strategy is how you map your learning objectives to your course materials, activities, and assessments, as well as how you keep your learners excited about learning along the way and how you reward them when they complete the module or course.

As you start to organize the course, follow these steps:

1. Review the overall goals of your course.
2. Review the learning objectives.
3. Describe how you will measure the outcomes.
4. Review the activities that connect to the learning outcomes and the course content.
5. Review the activities that are most appropriate for your learners.
6. Determine how you would like to best motivate your learners by developing badges.
7. Determine whether or not your institution requires you to align with competency frameworks. This is particularly vital if you seek accreditation or approval to offer certificates.

Following these steps will help you organize your assignments and also create a template that you can use for your other courses.

As you prepare for accreditation reviews, be sure that your instructional strategy is consistent across the institution. This means that your levels of difficulty and the types of instructional material should be consistent. Furthermore, when it comes to the assessments themselves, be sure that they not only align with Bloom's Taxonomy, but also reflect the vision and mission of the institution.

Your instructional strategy should be anchored by learning objectives. In the next section, we will review how to use and write learning objectives.

Learning objectives

We mentioned learning objectives at a high level earlier in this book. Now, we will look at how to apply the concept as we focus on activities. The learning objectives you select should clearly and concisely express the performative outcomes of your course. They will appear in the syllabus as well. Keep in mind that effective learning objectives use action verbs that tie to Bloom's Taxonomy, and they result in actions that are measurable and tie directly to the course unit or the entire course. Bloom's Taxonomy is arranged as a hierarchy, with the more fundamental outcomes such as **Identify forming** at the base and more complex and abstract ones such as **Create** at the top. Think of the different levels of the hierarchy as building blocks.

You can use the following process to write learning objectives:

1. Identify what you want the learner to be able to do.

2. Identify the level of knowledge of Bloom's Taxonomy.

3. Select a verb that ties to a measurable, observable action.

4. Add criteria to refine the outcome so that it has qualitative or quantitative specifics.

Let's review Bloom's Taxonomy. As you may recall, Bloom's Taxonomy was developed as a building-block sequence of ever-increasing levels of complexity. Simply put, it is a hierarchy that helps you describe, map, and measure knowledge in the cognitive domain.

We'll start with the learning objectives. Bloom's Taxonomy is a pyramid; the base is the most foundational, and it has to do with remembering. So, we can start with learning objectives that have to do with remembering. For example, we can say, `Identify five places in the world that use geothermal energy`.

As shown in *Figure 6.1*, we move up from the base of the pyramid to tasks of increasing complexity. Each task has affiliated verbs, which will make assessing and determining whether or not an individual achieved the learning objective much easier.

The top of the pyramid is **CREATING**. It is at the pinnacle of the hierarchy because it brings together the lower-domain cognitive activities and requires both synthesis and analysis. The learning objective for a course that will ascend as high as the sixth level will be easier than it may seem at first. The key is to consider an activity that will allow you, as the instructor, to properly evaluate or assess. For example, creating the corresponding activity could be to "develop a project" or "invent a new type of magazine":

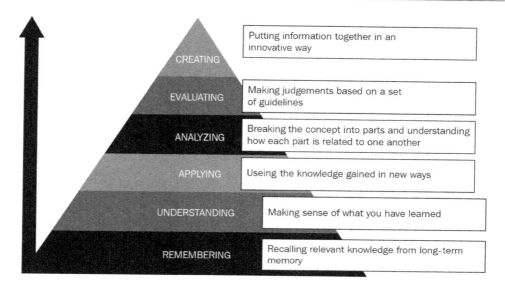

Figure 6.1 – Bloom's Taxonomy's pyramid shape contains the most basic verbs, which measure the cognitive domain, the base, and the most complex at the pinnacle

Now that we have reviewed the learning objectives and the functionality of Bloom's Taxonomy as a starting point in developing an instructional strategy, we will learn about using a competency learning or mastery learning strategy.

Competency learning definitions

Competency learning (often referred to as **mastery learning**) is an approach to learning that sets out a set of criteria that are learning outcomes that correspond to a course, as well as to the outcomes of a program. A competency framework can be imported into Moodle.

Competency learning is often required by regulatory agencies or governing bodies to ensure consistency in schools and learning organizations. When that is the case, there is a special emphasis on assessments. Many times, they are standardized tests rather than essay tests or demonstration projects. Great care is taken in assuring that the exams are psychometrically valid since completing the exam means that a person has demonstrated competence or even mastery of the concepts.

Competency learning uses the course outcomes (which tie to Bloom's Taxonomy) as the foundation for the course material and, above all, the standardized test.

External affirmation of the competency having been achieved can appear in the form of badges that are generated upon completing an activity. They can also be achieved by a report that is generated directly in Moodle within a competency framework.

Now that we have examined the different ways in which you can demonstrate mastery or competency concerning knowledge or skill, let's learn how to build assignments that will tie to the learning outcomes.

Moodle activities

Moodle 4.0 has dramatically changed the available icons and has enhanced the functionality of its activities so that they connect more closely to the dashboard and activity logs, as well as having more functionality with the mobile app. In the previous chapter, we looked at resources, as well as a few activities that can deliver course content because they deliver bundles of content, including interactive material. In Moodle, an activity is something that has an element that learners can interact with. Activities are used to deliver content in a certain sequence, to assess the learner's progress, and to keep the learner interested and engaged.

The following table contains a list of all the Moodle activities, which can serve as a "one-stop-shop" reference point as you build your course. Since activities are at the heart of your course, you'll need to select the activities well and make sure they align with your course goals and learning objectives.

You'll also want to keep Bloom's Taxonomy in mind. Note that the following table contains a thumbnail of the new icons for Moodle 4.0, as well as a brief description of each activity. Next to that, we have provided the advantages and disadvantages of each, along with a column that lists their common uses (which are also included in the description, advantages, and disadvantages).

Activities in Moodle 4.0 have been streamlined and expanded, which makes them easier to use. Some of the functionality has changed, which also streamlines them. For example, if you're used to using Moodle 3.11 (or earlier) in MoodleCloud, you'll notice that three activities no longer appear. **Attendance, Checklist,** and **Custom Certificate** are gone. Don't worry! That doesn't mean that you can't figure out who has attended the course. You can find out in the activity log if you use a **Lesson**. As for **Checklist**, all the required activities and due dates will now automatically appear in the dashboard, which will integrate everything that has a deadline into the calendar. If you wish you could automatically generate certificates and you miss the **Custom Certificate** activity that was included in MoodleCloud's paid packages, don't worry. Moodle 4.0 has updated the **Badge** plugin, which makes it much easier to generate badges that can be displayed on your website, LinkedIn page, social media, and more.

Let's review Moodle's activities now and take a close look at each one. We will start by looking at commonly used activities:

Activities	Description	Advantages	Disadvantages	Common Uses
Assignment	Instructors can use this activity to administer assessments that involve many steps, including describing the task, collecting work, and providing grades and feedback. Learners submit digital files, which can include documents, spreadsheets, images, audio, and video. Assignments can be individual and group-based. Instructors can leave feedback in many different forms: markups, as well as written and spoken feedback. Rubrics are accommodated. Grades are recorded in the gradebook.	Assignments can form the core element of the assessment strategy and can allow instructors to ask for more complex tasks. Assignments are ideal for the higher levels of Bloom's Taxonomy and collaborations. They allow instructors to give very specific feedback. The feedback is vital for developing learner self-efficacy. The feedback can consist of a marked-up document (tools are built-in), as well as written and recorded (spoken comments) feedback.	It can be tempting to use the same sort of assignment for all courses, which may not be an effective way to assess the achievement of all learning objectives. Assignments may not be ideal for all kinds of learners and learning styles because they can be hard to practice. Learners may not always be able to see comments or marked-up files if they do not realize they have to click in certain areas.	Assess the achievement of learning objectives.
Quiz	A popular assessment tool. The quiz types include matching, multiple choice, short answer, and numerical. There is quite a bit of flexibility as instructors can allow multiple attempts and shuffle the questions from the question bank. Grades are automatically recorded. Quizzes can be used for official assessments to achieve learning objectives, along with practice exams, feedback, and self-assessment.	Ideal for assessing the achievement of learning objectives, especially for objectives on the lower end of Bloom's Taxonomy. Can integrate seamlessly with the gradebook. Can help learners learn by providing background information about the correct answer.	Although they seem simple, quizzes are actually complex psychometric tools, and writing an effective quiz that actually assesses what you want it to assess is complex. Instructors who write their own quizzes should be provided with a guide.	Assess the achievement of learning objectives.

Activities	Description	Advantages	Disadvantages	Common Uses
Workshop	Learners submit work that they do individually and collaboratively for peer review. Learners submit files that are then assessed using a form developed by the instructor. Learners also peer-review each other's work.	This is one of the best activities for collaboration. It is fantastic for real-world activities or projects. It can even be used for hackathons. Learners can work by themselves or in groups. In either case, learners can peer-review each other, and they can receive grades for the peer review as well as for their work.	Learners can easily become confused as they try to complete the requirements for collaborative activities, peer reviews, and their own work. Clear instructions and guidance are critical to successfully deploy and administrate this activity.	Collaborative, project-based learning.
Lesson	Although classified as an "activity," a lesson can be considered a resource or an activity. It's a bundled set of pages or instructional activities that are designed as pathways to learning. They should align with your storyboard or course design document and fit into the overall learning plan to tie to learning objectives.	A lesson is a great way to bundle a module and make sure that learners follow a sequence of content and activities and that they stay engaged with a blend of content, interactive activities, and mini-assessments.	Lessons can take time to build and to be effective, they should be planned very carefully. Some of the content may become stale and it may be necessary to go in and update that content or activities. You must keep very well organized to keep track of the individual components in the lesson and their versions.	Blended delivery of static content with interactive content.

Figure 6.2 – Commonly used activities

Moodle has a number of activities that emphasize interactive communication and collaboration. Some emphasize interactive communication and others are easily incorporated into graded activities that can be used for assessment. The following table provides an overview of those activities:

Activities	Description	Advantages	Disadvantages	Common Uses
BigBlueButton	Web conferencing is integrated into Moodle. It is open source. Users can share audio, video, chats, and slides, and they can share their screens, use a whiteboard, collaborate in breakout rooms, participate in polling, and use emojis. Sessions can be recorded and archived.	BigBlueButton is easy to use, and it is fully integrated into Moodle. It has many built-in tools that allow for markup and demonstrations. It is easy to record and make the recording available. You can self/cloud host.	BigBlueButton can be slow and may not be allowed through a corporate firewall. It may be necessary to use Teams, Zoom, or another web-conferencing tool that the institution subscribes to.	"Live" instruction and engagement.
Chat	Text-based, real-time synchronous discussions. Chat sessions can be saved.	A very "lite" tool that provides the opportunity for questions, answers, and data sharing. It can be saved and archived.	It may be confusing if there is a "chat" function within web conferencing that is used at the same time. The code has not been maintained, so it's very out of date.	Interactive "lite" engagement, sharing content.
Choice	It looks like a quiz in the sense that there can be multiple-choice questions or polling. However, it is not connected to the gradebook.	This is a great place to engage learners, test their knowledge, and pique their curiosity by polling and then following up with a discussion.	It can be confused with a quiz. Overusing "choice" (check your knowledge, did you know?, and polling) can be distracting.	Assess the achievement of learning objectives. Can be used for engagement.

Activities	Description	Advantages	Disadvantages	Common Uses
Forum	This is an asynchronous discussion board. There is quite a bit of flexibility: forums can be open, with learners having the ability to launch new discussions; they can function for social interaction, asking and answering questions; and they can assess the course material.	If designed well, a forum can be very engaging. Be sure to ask learners to relate to their own experiences, add their opinions, and do research for websites on the topic.	Questions need to be developed well to avoid "yes/no" responses or ones that say the same thing. Questions need to be changed over time to avoid answers being published online.	Collaborative learning, maintaining engagement, and assessments.
Wiki	Learners add and edit web pages, often collaboratively, but wikis can also be individual. Wikis can be used in many ways – that is, as knowledge repositories, online creative writing journals, and comprehensive manuals for operations, a process, or an industry.	Very effective for collaborative activities, particularly those that involve areas that have new advancements or innovations.	Can be confused with a glossary or a database. Wikis are effective in areas that involve more than just definitions, but also questions regarding a process and its implementation.	Collaboration to build a knowledge base; can be part of a portfolio.
Glossary	Learners contribute content to create a dictionary-type product, organized in several different ways – from the category, to date and author, to alphabetically. Auto-linking allows entries to link automatically to where the concept words or phrases can be found in the course.	Ideal for low-level Bloom's Taxonomy, such as "remember." Learners can collaboratively develop a glossary and create interesting and innovative entries, especially if the entries include examples.	Can often be confused with a wiki or a database.	Collaborative activity, lower-level Bloom's Taxonomy.

Activities	Description	Advantages	Disadvantages	Common Uses
Database	The database consists of a repository of entries of many different possible types (numerical, text, images, URL, and more). For example, lab results or survey results can be entered by multiple participants to develop a database that can be used for analysis. It can also be used to create a digital showcase for learner work.	Databases have many uses. They can be used as repositories for learner work or entries and can be used in multiple courses. It can be used in conjunction with lab courses, programming courses, marketing, demographics, and more as the data is used for analysis.	This can be confused with a wiki or a glossary if it's used for items such as annotated bibliographies.	Collaborative projects, or data used in learning activities.

Figure 6.3 – Collaboration-focused activities

Moodle has a few apps that focus on gathering feedback from users. In addition, Moodle also makes it possible to import content in different preprepared packages. The following table provides an overview of those activities:

Activities	Description	Advantages	Disadvantages	Common Uses
External tool	Learners may access apps and other resources on other websites from within Moodle. Tool or app providers must support Learning Tools Operability (LTI).	It enables learners to use tools from another website. For example, a class based on programming in Python may need to use Jupyter Notebook. Instead of logging in and using it outside Moodle, it can be integrated.	It requires coordination with the site administrator for initial setup.	Higher-level activities or a programming framework.
Feedback	Feedback allows instructors to create customized questions to allow learners to provide their views. Feedback activities can be used for course evaluations, confidential "learning climate" assessments, signups for events, and more.	The Feedback activity is a great way to take the temperature off a course or institution and change the course before it's too late. It's also handy for signing up for modules or events.	Feedback is often confused with choice. Using feedback to register for an event or a module can be a bit cumbersome.	Instructional guidance.

Activities	Description	Advantages	Disadvantages	Common Uses
H5P	H5P stands for HTML5 Package, and it is the latest specification of the HTML markup language web framework, which accommodates interactive, self-playing content such as presentations, videos, questions, games, quizzes, and more. H5P packages are often acquired externally and can be uploaded to the Moodle site. Quiz activities are auto-graded and the grades go into the gradebook.	HTML5 packages are often professionally done and are available from educational material providers. The auto-grading aspect is very convenient. The materials are of high quality and are engaging. HTML5 templates are often responsive, so they look good and work on different devices and in different browsers (ideally).	HTML5 can be expensive, and since they often come as a package, you cannot customize or modify specific parts of it. Like Java, CSS, JavaScript, and other older languages, HTML5 will eventually become obsolete. It may also be vulnerable to security issues.	Deliver content and integrate assessments.
SCORM package	A SCORM package consists of bundled learning objects that can be zipped and added to a course. The learning objects are often pages, and the SCORM package contains a table of contents, consisting of the course content and quizzes, which, when graded, are recorded in the gradebook.	SCORM packages are often used for presenting content, including multimedia and animations. They can also include assessments. Many institutions require content that has been uploaded to be SCORM-compliant.	SCORM packages can contain animations and multimedia in old formats that will no longer play, or that require external drivers. You must be aware of this when evaluating pre-packaged SCORM bundles.	Deliver content, integrate assessments, and maintain an archive of individual learning objects.
Survey	Survey instruments can be used to gather data, ask questions, and express their opinions.	Surveys can be effective in engaging learners and finding out what their fellow learners think.	The survey is not configurable. For customizable surveys, use Feedback. Surveys need to relate to the course objectives. Surveys can, unwittingly, be a place of unconscious bias.	Engagement, instructor interaction.

Figure 6.4 – Tools to assist importing packages and obtaining feedback

Now that we have reviewed the functionality of the activities, along with their uses and the advantages and disadvantages for using them, let's look at how to add activities.

Adding an activity

Adding one activity is the same as adding any other activity, so let's go through this now. We'll address what all the activities have in common in this section as well.

Let's consider a course called *Dog Grooming for Everyone*. Once we've created the course and identified its topics, we can add activities.

As always, let's start by turning on **Edit mode** in the top right-hand corner:

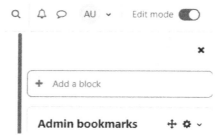

Figure 6.5 – Turning on Edit mode

Now, let's take a look at the topics. Click on **Add an activity or resource** and then select one from the menu:

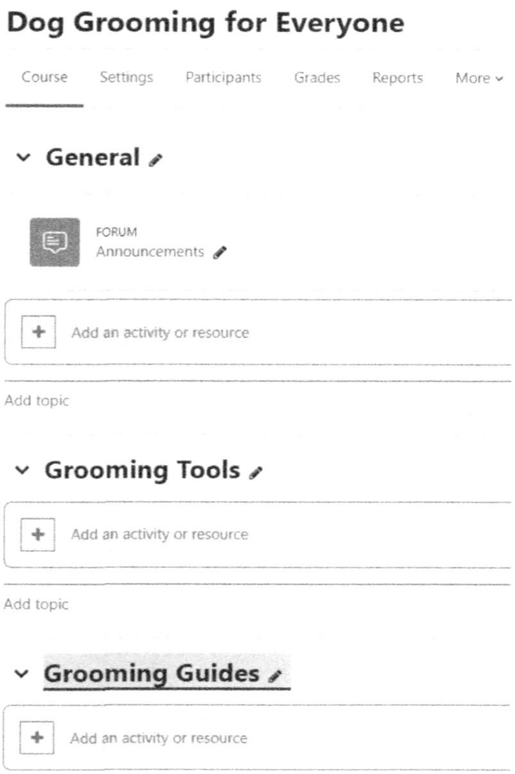

Dog Grooming for Everyone

Course   Settings   Participants   Grades   Reports   More ⌄

⌄ **General** ✎

FORUM
Announcements ✎

✚ Add an activity or resource

Add topic

⌄ **Grooming Tools** ✎

✚ Add an activity or resource

Add topic

⌄ **Grooming Guides** ✎

✚ Add an activity or resource

Figure 6.6 – Modifying the topics to customize their content

When you click on **Add an activity or resource**, the respective menu will pop up. I've selected **Activities** so that I only see activities. If you forget what each activity is about, you can click the little **i** icon for more information. Note that it only provides information and does not include the advantages or disadvantages, or common uses, that are shown in the handy "one-stop-shop" table:

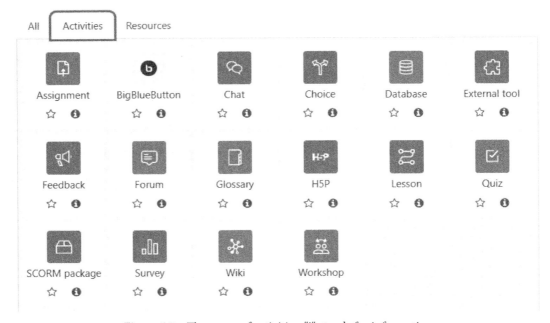

Figure 6.7 – The menu of activities. "i" stands for information

Now that we have provided an overview of all the activities, let's learn how to select one and build it. Let's start with Moodle's Assignment activity.

Selecting assignments

If you want the learner to do or create something and then grade the results, you will want an assignment. Keep in mind that if you are developing a blended course that contains synchronous content in the form of web conferences (BigBlueButton, Teams, or Zoom, for example), you may wish to put together assignments that can be done in conjunction with that "live" lecture. They may involve collaboration and group solutions. For peer review, use the Workshop activity.

Let's start with the Assignments activity in Moodle, which will give us a chance to bring together several activities to create an assessment strategy.

Understanding assignments in Moodle

If you would like your learner to demonstrate that they have achieved mastery of a skill set or a body of knowledge, you will need to develop a way of assessing it. One good approach is to develop an assignment. The Assignment activity in Moodle gives you space to check the learner's knowledge using a quiz, allow the learner to practice until they achieve the passing score, and show they have achieved the learning objective.

Adding an assignment

Let's start by creating an assignment. We can do that by clicking **Adding an assignment** and then selecting **Assignment** from the menu that includes the full list of Moodle activities. In this case, we will be adding the assignment to the *Dog Grooming for Everyone* course. We will name the assignment *Review of Dog Grooming Tools*.

This is where you can add the description of the assignment and also the assignment's instructions. Notice that the verb aligns with Bloom's Taxonomy and is measurable. In this case, the verb is "explain."

As you add your description, you can include a graphic to illustrate it. Please keep in mind that Moodle is powerful and incredibly flexible. We are addressing basic skills here and are not getting into some of the more complex ways to customize it:

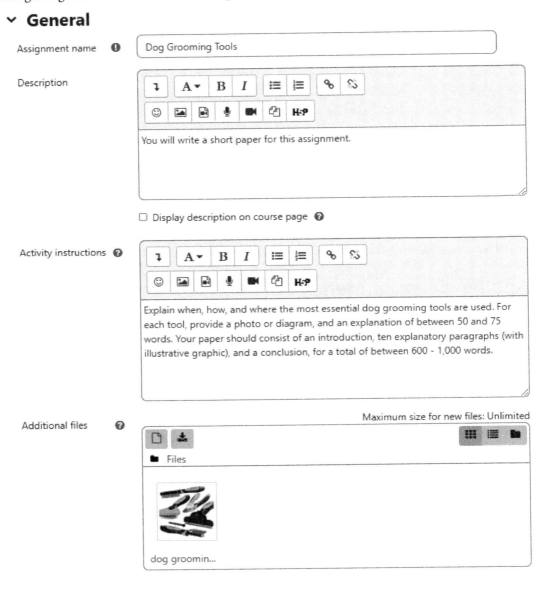

Figure 6.8 – Adding a name, description, activity instructions, and additional files

Once you have added the assignment, you'll need to customize it. You can do so by clicking on **Settings**, which allows you to edit the assignment. It will indicate that you are **updating the assignment in Dog Grooming Tools**. A screen will open containing a list of topics that expand when you click on them. Each will allow you to modify aspects of your assignment Keep in mind that this general approach is uniform across Moodle 4.0, so once you feel comfortable with it when creating an assignment, you'll feel comfortable with it in the other activities too:

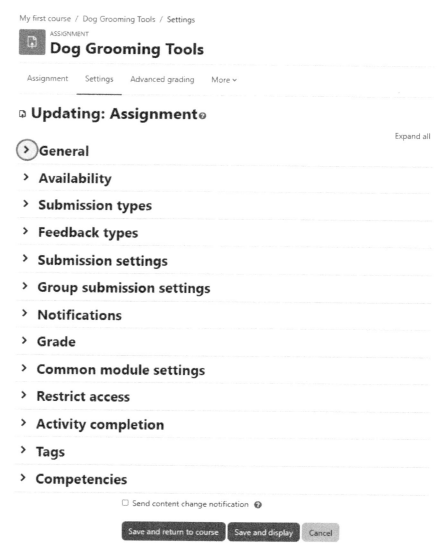

Figure 6.9 – Menu of options for the Assignment activity

As you look at your course design document or storyboard, and you match the assignment with the learning objective and the level of Bloom's Taxonomy, you'll find that assignments are very good at the middle to higher levels of the Taxonomy. For example, you may ask a learner to write a paper that explains when, how, and where each dog grooming tool is used.

Requirements of the assignments

In our case, we're going to ask a learner to write a paper that explains when, how, and where to use dog grooming tools. However, we could also ask the learner to submit images of each or explain through a video presentation. In short, in an assignment, you can require the learners to do the following:

- Submit one or more digital files.
- Write something.
- Do something outside of Moodle.

Availability

An aspect of understanding assignments involves being able to make assignments available to learners. Being able to make assignments available upon mastery can be very motivating, and it can also help you to avoid the trap of overwhelming learners with content they're not ready for. A key to learner success is keeping on track and making progress in the course. How you make assignments available can help motivate learners by clarifying the workflow and helping them manage their time so that they succeed. So, the **Availability** setting can be the cornerstone of your approach to helping learners develop a clear approach to not only maintaining awareness of what they should be doing but also prioritizing tasks:

Figure 6.10 – The Availability settings screen

You can use the **Availability** setting to set limits for when the learner can submit work.

Do not confuse this with the **Allow access** settings under **Restrict access**. The **Allow access** settings determine whether the learner can see the assignment on the course page, or whether the assignment is completely hidden from the learner. After the learner sees and selects the assignment, the **Availability** setting determines whether the learner can submit work to the teacher.

Note that there is a **Due date** and a **Cut-off date**. If you do not enable a **Cut-off date**, the assignment will stop accepting work on the due date. If you enable and enter a **Cut-off date**, the assignment will accept work between the due date and the cut-off date. That work will be marked as late.

When a learner clicks on an assignment, Moodle displays the assignment's description. You usually use the description to tell the learner how to complete the assignment. If you enable the **Always show description** setting, if a learner enters the assignment at any time, the learner will see the description. If you want a learner to be able to prepare and work ahead, this is fine. If you disable the **Always show description** setting, if a learner enters the assignment before the **Allow submissions from** date, Moodle will hide the description for the assignment. You can use this feature to prevent learners from working ahead.

Assignments that are due soon will appear in the **Upcoming events** block. If you do not set a **Due date**, by default, it will be set to today (the day you created the assignment). This will make the assignment show up in the **Upcoming events** block as if it's overdue. Ensure that you set an appropriate **Due date** for the assignment.

Submission types

As we start to think about the kind of paper or presentation we'd like our learners to do, let's take a moment to think about the kinds of submission types that are available under **Assignments**:

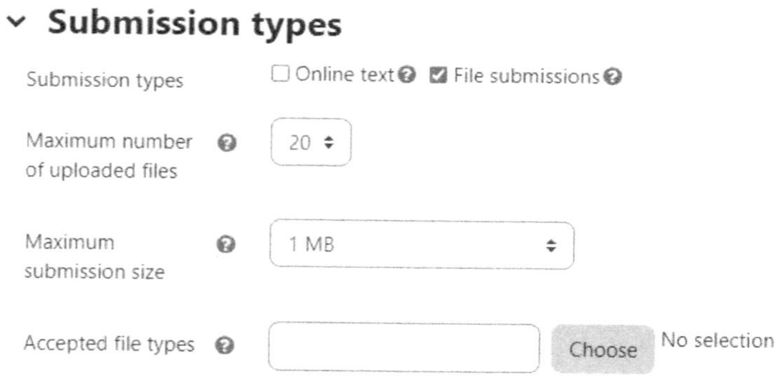

Figure 6.11 – The Submission types settings screen

Notice that you can ask people to type into a text box (**Online text**) or you can enable **File submissions**.

Submitting a digital file

Anything that can be uploaded on a computer can be uploaded into an assignment. However, Moodle will enforce its limit on the size of uploaded files. This is an important aspect to keep in mind as you plan your course. For example, if you require your learners to create a digital photograph, this option may work well.

Remember that a Moodle site is configured with a limit on the size of files that can be uploaded into Moodle. If you require your learners to create a video, you may need to find another way for them to send you their large video files. You can ask learners to submit digital files uploaded to the cloud (Google, Dropbox, and so on), or you can ask them to create audio or video using a platform you can link to that the institution provides, such as Zoom or Teams, and then view the video or listen to the audio from that platform. Another option is for them to create a video and then upload it to their account on YouTube, and then link to it. This is a good time to mention that antivirus software may make the upload fail. Be sure to check with the site administrator to ensure that everything is configured to avoid being blocked.

Requiring learners to submit online text

In an online text assignment, you will require the learner to enter text into an online text editor. This text editor is part of the assignment activity.

If learners are more comfortable writing the text in a word processor, they can copy and paste it into the text editor.

You cannot paste graphics into Moodle's online text editor. Each graphic must be uploaded and placed into the document using the text editor's **Insert or edit image** icon. Alternatively, instead of copying and pasting into the text box, you can click the **Manage Files** icon to submit a file, so that the graphics can be uploaded as separate files. The advantage of this approach is that you can easily make comments and provide feedback in the box.

Submitting work done in the real world by taking advantage of Zoom

Let's look at a way to use Moodle to track learning "in real life." You can use an assignment to require learners to tell you that they have completed an activity outside of Moodle. For example, you can instruct your art learners to build an outdoor sculpture. Then, their submission will consist of notifying you, **It's built and ready for you to review**.

Another approach would be for them to take a photo and then create a blog post that incorporates the textual part of their project, as well as photos. Here is an example that was posted on an account on *Blogger*: `http://fringejournal.blogspot.com/2018/04/installation-1-i-heard-voices-of-angels.html`.

If learners worked in teams (virtual or in person) on the projects, they can then record their experiences by starting a Zoom session where they take turns discussing their experience and then sharing their screen, where they can include photos, PowerPoint presentations, or screenshots. The key to this type of real-world project is to have a Zoom meeting that is recorded. Then, the MP4 video file can be downloaded and saved, and the video can be shared within Zoom itself.

Grading an assignment

This section shows the flexibility that Moodle offers in terms of grading assignments and how to make it more effective for providing specific feedback and timely responses that will motivate learners.

In the previous section, you learned how a learner submits an assignment. When assignments need to be graded, Moodle will notify the teacher by displaying a message on the teacher's **Dashboard**. They can then open the assignment and grade it. The submitted assignment can be opened for grading and providing feedback.

The assignment can also be configured to send an automated email to each teacher to alert them of the submitted assignments.

Moodle does not supply a link directly to the assignments that need grading but does supply a link to the course.

> **Tip**
> The system administrator can configure Moodle so that when a user logs in, they are automatically taken to the user's **Dashboard** page. This can be done in **Administration** | **Site administration** | **Appearance** | **Navigation**, and by selecting **My home** as the default home page.

The **Grading** page for the assignment enables the teacher to open all the submissions and enter a grade for each submission:

Figure 6.12 – The grading summary shows the instructor the status of the learners' work

When you create the assignment, you can enable feedback comments and feedback files. If you do that, the teacher will be able to enter the comments and files while grading the assignment.

Feedback types

Even though feedback is given after assignments have been turned in, you must anticipate what kind of feedback is to be given. This is generally done when you set up availability because you're not only setting the parameters for the availability of the instructional material and assessments, but you're also setting up how the learners will receive feedback.

In the preceding example, the learner received not only a grade but also additional feedback from the teacher. The feedback was in the form of comments that the teacher wrote, and also a file that the teacher uploaded. The instructor can give feedback comments, annotate a PDF, and upload Feedback files. You can also check the box to enable an Offline grading worksheet. This is enabled under the **Feedback types** setting:

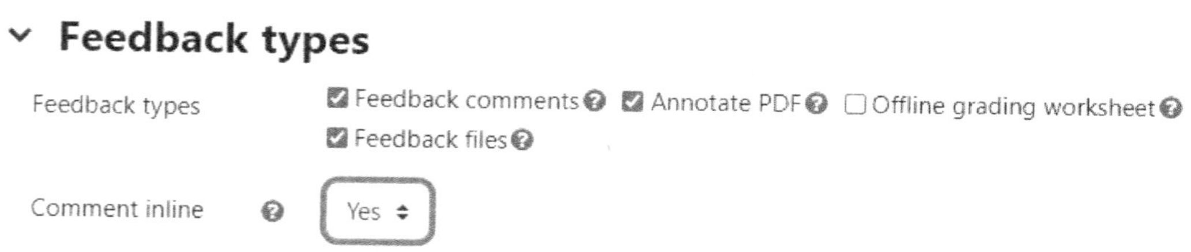

Feedback types

Feedback types   ☑ Feedback comments ❓ ☑ Annotate PDF ❓ ☐ Offline grading worksheet ❓
                   ☑ Feedback files ❓

Comment inline   ❓   [Yes ⬍]

Figure 6.13 – Feedback types settings

The **Offline grading worksheet** option allows the teacher to download a **comma-separated file** (a .csv file) that contains a list of all the assignments and a place for the teacher to enter grades. However, downloading the grading worksheet does not download the material that the learners submitted. If the teacher wants to see the submissions offline, they must download them separately.

If offline grading is enabled, when the teacher clicks on **Submissions** there will be a dropdown menu, **Grading action**. You will have all the options, including the teacher will see the **Download grading worksheet** option in the grading page for the assignment as shown in *Figure 6.12*. The path is **Course Name | Assignment name | View all submissions | Grading action**.

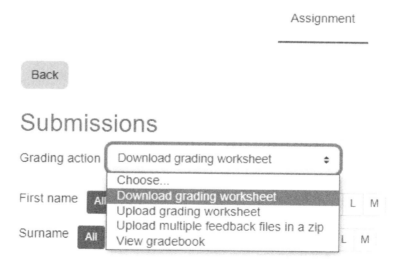

Figure 6.14 – The Download grading worksheet option for grading the assignment

Submission settings

Submission settings determines how Moodle behaves while the learner is submitting their work:

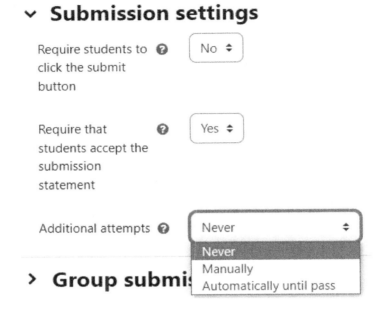

Figure 6.15 – Submission settings

The **Require students to click the submit button** setting determines whether the learner must submit the assignment all at once or whether the learner can save their submission as a draft and submit it later. If you select **Yes** for this setting, when the learner is creating a submission, Moodle will display a **Save** button. After the learner saves the submission, when the learner enters the assignment, they will have the option to either edit what was saved or submit it.

The **Require that students accept the submission statement** setting determines whether Moodle displays a statement that the work belongs to the learner. You can add automatic feedback upon submission to require the student to assure academic honesty. Note that this is a sitewide setting. The navigation path is **Site administration | Plugins | Activity modules | Assignment | Assignment settings**.

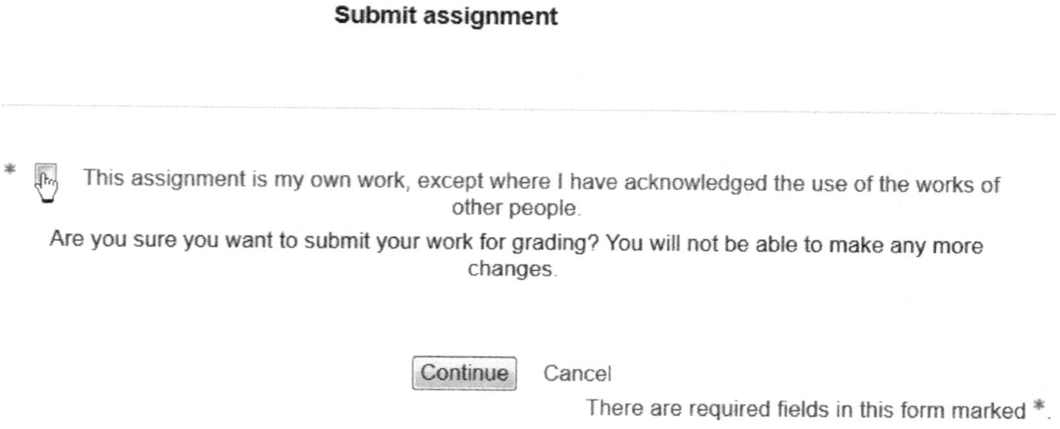

Submit assignment

 This assignment is my own work, except where I have acknowledged the use of the works of other people.

Are you sure you want to submit your work for grading? You will not be able to make any more changes.

 Cancel

There are required fields in this form marked *.

Figure 6.16 – Requiring learners to accept a submission statement,
which can include a statement of academic honesty

In the *Allowing learners to change their minds section*, we saw what it looks like for the learner when the teacher reopens an assignment. The **Additional attempts** setting determines whether, and how, the teacher can allow a learner to resubmit the assignment. Note that a resubmission replaces the original submission.

Selecting **Never** means the teacher cannot reopen the assignment to allow the learner to resubmit their work. **Manually** means that the teacher can reopen the assignment.

Automatically until pass means that the assignment will remain open until the learner achieves a passing grade – that is, if the teacher gives the learner less than a passing grade for the learner's submission, Moodle will automatically enable the learner to resubmit.

To use **Automatically until pass**, you must set a passing grade for the assignment:

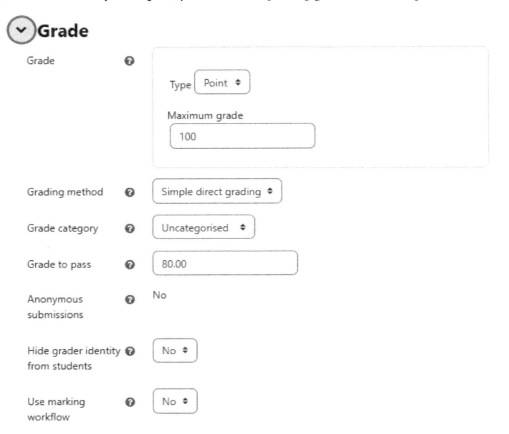

Figure 6.17 – Editing Grade to set a passing grade for the assignment

Then, select the *Edit* icon (the one shaped like a gear) for the assignment. That will bring you to a page where you can enter a passing grade for the assignment.

Group submission settings

Moodle allows you to assign the learners and teachers in a class to different groups.

For more about groups, please refer to *Chapter 11, Groups and Cohorts*.

In an assignment, setting **Learners submit in groups** to **Yes** means that each group the teacher created will submit their work together as a group and that all the members of a group will receive the same grade.

If you set **Require all group members submit** to **Yes**, every member of a group will need to click on the **Submit** button to finalize a submission. If you set this to **No**, any member of a group can submit the assignment for the whole group. However, even though only one member of the group may have submitted the assignment, the feedback and grade are applied to all members of the group.

Notifications

The **Notifications** settings determine whether the graders will receive messages when a learner (or group) submits an assignment.

Each user in Moodle can choose how they want to receive messages. This is done under **Preferences | User account | Message preferences**.

Then one can restrict to contacts and also indicate email preference.

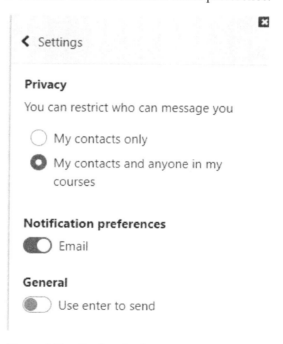

Figure 6.18 – Configuring how to receive messages

If your email application allows you to filter emails based on their subject line and sender, you can use that feature to automatically put all the notices about assignment submissions into a specific folder.

> **Tip**
> Email alerts are especially useful in courses where you allow learners to proceed at their own pace since you won't know what activities they have completed unless you check the course and look at the grade book.

Common module settings

This screen will let you determine whether or not the course can be seen by learners on the course page. It also includes an ID number and allows you to set it to **Group mode**, which means that the assignment will be completely different for groups.

Restrict access

You can restrict learner access by **Date**, **Grade**, or **User profile**, or via your own nested set of restrictions to make access apply only under specific conditions.

Activity completion

This screen is a helpful tool for learner success because it allows learners to manually mark whether or not the activity is complete. Alternatively, you can set conditions to let the activity appear as completed once the conditions that you've set have been met. Learners are often very motivated by seeing their progress through the course:

Figure 6.19 – The Activity completion settings screen

Tags

Moodle 4.0 takes advantage of metatags and the types of approaches used in social media. Adding tags to the assignment can help learners identify which content items and activities align with their learning objectives and course goals:

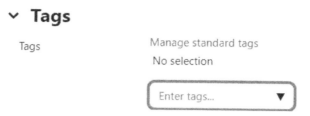

Figure 6.20 – The Tags configuration settings screen.

Competencies

If your institution uses outcome assessments or requires competencies toward a certificate or a degree, Moodle 4.0 allows you to add them, and then align the assignments to them. Once you've added competencies and set passing grades, the learner will see that the **Competency** box is checked when the assignment has been completed:

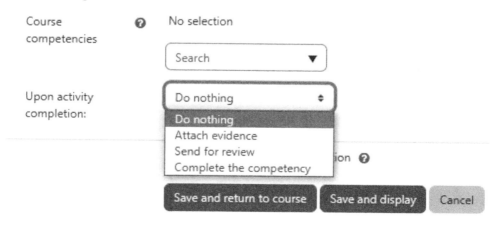

Figure 6.21 – The Competencies settings screen for the Assignment activity

After putting together assignments, you may wish to organize them so that they flow adaptively so that learners can automatically review and do remedial activities when needed. In the next section, you will learn how to do that by setting up lessons.

Setting up lessons

A lesson is a complex and powerful type of activity. Essentially, a lesson is a series of web pages that presents information and questions. Lessons take a bit of time to set up, but they are well worth the investment because they incorporate adaptive learning and can direct learners to remedial activities if they do not demonstrate mastery. It will advance them to other content and activities if they complete an activity. Lessons are useful in hybrid courses that incorporate synchronous tutoring or even face-to-face delivery because they can flag where learners may need more help.

Before you decide to use a lesson, familiarize yourself with its pros and cons.

A Moodle lesson can be a powerful combination of instruction and assessment. Lesson activities offer the flexibility of a web page, the interactivity of a quiz, and branching capabilities. The key is to plan your lesson and storyboard the sequence. For example, for our course, *Dog Grooming for Everyone*, you can create a lesson entitled *Dog Grooming Basics: The Breeds and their Characteristics*. You can require different content items and activities. Once learners achieve a passing score on the quiz, they can progress.

To add a **Lesson**, click on **Add an activity or resource** and then select **Lesson** from the menu:

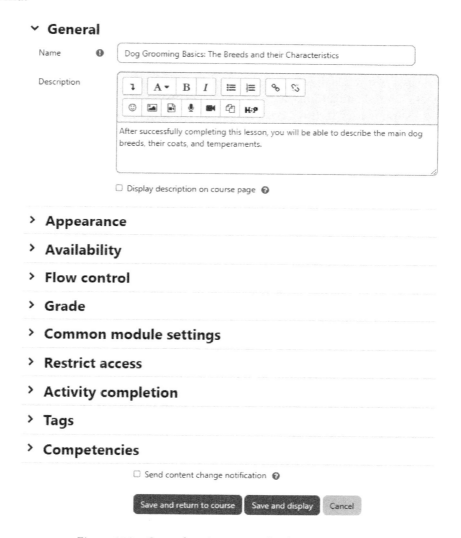

Figure 6.22 – General settings screen for the Lesson activity

You will have a chance to name your lesson and add a description. Below the **General** tab are other items that expand when clicked. Notice that several are the same as in the **Assignment** activity. However, the **Appearance** and **Flow control** tabs are different.

Planning, creating pages, and adding content

A lesson consists of a series of web pages. Usually, a lesson page contains some instructional material and a jump question about the material that the learner just viewed. The jump question is used to test a learner's understanding of the material. Get it right, and you proceed to the next item. Get it wrong, and you're taken back either to the instructional page or jump to a remedial page.

If you intend to create a lesson that has jumps, clusters, and branches, draw a diagram of the lesson. This type of flowchart or storyboard can tell you what kind of pages you will need to create. You can also use your course map to show where your files should go in the modules, and how they align with learning objectives.

Then, gather and organize your material in a file. After that, create the pages in the lesson.

Once the pages are in the Moodle lesson, you can create the jumps. Once you have the pages and jumps, go to the **Edit Lesson** page and look at the list of all the pages in the lesson. You can compare that list to the diagram that you created when planning the lesson.

Finally, you can test the lesson from the learner's point of view.

Types of lesson pages

Once you have named your lesson and saved it, the menu will close and you will go to another screen. Here, you will be able to edit the lesson and add questions, clusters, content pages, and question pages:

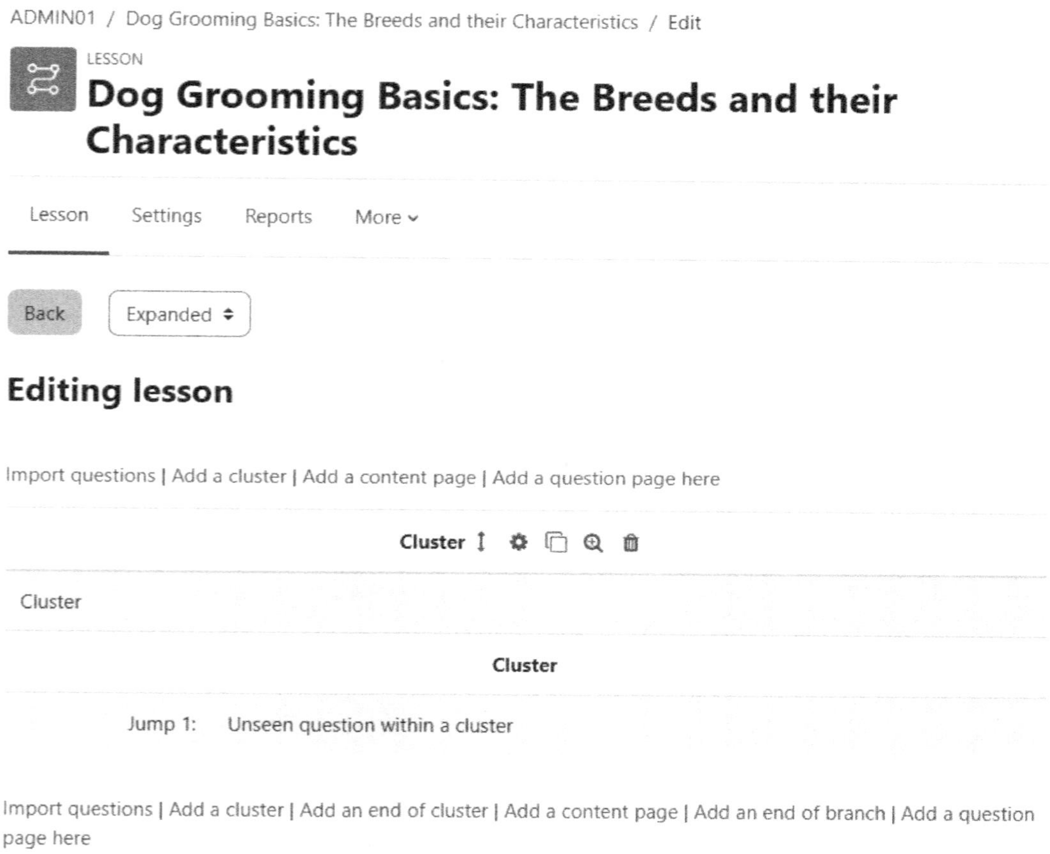

ADMIN01 / Dog Grooming Basics: The Breeds and their Characteristics / Edit

 LESSON
Dog Grooming Basics: The Breeds and their Characteristics

Lesson   Settings   Reports   More ⌄

Back   Expanded ⇕

Editing lesson

Import questions | Add a cluster | Add a content page | Add a question page here

Cluster I ⚙ ⧉ ⊕ 🗑

Cluster

Cluster

Jump 1:   Unseen question within a cluster

Import questions | Add a cluster | Add an end of cluster | Add a content page | Add an end of branch | Add a question page here

Figure 6.23 – Setting up the structure of the lesson and its jumps

Let's look at each type of page.

Content pages

A content page displays some information and then offers one or more buttons for the learner to click on to navigate to a different content page or question page.

Here's the second page from the preceding lesson:

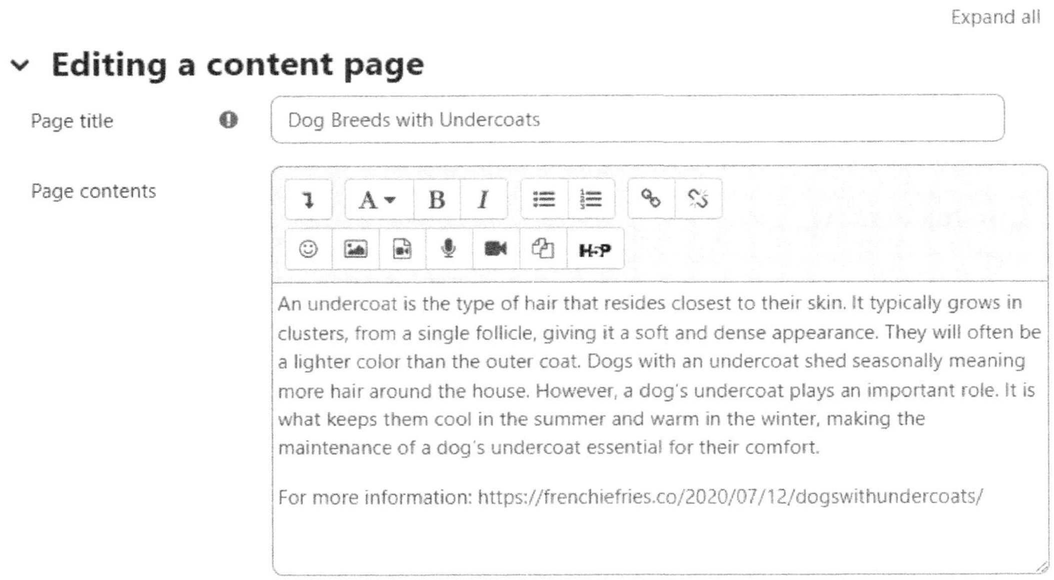

Expand all

Figure 6.24 – The content page of a lesson

The buttons at the bottom of this page are added by the course creator. Note that one of the buttons takes the learner to the next page. However, what if, when you are creating this page, the next page hasn't been created yet? That's not a problem. Once you have created all the pages in your lesson, you can go back to the content pages and add all the jump buttons. Using the relative jumps (previous page, next page, and so on) is a big time-saver.

Cluster with questions

A cluster page, end-of-cluster page, and the pages in between them act as a single unit. In our example, we have a cluster with two question pages.

On the first cluster page, a setting directs Moodle to display an unseen question page in this cluster. You can select other options for a cluster page:

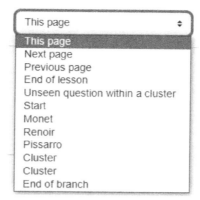

Figure 6.25 – Drop-down menu of options for the cluster page

Using the **Unseen question within a cluster** option turns the cluster into a random question test.

Between the cluster and the end of the cluster are two question pages. These question pages will jump the learner out of the cluster if they answer correctly, and to a remedial page if they answer incorrectly.

If you use a cluster like the preceding one, be careful that you do not create an impossible situation. In this case, if the remedial page sent the learner back into the cluster, and the learner had seen both questions, then there is no way the cluster could display an unseen question page. Moodle would give the learner an error message. Again, the key is to plan.

Instead of sending the learner back into the same cluster, create several clusters in a row. If a learner gets a question correct, you can skip over all the unseen clusters and move on to the next topic. If the learner gets a question incorrect, then you can send them straight to the next cluster.

Configuring lesson settings

When you first create a lesson, you will be presented with a window where you can choose settings for the entire lesson. Before you can add even a single page to a lesson, you must select the lesson settings. If you're not sure about any of these settings, just take your best guess. You can always return to this page and change the settings.

> **Tip**
>
> Remember that one of the advantages of Moodle is the ease with which you can experiment with and change your course material. Get accustomed to taking a bolder, more experimental approach to using Moodle, and you will enjoy it a lot more.

This window is broken into the following areas:

- Appearance
- Availability
- Flow control
- Grade
- Common module settings
- Restrict access
- Activity completion
- Tags
- Competencies

In this section, I'll go through the **Editing Lesson** page from top to bottom. I'll focus on the settings that are unique to the lesson activity. So, by the end of this section, you will understand how most of the settings on the **Editing Lesson** page affect the learner's experience.

General settings

This section consists of only the name of the lesson, which learners will see on the course's home page. If you want the learners to see a description of the lesson before they enter the lesson, you will need to complete the **Description** field and also add a label to the course home page to describe the lesson.

Appearance

This section contains settings that affect how the lesson is presented.

Linked media

You can upload a file into this field. When the learner enters the lesson, the file will be displayed in a pop-up window. This enables the learner to refer to the file as they proceed through the lesson.

The pop-up window might be blocked by the learner's browser. To ensure that the learner knows that there is a file they should see, consider adding a message to the first page of the lesson that tells the learner to open the file if it has not opened automatically.

While you are reading this lesson, they will need to refer to a diagram. To show that diagram, on the left menu bar, under **Linked Media**, click on **Click here to view link**.

After you display the diagram, proceed to the next page.

Display ongoing score

When this is set to **Yes**, each page of the lesson displays the learner's score and the number of possible points so far.

> **Tip**
> This displays the number of points that the learner could have earned for the pages that they have viewed so far.

If a lesson is not linear and it branches, the path that each learner takes through the lesson can change. This means that each learner can have the chance to earn a different number of points. For example, you may create a lesson with many branches and pages and then require the learner to earn at least 200 points on that lesson. This will encourage the learner to explore the lesson and try different branches until they have earned the required points.

Display left menu and Minimum grade to display menu

Display left menu displays a navigation bar on the left of the slideshow window. The navigation bar enables the learner to navigate to any slide. Without that navigation bar, the learner must proceed through the slideshow in the order that Moodle displays the lesson pages and must complete the lesson to exit (or the learner can force the window to close).

Sometimes, you may want a learner to complete the entire lesson, in order, before allowing them to move around the lesson freely. The **Minimum grade to display menu** setting accomplishes this. Only if the learner achieved the specified grade will they see the navigation menu. You can use this setting to ensure that the learner goes completely through the lesson the first time, before allowing the learner to freely move around the lesson.

Maximum number of answers

At the bottom of each question page in a lesson, **Maximum number of answers** determines the maximum number of choices that each question can have. For example, if this were set to **4**, each question could have, at most, four choices: **a**, **b**, **c**, and **d**.

If each answer sends the learner to a different page, the number of answers is also the number of branches possible. Set this to the highest number of answers that any of your questions will have. After creating question pages, you can increase or decrease this setting without affecting the questions that you have already created.

Use default feedback

If this is set to **Yes**, Moodle does not see any custom feedback that you created for a question; it will display a default message, such as **That's correct** or **That's incorrect**, instead. The default feedback is set in Moodle's language file, so it will be translated into whatever language the course is using. If you set this to **No**, and Moodle does not see any custom feedback that you created for a question, Moodle will not display any feedback when the learner answers.

Link to next activity

This setting allows you to put a link to another activity in the course at the end of the lesson. For example, you can link to a quiz.

Prerequisite lesson

The settings in this section allow you to require the learner to view another lesson before this lesson is open to the learner. One of the settings allows you to specify how many minutes the learner must spend on a previous lesson. You can use that setting to ensure that the learner spends a certain amount of time watching a video before moving on to the next lesson. You can do this by embedding the video in the prerequisite lesson.

The prerequisite lesson settings are in addition to the **Restrict access** settings that are available for all activities. With the **Restrict access** settings, you do not have the option to specify the amount of time that must be spent on another activity as a condition for access.

Flow control

This section contains settings that affect how a learner moves through the lesson:

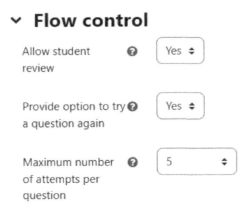

Figure 6.26 – The Flow control screen for the Lesson activity

Allow learner review

Allow learner review enables a learner to go backward in a lesson and retry questions that they got wrong. This differs from just using the **Back** button on the browser, in that this setting enables the learner to retry questions, whereas using the **Back** button does not.

Provide option to try a question again

Provide option to try a question again displays a message after the learner incorrectly answers a question. The message invites the learner to try the question again, but for no points.

When you create a question in a lesson, you can create feedback for each of the answers to that question. However, if you set **Provide option to try a question again** to **Yes**, Moodle will override the feedback that you created for the answers. Instead, it will display a message asking you to try a question again.

> **Tip**
>
> If you have created custom feedback for the answers in your lesson but Moodle is not displaying the feedback that you created, check the **Provide option to try a question again** setting. It might be set to **Yes**. Set it to **No**.

Maximum number of attempts

Maximum number of attempts determines how many times a learner can attempt any question. This applies to all the questions in the lesson.

Number of pages to show

Number of pages to show determines how many pages are shown. If the lesson contains more than this number, the lesson ends after reaching the number set here. If the lesson contains fewer than this number, the lesson ends after every page has been shown. If you set this to zero, the lesson ends when all the pages have been shown.

Grade

A lesson can be graded or ungraded. You can also allow learners to retake the lesson. While Moodle allows you to grade a lesson, remember that a lesson's primary purpose is to teach, not test.

> **Tip**
> Don't use a lesson to do the work of a quiz or assignment.

The lesson's score is there to give you feedback on the effectiveness of each page and to enable learners to judge their progress:

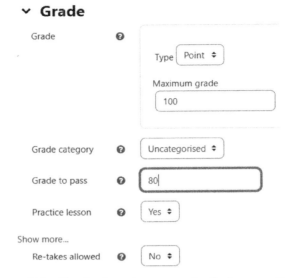

Figure 6.27 – The Grade settings screen for the Lesson activity

Practice lesson

If you set **Practice lesson** to **Yes**, this lesson will not show up in the grade book. In a practice lesson, learners see a grade after completing the activity, but this grade is only for them. It is not recorded or displayed in the grade book, and teachers cannot see it. It's a pure self-studying option.

Custom scoring

Normally, a correct answer to a question is worth the entire point value for the question, and each wrong answer is worth zero. Enabling **Custom scoring** allows you to set a point value for each answer to a question. Use this if some answers are *more right* or *more wrong* than others. For example, you could develop history quizzes in which the distractors range from almost correct to completely wrong, such as the same century versus the wrong century. You can also use this to set the point value for a question. If a question is more important, use custom scoring to give it more points.

Handling retakes

This setting is only relevant if the learner is allowed to repeat the lesson (the setting is set to **Yes**). When learners are allowed to retake the lesson, the grades shown on the **Grades** page are either the average of the retakes or the learner's best grade.

Minimum number of questions

Minimum number of questions sets the lower limit for the number of questions used to calculate a learner's grade on the lesson. It is only relevant when the lesson will be graded. If the learner doesn't answer this minimum number of questions, the lesson is not graded.

If you don't see this setting, it is probably because you have **Practice lesson** set to **Yes**. Set **Practice lesson** to **No** and save the page; you should see this setting appear.

Adding a content page

A content page consists of a page of links to the other pages in your lesson. At this point, immediately after you've finished the lesson settings page, your lesson won't have any pages. However, if you want to begin your lesson with a page of instructions, you can add a content page and make it jump to the next page. When you're creating a content page, you will see something similar to the following:

Figure 6.28 – Setting up a content page

When the learner runs the lesson, the content page will look like this:

Start

In this lesson you will be shown a series of Impressionist paintings and asked to reflect upon them and write your responses in the text box provided. This lesson will be manually graded so you may have to wait for your teacher to give you feedback.

(Source of questions: Monet Exhibition NZ 2009)

Figure 6.29 – Learner view of the content page to initiate the lesson

Adding a cluster

A **cluster** is a group of question pages. Within this cluster, you can require the learner to correctly answer several questions before they're allowed to proceed out of the cluster. This enables you to test that a learner understands a concept before moving on.

Alternatively, you can display a random page from the cluster, and from that page, proceed to any other page in the lesson. This enables you to send each learner down a different random pathway in the lesson so that not all learners have the same experience. For example, you can let them take different paths to cover Mesoamerican history.

A cluster consists of a beginning cluster page, an end-of-cluster page, and pages in between them.

Adding a question page

This option enables you to add a question page to your lesson using Moodle's built-in editor. The process of creating a question page will be covered in the next section.

Try adding your question pages first. Then, put a content page with instructions at the beginning of the lesson. If needed, organize your question pages into branches or clusters. Finally, end the lesson with a content page to say goodbye to the learner.

Creating a question page

Once you've filled out and saved the **Settings** page, it's time to create the first question page. Even though it's called a *question page*, the page can contain more than just a question. It's a web page, so you can add any content to it. Usually, it contains information and a question to test the learner's understanding. You can choose different types of questions:

- Multiple choice
- True/false
- Short answer
- Numeric
- Matching
- Essay

These can be found under **Select a question type**:

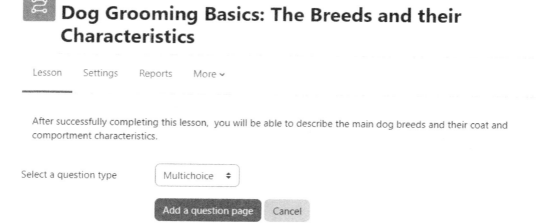

Figure 6.30 – Adding a question type screen for the Lesson activity

You can also create feedback for each answer to the question, similar to creating feedback for the answers to a quiz question. In addition, you can make the lesson jump to a new page, based on the answer the learner selects.

In the following screenshot, you can see that the question page contains a question that lets you jump to another location. Note that for each answer, there is a **Response** field that the learner sees immediately after submitting the answer. There is also a **Jump** field for each answer. For the incorrect answer that you see, **Jump** can take the learner to a remedial page or redisplay the current page so that they can try again. For the correct answer, **Jump** can display the next page in the lesson, as shown here:

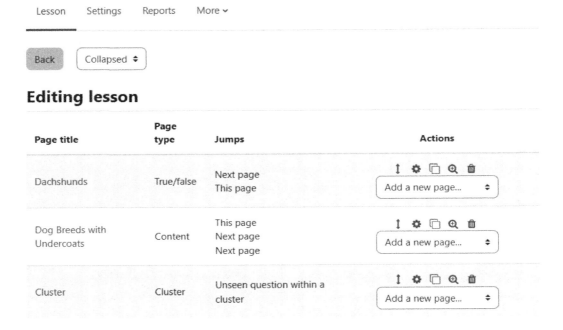

Figure 6.31 – Configuring the answers so that they jump to the appropriate page

Let's look at what's available on this page in more detail:

- **Page Title**: This will be displayed at the top of the page when it is shown in the lesson.

- **Page Contents**: As we mentioned previously, a lesson page is a web page. It can contain anything that you can put on any other Moodle web page. Usually, it will contain information and then a question to test the learner's understanding.

- **Answers**: This will be displayed at the bottom of the lesson page, after **Page Contents**. The learner can select an answer in response to the question posed in the **Page Contents** area.

- **Responses**: For each answer that the learner selects, its response is shown before the learner is taken to a new page.
- **Jumps**: Each answer that a learner selects results in a jump to a page.
- **This page**: If the jump is **This page**, the learner stays on the same page. The learner can then try to answer the question again.
- **Next page or Previous page**: If the jump is **Next page** or **Previous page**, the learner is taken to the next or previous page, respectively. After you rearrange the pages in a lesson, this jump may give you different results. Just be aware that this is a **relative** jump. This is best for a linear lesson:

Editing lesson

Import questions | Add a cluster | Add a content page | Add a question page here

Dog Breeds with Undercoats

An undercoat is the type of hair that resides closest to their skin. It typically grows in clusters, from a single follicle, giving it a soft and dense appearance. They will often be a lighter color than the outer coat. Dogs with an undercoat shed seasonally meaning more hair around the house. However, a dog's undercoat plays an important role. It is what keeps them cool in the summer and warm in the winter, making the maintenance of a dog's undercoat essential for their comfort.

For more information: https://frenchiefries.co/2020/07/12/dogswithundercoats/

Content

Content 1:	German Shepherds
Jump 1:	This page
Content 2:	Huskies
Jump 2:	Next page
Content 3:	Malamuts
Jump 3:	Next page

Figure 6.32 – Editing screen for the Lesson activity

- **Specific pages**: You can also select a specific page to jump to. The pull-down list displays all the lesson page's titles. If you select a specific page to jump to, the jump will remain the same, even if you rearrange the pages in your lesson.

For a jump, if you select **Unseen question with a branch**, the learner will be taken to a question page that they have not answered correctly in this session. That question page will be in the same cluster as the current page.

> **Tip**
> An unseen question with a branch takes the learner to a question page that they haven't answered correctly. The learner may have seen the page before and answered incorrectly.

Editing the lesson

Once you've created several lesson pages, you may want to see and edit the flow of the lesson. You can do this under the **Edit** tab.

Collapsed and expanded

The **Edit** tab is where you edit the content of your lesson. From here, you can add, delete, rearrange, and edit individual lesson pages.

Under the **Edit** tab, when you select **Collapsed**, you will see a list of the pages in your lesson, such as the one shown in the following screenshot:

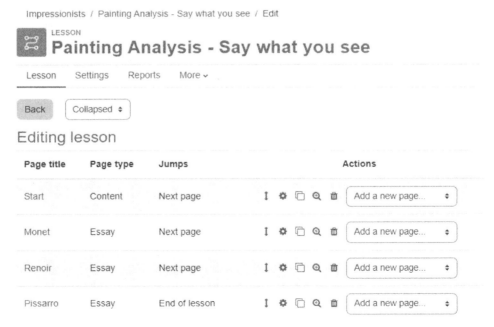

Figure 6.33 – After selecting the Collapsed option, you will see a list of pages in your lesson

The pages display in their logical order, which would be the shortest path through the lesson if a learner got all of the questions correct. Note that the content of the pages is not displayed. The purpose of this screen is not to edit individual questions but to help you see the flow of the lesson.

Rearranging pages

To rearrange the pages, click on the *up/down* arrow, ■, for the page that you want to move. Note that it is the jumps that determine the order in which Moodle presents the pages. If a question is set to jump to the next page, rearranging the pages can change the jumps. A question can also be set to jump to a specific, named page. In that case, the order in which the pages appear doesn't determine the landing point for the jump, so rearranging the pages here won't affect that jump.

Editing pages

From the **Edit** tab, to edit a page, click on the *edit* icon, which usually looks like this: ■ . Clicking on this takes you to the editing page for that page. The previous section provided detailed instructions for editing a lesson page.

Adding pages

The **Add a page here** drop-down list enables you to insert a new page into the lesson. You can choose from several different kinds of pages.

In this section, you learned how to create adaptive lessons, which will enhance the learning experience by providing remedial content. After putting together the lessons, it is a good idea to motivate learners by giving them a chance to provide feedback. In the next section, you will learn how to develop feedback modules.

Developing feedback modules

The **Feedback** activity allows you to create surveys for your learners. The **Feedback** activity is often confused with the **Survey** activity. In a **Survey** activity, you must choose from several pre-made surveys; you cannot build surveys. Also, do not confuse this with the questionnaire module. A questionnaire is an add-on, while **Feedback** comes as standard with Moodle.

Feedback isn't just for learners

Of course, you can use a **Feedback** activity to survey your learners. You can also use it to do the following:

- Survey the employees in your workplace.
- Collect data from people who have agreed to be research subjects.
- Conduct public opinion surveys of the visitors to your site.

The **Feedback** activity allows you to create different kinds of questions: multiple choice, dropdown, short answer, and more. You can share the results of feedback with the learners or keep them confidential.

Creating a Feedback activity

Let's imagine that we're developing a course called *Dog Grooming for Everyone*. In the course, we have a module called *Dog Grooming Tools*. Creating a **Feedback** activity is similar to adding a quiz. First, you add the activity, and then you add the questions. We'll cover each in the following sections separately.

To add a **Feedback** activity, follow these steps:

1. From the **Add an activity or resource** menu, select **Feedback**.
2. Moodle will display the **Settings** page for the activity.
3. Add a **name** for the feedback. Your learners will see this on the course home page:

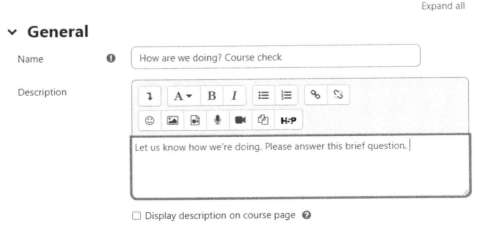

Figure 6.34 – Adding a new Feedback activity

4. Text and graphics that are entered into the **Description** field are displayed to learners before they begin the activity. Use this to explain the activity. Remember that this is a full-featured HTML editor, so you can put text, graphics, and media into the description.

5. Under **Availability**, you can enter a time to open and close the activity. If you don't enter a time to open the activity, it will be available immediately. If you don't enter a time to close the activity, it will remain open indefinitely:

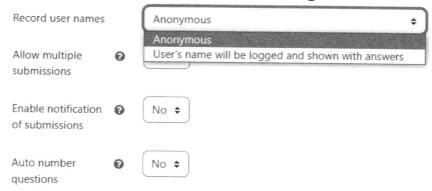

Figure 6.35 – The Availability and Question and submission settings screens for the Feedback activity

6. The **Record user names** option only affects what the teacher sees. Learners do not see each other's responses. If **Record user names** is set, then users' names will be logged and shown with answers. The teacher will be able to see a list of users who completed the feedback and their answers:

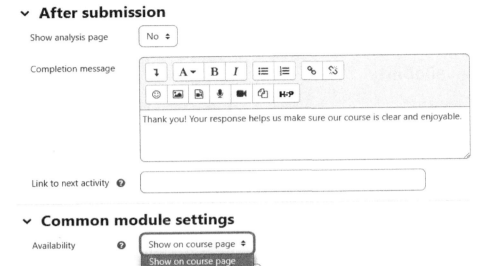

Figure 6.36 – Response screen for the Feedback activity

7. The **Allow multiple submissions** setting affects the activity, but only if you have allowed anonymous responses. If so, any user can submit the feedback survey as many times as they want.

8. If **Enable notification of submissions** is set to **Yes**, course administrators are emailed whenever someone submits feedback. This includes teachers and course managers.

9. If you want Moodle to number the questions in your feedback activity, select **Yes** for **Auto number questions**.

10. If **Show analysis page after submit** is set to **Yes**, a summary of the results so far is shown to the user after they submit their feedback.

> **Get This Setting Right the First Time**
> Moodle doesn't allow you to change the multiple submissions setting after someone has answered the feedback activity, without you losing the previous responses. So, be sure to get this setting right before people start answering. If you do need to change this setting, you must first set **Reset feedback responses** under the **Course administration** menu.

11. If you enter a **link to next activity**, that page will be displayed immediately after the users submit their answers. You can use this page to explain what happens after the activity. If you leave this blank, Moodle will display a simple message telling the user that their answers have been saved. At the bottom of this page, Moodle displays a **Continue** button.

Common module settings restrict availability work as they do for other activities.

> **Be Careful with the URL for Link to Next Activity**
>
> You might be tempted to use the URL to send the user to another page on your site. Remember that if you move this activity to another course or another Moodle site, that URL may change.

12. Click on the **Save and display** button to save the settings. Now, it is time to start adding questions.

To add questions to a feedback activity, follow these steps:

1. Select the **Feedback** activity.

2. From the left menu, select **Feedback activity name | Feedback | Edit questions**. You will see a dropdown button menu that has the following options: **Add question | Use a template | Import questions**.

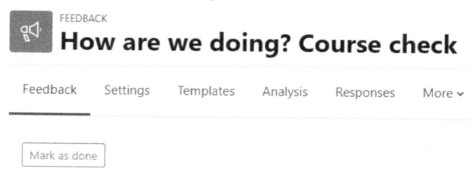

Figure 6.37 – Editing questions in the Feedback activity

3. From the **Choose** drop-down list select the type of question to add.

> **Tip**
> Specific types of questions will be described in the next section. The rest of this procedure covers settings that are common to almost all question types. For settings that are specific to a question type, please refer to the next section.

4. If you mark a question as **Required**, the user must answer it to submit the feedback. The question will have a red asterisk next to it.

5. The **Question** field contains the text of the question. Unlike a quiz question, a feedback question can only consist of text:

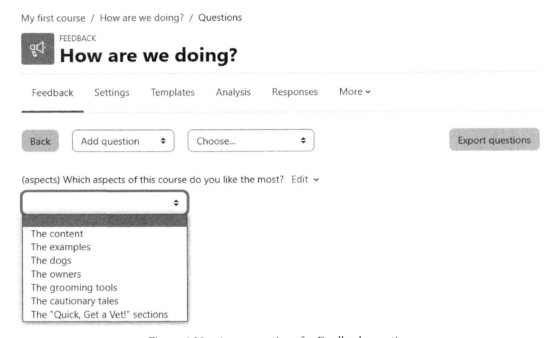

Figure 6.38 – Answer options for Feedback question

6. The **Label** field contains a label that only teachers will see when viewing the results of the feedback. The most important reason for the **Label** field is when you plan to export the results of the feedback to an Excel worksheet. The label is exported with the results. This allows you to match the feedback results with a short label in your database.

7. The **Position** field determines the order of the question when you first add it to the feedback page. Once the question has been added, you can override this number and move the question to any position on the page.

8. **Depend item** and **Depend value** can be used to make the appearance of a question dependent on the answer to a previous question. For example, you may first ask someone, **Do you have a Twitter account?**.

   If they answer with **Yes**, you might display a question such as **How often do you tweet?**. If they answer with **No**, you would hide that question. From the **Dependence item** drop-down list, select the question whose answer will determine whether this question appears. Then, in the **Dependence value** field, enter the answer that is needed to make this question appear.

9. For a discussion of fields that apply only to one type of question, check out the following section.

10. Save the question.

Question types

The **Feedback** activity allows you to add several types of questions. Some of these are not questions, but you can still add them from the same drop-down menu:

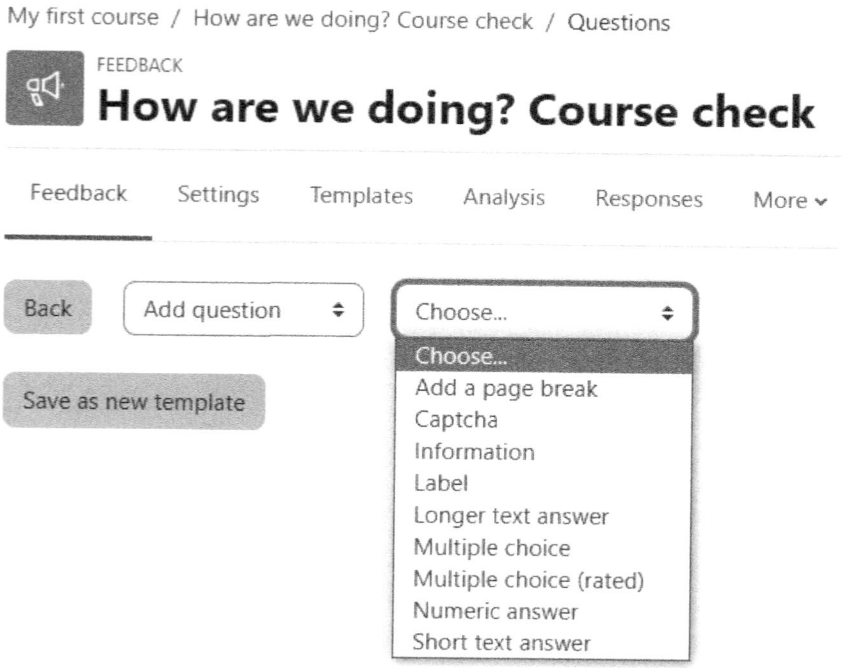

My first course / How are we doing? Course check / Questions

FEEDBACK

How are we doing? Course check

Feedback   Settings   Templates   Analysis   Responses   More ∨

Back   Add question ⬍   Choose... ⬍

Save as new template

Choose...
Add a page break
Captcha
Information
Label
Longer text answer
Multiple choice
Multiple choice (rated)
Numeric answer
Short text answer

Figure 6.39 – Drop-down menu of question types

Adding a page break

Add a page break inserts a page break into the **Feedback** activity.

Avoiding bots with CAPTCHA

If you allow guests to complete the form for access, you may need a level of security to avoid bots. A **CAPTCHA** is a test that ensures that a human is filling out an online form. It displays a picture of some text, and the user must read and type in that text. If the user doesn't type the text correctly, the feedback form is rejected. This prevents software robots from automatically filling in your feedback and spamming your results.

Inserting information

You can use this option to insert information about the feedback into the form. That information is added by Moodle and submitted with the user's answers. At the time of writing, the options are as follows:

- **Response time**: The date and time at which the user submitted the feedback
- **Course**: The short name of the course in which this feedback appears
- **Course category**: The short name of the category in which this feedback appears

Adding a label

This is the same as adding a label to a course home page. The label can be anything that you can put on a web page. This is a good way to insert an explanation, instructions, and encouragement into the activity.

Creating a text box for a longer text answer

Use this question type to create a text box where the user can type in an answer. Here, you can specify how many characters wide and how many lines high the text box is. If the user runs out of space, Moodle adds a scroll bar to the box so that the user can keep on typing.

Displaying multiple-choice questions

A multiple-choice question displays a list of responses. There are three subtypes of multiple-choice questions:

- **Multiple choice – multiple answers**: In this question, Moodle displays a checkbox next to each response. The user can select as many as they want.
- **Multiple choice – single answer**: In this question, Moodle displays a radio button next to each response. The user must select only one response.

- **Multiple choice – single answer allowed** (drop-down list): In this question, Moodle displays a drop-down list of the responses. The user must select only one response.

You create the responses for a multiple-choice question by entering one response on each line in the **Multiple choice values** field. For example, consider the following settings:

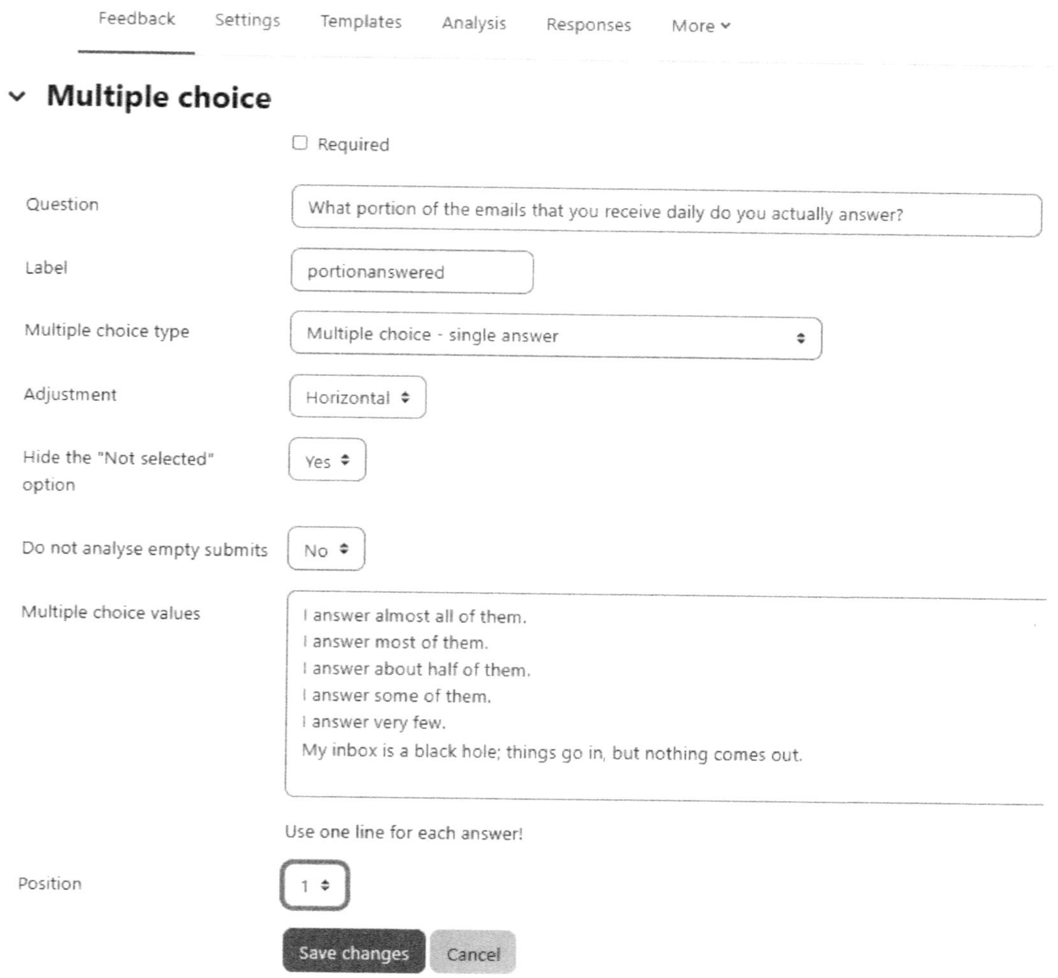

Feedback   Settings   Templates   Analysis   Responses   More ˅

˅ Multiple choice

☐ Required

Question — What portion of the emails that you receive daily do you actually answer?

Label — portionanswered

Multiple choice type — Multiple choice - single answer

Adjustment — Horizontal

Hide the "Not selected" option — Yes

Do not analyse empty submits — No

Multiple choice values —
I answer almost all of them.
I answer most of them.
I answer about half of them.
I answer some of them.
I answer very few.
My inbox is a black hole; things go in, but nothing comes out.

Use one line for each answer!

Position — 1

Save changes   Cancel

Figure 6.40 – Setting up Multiple choice

Create the following question:

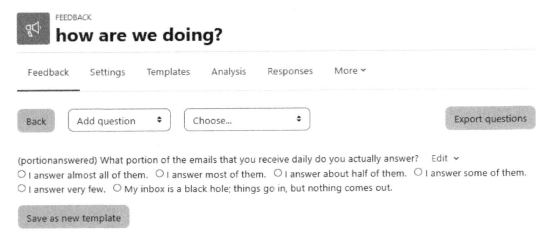

Figure 6.41 – Configuring the answers so that they jump to the appropriate page

> **Important Note**
>
> Note that the **Adjustment** setting for this question is set to **Horizontal**. This causes the responses to be listed horizontally, across the page, instead of in a vertical list.

Also, note the setting for the **Hide the "Not selected"** option. If this is set to **No**, Moodle will add a **Not selected** response to the list of responses that you create. When set to **Yes**, Moodle will only display the responses that you create.

Creating multiple-choice questions

To the user, this type of question appears identical to a multiple-choice single-answer question. However, when you review the results, you will see a number that is associated with each answer. This allows you to calculate averages and perform other calculations with the data that you collect.

In this example, the answers are rated **4** through **0**:

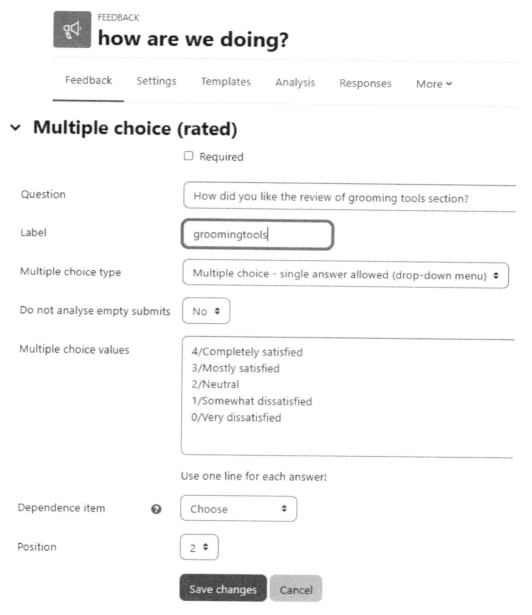

Figure 6.42 – Text for the feedback options

The user doesn't see these numbers when they select an answer, but when the teacher looks at the analysis for the question, the average is displayed. Also, when the results of the feedback are exported to Excel, the rating numbers are exported. This enables you to do an advanced analysis of your results using a spreadsheet.

Numeric answer

Use this type of question to ask the user to enter a number. You can specify a range that you will accept.

Short-text answer

A short-text-answer question lets you limit the amount of text that the user enters. You specify the size of the text entry box and the amount of text that the box will accept.

Viewing feedback

Teachers and administrators can view the responses to a **Feedback** activity. You can view the responses one at a time or a summary of all responses.

Seeing individual responses

If **Record User Names** is set to **User's Names Will Be Logged and Shown With Answers**, the teacher will be able to see a list of users who completed the feedback and their answers. To see this list of responses, follow these steps:

1.   Select the **Feedback** activity.

2.   From the left menu, select **Settings** | **Feedback administration** | **Show responses**.

3. For the learner whose responses you want to see, click on the date:

Figure 6.43 – Selecting learner answers to see

Analyzing responses with the Analysis tab

Under the **Analysis** tab, you can see a summary of all the responses. On this page, you also have an **Export to Excel** button, which will download all the data to an Excel spreadsheet.

It is good to keep in mind that feedback is important not only after a lesson or set of assignments but also after a synchronous web conference or tutoring session. The advantage of using Moodle for the feedback over using it within BigBlueButton or Zoom is that you will have a more durable record of it within the current and archived courses in Moodle. For more involved questions or surveys, the ideal tool is **Choice**. You can use **Choice** for feedback as well as for engagers, such as "Check Your Understanding" types of quizzes or engagers.

Exploring Choice

Moodle's **Choice** is the simplest type of activity. In a **Choice** activity, you create one question and specify a choice of responses. You can use **Choice** to do the following:

- Take a quick poll.
- Ask learners to choose sides in a debate.
- Confirm the learners' understanding of an agreement.
- Gather consent.
- Allow learners to choose a subject for an essay or project.

Before we look at how to accomplish this, let's look at the **Choice** activity from the learner's point of view and then explore the settings available to the teacher while creating a **choice**.

The learner's point of view

From the learner's point of view, a **Choice** activity looks like this:

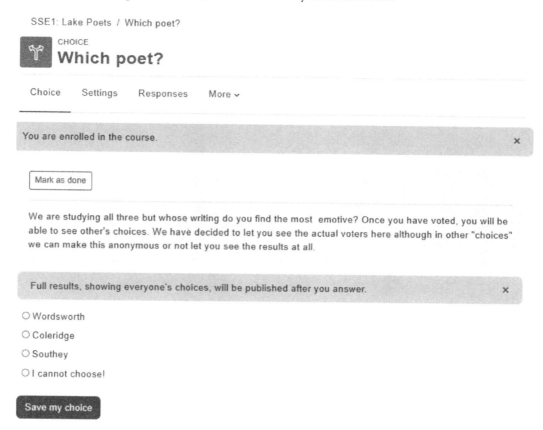

Figure 6.44 – View of the Choice activity from the learner's view

There are a few things to note about this choice activity:

- The learner can see how many other learners have chosen a response.
- There is a limit on the number of learners who can choose each response.
- The learner can remove their choice and submit again.

These are options that you can set for the activity. The teacher could have also hidden other learners' responses, placed no limit on the number of learners who can choose each response, and prevented the learner from changing their response:

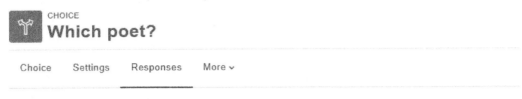

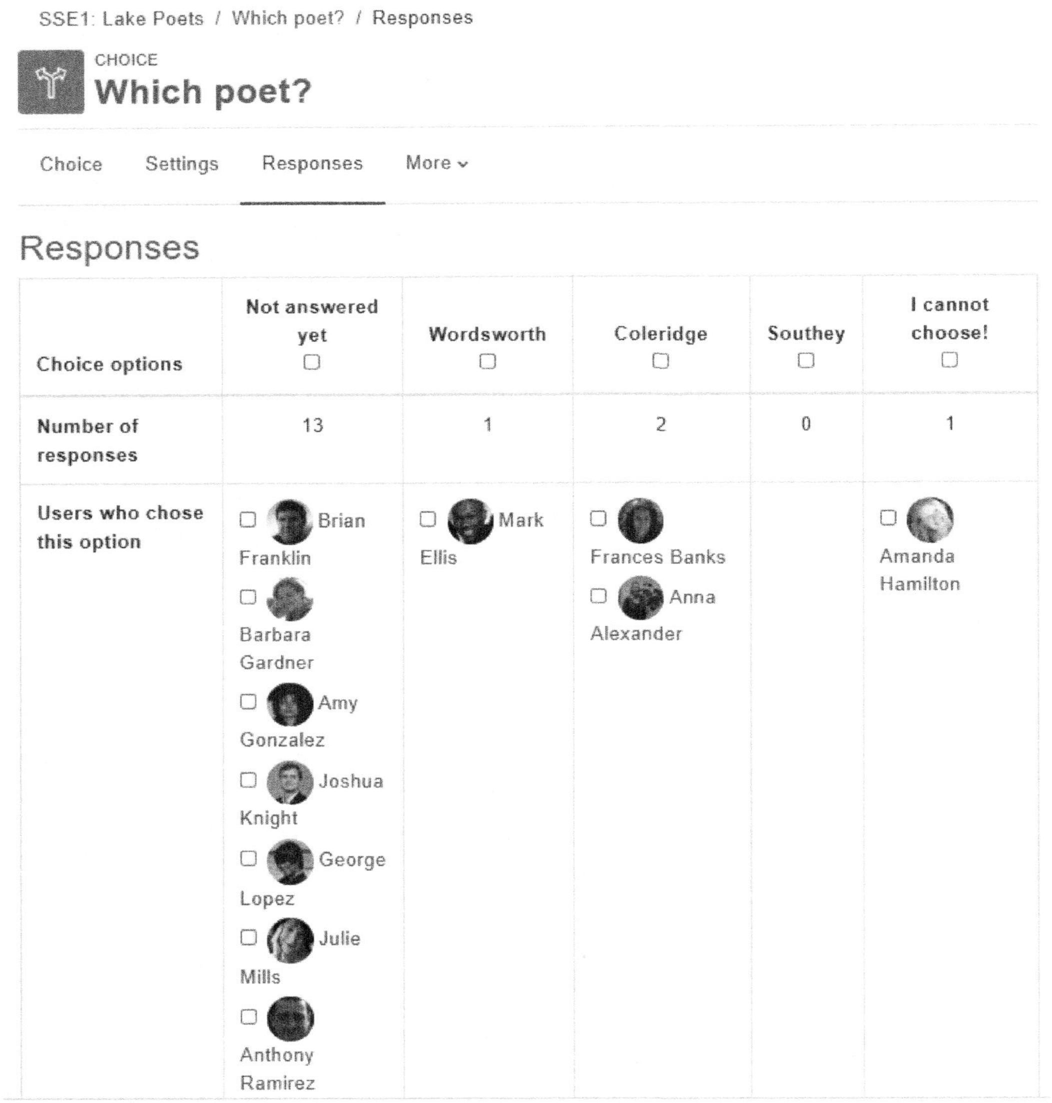

SSE1: Lake Poets / Which poet? / Responses

CHOICE
Which poet?

Choice   Settings   Responses   More ˅

Responses

Choice options	Not answered yet ☐	Wordsworth ☐	Coleridge ☐	Southey ☐	I cannot choose! ☐
Number of responses	13	1	2	0	1
Users who chose this option	☐ Brian Franklin ☐ Barbara Gardner ☐ Amy Gonzalez ☐ Joshua Knight ☐ George Lopez ☐ Julie Mills ☐ Anthony Ramirez	☐ Mark Ellis	☐ Frances Banks ☐ Anna Alexander		☐ Amanda Hamilton

Figure 6.45 – Combined Choice results

The teacher's point of view

Before we discuss some of the uses for a **Choice** activity, let's look at the settings that are available on the **Editing choice** page. Then, we'll learn how to make creative use of these capabilities.

Limit

The **Limit** option next to each choice allows you to limit how many learners can select that choice. In the preceding example, no more than four learners can select each choice, so after four learners have selected a team, that choice becomes unavailable.

For limits to take effect, **Limit the number of responses allowed** must be set to **Yes**:

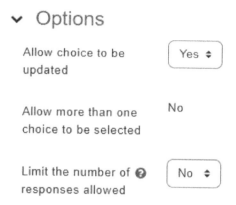

Figure 6.46 – The Options settings screen in the Choice activity

Display Mode

In the preceding example, **Display Mode** is set to **Vertical**. You can also arrange the choices horizontally.

Publish results

You can choose whether to reveal the results of the choice to the learners and, if so, when.

In the example at the beginning of this section, **Publish results** was set to **Always show results to learners**; this is why the learner could see how many learners had chosen each response. If it had been set to **Do not publish results to learners**, the activity would not have shown how many learners had selected each response:

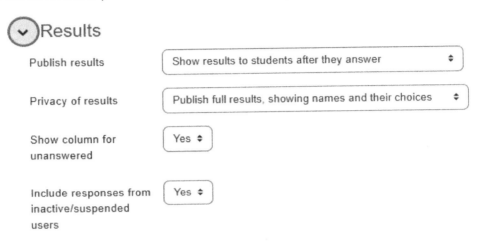

Figure 6.47 – The Results settings screen in the Choice activity

If you limit the number of learners who can choose a response, consider using **Always show results to learners**. That way, the learner can see how many others have chosen the response and how many slots are left for each response.

Privacy of results

If you publish the results of the choice, you can choose whether to publish the names of the learners who have selected each response. In the example at the beginning of this section, **Privacy of results** was set to **Publish full results**, so the learner could see who had selected each response.

Allowing learners to change their minds

The **Allow choice to be updated** setting determines whether a learner can change their answer after submitting it. If this is set to **Yes**, a learner can retake the **Choice** activity until the activity is closed.

In an environment where instructors use a combination of synchronous and asynchronous delivery, having the ability to include survey and feedback tools can be vital in maintaining engagement and determining the effectiveness of content, activities, and lessons.

Summary

Activities are very important in the Moodle framework because they allow learners to demonstrate competency, as well as staying engaged and motivated. They also allow course designers to connect learning outcomes to the overall competency frameworks that may be required by governing bodies.

In Moodle 4.0, the activities have been streamlined so that there are not as many, but many have increased their functionality to be even more collaborative and interactive to keep learners engaged and motivated. Moodle 4.0 has made it easier for learners to see where they are in a course by making enhancements to the Assignment activity, as well as others, to indicate whether an activity has been completed, and whether or not the minimum passing score has been achieved.

Moodle's **Assignment** and **Lesson** activities allow you to create course material that learners can interact with. This interaction is more engaging, and usually more effective, than courses consisting of static material that the learners view. While you will probably begin creating your course by adding static material, the next step should usually be to ask, "How can I add interactivity to this course?"

There are many ways to build engaging assignments and Moodle provides many different activities to help you do so. You can customize your solutions, so as you work through this unit, please take a moment to experiment. Remember, you can always delete and modify your work. So, play in the sandbox!

Lessons can take the place of many static web pages since they consist of web pages with a question at the end of each page. A lesson allows you to present information to a learner, test the learner on the information, and then either present remedial information or continue to the next topic.

The **Feedback** and **Choice** activities allow teachers to assess learners, their attitudes, and their satisfaction with a course. Feedback is especially useful for assessing the class's attitude and experience at the beginning of the course. You can also use feedback to create surveys for people who are not even taking a course, such as an employee survey or research data.

The **Choice** activity is especially useful for having a structured, ongoing conversation between the learners and teacher. You can create several of these, keep them hidden, and reveal them when you want to measure the learners' attitudes.

In the next chapter, you will learn how to evaluate learners using the **Quiz** activity.

7
Evaluating Students with Quizzes

A foundational part of any assessment strategy in an online course often relies heavily on different types of automatically scoring quizzes. However, quizzes can often be the Achilles heel of a course or educational program if they are not designed well, and do not tie in well with overall course learning objectives. Planning with storyboarding is critical. Furthermore, in an environment where there is a need for "live" (synchronous) lectures via Zoom, Teams, BigBlueButton, or other platforms, quizzes are often overlooked. Nevertheless, they can be an ideal way to take stock of how and where the students are concerning learning goals, and to keep them engaged.

A well-designed use of quizzes can help learners achieve learning objectives, and they also satisfy **Universal Design for Learning (UDL)** guidelines that have to do with building a structure for student success. Quizzes can help with goal setting, self-regulation, and developing a positive "I can do it!", believe-in-yourself attitude (self-efficacy).

Moodle 4.0's redesigned look and feel, as well as its responsive themes, make it easy to use on many different devices, including smartphones. This fact is critical because many learners will be relying on their phones to do coursework, particularly in situations where they cannot access the Moodle course on a laptop or desktop. In situations where learners are relying on cell phones, it's important to use assessment strategies that can display well on small screens. In that case, Moodle's Quiz activity is ideal, particularly for multiple-choice quizzes.

Coupled with certificates and badges to be awarded once mastery has been demonstrated, quizzes can be a key building block for academic and career milestones.

In this chapter, we will examine how Moodle offers a powerful solution that allows well-designed and well-placed quizzes, and the ability to tie the quizzes in with mastery learning, competency frameworks, certificates, and badges. In this chapter, you will learn how to do the following:

- Develop graded assignments
- Create quizzes with question banks
- Integrate certificates and badges

After completing this chapter, you'll know which strategies to use for Quiz activities in Moodle. You'll also have a foundational knowledge of how to develop different types of quizzes and how to write effective questions.

Moodle 4.0's Quiz activity

In Moodle 4.0, **Quiz** is a powerful and highly flexible activity that allows you to achieve learning objectives by creating assessment tools ranging from simple, multiple-choice tests to complex, self-assessment tasks with detailed feedback. The following screenshot shows the newly redesigned icon for Quiz in Moodle 4.0:

Quiz

Figure 7.1 – Icon for the Quiz activity in Moodle 4.0

As is the case with all resources and activities in Moodle, once you have turned on **Edit** in the top right-hand corner and selected **Add activity or resource**, select **Quiz**. You will see a screen called **Updating: Quiz**, which will include the fields you need to complete to add a name and description, as shown in the following screenshot:

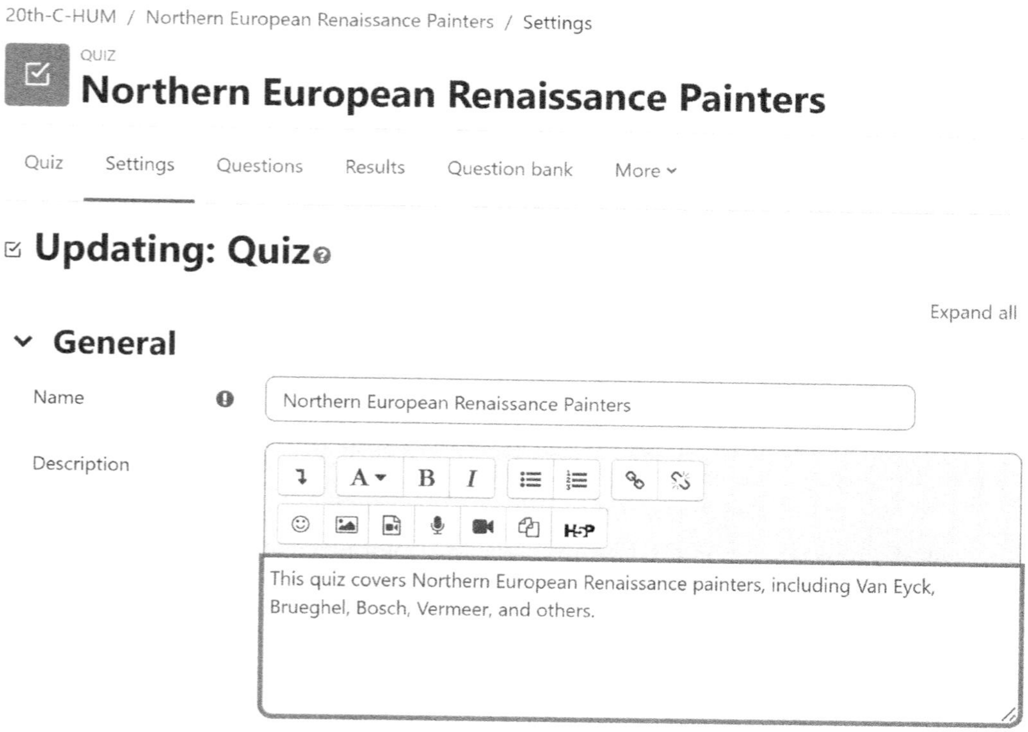

20th-C-HUM / Northern European Renaissance Painters / Settings

QUIZ
Northern European Renaissance Painters

Quiz   Settings   Questions   Results   Question bank   More ⌄

☑ Updating: Quiz❓

Expand all

⌄ General

Name   ❶ | Northern European Renaissance Painters |

Description

| ⤵ | A ▾ | B | I | ≣ | ≣ | ⚭ | ⚬ |

| ☺ | 🖼 | 🎞 | 🎤 | 🎥 | ⎘ | H5P |

This quiz covers Northern European Renaissance painters, including Van Eyck, Brueghel, Bosch, Vermeer, and others.

Figure 7.2 – You can name your quiz and describe it in the General settings area

Once you've created your Quiz description, scroll down the page to see the other aspects of the Quiz activity that you will configure. Each topic is clickable and opens a screen that allows you to customize the quiz. The following is what you will see when you scroll down the screen:

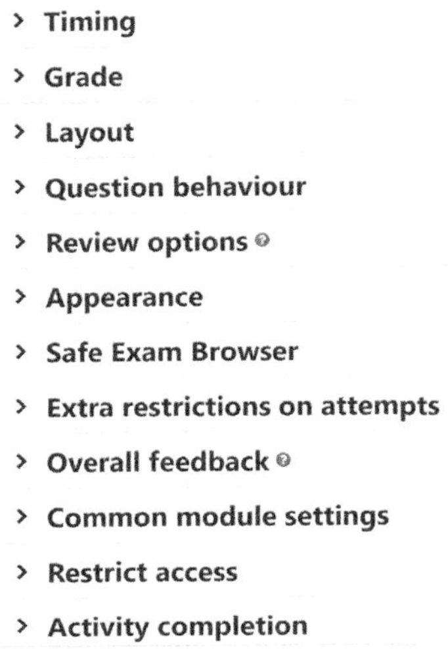

> **Timing**

> **Grade**

> **Layout**

> **Question behaviour**

> **Review options** ⊘

> **Appearance**

> **Safe Exam Browser**

> **Extra restrictions on attempts**

> **Overall feedback** ⊘

> **Common module settings**

> **Restrict access**

> **Activity completion**

Figure 7.3 – Categories of settings you can use to configure your Quiz

Now that we know where to find the Quiz activity, what it looks like, and the basic options, let's look at the best way to use quizzes.

Developing graded assessments using quizzes

As you put together your lessons and assignments, you will need an assessment strategy. In online courses, it is very useful to be able to incorporate self-grading quizzes. Moodle offers a flexible quiz builder. Each question can include any valid HTML code, such as graphics, formatted text, and media. A question can include anything that you can put on a Moodle resource page.

In most instructor-led courses, a quiz or test is a major event. Handing out the quizzes, taking them in the middle of a class, and grading them can take up a lot of the teacher's time. In Moodle, creating, taking, and grading quizzes can be much faster. This means that you can use quizzes liberally throughout your courses. Here are some instances where you can use quizzes:

- You can use a short quiz after each reading assignment to ensure that the students complete the reading. You can shuffle the questions and answers to prevent sharing among the students. You can also make the quiz available only for the week/month in which the students are supposed to complete the reading.

- You can use a quiz as a practice test. You can allow several attempts and/or use adaptive mode to allow students to attempt a question until they get it right. Then, the quiz functions both as practice and learning material.

- You can use a quiz as a pretest to confirm prior learning, as well as for determining where there is a knowledge or skills gap. You can ask the students to complete a quiz even before they come to the course. The students can complete this pretest at a time and place that is convenient for them. Then, you can compare their scores on the pretest and final test to show that learning has occurred. The skills gap analysis that you will have can help you measure the effectiveness of the course.

- You can use a quiz in conjunction with mastery learning to help students achieve the minimum score to demonstrate mastery.

- You can tie quiz scores/performance to competency frameworks to help satisfy institutional or accreditation requirements.

- You can automatically generate badges and certificates based on the achievement of certain scores. Note that you can restrict access to further modules, courses, resources, or activities until a sufficiently high quiz score has been achieved.

In Moodle, after setting up a new Quiz, you will need to develop a question bank. The kinds of questions you develop depend on the type of Quiz you've decided to use, depending on your instructional strategy. You'll want to develop a sufficient number of questions to allow you to rotate the questions and assure academic honesty.

The Quiz activity includes several different types of quizzes, but we will start with multiple choice because it is the one you are likely to use the most. To be effective, you should follow psychometric standards, which can be complicated. We will provide easy-to-follow guidelines here, which will help you write multiple-choice questions that you can feel confident about. Now, let's start building a question bank, where you will store your classified and tagged questions that correspond to the kind of quiz you plan to administer.

Building question banks

Let's build a question bank. Building the quiz is a three-step process. First, create a quiz. Second, create questions in the question bank. Third, add questions to the quiz. You can create the questions first, but it is often best to storyboard your course and list the Quiz activities first.

Moodle 4.0 makes it easier to access question bank global configurations by accessing them through plugins. There are three question-related areas: **Question bank plugins**, **Question behaviors**, and **Question types**. You can enable site-wide access, and also configure the behaviors across the site by making changes on the **Plugins** page.

A question bank in Moodle is a collection of questions that you can organize in different ways in a database so that you can use them in the future. You'll use your questions in different "contexts" – some will be used across the entire system. Others would be used in all quizzes in a course category. Others would be used in a course, and others would be used only in a single quiz. You can also think of it as a tree of categories.

So, let's get started! The question bank is a collection of questions and corresponds to one of four contexts. The contexts are *system*, *course category*, *course*, and *quiz*. In this case, we are using the course context:

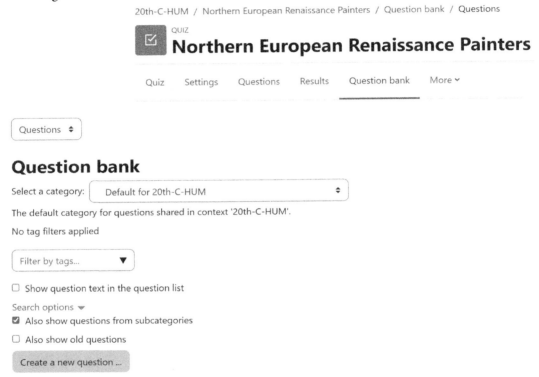

Figure 7.4 – The Question bank screen, which includes the option to create a new question

In this chapter, you will learn how to create a quiz and add questions to it. While completing this process, keep in mind that when you create a question, you are adding that question to Moodle's question bank. In the preceding screenshot, you can see that when you select a category, a course has already been selected (**20th-C-HUM**). At the same time, you can make sure that your question shows up when you search in the subcategories by checking **Also show questions from subcategories**.

It is useful to keep in mind that Moodle 4.0 has built-in functionality boosters for the Moodle Quiz activity.

> **Tip**
> There is a new setting that allows you to have your settings automatically saved when you create a Quiz question, and they are applied to the next question. This saves time and allows you to be consistent.

The questions in the question bank can be categorized and shared. The real asset in your learning site is not the quizzes, but the question bank that you and your fellow teachers build over time.

So, to recap, building the quiz is a three-step process. First, create questions in a question bank. Second, create a quiz. Third, add questions to the quiz.

Functionality booster

Once you have developed your quiz and you want to deploy it, you can add it to Moodle's Calendar. In Moodle 4.0, you can color-code categories of events and activities and add them directly to the Calendar. For example, you can color-code the quizzes red and the review webinar sessions green so that students can plan their studies more efficiently.

Question types

The following table explains the types of questions you can create and gives some tips on using them. These question types are included in the default installation of Moodle. You can obtain plugins from `https://moodle.org`. These plugins add more question types to your system. This table provides an overview of some of the types of questions that you can use when you are creating a Quiz. Here is a link to the **Plugins** directory: `https://moodle.org/plugins/?q=type:quizaccess`. You can also create your own question types (`https://docs.moodle.org/dev/Question_types`):

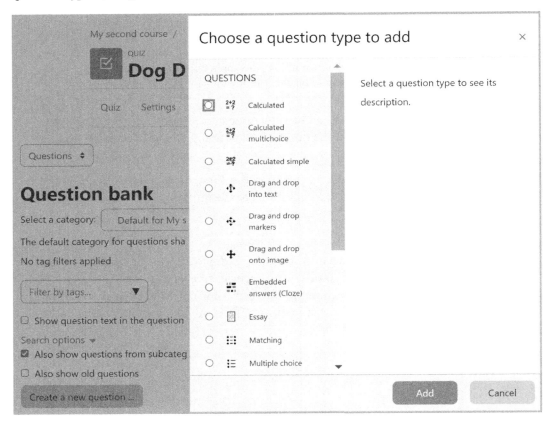

Figure 7.5 – Selecting the type of question to add

Take a look at the question types shown in the menu in the preceding screenshot. Now, we will describe each type of question and provide a few tips for using them:

Type of Question	Description and Tips for Using Them
Calculated simple	When you create a calculated question, you enter a formula that gets displayed in the text of the question. The formula can contain one or more wildcards. These wildcards are replaced with numbers when the quiz is run. Wildcards are enclosed in curly brackets. For example, if you type the question What is 3 * {a}?, Moodle will replace {a} with a random number. You can also enter wildcards into the answer field so that the correct answer is 3 * {a}. When the quiz is run, the question will display What is 3 * {a}?, and the correct answer will be the calculated value of 3 * {a}.
Calculated multichoice	Like the calculated simple question, this question consists of an equation that gets populated with a value(s) when the question is delivered. Then, the question displays several choices for the student via a multiple-choice question.
Description	This is not a question. It displays whatever web content you enter. When you add a description question, Moodle gives you the same editing screen that you get when you create a web page. Recall that under the **Quiz** tab, you can set page breaks in a quiz. If you want to break your quiz into sections and fully explain each section before the student completes it, consider adding a description on the first page of the section. For example, the description can say, The following three questions are based on this chart and show the chart just once.
Essay	When the student is given an essay question, they use Moodle's online rich-text editor to answer the question. Also, you may want to instruct your students to save their essays every few minutes. Be sure to include a minimum and maximum word count.
Matching	After you create a matching question, you create a list of subquestions and enter the correct answer for each subquestion. The student must match the correct answer with each subquestion. Each subquestion receives equal weight for scoring the question.

Figure 7.6 – Types of questions

Notice that **Embedded answers (Cloze)** types of questions are in the form of a paragraph with missing text. The missing text blocks are the "embedded answers," which differ from multiple choice in that the paragraph creates an envelope of context, which can help trigger a student's recall and also properly contextualize the material being tested. This type of question is also called a **Cloze** test or **Cloze deletion test**. Cloze is a kind of reading comprehension test that involves asking the person to supply words that have been systematically deleted from a piece of text:

Type of Question	Description and Tips for Using Them
Embedded answers (Cloze)	An embedded answers question consists of a passage of text, with answers inserted into the text. Multiple-choice, fill-in-the-blank, and numeric answers can be inserted into the question. Moodle's help file gives the following example:

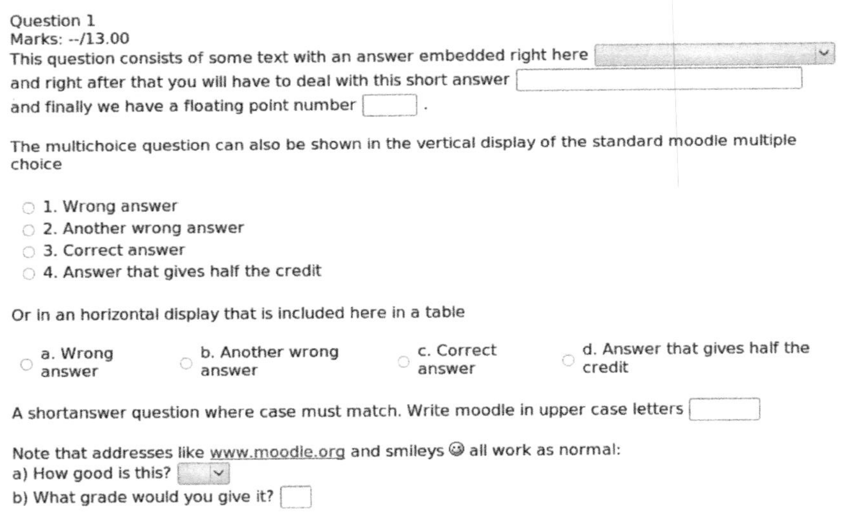

Question 1
Marks: --/13.00
This question consists of some text with an answer embedded right here [   ]
and right after that you will have to deal with this short answer [   ]
and finally we have a floating point number [   ] .

The multichoice question can also be shown in the vertical display of the standard moodle multiple choice

 ○ 1. Wrong answer
 ○ 2. Another wrong answer
 ○ 3. Correct answer
 ○ 4. Answer that gives half the credit

Or in an horizontal display that is included here in a table

 ○ a. Wrong answer   ○ b. Another wrong answer   ○ c. Correct answer   ○ d. Answer that gives half the credit

A shortanswer question where case must match. Write moodle in upper case letters [   ]

Note that addresses like www.moodle.org and smileys ☺ all work as normal:
a) How good is this? [▼]
b) What grade would you give it? [   ]

Note that the question presents a drop-down list first, which is essentially a multiple-choice question. Then, it presents a short answer (fill in the blank) question, followed by a numeric question. Finally, there's another multiple-choice question (the Yes/No dropdown) and another numeric question.

There is no graphical interface to create embedded answers to questions. You need to use a special format, as explained in the help files at `https://docs.moodle.org/29/en/Embedded_Answers_%28Cloze%29_question_type`.

Figure 7.7 – Embedded answer type of Quiz

Multiple-choice, short answer, numerical, and true/false are very popular types of quiz questions. When developing your assessment strategy, try to limit the number of true/false questions because they tend to disproportionately reward students who guess. Short answer questions can be difficult to prepare because the responses must be a perfect match. For that reason, it is often best to use short answer questions that require a numerical response or a vocabulary term:

Type of Question	Description and Tips for Using Them
Multiple choice	Multiple-choice questions can allow a student to select a single answer or multiple answers. Each answer can be a percentage of the question's total point value. Multiple-choice questions are best used for learning objectives that correspond with the lower levels of Bloom's Taxonomy: Remember and Understand.
Short answer	The student types a word or phrase into the answer field. This is checked against the correct answer or answers. There may be several correct answers with different grades. Short answers are most effective for learning objectives that correspond to Understand, Apply, and sometimes Analyze in Bloom's Taxonomy.
Numerical	Just as in a short answer question, the student enters an answer into the answer field. Numerical answers are most effective for learning objectives that correspond to Understand and Apply in Bloom's Taxonomy.
True/False	The student selects from two options: True or False. True/False questions are most effective for learning objectives that correspond to Remember and Understand and Apply in Bloom's taxonomy.

Figure 7.8 – Types of questions and when to use them

Once you've created your quizzes, be sure to add feedback. Feedback is very important to the learning process because it allows a student who has missed a question to learn the answer, and also to refer back to the text where a lengthy explanation is available.

Tip

On the **Editing quiz** page, if you have chosen to shuffle answers, check all the multiple-choice questions that you use in the quiz. If any of them have answers such as **All of the above** or **Both A and C**, shuffling answers will ruin these questions.

Instead, change them to multiple answer questions and give partial credit for each correct answer; for example, instead of **Both A and C**, you would say **Select all that apply** and then give partial credit for A and C.

There should be clear connections between the learning objectives, Bloom's Taxonomy level, and the types of quizzes. The following table will help you match learning objectives, Bloom's Taxonomy level, and quiz type. Bloom's Taxonomy has been widely adopted as a tool for making sure that course assessments align with certain assessment types and learning objectives. They are particularly helpful in the sense that they require the use of verbs with measurable outcomes. It is good to keep in mind that Bloom's Taxonomy is a useful tool:

Type of Quiz	Learning Objectives	Bloom's Taxonomy	Ideal Size of Question Bank	Blend with Webinars and Synchronous Delivery?
True/False	Can start with List, Name, or Define.	Remember.	Include the key glossary terms you need to cover.	Yes, can use this for polling as well as identifying terms.
Multiple-Choice	Can start with Define, Identify, Select, or Solve.	Remember and Understand, Apply.	At least four questions per learning objective and Bloom's Taxonomy level; for lower-division college courses, at least 60 percent in Remember and Understand.	Yes, can use as a "check your knowledge" engager.

Numerical	Best with Define, Name, Identify, or Solve.	For science classes, it can be used at all levels, but it's better at low levels since it is often important to include diagrams and equations.	Make sure that the distractors (the wrong answers) are reasonable. Although they are easy to auto-grade, the questions need to be written with absolute clarity	Yes, can use this for polling and "check your knowledge" engagers.
Short Answer	Could be ideal with Explain, Describe, Define, List, Interpret, and Solve for short answers and multi-paragraph responses. Good with Compare, Contrast, and Examine.	Remember and Understand, Apply, and sometimes Analyze if the "short answer" consists of several paragraphs.	These are not auto-graded so it is a good idea to provide a rubric and give sample answers to guide students through the length and level of specificity in the responses.	No, except when short answers consist of a few words.

Figure 7.9 – Grid to help determine when and where to use types of quizzes

As you plan your course and your use of quizzes, always consider the learning objectives and also the learning characteristics of your students. Adjust your quiz types as well as their content to accommodate their learning levels as well as prior knowledge. Courses need to be learner-centric. In addition, take into consideration that you may have students with different learning preferences and levels of mobility. Be sure that your quizzes follow Universal Design for Learning concepts and that they can be used to enhance the student experience and self-regulation.

Adaptive mode

The **Adaptive mode** setting allows multiple attempts *for each question*. This is different than **Attempts allowed**, which allows multiple attempts at *the whole quiz*.

In an adaptive quiz, when a student answers a question incorrectly, the quiz redisplays that question and gives the student another chance to answer it correctly. How many attempts the student gets is determined by how much you penalize the student for each wrong attempt.

For example, let's assume that you penalize the student 50 percent for a wrong answer. If the student gets a question wrong, they can try once more for half points. If the student gets the second attempt correct, they get half credit. If they get it wrong again, the system subtracts another 50 percent from the score. Now, the question is worth zero points. The system will not redisplay the question for a third attempt, because it's now worth zero points.

If you penalize the student 33.33 percent for a wrong answer, the student will get three attempts to answer the question. The first attempt is worth 100 percent, the second is worth 66.66 percent, and the third is worth 33.33 percent. There will be no fourth attempt because, after the third wrong answer, the question is worth zero points.

The **Adaptive mode (no penalties)** setting also gives the student multiple attempts at answering a question. However, the student gets an unlimited number of tries, because there are no penalties for wrong answers.

Interactive with multiple tries

When you make a quiz interactive with multiple tries, you allow the student to try each question multiple times. After each wrong attempt, Moodle will display a **Check your answer** message. You can create these messages for each question. For example, if it is a question about the definition of the word "caldera" in an Earth Science course, you can link to a glossary entry if your course includes a glossary and also provide a link to the section in the text that covers that topic.

This differs from **Adaptive mode**, where the student gets multiple attempts but no feedback.

Immediate feedback

When you select **Immediate feedback**, the student submits each question as they answer it. The quiz immediately displays a message based on the student's answer. You can create separate feedback messages for each answer, any wrong answer, any right answer, and the question, regardless of the answer.

At this point, let's look at a comparison between the options we've discussed:

	Adaptive Mode	Adaptive Mode (No Penalties)	Interactive with Multiple Tries	Immediate Feedback
Multiple attempts at the same question?	Yes	Yes	Yes	No
Feedback after each attempt?	No	No	Yes	Yes
Reduced score for wrong answers?	Yes	No	Yes	Yes

Figure 7.10 – Settings for the Adaptive and Interactive modes with multiple tries

Deferred feedback

If a quiz uses **Deferred feedback**, the student submits the entire quiz after answering all the questions. Then, the quiz displays the student's score and any feedback that you have created for the questions.

Each attempt builds on the last

Each attempt builds on the last only has an effect if multiple attempts are allowed. When this setting is enabled, each attempt that a student makes will display the results of the student's previous attempt. The student can see how they answered and scored on the previous attempt.

The **Attempts allowed** option allows the student to keep trying the quiz. **Each attempt builds on the last** retains the answers from one attempt to another. Taken together, these two settings can be used to create a quiz that the student can keep trying until they get it right. This transforms the quiz from a test into a learning tool.

Adding existing questions from the question bank

As you saw earlier, you can create a new question and add it to the question bank. You can also add existing questions to a quiz. These questions come from an existing question bank. So, what we are creating is a way to think of the outcomes of your course, develop an assessment strategy, and then create questions to add to the question bank that can be deployed in the most effective ways in course categories, courses, and individual quizzes.

To add a question from an existing question bank, follow these steps:

1. With the named quiz selected, go to **Quiz | Questions**.

2. In the lower right-hand corner, click on **Add**. A pop-up window is displayed with + **a new question** | + **from question bank** | + **a random question**. Select from question bank.

    The question bank will be displayed. The questions in the bank are categorized. They can belong to this quiz, to this course, to the category that this course is in, or to the system overall. In the following screenshot, the user is selecting the course's category

    Select the category and question, and then select **Add selected questions to the quiz**.

Configuring quiz settings

When you first create a quiz, you need to go to the **Settings** page. The settings that you select only affect that particular quiz. The settings affect things such as the number of questions displayed on each page of the quiz, whether a student can retry the quiz, whether the quiz has a time limit, and more. The settings affect the look and behavior of the quiz:

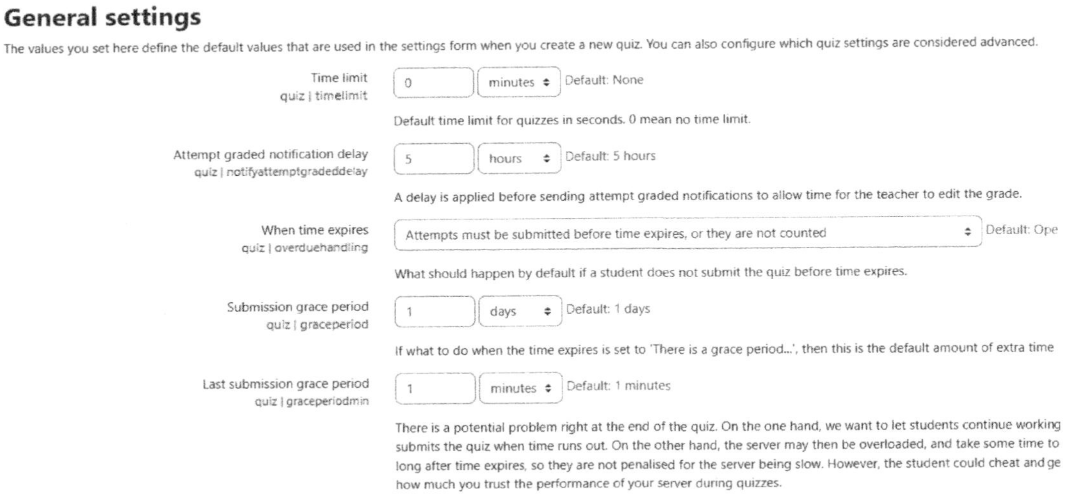

General settings

The values you set here define the default values that are used in the settings form when you create a new quiz. You can also configure which quiz settings are considered advanced.

Time limit quiz | timelimit	0	minutes ⬍	Default: None

Default time limit for quizzes in seconds. 0 mean no time limit.

Attempt graded notification delay quiz | notifyattemptgradeddelay	5	hours ⬍	Default: 5 hours

A delay is applied before sending attempt graded notifications to allow time for the teacher to edit the grade.

When time expires quiz | overduehandling	Attempts must be submitted before time expires, or they are not counted	⬍	Default: Ope

What should happen by default if a student does not submit the quiz before time expires.

Submission grace period quiz | graceperiod	1	days ⬍	Default: 1 days

If what to do when the time expires is set to 'There is a grace period...', then this is the default amount of extra time

Last submission grace period quiz | graceperiodmin	1	minutes ⬍	Default: 1 minutes

There is a potential problem right at the end of the quiz. On the one hand, we want to let students continue working submits the quiz when time runs out. On the other hand, the server may then be overloaded, and take some time to long after time expires, so they are not penalised for the server being slow. However, the student could cheat and ge how much you trust the performance of your server during quizzes.

Figure 7.11 – Quiz settings

Once you've chosen your settings, you can add questions to the quiz; the questions are the content of the quiz.

In Moodle, think of a quiz as a combination of the settings (display and behavior), the container (the quiz pages), and the questions (content).

The **Settings** page is divided into nine areas. Let's look at the settings under each area, top to bottom.

General

The **General** settings include the name and description of the quiz:

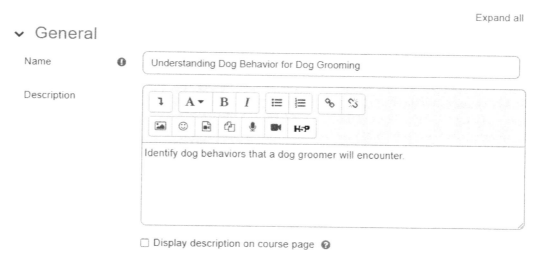

Figure 7.12 – Quiz name and description in the General settings

The **Name** property of the quiz is displayed on the course's home page, while the **Description** property is displayed when a student selects the quiz.

The description should explain why the student is taking the quiz. It should also inform the student of any unusual features of the quiz, for example, or whether it uses a pop-up window. Remember that once the student clicks on the **Attempt quiz now** button, they are in the quiz, so give the student everything they need to understand why and how to take the quiz before clicking on the **Attempt quiz now** button.

Optionally, you can display the description on the course's home page. If you do this, it will continue to display when the student selects the quiz.

Timing

The **Open** and **Close** dates determine when the quiz is available. If you do not select the **Enable** checkbox for **Open the quiz**, the quiz will be permanently open, instead of becoming available on a given date. If you do not select the **Enable** checkbox for **Close the quiz**, then once the quiz is open, it will stay open permanently instead of becoming unavailable on a given date. Moodle 3.10 includes a built-in timer for students to see and be aware of how much time they have left in a quiz.

Tip

Even if the quiz is closed, it will still show on the course's home page, and students may still try to select it. When they select a closed quiz, the students will see a message saying that it is closed.

If you want to hide a quiz, further down on this page, under **Common module settings**, you will see the **Visible** setting; change this setting to **Hide**.

By default, a quiz does not have a time limit. If you want to set a time limit, use the **Time limit** setting. When time runs out, the quiz is automatically submitted with the answers that have been filled out. A time limit can help prevent the use of reference materials while taking the quiz. For example, if you want students to answer the questions quickly from memory with minimal interaction with the course textbook, setting a timer may encourage students to review the material more extensively before taking the quiz.

When students are taking a timed quiz, they see a countdown timer on the quiz page. With Moodle 4.0, the countdown timer follows the students as they scroll down the questions.

If you set a time limit for the quiz, in the quiz's description, inform the students about what happens when the time limit is reached. For example, if you configure the quiz to discard the student's answers if the student has not submitted the quiz in time, inform the student about this.

Grade

If you allow several attempts, the **Grading method** option determines which grade is recorded in the course's grade book: **Highest**, **Average**, **First**, or **Last**. If you do not allow multiple attempts, then **Grading method** will have no effect.

Attempts allowed can be used to limit the number of times a student takes the quiz. Further down the page, you can choose settings that require the student to wait between attempts. The time delay settings will only take effect if you enable multiple attempts.

Layout

The settings under **Layout** control the order of the questions on the quiz and the number of questions that appear on a page.

Question order determines whether the questions appear in the order that you placed them while editing or randomly. The random order will change each time the quiz is displayed. This does not allow students to share quiz answers and encourages them to focus on the wording when they retake a quiz.

New page determines where page breaks will fall. It determines whether you will have a page break after every question, every two questions, and so on:

Figure 7.13 – Configuring the layout for every 6 questions

Tip

The **New page** setting determines where Moodle automatically puts the page breaks. While you create the quiz, you can move these page breaks to the page where you edit the questions for the quiz.

By default, all questions in a quiz are displayed on separate pages. **New page** breaks up the quiz into smaller pages. Moodle inserts the page breaks for you. On the **Editing quiz** page, you can move these page breaks. If you want to break up your quiz into pages that hold the same number of questions, this setting will work for you. If you want each page in the quiz to hold a different number of questions, use this setting anyway and edit the page breaks that Moodle creates for you.

The **Navigation method** setting determines whether the student can go back and forth between questions. If this setting is set to **Sequential**, the student must answer the questions in order. If questions near the end of the test give clues to the answers to questions at the beginning, you may want to change this setting to **Sequential**.

Review options

The **Review options** setting determines what information a student can see when they review a quiz. These options also determine when they can see this information. You can see these options in the following screenshot:

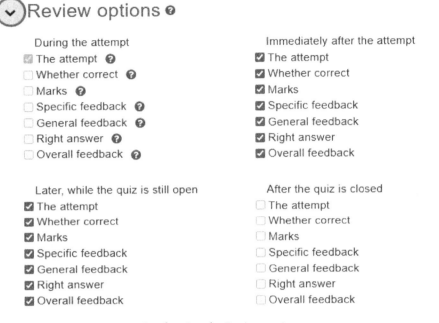

Figure 7.14 – Configuring the Review options screen

Here is what the different options mean:

Setting	Type of Information Displayed to the Student
Responses	These are the answers that the student had to choose from for a question.
Answers	These are the answers that the student chose.
Feedback	Each response to a question can have feedback. This setting refers to the feedback for each response that the student selected (that is, the feedback for each of the student's answers).
General feedback	Each question can have feedback. This feedback is displayed regardless of how the student answered the question. This setting displays general feedback for each question.
Scores	These are the student's scores, or points earned, for each question.
Overall feedback	The overall feedback that's given for the student's score on the quiz.

Figure 7.15 – Review options and what they mean

When the information is revealed, the settings have the following meanings:

Time period	Meaning
During the attempt	With this setting, the information appears while the student is attempting the quiz. This setting only has meaning if immediate feedback is enabled.
Immediately after the attempt	With this setting, the information appears within 2 minutes of the student finishing the quiz.
Later, while the quiz is still open	With this setting, the information appears 2 minutes after the quiz is finished.
After the quiz is closed	With this setting, the information appears after the date and time that's been set in **Close the quiz** has passed. If you never close the quiz, this setting has no effect.

Figure 7.16 – The timing of when response information is revealed

Appearance

Here, you can customize the appearance of the Quiz activity:

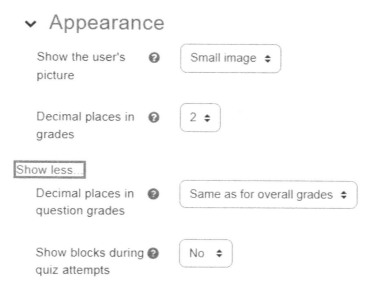

Figure 7.17 – Configuring the appearance of the Quiz

The settings under **Appearance** affect the information that is displayed while the student is taking the quiz.

If **Show the user's picture** is set to **Small image** or **Large image**, while the student is taking the quiz, the student's picture and name will be displayed in the quiz window. This makes it easier for an exam proctor to confirm that the students have logged in themselves. The proctor can just look over the student's shoulder and see the student's picture and name on the screen.

The settings for **Decimal places in grades** and **Decimal places in question grades** affect the grades that are shown to the student. The first setting affects the display of the overall grade for the quiz, while the second setting affects how the grade is displayed for each question.

No matter how many decimal places you display, Moodle's database calculates the grades with full accuracy. When you create a course, you can add blocks to the left and right sidebars. The **Show blocks during quiz attempts** setting determines whether these blocks are displayed while the student is taking the quiz. Normally, this is set to **No** so that the student is not distracted while taking the quiz.

Safe Exam Browser

Moodle 4.0 allows you to require the use of **Safe Exam Browser** (**SEB**). SEB is a web browser environment that allows you to carry out e-assessments in a secure manner. The software turns any computer into a secure workstation and controls access to resources such as system functions, websites, and applications so that they cannot be used during an exam. Not every institution uses this approach since it is easily circumvented, both by smartphones and written notes and printed publications. You can configure SEB manually, or you can upload your own configuration. An exam configuration, as the name implies, is done for an exam and contains most of the known configuration attributes from the latest SEB configuration tool. It is outside the scope of this book to go into system administrator configurations in detail. If your institution uses SEB, obtain the configuration from your system administrator:

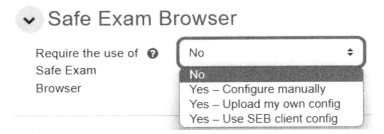

Figure 7.18 – Safe Exam Browser configuration

Extra restrictions on attempts

You may want your students to have additional restrictions on attempts for the quiz. Sometimes, it's a good idea to add more restrictions if you want to pace the students and add a level of security:

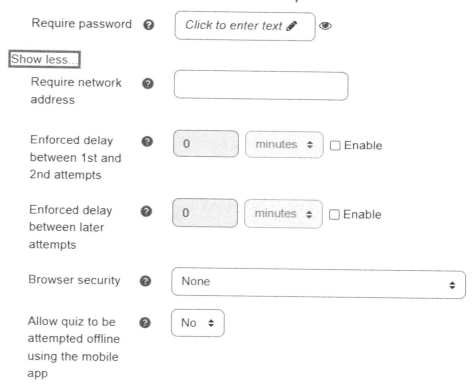

Figure 7.19 – Configuring Extra restrictions on attempts

If you enter anything into the **Require password** field, the student must enter that password to access the quiz.

With **Require network address**, you can restrict access to the quiz to particular IP address/addresses. For example, you can restrict the quiz's access to the following IP addresses:

- **146.203.59.235**: This is a single IP address. It will permit a single computer to access the quiz. If this computer is acting as a proxy server, the other computers *behind* it can also access the quiz.

- **146.203**: This is a range of IP addresses. It will permit any IP address starting with those numbers. If those numbers belong to your company, you effectively limit access to the quiz to your company's campus.

- **146.203.59.235/20**: This is a subnet. It will permit the computers on that subnet to access the quiz.

The **Enforced delay** settings prevent students from attempting the quiz without waiting between attempts. If you show the students the correct answers after they submit the quiz, you may want to set a delay between attempts. This prevents students from attempting the quiz, seeing the correct answers, and then immediately trying the quiz again while those answers are fresh in their memory.

If **Browser security** is set to **Full-screen popup...**, the quiz will be launched in a new browser window. It uses JavaScript to disable copying, saving, and printing. This security is not foolproof.

Techniques for greater security

Your organization may require proctoring. There are several ways to build virtual proctoring into Moodle. For example, you can link out to a virtual test-taking proctoring platform such as Meazure Learning (formerly ProctorU – `https://www.meazurelearning.com/`). You will need a subscription to their service, and all the students will need a built-in camera and microphone. Once you've subscribed, you can create a link so that they can log into the platform from within their course in Moodle.

You can also devise a solution by asking the students to take the exams and have the camera on them at all times. You can do that by simultaneously asking them to log into Zoom, Teams, or BigBlueButton so that all the individuals in the class will show up on the same screen.

Here are a few strategies for developing effective proctored exams:

- Create numerous questions, but have the quiz show only a small set of them; this makes sharing questions less useful.

- Shuffle the questions and answers. This also makes sharing questions more difficult.

- Apply a time limit. This makes using reference material more difficult.

- Open the quiz for only a few hours. Have your students schedule the time to take the quiz. Make yourself available during this time to help with technical issues.

- Place one question on each page of the quiz; this discourages students from taking screenshots of the entire quiz.

Overall feedback

Moodle enables you to create several different kinds of feedback for a quiz:

- You can create feedback for the entire quiz, which changes with the student's score. This is called **Overall feedback** and uses a feature called **Grade boundary**:

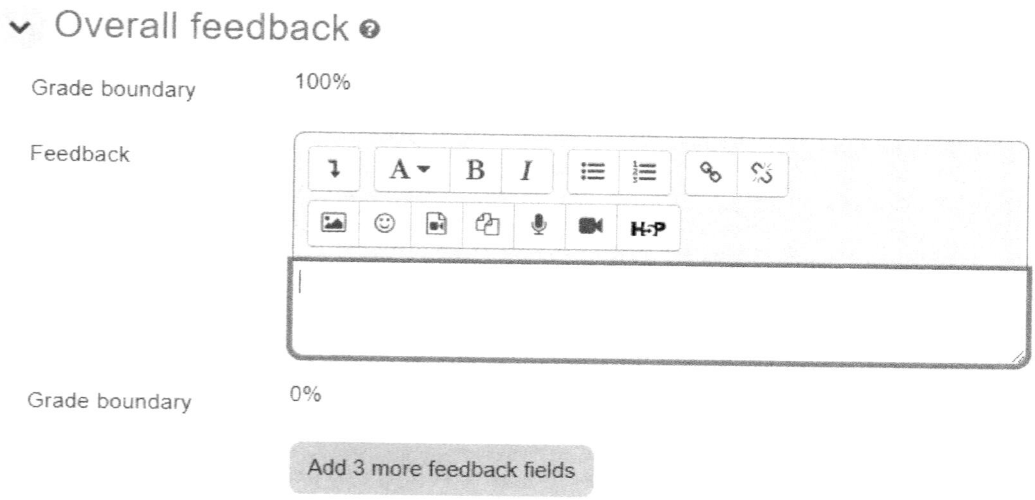

Figure 7.20 – The Overall feedback configuration screen

- You can create feedback for a question, no matter what the student's score on that question is. All students receive the same feedback. This is called **General feedback**. Each question can have **General feedback**. The type of feedback that you can create for a question varies with the type of question.

- You can create feedback for a response. This is the feedback that the student receives when they select that response to a question.

The following screenshot shows **Overall feedback** with a **Grade boundary** set:

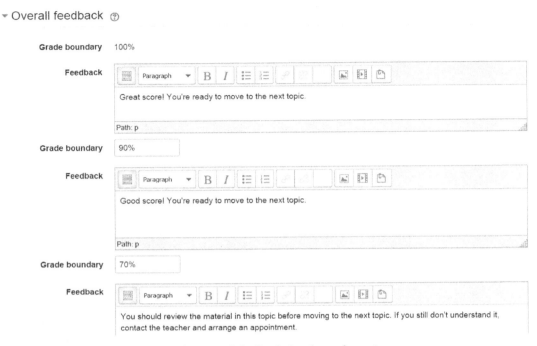

Figure 7.21 – The Overall feedback details configuration screen

Common module settings

Group mode works in the same way as it does for any other resource. However, since students take the quiz themselves, the only real use for this group setting in a quiz is to display the high score for a group in the **Quiz Results** block.

Visible can show and hide the quiz from students. However, a teacher or course creator can still see the quiz. Now that we've configured the feedback for a quiz, let's look at adding questions to a quiz.

Adding questions to a quiz

Once you've selected the quiz from your course home page, you can add questions to the question bank that is used when constructing the quiz. First, go to **Administration | Quiz administration | Edit quiz**. On the **Editing quiz** page, you can see the **Add a question...** button:

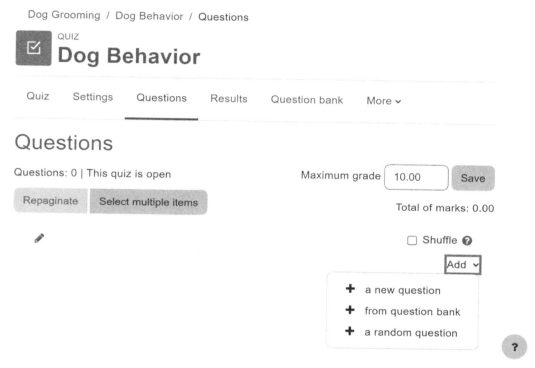

Figure 7.22 – Adding questions to a quiz

Before we look at the detailed instructions to create new questions, let's look at the **Question bank contents** button. Also, on the **Quiz administration** menu, you can see the options for **Question bank**; these options enable you to work with the question bank.

> **Functionality Booster**
>
> An essay is a question type in Moodle. Moodle 4.0 incorporates a word count feature for Essay questions, which allows you to set minimum and maximum word counts for answers. When the minimum word count has not been satisfied, a message will automatically appear and alert the learner.

Multiple-choice questions in the question bank

Multiple-choice quizzes are some of the most widely used types of quizzes in online courses. Given their pervasive presence, it is important to know how to write robust, psychometrically sound multiple-choice questions. Let's review multiple-choice questions to see what they contain and how they're written. Each multiple-choice question consists of the following:

- A stem (the question)
- The key (the correct answer)
- Distractors (the incorrect choices)

Your stem should be clear and simple. The stem should be as follows:

- Be phrased as a question
- Have meaning by itself
- Contain only relevant material
- Avoid being negatively stated

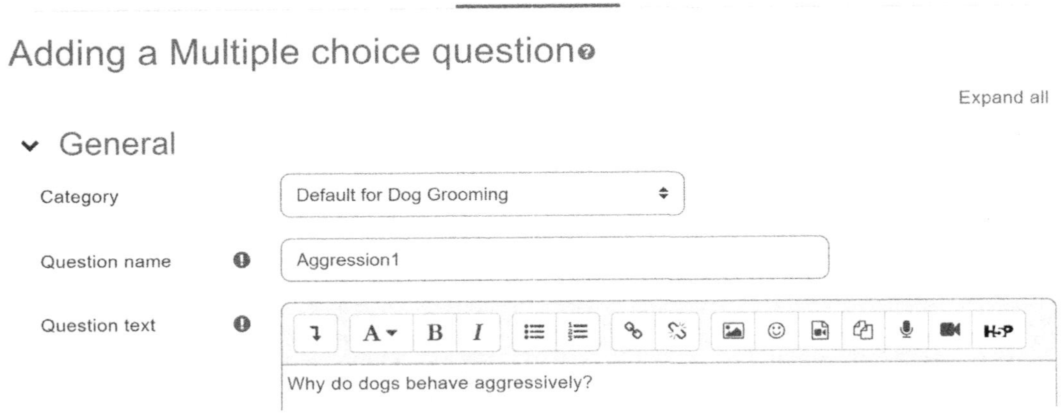

Adding a Multiple choice question❓

Expand all

✓ General

Category		Default for Dog Grooming ⬍
Question name	❶	Aggression1
Question text	❶	↲ A▾ B I ☰ ☷ ⚲ ⚲ 🖼 ☺ 🎬 🗂 🎤 🎥 H-P
		Why do dogs behave aggressively?

Figure 7.23 – The Adding a Multiple choice question page

Once you've added the multiple-choice question, you'll need to configure the answers. You have several options, as shown here:

Figure 7.24 – Configuring the structure of the answers

A single idea or concept should form the foundation of the stem, and it should contain verbs that correspond to the correct level of Bloom's taxonomy. The reason why you should shape the stem as a question is because it allows the learner to focus on answering the question. It also has less cognitive load than if you ask the learner to keep a partial sentence in working memory and complete the sentence.

The answers should have the key (the correct answer) and wrong answers, which are distractors. The distractors should be plausible. In addition, they should be as follows:

- Be clear and concise
- Not contain clues to the answer
- Not include absolutes such as "always" or "never"
- Not contain overlapping content
- Not include "all of the above" or "none of the above"

- Be presented in a logical order (alphabetical, for example) to avoid the tendency to place it in a preferential answer position

Answers

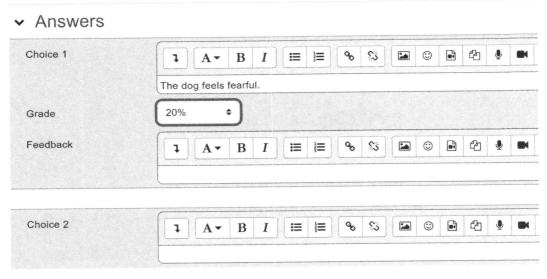

Figure 7.25 – Configuring the answers

The distractors should be plausible and not be absurd or comical (however tempting it is to include them). They should be similar in length. You should also include feedback for each incorrect answer or distractor so that the experience provides a learning opportunity:

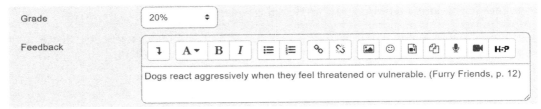

Figure 7.26 – Configuring feedback

Guessing games

As you develop your quiz, it's useful to know the kinds of guessing games that students taking multiple-choice quizzes typically employ. Here are a few, along with strategies for countering them:

- "The correct answer is usually second or third."

  Solution: Make sure that your answers are random, or in a meaningful order (alphabetical, for example).

- "The longest answer is always the correct one."

  Solution: Make sure that all the choices are of about the same length.

- "Pick the most technical-sounding term."

  Solution: All choices should be of the same technical level.

- "Pick the one that has key terms you recognize."

  Solution: Include key terms in all of the distractors.

Developing quiz questions that align with the higher-order levels of Bloom's Taxonomy

Creating questions that correspond to the levels of Bloom's Taxonomy is perhaps the most challenging aspect of developing multiple-choice questions and choices. To create higher-level multiple-choice questions, you must consider three key elements:

- Sequential reasoning

- Incorporating high cognitive levels, including application, analysis, and synthesis

- Using a unique or novel but always realistic case, scenario, chart, or graph

It may interest you to know that if you use a case, scenario, chart, or graph, it is referred to as the "stimulus." You can use it for a cluster of related multiple-choice questions, which may have benefits for you as you look at the course objectives. You can write a cluster of questions based on a single stimulus (case, scenario, chart, or graph).

Another strategy for employing higher-order cognitive skills is to use a "multiple response, multiple choice" question. In such a question, you can ask learners to "select all that apply" and to receive credit, they must select all the correct answers. The advantages are that you will allow for several correct answers, there is less opportunity for guessing, and it avoids the "all of the above" option. The downside is that it requires 5 or 6 options, and it is more difficult to construct because it contains more distractors.

If you would like to learn more about developing psychometrically valid multiple-choice exams, you may enjoy Cohen and Wollack's handbook on test development.

Cohen, A., & Wollack, J. (2000). *Handbook on test development: Helpful tips for creating reliable and valid classroom tests*. Madison, WI: University of Wisconsin, Center for Placement Testing. Retrieved October 13, 2003, from http://testing.wisc.edu/ Handbook%20on%20Test%20Construction.pdf.

Matching

A matching question consists of two lists of related words, phrases, pictures, or symbols that appear in columns adjacent to each other. Each item corresponds to at least one item in the other list.

Matching is used to recognize relationships and make associations. It aligns with Bloom's taxonomy's "Remember" level, which requires learners to identify, list, and make connections. They can be used in a wide range of subject matter, and they can be used for terms, definitions, symbols, names, cause and effect, parts with functions, procedures with operations, and principles that apply to situations.

In Moodle, we can start by configuring the matching options:

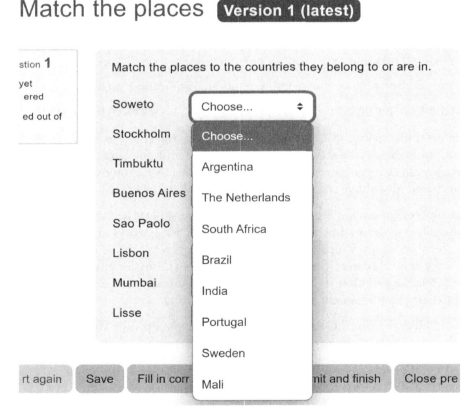

Figure 7.27 – Configuring matching options

The next step would be to configure the answers. Make sure that you always include feedback so that the student can learn and reinforce the correct responses:

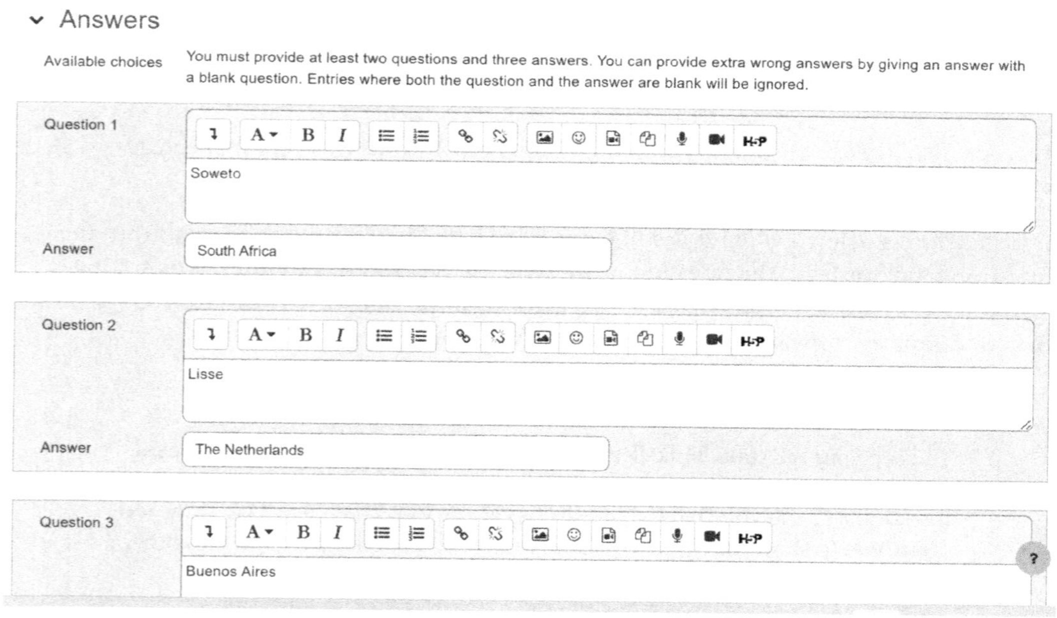

Figure 7.28 – Configuring answers

Once you have configured the answers, you can add feedback. Note that the editing menu allows you to embed images, video, audio, and HTML5 content so that your matching questions can incorporate more complex content, such as specific procedures or situations.

Sharing Questions

If you want the questions that you create for this quiz to be available to other users of the site, create the questions and then add them to the question bank and the quiz at the same time by selecting the correct contexts. Note that your role determines your ability to manage questions.

As shown in the *Adding questions to a quiz* section, you can create questions and add them directly to a quiz and the question bank at the same time. As shown earlier in the *Adding questions to the question bank* section, you can also change the category/contexts for the questions later so that you can use the questions for more than one purpose. If you're in a hurry to create questions for a quiz, select **Edit quiz** and start creating them. You can rearrange them in the question bank later.

You can also display questions from one category at a time. To select that category, use the **Category** drop-down list.

If a question is deleted when it is still being used by a quiz, it is not removed from the question bank; instead, the question is hidden. The **Also show old questions** setting enables you to see questions that were deleted from the category. These deleted (or hidden or old) questions appear in the list with blue boxes next to them.

> **Tip**
> To keep your question bank clean and to prevent teachers from using deleted questions, you can move all the deleted questions into a category called **Deleted questions**. Create the **Deleted questions** category and then use **Also show old questions** to show the deleted questions. Select these questions and move them into **Deleted questions**.

Moving questions between categories

Every question in the question bank belongs to a category. If a question belongs to a category for the course, only teachers with access to that course can see and reuse the question. If a question belongs to a category for the system, the question can be seen and reused by all teachers in the system. To let your questions be used by other teachers, you may want to move them to a category that is accessible by other teachers.

Select the question(s) to move, select the category, and then click on the **Move to** button.

Managing the proliferation of questions and categories

As the site administrator, you may want to monitor the creation of new question categories to ensure that they are logically named, don't have a lot of overlap, and are appropriate for your site. As these question categories and the questions in them are shared among course creators, they can be powerful tools for collaboration.

Creating and editing question categories

Every question belongs to a category. You can manage question categories under the **Categories** tab. There will always be a **Default** category. However, before you create new questions, you may want to check to ensure that you have an appropriate category to put them in.

To add a new category, follow these steps:

1. To add a new question category within a system context, go to **Course administration | Question bank | Categories**.

2. Scroll to the bottom of the page to the **Add category** section.

3. Select **Parent** for the category. If you select **Top**, the category will be a top-level category. Alternatively, you can select any other category that you have access to. Then, the new category will be a child of the selected category.

4. In the **Name** field, enter the name for the new category.

5. In the **Category Info** field, enter a description of the new category.

6. Click on the **Add category** button.

To edit a category, follow these steps:

1. Go to **Quiz** (name of the quiz) | **Question bank | Categories**.

2. Next to the category, click on the icon. The **Edit categories** page will be displayed.

3. You can edit the **Parent**, **Category**, and **Category Info** settings here.

4. When you are finished, click on the **Update** button. Your changes will be saved, and you will be returned to the **Edit categories** page.

> **Tip**
>
> For an explanation of the different types of questions, please refer to the *Question types* section.

Types of feedback for a question

In a multiple-choice question, you can create three kinds of feedback, as described in the following table:

Type of Feedback	Explanation and When to Use it
General feedback	If you create general feedback for a question, no matter what answer the student chooses, they will receive that feedback. Every student who answers the question gets general feedback. If you think the student may get the correct answer by guessing, you can use general feedback to explain the method of arriving at the correct answer. Also, consider using general feedback to explain the importance of the question.
For any correct response	A multiple-choice question can have two or more answers that are 100 percent correct. For example, from the list of people below, select one person who signed the Declaration of Independence. This list could include several people who signed, and each of them would be 100 percent correct. If the student selects any of those correct answers, they will see the feedback for **Any correct response**. This is useful when you want to teach the student which answers are 100 percent correct and why they are correct.
For any partially correct response	You can create a multiple-choice question that requires the student to select several choices to get full credit. For example, From the list of people below, select the two people who signed the Declaration of Independence. In this case, you could give each response a value of 50 percent. The student needs to choose both responses to receive the full point value for the question. If the student selects one of the correct choices, they will see the feedback for **Any partially correct response**. This is useful when you want to teach the student the relationship between the correct responses.
For any incorrect response	Any response with a percentage value of zero or less is considered an incorrect response. If a student selects an incorrect response, they will see the feedback for **Any incorrect response**. This is useful when all incorrect responses have something in common and you want to give feedback about this commonality.

Figure 7.29 – Feedback for multiple-choice questions

Remember that these types of feedback are not activated because the student chose a specific response – they are activated because the student chose any correct, partially correct, or incorrect response.

We will discuss the process of creating feedback for individual responses in the *Feedback for individual responses* section.

Now, let's learn how to add random questions to a quiz.

Adding random questions to a quiz

You can add several random questions to your quiz. In the following screenshot, note that there are three questions in the selected category. The maximum number of questions that can be added depends on the number of questions in the category:

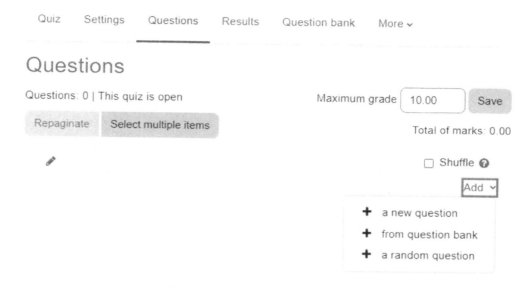

Figure 7.30 – Adding random questions

You can add random questions from several categories to the same quiz.

In the same attempt, students will never see the same random question twice. The questions are reset between attempts, so students can see the same question twice if they attempt the same quiz twice.

To add a random question(s), follow these steps:

1. With the quiz selected, go to **Questions**.

2. A pop-up window will be displayed; select **Add random question**.

3. A dialog box will be displayed. Select the category that you want to draw the random question(s) from:

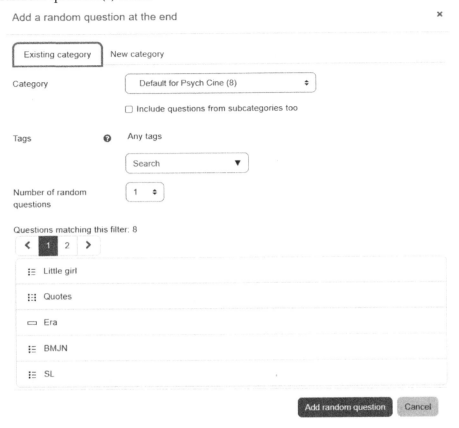

Figure 7.31 – Configuring random questions

4. Select the number of questions to add, and then select the **Add random question** button.

Let's look at some other functions available under the **Questions** tab.

Maximum grade

The quiz's maximum grade is the quiz's point contribution toward the course. In this example, the quiz is worth 10 points toward the student's total for the course.

The grade for each question will be scaled to the quiz's maximum grade. For example, if this quiz had two questions worth **1** point each but **Maximum grade** is **10**, each question will contribute **5** points to the student's total grade for the course.

The grade for each question

Each question has a point value, as shown in the following screenshot:

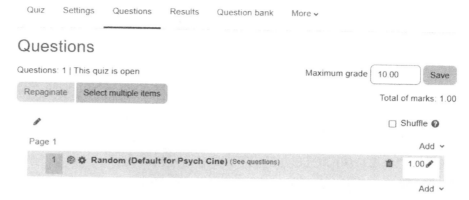

Figure 7.32 – Adding the point values to the quiz

The question's point value is scaled to the quiz's **Maximum grade**. For example, if a question has a grade of **2** and the quiz has a maximum value of **10**, that question is worth one-fifth of the quiz's grade.

Now that we have set up quizzes, let's learn how to use them in conjunction with mastery learning.

Mastery learning

Many organizations require learners to show that they have achieved mastery, which means they have achieved the minimum passing score (usually 80 percent) in knowledge and skills associated with the course outcomes. This is particularly important in the case of training and regulatory compliance.

Moodle allows you to develop a question bank that is specific to the statutes, standards, or codes for regulatory compliance. Be sure to plan the sequence (storyboard) and also to provide responses that refer to the correct answers in the text. The following steps are important to follow when you're applying mastery learning:

1. Clearly state the grade or score that must be earned.

2. Allow students to repeat the questions or the quiz if they failed until the qualifying score or grade is earned.

3. Incorporate the regulations as a link, file, or embedded player.

4. Provide explanations for incorrect answers and point them to the passages that provide the correct responses.

5. Categorize and classify the questions according to the nomenclature used in the codes.

6. Ensure that the form of the questions is similar to that used in the test, which they will be required to take if there are further exams or skills demonstrations that must be performed.

After demonstrating mastery, it is time to incorporate them into a larger set of assessments, which we refer to as "competency frameworks." They are vital for establishing specific types of learning outcomes, particularly when they relate to a specific type of skill or job-related competency.

Quizzes and competency frameworks

Moodle allows you to tie to competency frameworks, which are external performance standards. For example, if your organization has an overall rubric that lists types of competencies, you may classify your questions so that they align with the competency categories. Then, when the student correctly performs the tasks in the quiz, a positive score is received, and a box is checked in the competency framework.

It is possible to automate this process so that the competency framework is automatically updated for the student. However, it is easier to simply code the questions so that they reflect the competency categories and to independently calculate a score for the competency framework.

Quiz questions can tie to the competency frameworks you may be using. Alternatively, entire quizzes can tie to them and incorporate a single aspect of the framework:

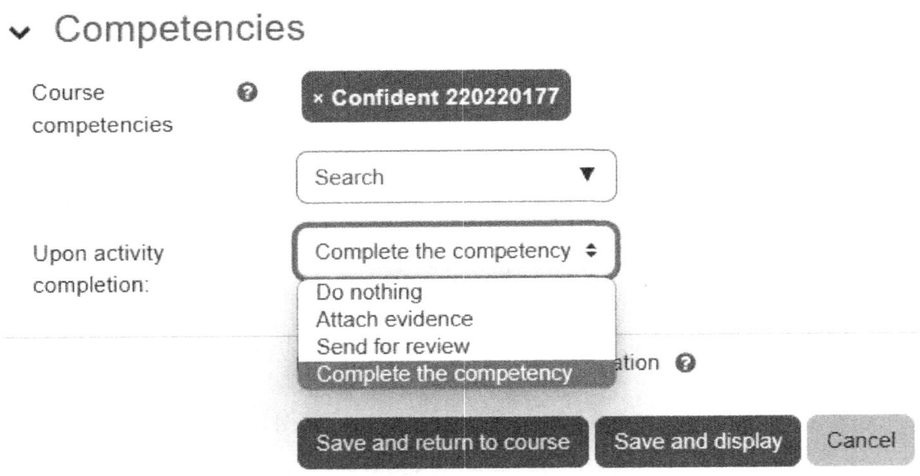

Figure 7.33 – Adding competencies

Certificates

Certificates are important for talent management functions (universities, associations, and individual record-keeping). Certificates can be digital, and they can be printable. Moodle 4.0 has several plugins for certificates that you can import. Certificates can be generated upon successfully completing a quiz or a series of quizzes.

Badges

Badges are earned when a student demonstrates successful completion of a course, which can also relate to mastery learning. Because mastery learning is often tied to completing quizzes, it often follows that to earn a badge, the student will need to successfully complete quizzes. An **Open Badge** is a verifiable, portable digital badge with embedded metadata about skills and achievements. It complies with the Open Badges standard and can be shared via social media across the web. Each Open Badge is associated with an image and information about the badge, the organization that issued it, the subject matter, and other key evidence (number and so on).

Badges are similar to certificates, but they can also be displayed on social media, which makes them ideal for promoting and publicizing courses and programs. Badges are earned upon successfully completing a quiz or series of quizzes. Certificates can be specifically tied to an organization or board, while badges are more informal and are intended to be displayed on social media.

Moodle's Badge plugin allows you to design a badge and also make it portable so that it can be displayed on social media. Instead of having to upload them to all your social media sites, it's possible to utilize the Open Badges project (`https://openbadges.org`) and include the social media in the Open Badges Backpack, which is provided by Mozilla's Badgr. Badgr Backpack is an app that helps you organize and share your badges from a single place (Badgr | Achieve Anything, Recognize Everything, `https://info.badgr.com/`).

Incorporating badges is easier than ever since Moodle 3.11 supports Open Badges v2.1 (Open Badges Version 2.1) | IMS Global Learning Consortium, `https://www.imsglobal.org/spec/ob/v2p1/`).

You can set your quizzes so that they automatically generate badges when the student achieves a qualifying score. Badges can indicate course completion, as well as certifications:

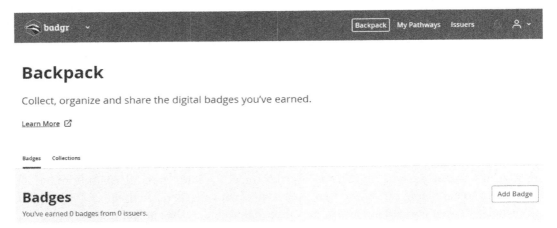

Figure 7.34 – Badgr Backpack

You can learn more about them by referring to `https://support.badgr.com/en/knowledge/using-the-badgr-backpack`:

Figure 7.35 – Mozilla Badgr open badges Backpack

Being able to successfully complete assessments to demonstrate mastery of a topic or course is critical. Being able to generate badges and certificates will allow you to meet your learners' need to demonstrate that they have achieved a certain skill level or knowledge for a specific course, skill, or job.

Summary

Moodle's Quiz activity is flexible and can be used in several settings to assess students, particularly those in the lower levels of Bloom's taxonomy. That said, Moodle 4.0 is designed to make learning in many settings and with numerous devices and delivery methods possible, and the Quiz activity is often the most expedient method for assuring the attainment of learning objectives. That said, it is very important to know how to write psychometrically sound multiple-choice questions.

One aspect of the Quiz activity in Moodle 4.0 is that it is rich in feedback. The different types of feedback enable you to turn a quiz into a learning activity. Consider using the Quiz activity not just for testing but also for teaching. It can also be used for demonstrating competency, mastery of learning, and compliance. Accomplishments can be recorded and displayed automatically using plugins such as certificates and badges.

The site administrator and teachers should work together to organize questions in the question bank and give teachers access to the categories of questions they need.

In the next chapter, you'll learn how to make a course more social with forums and chats.

8
Getting Social with Chats and Forums

At the heart of Moodle is the theory of learning that people learn best when they learn from each other, through meaningful interaction. Some of this interaction occurs in collaborative activities. However, the bulk of this interaction will occur in social settings, in synchronous or live chats or in asynchronous discussion board areas, called **forums** in Moodle.

Social course activities encourage student-to-student interaction. Peer interaction is one of the most powerful learning tools that Moodle offers. It not only encourages learning but also encourages exploration. This tool also makes courses more interesting, because students can share their knowledge, which increases student participation and satisfaction. Peer sharing is part of the social constructionist approach to learning and forms the foundation of Moodle. This chapter will teach you how to add communication activities to a course and how to make the best use of them. This includes chats, forums, and other forms of social media. Moodle 4.0 takes a social approach and allows notifications and communications in the same way as social media apps. It also uses redesigned, attractive navigation icons. In addition to enhancing engagement and ease of navigation, Moodle 4.0 also provides more ways for the teacher or manager to keep the student on track and not allow them to move ahead before they're ready.

In this chapter, you will learn how to create learning activities that allow people to learn from each other. We will cover the following topics:

- Designing an instructional strategy that incorporates active discussion boards (forums)
- Incorporating synchronous communication using Chat, and then keeping a record of it
- Designing the right kinds of forums for your learning objectives
- Providing evidence of achievement (as it would in a face-to-face classroom)
- Boosting functionality by incorporating collaboration platforms

After completing this chapter, you'll feel confident in being able to engage your students and keep them motivated as they feel excited about sharing their perceptions and learning with each other.

An interaction-based instructional strategy

In Moodle, a **Forum** is an activity that enables participants to have asynchronous discussions over an extended period. It can also promote more inclusive learning in the case of a learner who may be reticent in a face-to-face classroom setting. They can also encourage engagement and collaboration and are a place where the instructor can be very creative. In Moodle, a Chat is an activity that allows real-time, synchronous text-based interactions. Both focus on communication among students and instructors, and they allow digital materials and direct conversations to be shared. In Moodle 4.0, the icons have been updated:

Figure 8.1 – Updated icons in Moodle 4.0

Let's consider the most effective uses of the **Forum** and **Chat** activities. As you review your learning objectives and seek to map the course materials with the course activities, think about how you can make your course structured around forums and chats so that the focus stays on student engagement. This sets up a sense of wonder and discovery as students dig into the content, and then share their ideas and impressions. If you create a forum around solving a problem together or exploring aspects of something mysterious, you will create an unforgettable learning experience.

It may seem hard to envision at first, but in practice, it's quite simple. As you set up your course, ensure that you include a forum in each of your units. Then, you can use the forum for the following purposes:

- Set up a problem for individuals or teams to tackle and share. Create a sense of mystery, or tackle something that is an actual problem in the world today, which could include roleplay. It can be local or global. For example, you could ask students to tackle the problem of stray dogs and cats that owners just simply abandon. Or you could pose a question that requires some digging and some imagination: *Imagine that you time-traveled to a time and place where you had to become a pirate to survive. Where would you be? When? What would your daily life look like? What would you wear? How would you do your pirating?*

- Make relevant instructional materials available. The advantage of having them in the forum is that you can let the instructors comment and add more materials, commentary, and so on.

- Demonstrate achievement of learning objectives by tying the questions to learning objectives.

- Assure comprehension of the unit content by asking instructional materials-focused discussion questions. The students can read the materials and immediately comment and share their impressions.

- Post drafts and peer reviews. This is a great place to post drafts of papers or comments and include rubrics, both for peer reviews and final grading. Moodle makes incorporating rubrics easy. This could tie to a workshop peer review activity.

- Post current controversies, links to articles, and multimedia links.

- Set up projects that require collaboration and encourage the use of collaboration platforms such as Google Docs in Google Drive.

The advantage of thinking about what you'd like to have students do helps you consider how they will interact with each other and demonstrate that they are achieving the unit learning objectives. In doing so, they will be learning from each other.

In the next section, we will put learning from each other into practice by setting up engaging forum and chat modules that include positive reinforcement and motivating content.

Learning from one another

You can set up the forum and chat modules so that students have the optimal conditions to learn from one another:

- First, you can ensure that the prompts are engaging and do not result in *yes* or *no* answers. Be creative and inspire a sense of wonder and discovery.

- Second, you can ask students to share their work and comment in a positive, constructive way. For example, you can ask students to post drafts of presentations. You'll be setting up positive reinforcement, which is very motivating.

- Third, you can encourage students to share experiences and things from current events. All of these activities and prompts will be very engaging, and they will serve as excellent motivation as well. If they are tackling a current local problem, such as the problem of stray cats and dogs, they may even decide to organize a pet adoption day for the strays that have been captured, cleaned up, vaccinated, and ready for their new, happy "forever" homes.

- Finally, you can remind students of deadlines and include checklists of things to do. This will help students organize their work and manage their time effectively.

In the next section, we'll learn how to bring forums and chat together so that there is an integration of both synchronous and asynchronous communication.

Setting up Chat

Chat is great when you need quick, immediate feedback. In Moodle 4.0, Chat can be set so that messages can be received, even if you do not have Moodle open in your browser. Keep in mind that Chat is a feature that has been in Moodle since its early versions, and it is not as up-to-date as other activities in Moodle. Nevertheless, it is integrated into Moodle and thus can be convenient, especially if you don't want to go outside of Moodle (into Teams and so on) for a chat or messaging feature. Chats are automatically saved, so they can help an instructor make sure they have responded to the student's questions. So, let's get started:

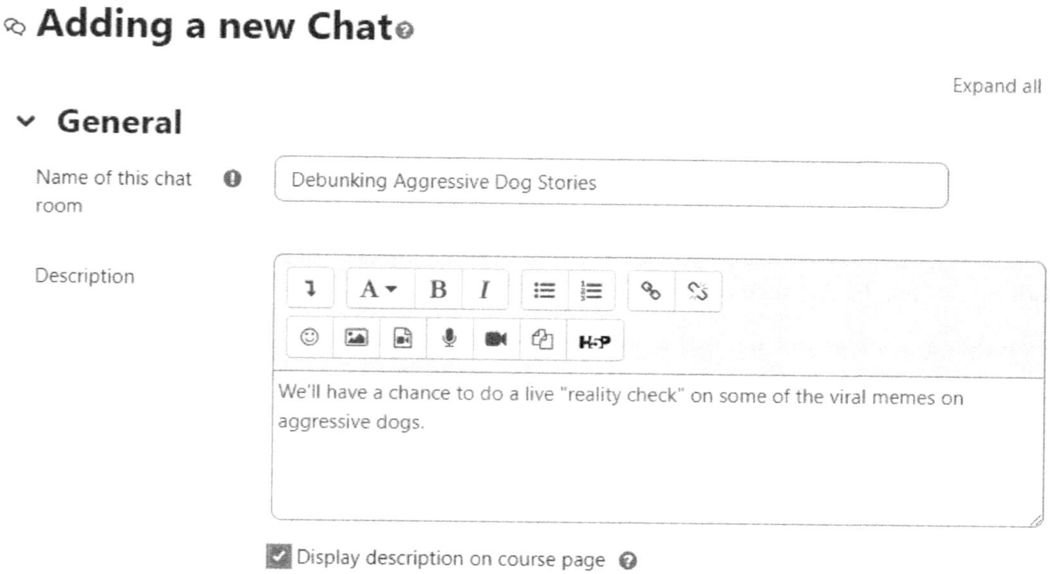

⟜ **Adding a new Chat**⊘

Expand all

⌄ **General**

Name of this chat   ❶ | Debunking Aggressive Dog Stories |
room

Description

| ↧ | A ▾ | B | *I* | ≡ | ≣ | % | ⌇ |

| ☺ | 🖼 | 🖻 | 🎤 | 🎥 | ⎙ | **H-P** |

We'll have a chance to do a live "reality check" on some of the viral memes on
aggressive dogs.

☑ Display description on course page ❷

Figure 8.2 – Adding a new Chat

Sometimes, it is helpful to have synchronous or real-time communication. We often
use our smartphones for texting when we need a quick answer or want to ask a rather
informal question. Now that many institutions use Teams, Google products, or Zoom for
chat and real-time video conferencing, Chat can be built into Moodle. Moodle has its own
Chat, but there are advantages to using your institution's platform, such as Teams. In this
case, you would log into Moodle, but your Teams application would be simultaneously
running (as it usually is) at the same time on your desktop, tablet, or phone.

If your institution does not use Teams or another cloud-based productivity or collaboration
app and prefers that everyone participate only in Moodle, Moodle's Chat function is a
good option. For example, if you are a training organization and you are attracting students
from many organizations, groups, or schools, it will be impossible to communicate through
everyone's Teams, Zoom, or Google accounts. Instead, it is better to use Moodle's Chat.
Also, individuals may use WhatsApp or phone texts. However, if you use Moodle's Chat
module, you can save the chat conversations within Moodle. Saving the transcripts of chats
can be very important for instructors who want to ensure that they are communicating, and
also for students who may wish to keep a record of what they have said.

Perhaps the most popular form of text generated in an online course is that which is generated through live captioning, which is available through Zoom and PowerPoint, just to name two. The transcript can be saved and used as notes. Instructors who find they say their most insightful things while giving a lecture can use the live transcript chat text as a source of ideas for their next article or book. It is useful to keep in mind that collaborative chat was the method used to write the book *Angrynomics* (`https://www.gapingvoid.com/blog/2020/02/27/why-we-wrote-angrynomics-by-mark-blyth/`), which came about as two authors recorded their conversations and used speech-to-text to transcribe them.

Another advantage of Chat is that your students may use speech-to-text applications (built-in as closed-captioning in Zoom, YouTube Live, and Google, for example), which automatically inserts a microphone avatar or logo. You can use it as an assistive technology as it is a good way to have students practice speech-to-text and can also be very helpful for those students who may have limited vision or limited physical mobility.

A chat room can be useful for students who are in a group. However, it's not necessarily a good idea to have a chat with the entire class, because threads can get lost fairly quickly if people are commenting at the same time.

When you add a chat room to a course, by default, any student in the course can enter this chat room at any time. As with other activities, access restrictions can be set to override this default. The **Course Chat Room** area can become a meeting place for students in the course, where they can come to collaborate on work and exchange information. If you give group assignments or have students rate other students' assignments, consider adding a chat room to the course and encouraging students to use it. Also, consider saving transcripts of the chat sessions so that they can act as other reference tools for students.

When you schedule a chat session, the scheduled time appears in the **Course Calendar** area and is also displayed in the **Upcoming events** block:

⌄ Chat sessions

Next chat time	19 ⬍	May ⬍	2022 ⬍	20 ⬍	30 ⬍ 🗓
Repeat/publish session times	Don't publish any chat times ⬍				
Save past sessions	Never delete messages ⬍				
Everyone can view past sessions ❓	No ⬍				

Figure 8.3 – Scheduling a chat session in the calendar

As the chat module is open all the time, when you put a chat on the calendar, you are not restricting access to the chat module. You are just creating a reminder to inform students when they should click on the chat module. You can also hide the chat when you don't want students to enter it.

If a group of more than five or six wants to communicate, it's usually much better to use a discussion board rather than a chat. That said, if you are launching a webinar, it is always good to have Chat available to send questions and comments and to alert the instructor if there are technical difficulties. BigBlueButton and Zoom have Chat built-in so that people can communicate via Chat as they also converse with each other via video or pure audio.

When a student selects a chat, they see the description that you entered when you created the chat. You can use this **Description** to instruct the student about the purpose of the chat:

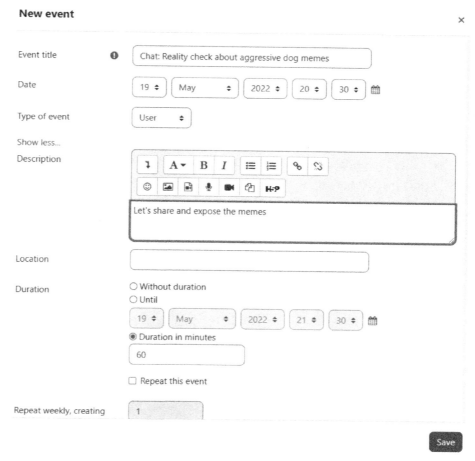

Figure 8.4 – Developing a description for the chat

When you enter a chat, it launches a pop-up window. You can choose between two themes: **Bubble** or **Compact**, I've selected **Bubble**. Ensure that your students don't have popups blocked:

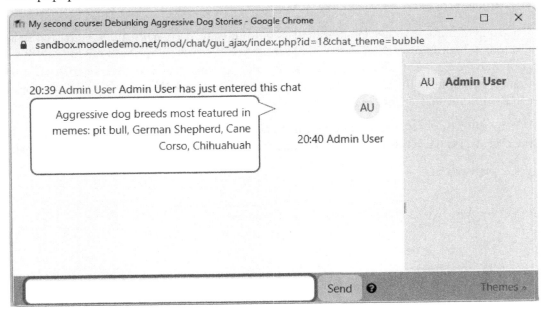

Figure 8.5 – Using the Bubble theme for a chat

Let's look at the settings that you will use to create a chat.

The chat settings page

The **Adding a new Chat** page is where you create and select settings for a chat. When you first add a chat, you will be taken to this page. To edit the settings for an existing chat, select the chat. Then, from the horizontal top menu bar, select **Settings**. This will take you to the same page, but it will be called **Updating Chat** instead of **Adding a new Chat**. Both pages have the same settings.

Keep in mind that entering a name for a chat room generates a pop-up window. As you add a chat, you'll need to add it to the calendar so that it shows up from the student's **Dashboard** in the **Calendar** block:

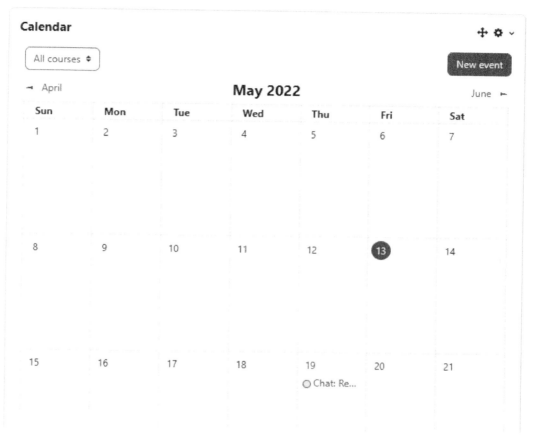

Figure 8.6 – How the chat appears in the Calendar block in the Dashboard

Let's consider the options you have for settings on this page. Note that as in all the activities, you now have a chance to tie the chat so that it fulfills competencies. You can also tag the topics for use in social media, and you can also restrict access so that the chat takes place within groups.

The following screenshot shows how to describe the chat room and also where to click to restrict access. Note that in Moodle 4.0, you can restrict access based on achieving a passing grade. While this restriction may seem more important for activities such as quizzes, it does keep the student from moving ahead before they're ready and have demonstrated mastery of the learning objectives:

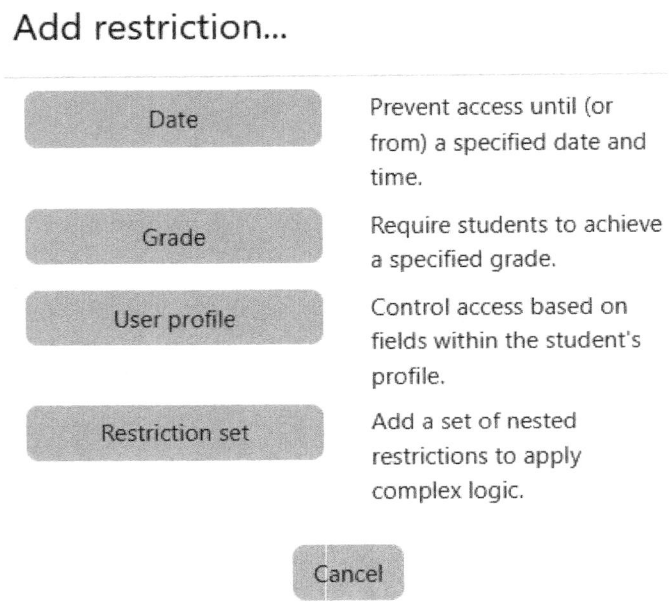

Add restriction...

Date	Prevent access until (or from) a specified date and time.
Grade	Require students to achieve a specified grade.
User profile	Control access based on fields within the student's profile.
Restriction set	Add a set of nested restrictions to apply complex logic.

Cancel

Figure 8.7 – Ways to restrict access to the chat

Once you've named the chat room, it will appear on your course's home page.

The name of the chat room

This is the name that students will see on the course's home page:

CHAT
Debunking Aggressive Dog Stories ✏

Mark as done   ⋮

We'll have a chance to do a live "reality check" on some of the viral memes on aggressive dogs.

Figure 8.8 – How the chat room appears on the course's home page

Description

When the students enter the room, its **Description** will appear. Ensure that the description makes sense and does not confuse or distract your students.

When a student selects a chat, they will see the introduction text before clicking on the chat room. You can also display the description on the course's home page.

Scheduling office hours

It's often a good idea to schedule virtual office hours before a high-stakes test or a big project. One good way to do so is to make a calendar entry for the chat session and then make it available to all the members of the course. Then, you can be available for questions. Ensure that you save the transcript, because many people may have the same questions but, perhaps, cannot attend at the same time. In this case, the forum could be used as an exam review or FAQ site. You can post your chat transcript here. Keep in mind that your chat room will be open all the time, not just during office hours. Your office hours' notice on the calendar simply means that you'll be there and waiting for questions.

The next chat time and repeat/publish sessions

As stated at the beginning of this section, so long as a chat is visible to the student, they can enter that chat room at any time. Due to this, the settings for **Next chat time** and **Repeat sessions** don't open and close the chat. Instead, these settings put a time and date for the chat on the class calendar.

Chat times are listed in the **Calendar** and **Upcoming Events** blocks. Note that chats are not restricted to these times; they are only announced as a way for people in the course to *make a date* for the chat. However, this is a good way for the teacher to announce online office hours and also help students manage their time by scheduling times to pop into the chat and discuss their work and possible collaborative projects.

Spontaneous chats have the best chance of happening if the course has a lot of students who frequent the course's home page. Also, consider adding the **Online Users** block so that when students visit the site, they will know who is online and can invite others to the chat room.

Saving past sessions – Save past sessions and Everyone can view past sessions

Past chats are automatically saved. The **Save past sessions** setting enables you to choose how long the system saves the chats. The **Everyone can view past sessions** setting determines whether students can view past chats (**Yes**) or whether only teachers can (**No**).

Chat logs

The only security for a chat room is turning the group mode on so that only students in a selected group can see each other in this chat room. You can find the group settings under **Common module settings**.

Remember that on the **Course settings** page, you can set **Enrolment duration** to **Unlimited**. This means that once a student is enrolled in the course, they are always enrolled until you manually unenroll the student. If you leave the course open to all the students who were ever enrolled, consider segregating your chat into groups. Then, create a group that only includes the currently enrolled students:

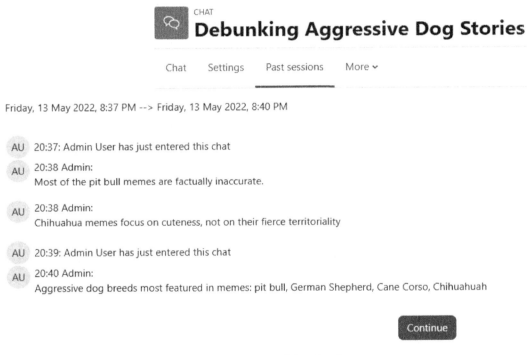

Figure 8.9 – A view of the Chat log

Once you've set up synchronous communication in the form of chats, you can look at developing asynchronous student engagement and communication in the form of discussion boards, called forums in Moodle.

Adding and running forums

Discussion boards, also known as forums, are at the heart of Moodle, and they provide you with a way to organize and launch group projects and investigations, add student interaction, provide peer review, share information, and disseminate course content. You can also use forums to provide links to assessments. Many instructors use forums as the primary method for organizing content in the course. For example, in an eight-module course, you can lead each week with a forum. In the forum's description, you can include links to the readings and multimedia (audio, images, and videos). Then, you can ask students questions to respond to them in the forum.

We can get started by creating a **Forum** activity. After you select **Forum** from the activity menu, you'll be asked to give the forum a name.

To add the **Forum** activity, we can follow the same procedure as in the other activities. Click on **Add an activity or resource** and then select the **Forum** icon. As shown in the following screenshot, you can name and describe the forum, and also review the different settings:

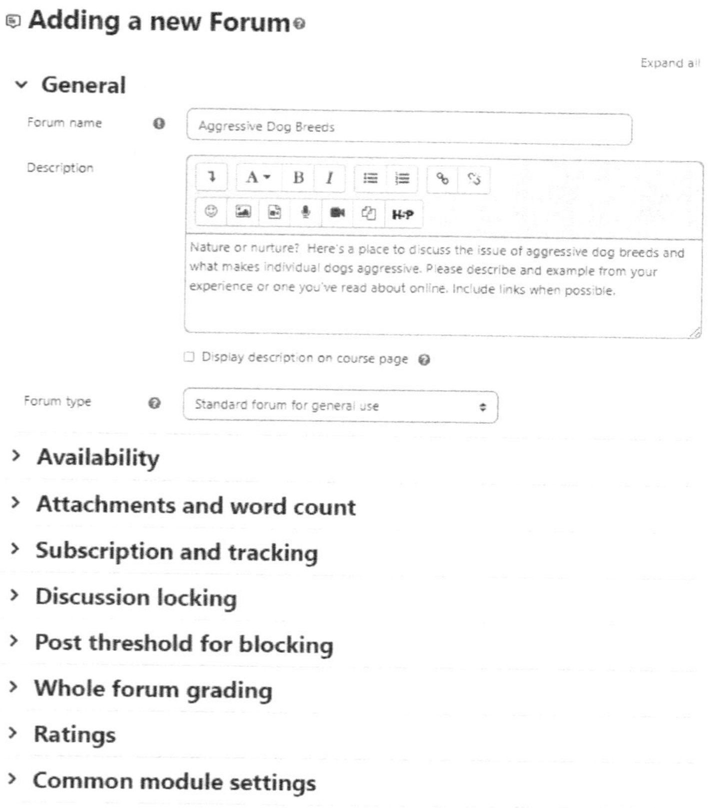

Figure 8.10 – The Adding a new Forum screen, with places to add a name and description

By tying the course content to a forum, you're emphasizing interaction and engagement. Engagement is what keeps people making satisfactory student progress, so this is a good thing to do. If you run the forum well and incentivize students to interact positively with each other, you can stimulate thoughtful discussion and motivate students to become involved, which will result in unexpected and intriguing insights.

Taking the idea of active and ongoing engagement through forums to an extreme, you can also create a course that consists only of a forum. The course's home page is the forum. The course will consist of only discussion topics. You can do this using the **Social** course type under the course settings.

With this structure, you will need to plan carefully. The discussion topics will need to correspond to units, and you will need to be consistent as you place the course readings, videos, student responses, and links to assessments.

Multiple forums

Remember that a class can have as many forums as you want. If your course uses groups, you can use groups in the forum. Also, you can hide old forums and create new ones. This is useful if you run students through a course on a schedule. Just turning off old forums and creating new ones enables you to refresh parts of the course.

Forum settings

The **Settings** page is where you select settings for a forum. It can be accessed by going to **Administration | Forum administration | Settings**. Let's take a look at how each of these settings affects the user experience.

General settings

The general settings affect the appearance and function of the forum.

Forum name

This is the name that students will see when a forum is listed on the course's home page.

Forum description

When a student enters a forum, they will see **Forum description** at the top of the forum's page. This text should tell the student what the forum is about. You can also use this introduction to tell the student if they can rate posts by other students. It also tells the student how to link to a document with more extensive instructions on how to use the forum. This is possible because the description is a full-featured web page that can hold anything you put on a web page.

As with other activities, if you check the **Show description** box, the description will be displayed on the course page.

The forum type

On Moodle, you can create several types of forums. Each type can be used differently. The different types of forums can be seen in the following screenshot:

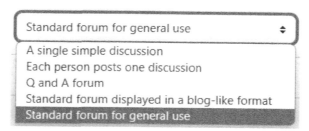

Figure 8.11 – Drop-down menu for you to select the forum type

The following table looks at each type of forum in more detail. **Standard forum for general use** is probably the most popular for courses. However, a forum for **Q&A** is also very important to include, particularly for student success:

Forum Type	Description
A single simple discussion	The entire forum appears on one page. The first posting at the top of the page is the topic for the forum. This topic is usually created by the teacher. The students then post replies under this topic. A single-topic forum is most useful for short and highly-focused discussions.
Each person posts one discussion	Each student can create one – and only one – new topic. Everyone can reply to every topic. You may need to explain that students only get one new topic, so they should choose their topic wisely.
Q&A	This is like a single-topic forum. Here, the teacher creates the topic for the forum. Students then reply to this topic. However, a student cannot see anyone else's reply until they have posted a reply. The topic is usually a question posed by the teacher, and the students' replies are usually answers to this question.
A standard forum displayed in a blog-like format	In a standard forum, anyone can start a new topic. Teachers and students can create new topics and reply to the existing postings. Displaying the discussion in a blog-like format makes the title and body of each discussion visible. This is a great structure for stimulating discussion and sharing links and images and embedded social media posts.
A standard forum for general use	In a standard forum, anyone can start a new topic. Teachers and students can create new topics and reply to the existing postings. Only the titles of discussions are visible; you must click on a discussion to read the postings under it.

Figure 8.12 - Types of forums

The maximum attachment size

Students can attach files to forum postings. This sets the maximum file size the student can upload. One of the settings turns off the student's ability to upload files to the **Uploads are not allowed** forum.

The maximum number of attachments

This sets the maximum number of files that can be attached to one post, not the maximum for the whole forum.

The display word count option

When set to **Yes**, the forum will show how many words are in each post. The word count is shown at the bottom of the post, so you won't see the word count until you have clicked on the post. This is useful for an "explain in 100 words or less" type of activity. It can also connect to a rubric. We will discuss rubrics later in this book. For an excellent guide on rubrics, please check out the University of Oklahoma's useful checklist and guide for creating and using rubrics: `https://www.ou.edu/assessment/faculty-resources/creating-and-using-rubrics`.

The subscription mode

Selecting **Force subscription** subscribes all students to the forum automatically (even students who enroll in the course at a later time). Before using this setting, consider its long-term effect on students who took your class.

If you reuse the same course for a later group of students, the previous group will still be enrolled. Do you want previous students to be notified of new postings in the current class's forum? If not, there are several solutions:

- Don't force all students to be subscribed.
- Use groups to separate the current group of students in the class from the previous groups.
- Create a fresh instance of the course for each new group.
- Reset the course, which will unenroll past students.
- Create a new forum for a new group of students.

If you select **Auto subscription**, everyone in the course will be subscribed to the forum, but later, they can unsubscribe. With **Force subscription**, the student cannot unsubscribe so long as they are enrolled in the course.

Read tracking

When turned on, this highlights the forum posts that the students haven't read.

Once you have reviewed how to set up forums, you can take a step back and start thinking of the uses for your forums. In the next section, we will learn how to use forums for delivering content, as well as spurring interaction and engagement.

Using the Announcements forum for notifications

Moodle has simplified how to notify students of general news and announcements by setting up a special forum called the Announcements forum. It is automatically created in a new course, and there can only be one, except in very special occasions in which it has been imported from a different system.

Your new, automatically generated Announcement forum is placed at the top of the central section by default. Posting is restricted to teachers, managers, and administrators. The default subscription setting is the "forced subscription." You can set how many discussions appear in the Announcement forum.

If you do not want to have an Announcement forum, you can remove it in several ways. The easiest way is to simply hide the Announcements forum. This is recommended because you may want to post an announcement sometime in the future. Other ways include deleting the Announcements forum from the course home page or deleting the **Latest announcements** block.

If, for some reason, you do not want to have the auto-creation of Announcements by default, you can simply set **Number of announcements** to 0 in the **Course** default settings. You can still override this setting if there are one or two courses in which you would like to have Announcement forums.

Now that you know how to set up different types of chat and forum modules, you can think about how to take collaboration a step further. In the next section, you will learn how to set up links to the collaboration platforms that your organization makes available to learners.

Forum-based content delivery

As we mentioned previously, a very convenient way to deliver content is to create forums that correspond to the weeks in the course. For example, if you have an 8-week course, you can create eight separate forums. Each one can correspond to specific content (text, blocks, video, audio, presentations, and more) that you would like the students to read. By putting the links in the forum threads, you can ensure that everyone progresses through the course at the same pace and covers the same content. You can then include a few questions in the forum and open threads that allow students to ask questions, as well as reflect on the material. It's a good place to add a few reflective questions. As you develop your questions, make sure that they are structured so that each person can give a unique, personal answer. For example, you may ask students to find an example of an article or website that relates to the topic. You can also ask them to describe their own experiences. Avoid questions that can be provided with yes/no answers or ones that will result in the same response.

Forum-based assignments

By organizing assignments in your forums, you can ensure that you attach the necessary content and reviews to the assignments. For example, you may wish to have students write essays about readings. If you do so, you can open up a forum in which you describe the paper, include expectations, and even incorporate a rubric. For example, if you ask students to write a short response to a reading, you can post a link to the reading, a series of guiding questions, and a description of the structure of the paper they are to write. Then, you can include a checklist of the criteria (number of words, content, structure, organization, grammar, mechanics, and so on). You can open threads for students to ask questions, and you can put a link to Dropbox so that they can, with a single click, submit their assignments.

One advantage of using forum-based assignments is that if you have any changes you wish to make, you can be assured that most of your students will see the changes because they will occur in the same location that everyone is visiting. It's a "one-stop shopping" point for assignments.

It is a perfect place to create an assignment that encourages students to apply knowledge, such as in tackling a current issue or problem or doing research into topics that require creativity and imagination, as well as the ability to comprehend the learning materials and seek and find new content, potentially in your online library or web-based repositories and publications.

Forum-based peer review

Forums are an excellent way to boost student engagement because they can interact with each other in a meaningful way and thus humanize the online experience. Using forums for peer review is also a good idea, but you'll need to ensure that you establish good ground rules because the forum is, after all, a public place. If you want a more detailed and granular kind of peer review interaction, and you'd like to be able to easily grade each interaction, it is better to "upgrade" to Moodle's Workshop activity. If you use the forum as a place for students to start a thread, post a draft, and then respond to each other's drafts, you'll need to ensure that they keep their comments positive and productive. One good way to do that is to provide a checklist of items to respond to. If you want to grade each checklist item, it's better to use the Workshop activity rather than a Forum activity. For example, you can ask students to respond to a series of questions:

- What did you like about this post?

- How could the post have been more specific or have provided more details?

- As you were reading the post, when did you want to know more? What could the author have provided?

The key is to keep the peer review questions brief and avoid having too many. After all, you want to motivate your students to interact, not frighten them into avoiding the forum altogether.

Forum-based review and linking to assessments

Forums are a wonderful place to provide a self-contained place for quizzes, exam reviews, and practice before they take the full exam. The best way to organize forums for assessment review, practice, and performance is to tie the forum title to the topics covered in the assessment. Then, you can create a link to the key content covered and describe the learning goals or outcomes. After that, you can include a few review questions. Ensure that your practice or review questions are in the same format as the ones that they will be taking for their final assessments.

The practice forum is a great place for students to develop self-efficacy and an "I can do it!" attitude. The way to develop self-confidence is to allow feedback in the practice test and allow the students to take the test or quiz as many times as they like. Ensure that you always link back to the course content that contains the correct responses or the information they need.

Now that we have covered the structure and functionality of the Moodle Forum activity, we can take a deep dive into starting, posting, and communicating via a forum. Please keep in mind that as you work through the forum, you may wish to use a Workshop instead of a Moodle Forum. To make that determination, you'll need to review your goals in the course, and also evaluate how easily your students are managing the forum. If they are comfortable with the easy-to-navigate structure of the forum but are confused by more complex activities, it's best to stick to the Forum activity.

Starting and posting to a forum

When a student enters a general-purpose forum, they see the description that was entered during the creation of the forum, as shown in the following screenshot:

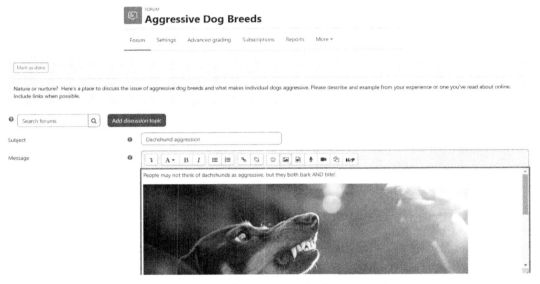

Figure 8.13 – Making a post in the Forum activity

Once you click **Save**, the forum will be listed under **Discussion**. Fellow learners will be able to click on the topic and then add a response. Notice that there are several options, which include **Permalink**, **Edit**, **Delete**, and **Reply**.

Encourage students to subscribe to the form by clicking the **Subscribe** button on the main **Discussion** screen. They will receive notices when people post, which can be very engaging, especially if a student is using a tablet or phone and they can respond quickly:

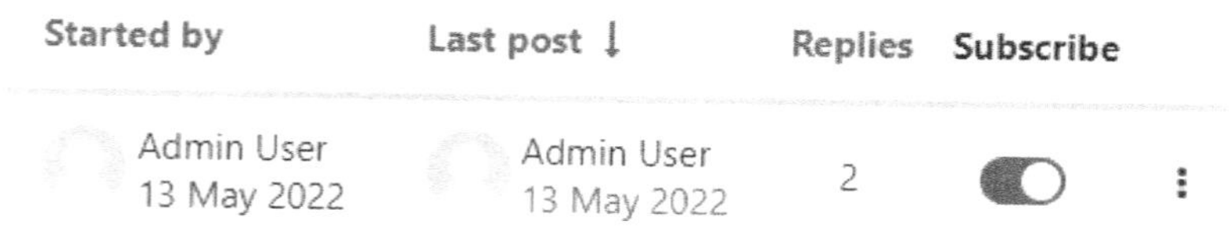

Started by	Last post ↓	Replies	Subscribe
Admin User 13 May 2022	Admin User 13 May 2022	2	⬤▶ ⋮

Figure 8.14 – Subscribing to the Forum activity to receive notices when someone has posted

You can set the way that responses are displayed. The available options are shown in the following screenshot:

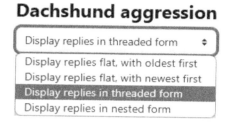

Figure 8.15 – How to configure the way the responses are shown

To post a reply, simply click **Reply** and type a response. The following screenshot shows the text box. To add images, files, links, emoticons, HTML5, and more, you will need to click on **Advanced** to open the full menu:

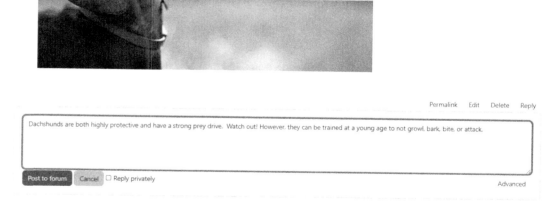

Figure 8.16 – The Forum activity without the formatting bar enabled

After clicking **Advanced**, the horizontal formatting bar will open, where you can select from different formatting and information-sharing options, as shown in the following screenshot:

Figure 8.17 – The student's view of a general forum with the formatting bar enabled

If you want to ensure your students see the discussion, you can star it. You can also pin it so that it appears at the top of the module. If you don't want any more posts, you can lock the discussion. In Moodle 4.0, you're automatically subscribed to the discussion so that you receive notices if people post. You can unsubscribe if you do not want to receive push notices:

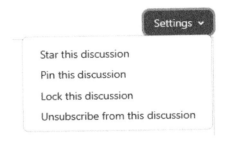

Figure 8.18 – Discussion settings that allow you to do things to the Forum activity that make it easier to see and avoid distractions

If you ask students to collaborate on assignments or ask them to review each others' work, consider adding a forum specifically to discuss the assignment. Some people may use a Workshop for that purpose, but a Forum works well because students have an informal way to read each other's drafts and thus feel more confident about their own. Furthermore, a Forum is a good place to discuss exemplar work. Then, for more granular peer reviews, you can use a Workshop.

To encourage collaboration, you may wish to display the forum postings in a flat format, with the newest first. This option shows the text, which can be engaging and pique the students' curiosity, inspiring them to engage and post:

Figure 8.19 – Forum displayed in a flat format

You may couple the forums with an occasional synchronous discussion on the topic to provide a hybrid experience that mixes synchronous with asynchronous contact with each other. In this way, you will be motivating students by creating an open, welcoming environment where students can use the forum to preview each other's work and informally share and collaborate on the assignments you complete via a forum.

Linking to collaboration platforms (Functionality booster)

Forums are interactive and often collaborative activities, and as such, they can encourage students to learn from each other. Sometimes, it is useful to have students collaborate on a single document. Students can collaborate in a shared document. In a Moodle Forum, having a collaborative document can encourage people to add content. It's not granularly peer-reviewed and assessed as in a Moodle Workshop, nor is it intended to be a wiki. It's simply to encourage engagement. It may seem complicated, but it's quite simple, especially if your school or organization uses Microsoft Office 365 products and OneDrive, or if students have a Google account that gives them access to Google Drive, Docs, Sheets, and more. They can also use other collaborative spaces, such as Dropbox. For more complex tasks, students may collaborate in a spreadsheet that has a timeline and critical path. Some organizations use project management tools such as Basecamp or Slack for informing team members of milestones and building in automatic alerts. Google Drive may be one of the easier approaches because it integrates with email and other applications.

They can use the following steps:

1. Log into their school shared drive account. Let's use Google for this example.
2. Go to Google Drive.
3. Set up a folder for the course.
4. Open the folder.

5. Within the folder, create a new Google document (this can be a document, sheet, or something else).

6. Name the document.

7. Obtain the link for the document and post it in the forum. You can set it so that anyone with the link can see the document. You can also grant permission for your partners to be able to edit the document. You'll need their Gmail email addresses. Non-Gmail addresses do not seem to play nicely with Google Drive, and Gmail will automatically send out an email requesting permissions.

Once you have set up the documents, you can let people in the class see what you're doing as you progress. If you'd like to keep the drafts and the progress private, you can simply change the settings so that only people with permission can view and/or edit the document.

One advantage to using a collaboration platform rather than sending documents back and forth in email is the fact that it's easier to keep up with version control. Furthermore, once you've finished one draft and everyone has included their contributions, you can start a new document that indicates that it's a new revision or version. Sometimes, it's easiest to keep separate folders within the main folder to keep everything clear and well sorted.

If your organization is using Teams, you can collaborate on documents in a folder you can set up in **Files**. Here, you can add documents, and anyone in your team can collaborate on them. If you are using Google Classroom, you can use it in conjunction with Moodle for access to shared Google documents. You'll simply need to include a link to a folder with shared documents in Google or Google Classroom.

Summary

In this chapter, you learned how to create a sense of adventure and excitement by creating places where students interact and learn from each other, both in real-time (synchronously) and on-demand (asynchronously), using chat and forums.

In learning about how best to use chat and forum activities to encourage engagement and motivate students, we've reviewed the different types as well as purposes. We also discussed how Moodle 4.0 makes it easier for students to interact with each other, and for the teacher to make sure that students are staying on track and not bounding ahead before they're ready. Moodle 4.0 focuses on student success.

In the next chapter, you will learn how to encourage collaboration among students using wikis and glossaries. You will learn how to use collaboration as an instructional strategy and how to select the collaborative activities that work particularly well in Moodle.

9
Collaborating with Wikis and Glossaries

Collaboration can be a cornerstone of social constructivism and a place where students truly learn from each other. They can share their insights, set goals and targets, and bring prior learning to their collaborations. In addition, collaborations allow students to develop a body of knowledge or a project plan that can be implemented in the real world.

One strategy for collaboration is to engage students in activities that require each person to contribute to the final product. Two popular activities are informative wikis and topic-based glossaries. While wiki and glossary activities can be completed individually, they are perfect vehicles for collaboration. The key is to examine the learning objectives and determine how best to implement them. In this chapter, we'll discuss various strategies for getting your students engaged in collaborations and excited about learning from each other.

This chapter teaches you how to develop effective collaborative activities that allow you to achieve your learning objectives by adding wikis and glossaries to your course. It is a way to build up social constructivism and implement the theories first developed by psychologist Lev Vygotsky, who discussed how people first learn in a group context and then, later, on an individual level. While such learning happens in any interaction (such as a forum, a workshop, and more), in wikis and glossaries, the focus is on a collaborative end product, so the interactions can be even more focused. These activities enable students to work together and build up a body of knowledge. The resulting collection of knowledge (the completed wikis and glossaries) can be reused by students in future courses. As the course evolves, the wikis and glossaries that past students created can be retained, edited, referenced, and grown.

Specifically, in this chapter, we will learn about the following topics:

- Determining the best collaborative activity to use with asynchronous, synchronous, and blended Moodle courses
- Aligning glossary and wiki activities with our learning objectives
- Developing glossary activities for collaboration in all kinds of delivery modes
- Developing wiki activities for collaboration in all kinds of delivery modes

In this chapter, we will bring together the emerging needs for synchronous, asynchronous, and blended delivery with collaboration, which is a powerful learning strategy. By the end of this chapter, you will be able to use Moodle's wikis and glossaries for effective collaborative learning.

Using collaboration as an instructional strategy that replicates today's work environment

In our distributed world, where people move from place to place and still communicate with each other and develop work products together, it is necessary to understand how to collaborate productively in a virtual environment. Therefore, there is a pragmatic side to the emphasis on collaboration. Moodle's wiki and glossary activities replicate how people use cloud-based collaboration in the workplace to generate reports, guides, marketing materials, and more.

While wikis and glossaries are often asynchronous, they can also incorporate synchronous web conferencing. This also replicates today's workplace, making the Moodle classroom even more effective for training people not only in the subject matter but also in new ways of working and learning.

We use Moodle precisely for its flexible architecture – a structure that encourages learning from each other. The ability to contribute to glossaries, wikis, and other collaborative activities allows students to contribute knowledge in a way that reinforces and rewards. Thus, it is an instructional strategy that brings together motivation, self-confidence, and curiosity, which creates conditions for learning. Additionally, it is a way to reinforce prior knowledge and build up experience as students recall past learning, add to what they already know, and reflect on what others are contributing. It's also a strategy for overcoming the negative effects of isolation and distance and for rehumanizing the experience of working in isolation, which can be disconcertingly difficult.

Therefore, collaboration can be a very effective instructional strategy, and glossaries, wikis, and other areas where students can contribute can form the cornerstones of the knowledge and skills that they will demonstrate in the future. As you work through this chapter, please refer to *Chapter 13, Features for Teachers: Logs, Reports, Guides* too. In that chapter, you will learn how to connect many different elements in Moodle. We'll start with the glossary activity.

Glossary

The **Glossary** activity is one of the most underrated activities in Moodle. On the surface, a glossary is a list of words and definitions that students can access. However, a course creator allows students to add entries to the glossary. Adding entries transforms the glossary from a static list of vocabulary words into a collaborative tool for learning purposes. It also has an auto-linking feature that means that any time the word is used in the course, it automatically links to the glossary entry:

Glossary

Figure 9.1 – Glossary icon

If your learning objectives require individuals to be able to identify, define, and describe items or phenomena, the **Glossary** activity is ideal. For example, you might have a course on tourism and wish to develop a glossary of terms that are specialized in a specific area; for example, the terms regarding *culture tourism*. Students can collaborate and make a customized glossary that can help them during the course and, later, in their careers.

A text filter, called **auto-linking**, creates links to the glossary entries in your course. When this is turned on by a site administrator and a word from the **Glossary** activity appears in the course, it's highlighted. Clicking on the word brings up a pop-up window with the word's entry in the glossary. The entry can consist of text, images, media, and links. It is a miniature page devoted to defining and elucidating the glossary term. The auto-linking feature makes collaborative possibilities even richer. For example, students might be assigned specific glossary terms that they will use as the basis of an illustrative paragraph or passage.

You can use a glossary to build a class directory, a collection of past exam questions, famous quotations, or even an annotated collection of pictures.

Let's take a look at how we enable glossaries and auto-linking in Moodle.

Enabling glossaries and auto-linking

Let's start with a bit of administrative housekeeping. Before teachers can set up a glossary assignment, it needs to be enabled on the system. So, please be sure that the site administrator sees this first. There are several places where a site administrator will need to enable **Glossary** and its features.

When **Glossary auto-linking** is turned on, a glossary term appears for the course and is linked to its glossary entry. This is what the link looks like:

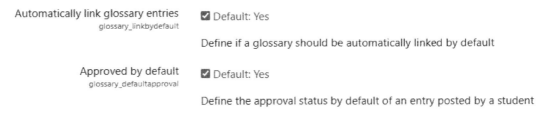

Figure 9.2 – Auto-linking in the glossary function

Auto-linking creates links when a glossary term is used in the same course in which the glossary is located.

Enabling glossaries for your site

First, under **Site administration** | **Plugins** | **Activity Modules** | **Manage activities**, the site administrator must enable the **Glossary** activity. By default, the **Glossary** activity is enabled on Moodle. Enabling it is only necessary if you do not see the glossary in the **Add Resource** or **Activity...** menu:

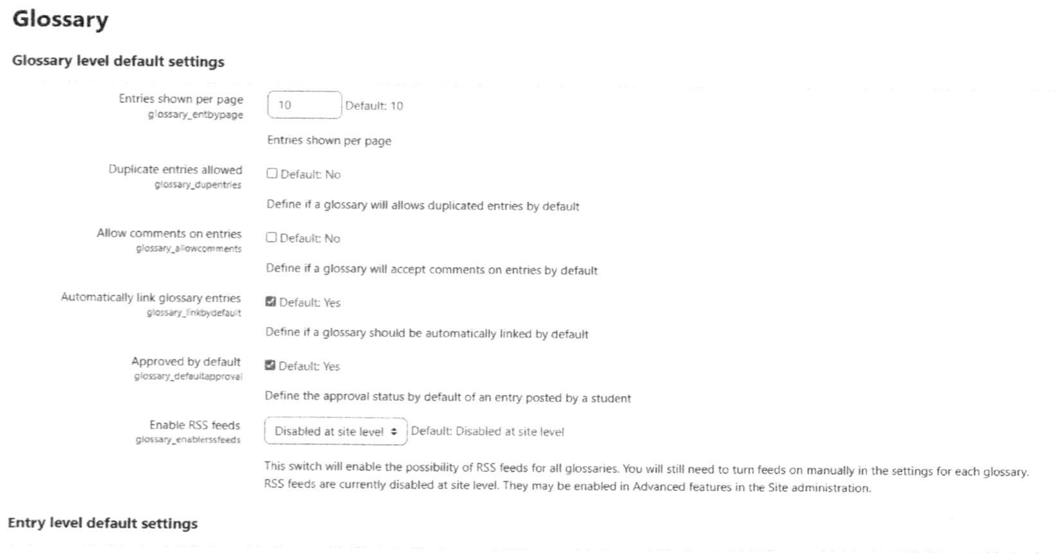

Glossary

Glossary level default settings

Entries shown per page glossary_entbypage	`10` Default: 10
	Entries shown per page
Duplicate entries allowed glossary_dupentries	☐ Default: No
	Define if a glossary will allows duplicated entries by default
Allow comments on entries glossary_allowcomments	☐ Default: No
	Define if a glossary will accept comments on entries by default
Automatically link glossary entries glossary_linkbydefault	☑ Default: Yes
	Define if a glossary should be automatically linked by default
Approved by default glossary_defaultapproval	☑ Default: Yes
	Define the approval status by default of an entry posted by a student
Enable RSS feeds glossary_enablerssfeeds	Disabled at site level ⇕ Default: Disabled at site level
	This switch will enable the possibility of RSS feeds for all glossaries. You will still need to turn feeds on manually in the settings for each glossary. RSS feeds are currently disabled at site level. They may be enabled in Advanced features in the Site administration.

Entry level default settings

Figure 9.3 – Enabling glossaries for your entire site

After you have enabled glossaries for the entire site, you can determine what happens with it.

Enabling auto-linking

Glossary auto-linking needs to be enabled in several places at the site, course, and activity level. If you create a glossary term and it's not being auto-linked to your course, check that glossary auto-linking is enabled at the site, course, and activity/resource level. Each of these levels will be covered as we proceed.

Enabling auto-linking for the site

Under **Site administration | Plugins | Filter | Manage filters**, the site administrator can turn on glossary auto-linking:

Figure 9.4: The site administration page showing Filters

When you see the filter options, click on **Manage filters**. You will be able to enable glossary auto-linking, as follows:

Figure 9.5 – The site administration page showing how to turn on Glossary auto-linking

The **Disabled** setting removes the teacher's ability to turn on auto-linking in the course. By default, the **Off, but available** setting turns off auto-linking, but it enables the teacher to turn it on during the course. The **On** setting turns on auto-linking for all courses on your site.

In the right-hand column, note that the user has chosen to have auto-linking in the content of activities and resources. Additionally, you can select **Content and headings**, which will turn on auto-linking for the content of an activity or resource along with the words in the heading of that activity or resource.

Enabling auto-linking for the course

If the site-wide setting for auto-linking is set to **On**, you do not need to enable it at the course level. If the site-wide setting is set to **Disable**, it's not possible to enable it at the course level. This setting is available and only necessary if the site-wide setting is **Off, but available**.

Under **Administration | Course administration | Filters**, the teacher must turn on **Glossary auto-linking**. If this is disabled, auto-linking will not work for any of the glossaries within the course.

Enabling auto-linking for the activity or resource

If you have auto-linking enabled for the site and the course and it's still not working, check the auto-linking setting for the activity or resource that you are in. In the **Administration** menu, look for the administration options for the resource or activity that you are in. Select **Filters**, and on the filters page, turn on **Glossary auto-linking**:

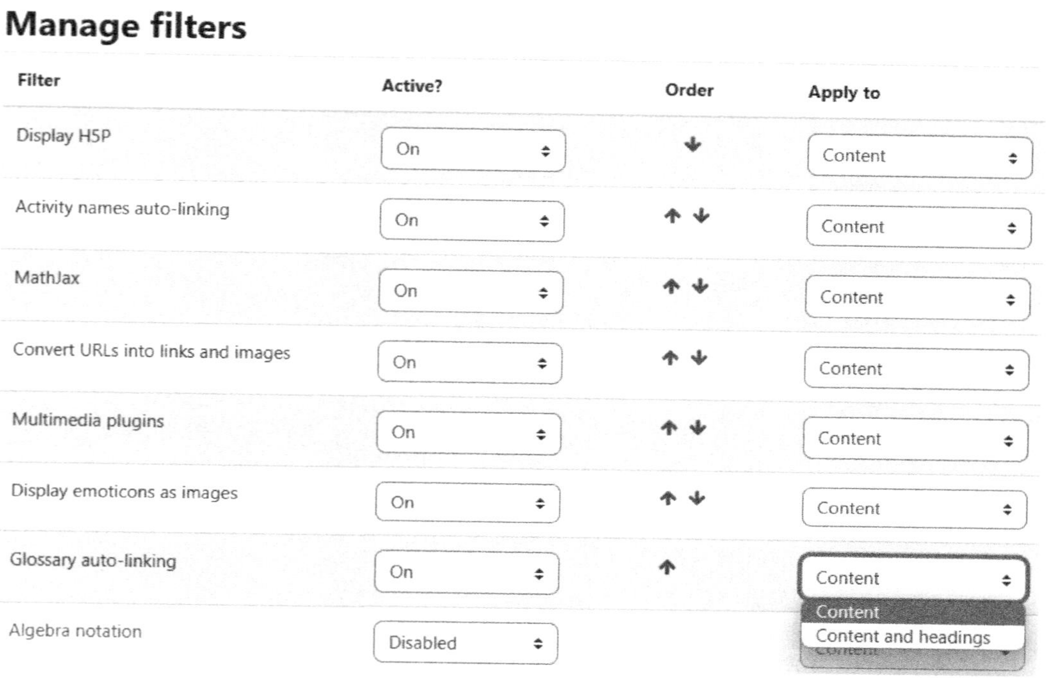

Manage filters

Filter	Active?		Order	Apply to	
Display H5P	On	⬍	⬇	Content	⬍
Activity names auto-linking	On	⬍	⬆ ⬇	Content	⬍
MathJax	On	⬍	⬆ ⬇	Content	⬍
Convert URLs into links and images	On	⬍	⬆ ⬇	Content	⬍
Multimedia plugins	On	⬍	⬆ ⬇	Content	⬍
Display emoticons as images	On	⬍	⬆ ⬇	Content	⬍
Glossary auto-linking	On	⬍	⬆	Content	⬍
				Content	
				Content and headings	
Algebra notation	Disabled	⬍		Content	

Figure 9.6 – Making sure that auto-linking is enabled within the site home page settings

After you've enabled glossaries on the site, you can start adding individual glossaries that align with the categories or topics covered by your course and are necessary to fulfill the learning objectives.

Adding and configuring a glossary

Now that the site administrator has enabled and configured the glossary activity, you are ready to start adding and configuring a glossary. Add a glossary by clicking on **Add an activity or resource** on your course page, and then select **Glossary**. When the glossary settings page is displayed, you will need to choose the correct setting to create the kind of glossary that you want for your class. Let's look at the settings that are unique to a glossary.

You will find these settings under **Administration | Glossary administration | Edit settings**:

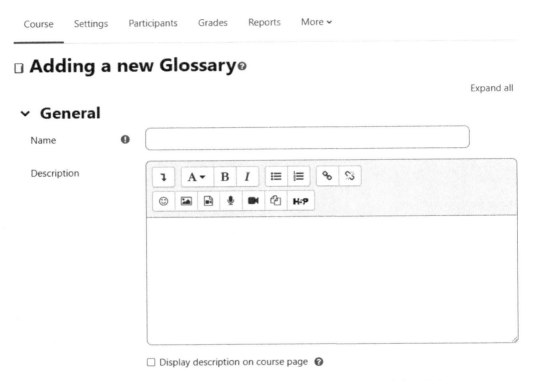

Figure 9.7 – Adding a new glossary and entering its name and description

Global glossaries versus local glossaries

By default, a glossary only applies to the course in which it resides. However, you can choose to make a glossary global. In this case, the words from this glossary will be highlighted and clickable wherever they are on your site. The work done in one course will then become available to all the courses on your site. If your site's subject matter is highly focused, consider using a global glossary. If your site's subject matter is very broad, such as in a university-wide learning site, you should use local glossaries to avoid confusion. For example, imagine that you have a course in chemistry and another in statistics. Both use the word *granular*, but chemistry uses the term to indicate a powdered substance, while statistics uses it to indicate a fine level of detail.

> **Important Note**
>
> Only an administrator can create a glossary in the global glossary. If you only have teacher rights, get an administrator to do this for you.

You may wish to empower your students to create their own glossaries and glossary terms. In that case, it's good to know about secondary glossaries.

Main glossaries versus secondary glossaries

The **Glossary type** setting enables you to designate a glossary as either **Main** or **Secondary**. The **Main glossary** setting refers to a glossary that will include terms from other glossaries. The **Secondary glossary** setting refers to a glossary that stands alone; it does not include terms from any other glossaries. For example, you might have an overall glossary for science terms and standalone glossaries such as physics, chemistry, biology, and geology as secondary glossaries. This is an important distinction when creating collaborative activities if you want the students to be able to add new terms. However, if you want to keep the glossary terms limited to the ones that align with your learning objectives, it's best to avoid secondary glossaries.

If you want students to be able to add entries to a glossary, you must make it a **Secondary glossary** type. Only teachers can add terms to a **Main glossary** type.

You can export terms from a **Secondary glossary** type to a **Main glossary** type, one at a time. So, you can create a secondary glossary that students will add terms to. Then, you and/or the students can export the best terms to the main glossary. Imagine a course with one main glossary and a secondary glossary each time the course is run. The main glossary will become a repository of the best terms added by each class.

However, sometimes, you might wish to have entries automatically approved. In that case, you can request Moodle to approve them. We will learn how to do that next.

Entries approved by default

If you turn on the setting for **Approved by default**, as soon as a student adds an entry to a glossary, this entry will appear in the glossary. If it's turned off, the teacher will need to approve each entry.

If you turn this setting on and students add entries that you think are inappropriate, you can always delete those entries and turn the setting off.

If **Approved by default** is turned off, new terms will await the teacher's approval before being added:

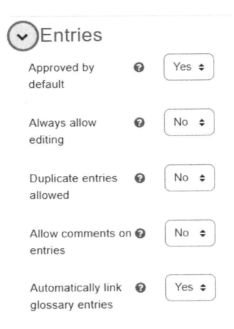

Figure 9.8 – Configuring entries in the glossary

If you would like the students to learn from each other by contributing definitions for the same term, you can set Moodle up so that they can contribute terms and then collaborate to come up with a final version. We'll discuss how to do that in an upcoming section.

Always allow editing and Duplicate entries allowed

Always allow editing and **Duplicate entries allowed** are two separate settings. However, they can work together in an interesting way.

If you turn on **Always allow editing**, students can edit entries that have already been made. So, if two students have different definitions for a term, they can each contribute their definition to the same entry. In this case, the second student will not need to create a duplicate entry; they can just add their definition to the existing entry.

If you turn the **Always allow editing** setting off, consider allowing duplicate entries. Then, if two students have different definitions for the same term, they can each create an entry for that term.

Allowing comments

If you turn the **Allow comments on entries** setting on, students and teachers can add comments to a glossary entry. These comments will appear at the bottom of the entry. Comments are visible to all the readers of the glossary.

Automatically linking glossary entries

If you turn the **Automatically link glossary entries** setting on, this will not always result in all entries becoming links on your course. Instead, when an entry is created, its editing page will have the option to turn on auto-linking for that entry.

As you develop your glossaries, you will need to think about how they will appear on the page. How many do you want to show on a page? Much depends on what the glossary entries are and how you plan to use them for collaboration.

Appearance settings

In the **Appearance** section, you will find settings that affect the presentation of the glossary. These settings affect the layout of the glossary page, how many entries are shown on a page, the links that users are given, and more.

Outcomes

Outcomes, also referred to as "competencies" or "goals," are descriptions of what the student has demonstrated after the completion of the activity or course.

Moodle 4.0 is flexible and designed to be used for courses in any possible delivery mode. The **Glossary** activity includes the outcomes, which enable you to indicate if you'll be using the glossary as a class participation activity, a supplement to a face-to-face course, or for team-based collaboration. Remember that to enable outcomes, you'll need to go to **Site administration** and select **Advanced features**. Then, click on **Enable outcomes** and save the changes. To add the course-level outcome, simply click on **Edit outcomes** from the link in **Course administration**. Then, click on **Add a new outcome**. Complete the form, and select **Save changes**.

After you've set up the outcomes, you might wish to set up the appearance. Here is the drop-down menu inside the **Appearance** menu:

Figure 9.9 – Configuring the Appearance menu in the glossary

To determine the best settings for your situation, experiment with the following steps:

1. Log in as a teacher.
2. Create a few glossary entries.
3. Open another browser, log in as a student, and open the glossary.
4. As a teacher, try different settings within the **Appearance** menu.
5. Each time you change the settings as a student, refresh the **Glossary** page:

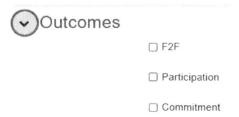

Figure 9.10 – Setting up the outcomes for the glossary

Including outcomes can be a great motivator. Three excellent ways to keep your students on track are to do the following:

- Connect the glossary to an assignment and include a due date so that it appears in the **Calendar** block of the dashboard.
- Manually add a calendar entry for the **Glossary** activity on specific days when you'd like students to add a glossary entry.
- Enable the **Check when complete** option in **Activity completion**, which will show up on the student's dashboard as a completed activity:

Figure 9.11 – Specifying how students track activity completion and making sure this shows up on the calendar in the student's dashboard

Functionality booster – enabling ratings

You can give students the ability to rate glossary entries, just like they can rate forum postings. The question is what do you want students to rate? The glossary entry's clarity, its helpfulness, or your writing skill in creating an entry? You'll need to consider what you want students to rate and create a custom scale that supports that rating. The criteria can align with the learning objectives and the learning plan. For example, they could tie to activities that align with "identify," "describe," and "explain." You can determine who can rate glossary entries, along with what scale to use, on the **Settings** page:

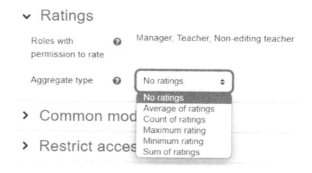

Figure 9.12 – Selecting the rating scale on the Ratings settings page

Note that only the **Manager**, **Teacher**, and **Non-editing teacher** roles can rate the entries in this glossary. In the next step, the teacher modifies the permissions to allow students to rate entries, too.

The following is the process to allow students to rate glossary entries. It consists of three parts:

- Creating the rating scale
- Selecting the scale for the glossary
- Giving students permission to use the ratings

In order to make it possible for the learners to easily rate the entries, it is necessary to create a rating scale. The following steps show you how to create a rating scale:

1. Select **Administration | Grade administration | Scales**:

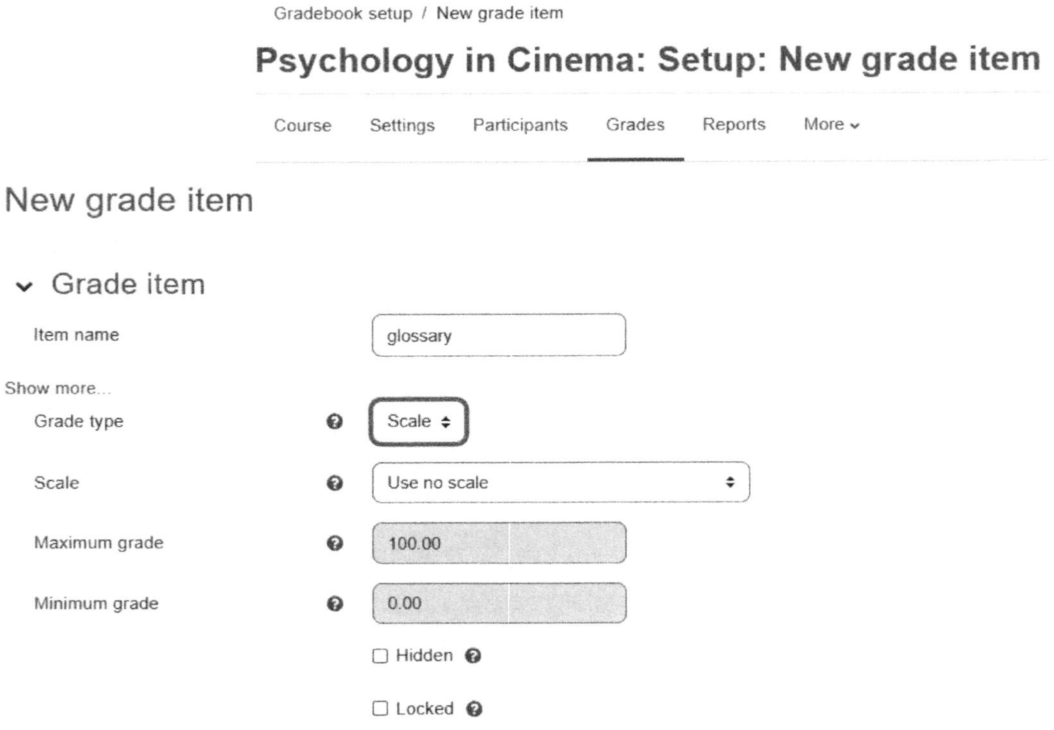

Gradebook setup / New grade item

Psychology in Cinema: Setup: New grade item

Course   Settings   Participants   Grades   Reports   More ⌄

New grade item

⌄ Grade item

Item name		glossary
Show more...		
Grade type	❓	Scale ⬍
Scale	❓	Use no scale ⬍
Maximum grade	❓	100.00
Minimum grade	❓	0.00
		☐ Hidden ❓
		☐ Locked ❓

Figure 9.13 – Setting up grading for the glossary

2. Click on the **Add a new scale** button.

3. On the new **Scale** page, give a name to the scale. Note that only the teacher can see this name.

4. In the **Scale** field, enter the values that the user will select in order to give the glossary definition a rating. The scale must have more than two items.

5. In the **Description** field, enter a short description. This will help you remember the purpose of this scale.

6. **Save** your changes.

The following steps show you how to select the scale for the glossary:

1. Navigate to the **Settings** page of the glossary.

2. In the **Scale** field, select the scale that you have just created.

3. Modify any other settings that you want on this page,

4. **Save** your changes.

For students to be able to actually implement the ratings, you'll need to turn on the permissions. To give students permission to use ratings, perform the following steps:

1. From the main menu, select **Administration | Glossary administration | Permissions**:

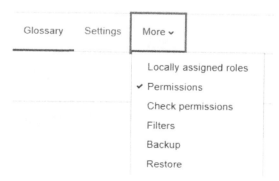

Figure 9.14 – Setting permissions for the glossary ratings

2. On the **Permissions** page, scroll down to the **Activity: Glossary** section.

3.   Click on the plus sign located next to **Rate entries**:

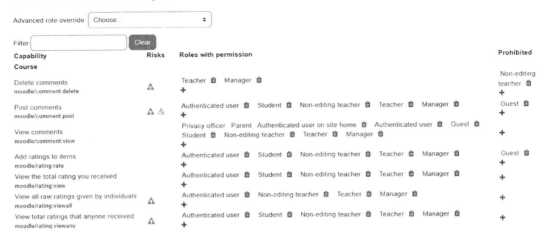

Figure 9.15 – Giving students permission to rate entries

4.   Select the role that you want to add to this permission, and then click on the **Allow** button.

Once roles have been enabled, students and anyone who has permission to create glossary entries can now begin adding glossary entries.

Adding glossary entries

Selecting a **Glossary** activity from the course menu displays the glossary's introductory page. From this page, you can edit and browse the glossary.

The following screenshot shows the **Add a new entry** button, which appears under every tab in the glossary:

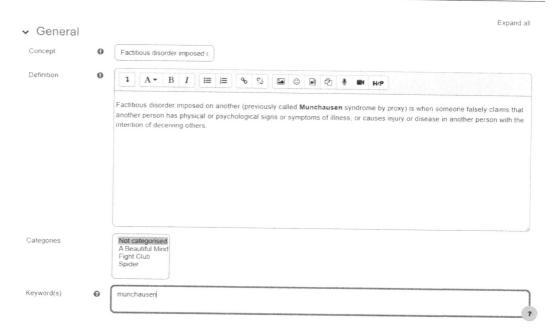

Figure 9.16 – The Add a new entry button allows you to create another glossary entry

Create new **Glossary** categories by navigating to the **Browse by category** page and then clicking on the **Add a new entry** button. This button appears under each of the tabs when you browse the glossary, so it's always available.

On this page, **Concept** is the term that you will add to the glossary. Keyword(s) are synonyms that are equivalent to a *See also* section in an index or dictionary. These terms will link to the same definition as the concept.

Note that you can add a picture or media file to **Description** using the icons in the toolbar:

You can also upload these kinds of files as an attachment, which is what this user chose to do.

If auto-linking has been enabled, the bottom half of **Add a new entry** contains the settings, as shown in *Figure 9.17*:

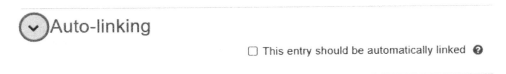

Figure 9.17 – Another auto-linking screen

When the glossary term appears within your course, you can have it linked to its glossary entry. The **Auto-linking** option determines if and when this word should link to its glossary entry.

Once you have a number of glossary entries, you might wish to use them in different applications and even share them with other instructors or put them on other courses. You can do that by importing and exporting entries, which we will address in the next section.

Importing and exporting entries

The **Import entries** and **Export entries** links enable the teacher to exchange glossaries between courses and even Moodle installations:

Figure 9.18 – The list of settings allows you to import and export glossaries
and glossary entries between courses

You might want to begin a course with a small glossary and let students add to it as they discover new concepts. If you do this, export the beginning glossary so that it is available for the next course. The next time you teach a course, you can choose to export everything from the completed course (except the student information and the glossary). In the new copy, just create a new and blank glossary and import the beginning glossary.

Also, note that the editing window enables you to include hyperlinks in the definition (via the ⚙ icon). This can be used to link to freely available information on the web, such as http://www.wikipedia.org/.

A glossary is effective for learning activities, whether individual or collaborative, that center around definitions. In this case, the learning objectives that are satisfied tend to be at the lower levels of Bloom's taxonomy, in the "Remember" category, which is at the base of the pyramid. To be able to satisfy higher-level cognitive skills and demonstrate mastery of the higher levels of Bloom's taxonomy, you can choose a wiki. Moodle has a very robust and flexible wiki that we will explore in the next section.

Wiki

The Moodle Wiki module enables students to collaborate on a group writing project, build a knowledge base, and discuss class topics. Students can also collaborate on developing rating criteria for a competition, a team-led event, or a business plan for a start-up company or organization.

Here is Moodle 4.0's redesigned Wiki icon:

Wiki

Figure 9.19 Wiki icon

As a wiki is easy to use, interactive, and organized by date, it encourages collaboration among its participants. This makes it a powerful tool to create group knowledge. The key difference between a forum and a wiki is that when users enter a forum, they see a thread devoted to a topic. Each entry is short. Users read through the thread, one entry at a time. The result is that the discussion becomes prominent. In a wiki, users see the end result of the writing. To see the history of the writing, they must select a **History** tab. The result is that the end result of the writing becomes prominent.

Older wiki content is never deleted and can be restored. Additionally, wikis can be searched just like other course material. In the following section, we'll look at the settings on the **Editing wiki** page and how they affect user experience. There are advantages to using the wiki in Moodle. Collaborating using Google Docs or Teams/Sharepoint is similar in the sense that everyone can contribute. However, if students lose access to the outside platform (Google or Microsoft), they're unable to continue to contribute.

Using a wiki for student contributions and explanations of a topic

A wiki can be used to help explain a topic. For example, let's say that a course on entrepreneurship is planning to have a start-up competition. It will be useful to include a list of criteria for judging. Additionally, it will be very useful to include a wiki that contains definitions, processes, and procedures. It's a useful tool for instruction because the instructor can provide guidelines and pointers.

Using a wiki to create a list of judging criteria for evaluating a competition

Shark Tank (or *Dragon's Den* in the UK) is a popular show on television in which entrepreneurs come before a panel of potential investors and make presentations to entice the panel members to invest. It is an entertaining and informative program, and having *Shark Tank/Dragon's Den* as a class project can be equally informative, entertaining, and engaging.

One good way to plan a student *Shark Tank/Dragon's Den* project is to use a wiki. The first step will be to set up a list of judging criteria along with a clear set of guidelines that indicate what is expected in an outstanding *pitch* that will convince the investor to put money into the project or start-up company. Then, the students can also share their evaluations of the start-up pitches in the competition:

Figure 9.20 – How the wiki appears on the course page

Another excellent use of a wiki is to keep a collaborative journal:

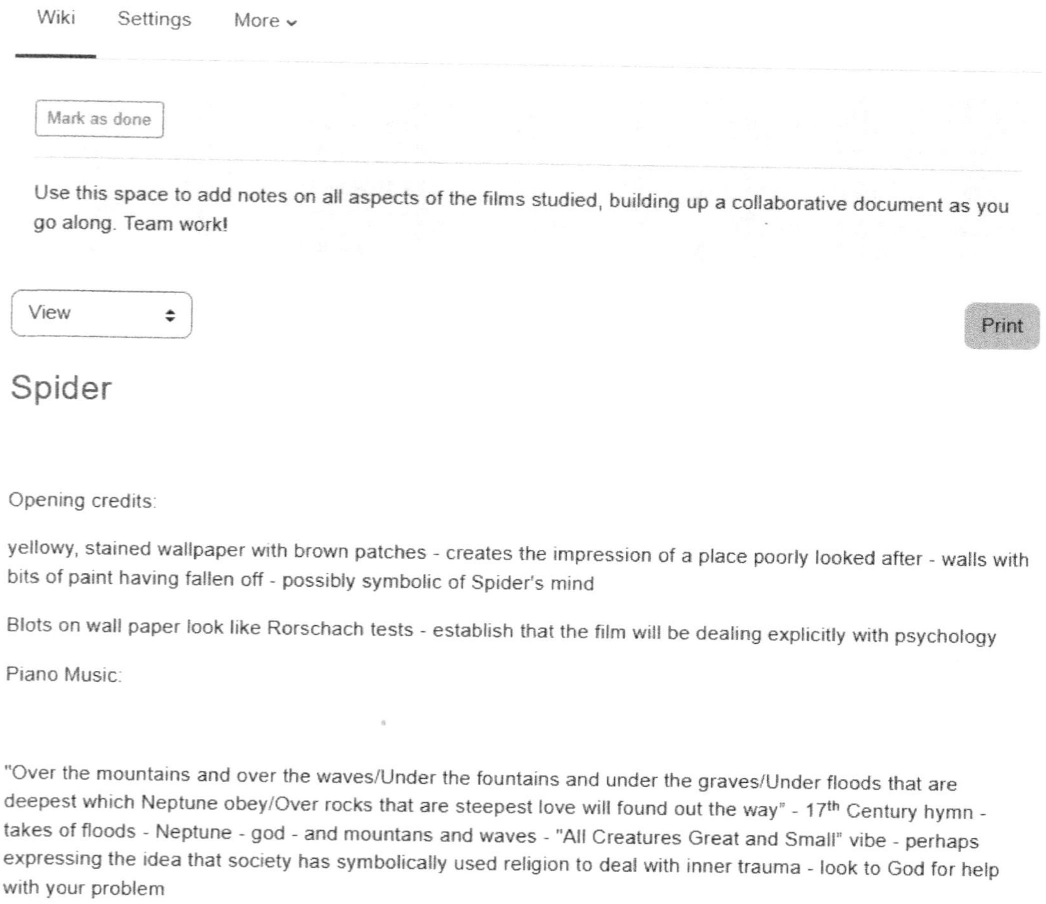

Wiki   Settings   More ⌄

Mark as done

Use this space to add notes on all aspects of the films studied, building up a collaborative document as you go along. Team work!

View   ⇕   Print

Spider

Opening credits:

yellowy, stained wallpaper with brown patches - creates the impression of a place poorly looked after - walls with bits of paint having fallen off - possibly symbolic of Spider's mind

Blots on wall paper look like Rorschach tests - establish that the film will be dealing explicitly with psychology

Piano Music:

"Over the mountains and over the waves/Under the fountains and under the graves/Under floods that are deepest which Neptune obey/Over rocks that are steepest love will found out the way" - 17th Century hymn - takes of floods - Neptune - god - and mountans and waves - "All Creatures Great and Small" vibe - perhaps expressing the idea that society has symbolically used religion to deal with inner trauma - look to God for help with your problem

Figure 9.21 – An example of a collaborative wiki

You can switch to the **History** view to see who has commented and when:

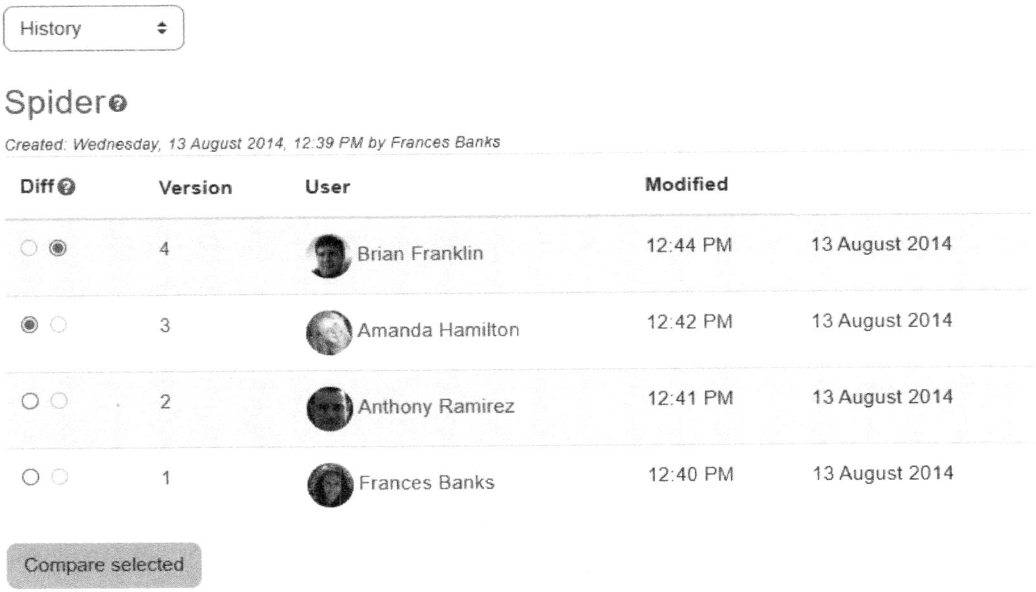

History   ⬍

Spider⊘

Created: Wednesday, 13 August 2014, 12:39 PM by Frances Banks

Diff⊘	Version	User	Modified	
○ ◉	4	Brian Franklin	12:44 PM	13 August 2014
◉ ○	3	Amanda Hamilton	12:42 PM	13 August 2014
○ ○	2	Anthony Ramirez	12:41 PM	13 August 2014
○ ○	1	Frances Banks	12:40 PM	13 August 2014

Compare selected

Figure 9.22 – The History view of the wiki allows you to see who has posted and when

Planning collaborative projects – using the wiki type and groups mode to determine who can edit a wiki

There are several ways to use wikis that focus on a collaborative, actionable project rather than creating a simple repository of knowledge. In the case of *Shark Tank*, one collaborative activity could be to develop a business plan. Another could be to develop a directory of potential financial backers, which could include angels, venture capital firms, private equity firms, and partners who will help commercialize the product.

Event planning

A wiki can be used to identify the tasks, roles, and resources of an event. For example, let's take the task of planning a wedding. There will be many different elements, ranging from the flowers, the decorations during the wedding ceremony, the reception, the catering, the invitations, and more. The wiki can be used to identify the different tasks, and then further define and refine the tasks as they are listed. Following this, the wiki can be taken one step further and be used for developing a timeline with action steps.

Business plan for a start-up

As mentioned earlier, a class in entrepreneurship that includes a *Shark Tank* competition would be the perfect place to have a collaborative business plan. The wiki can contain the following elements:

- Key elements of a business plan
- **Strengths, Weaknesses, Opportunities, Threats (SWOT)** analyses
- Financial projections
- Goals and desired outcomes
- Diagrams of the product
- Materials used to market the products

Using the wiki type and groups mode to determine who can edit a wiki

Wiki content is open to editing by the entire class, a group, the teacher, or a single student. Additionally, the wiki can be available for viewing by the entire class, a group, the teacher, or a single student. Note that the teacher determines who can see and edit the wiki content; the settings differ.

The settings for who can edit the wiki content are done using the **Wiki mode** drop-down box.

The settings for who can simply see the wiki content are done using the **Groups** mode.

In this case, the wiki can double as a learning journal, which is a great place for students to develop reflection-based knowledge. Making a wiki editable by only a single student appears to turn the wiki into a personal journal. However, the difference between a single student wiki and a journal is that a journal can be seen only by the student and the teacher. You can keep a single student wiki private, or you can open it to change the settings and make it collaborative for the student's group or the entire class:

Single Student Wiki	Journal
Private? Optional	Yes
Collaborative with class	No

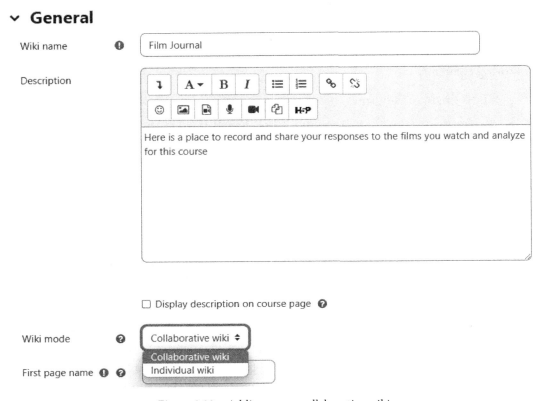

Figure 9.23 – Adding a new collaborative wiki

The first-page name

The name on the first page of the wiki will be taken from this field. A screen to add a page will pop up after you set up the new wiki. Teachers and administrators can delete pages. Students cannot.

If there is one wiki for the entire class, then when the first student enters the wiki, that student will see the starting page(s). If that first student edits any page, the next student who enters will see the edited version, and so on. If there is one wiki for each group in the class, each group will get a *fresh* wiki with the starting page(s) that you created. Also, if each student gets their own wiki, each student will see their starting pages when they enter their wiki:

Figure 9.24 – Adding the first-page name for the wiki

The default format

The **Default format** setting determines whether wiki authors use standard wiki markup or HTML code while editing. If you will use the HTML editor for other student activities, setting this to HTML can simplify this activity for your students. They will get familiar with the HTML editor and won't need to learn the wiki markup language. However, if your students are accustomed to wikis, you might want to select **Creole**. This enables them to use a common wiki markup, which is faster for experienced typists. Creole is a lightweight markup language, aimed at being a common markup language for wikis, enabling and simplifying the transfer of content between different wiki engines. **NWiki** is a wiki engine based on the SOA paradigm. It is a set of components and services to embed wiki capabilities in any .NET application.

If you do not select the **Force** format, then when a student enters the wiki, they will be able to use HTML for editing purposes. After you have created a new wiki, a screen will appear that allows you to start a new page. Take a look at the following screenshot:

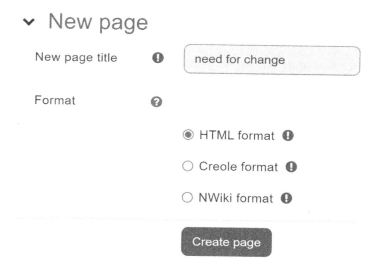

Figure 9.25 – Starting a new page with the Format options

As you can see, wikis are powerful and can be utilized in courses that require a group project, presentation, or proposal. The actual collaborative work can be done in both synchronous and asynchronous ways. For example, students can make contributions to the wiki asynchronously and then meet through Moodle's built-in web conferencing, BigBlueButton, or by linking to their own institution's subscribed platforms, such as Zoom or Teams.

Functionality booster

It is possible to collaborate using Google Docs, Microsoft Teams, or OneDrive, rather than doing all the collaboration within the glossary or wiki entries. This is highly recommended if several teams are collaborating or if there are different phases of a glossary or wiki entry (for instance, initial, revision, or an annotated bibliography). However, there are disadvantages if people are from different institutions, if they lose access to the outside platform, or if they run out of space there. There can also be security features and firewalls that could impede some users.

For example, one team could be in charge of posting the initial definitions. They could collaborate in Google Docs and then upload their final document to the glossary or wiki entry. The second team could go in and add references from refereed journals to specific terms. The third could add annotations:

Team 1: Enter the primary definition.

Team 2: Add key references from the refereed journals.

Team 3: Add annotations to the journals.

Each team would collaborate outside Moodle and then upload the clean, final version to add to the appropriate entries.

Now that we've taken a look at how glossaries and wikis work in Moodle, along with how they can blend with the cloud-based platforms that learners and institutions can use, we are ready to move on and work with them.

Summary

Moodle offers several options for students to collaborate on building a body of knowledge. For instance, a class can work together to build a glossary that can be imported and reused in future classes. They can work together to write a wiki, which provides an opportunity for them to organize their knowledge into a narrative. Moodle 4.0 is designed for maximum flexibility, and it puts social interaction at the heart of its core philosophy. That means that collaborative wikis and glossaries are perfect activities in Moodle 4.0, and they can be used in conjunction with 100% online activities alongside those that incorporate in-person, face-to-face interactions.

Both glossaries and wikis are very effective for a combination of synchronous and asynchronous learning. For example, group members can chat with each other as they develop their definitions (glossaries) or collaborative projects (wikis). Additionally, they can schedule synchronous web conferences by integrating and embedding BigBlueButton or linking to an outside platform such as Zoom, Google Meet, or Microsoft Teams.

Such engagement is highly motivating, and students will be more likely to stay involved with the course and also learn from each other. Incorporating collaborative glossaries and wikis can also help students feel more confident about learning and take their knowledge easily from coursework to real-world applications.

In the next chapter, you will learn how to use Moodle to run a workshop. In it, we will cover workshops, group projects, combinations of group and individual projects, workshop strategies, and the four phases of a workshop.

10
Running a Workshop

A workshop provides a place for students in a class to see an example project, upload their individual projects, and see and assess each other's projects. They are ideal for courses that include higher-level orders of Bloom's taxonomy of educational objectives, beginning with Analyze, Evaluate, and Create. When a teacher requires each student to assess the work of several other students, the workshop becomes a powerful collaborative grading tool. It is also an ideal tool for peer review.

Workshops are ideal for putting into practice a theory or a technique. They allow students to apply the concepts and also to take a building block approach, with guidance and help along each step of the way. In this chapter, you will learn about the following topics:

- Determining the best time to use a workshop
- Identifying when to incorporate group projects into the workshop
- Implementing various types of workshop strategies
- Detailing the main phases or parts of a workshop

In addition to applying knowledge, workshops encourage group projects and collaboration. The advantage of a workshop over using a wiki or a glossary as a collaborative project is that the workshops allow more options for bundling materials and activities, and there are also more options for assessment. Additionally, in the current learning environment that blends synchronous and asynchronous content, workshops can include "live" or synchronous presentations or panel discussions.

Moodle 4.0 has been designed for maximum flexibility. Workshops can be 100% online and also be done in conjunction with a face-to-face workshop with corporate or not-for-profit activities and training. They can be synchronous, asynchronous, or hybrid. Moodle 4.0's newly redesigned navigation helps students quickly find their way to the collaborative activities, and an updated dashboard can be configured so that students receive notice on the dashboard when a team member has posted. With one click, they're where they need to be. Furthermore, the workshop allows you to use a building block approach, where the concepts form the foundational underpinning, and group or individual projects, case studies, and presentations constitute the applications of the core concepts that are a part of the learning outcomes. By the end of this chapter, you will be able to design and configure a collaborative, peer-review workshop in Moodle.

Why use a workshop?

A workshop is a great way to boost the knowledge and skill level of a group very quickly. It helps people implement social constructivism by learning from each other, namely through peer review. Workshops in Moodle, such as those held in face-to-face settings, are great for getting students up to speed and functional with very little downtime. Usually, they focus on a single outcome, and they pare down the focus to ensure that the specific skill or knowledge set is achievable in a short period of time. For example, let's say that you have a course in entrepreneurship and the students are preparing to make group presentations on their start-up companies. A workshop gives them the perfect platform to develop and hone their presentations as a team and then present them to the overall class as a group.

The **Workshop** activity icon has been redesigned and deployed in Moodle 4.0. Notice how the new design emphasizes the idea that more than one person participates in a workshop, and that it involves communication and collaboration:

Workshop

Figure 10.1 – Workshop icon

In Moodle, the ideal workshops are collaborative and they require students to interact with peer reviews and share knowledge and information. Further, they involve creativity that is focused on the course learning objectives and outcomes. They are flexible and allow you to use both synchronous and asynchronous delivery. So, for example, if you have final presentations that are "live" and you'd also like to archive them, the Workshop gives you the perfect platform. Individuals work together to create their final products such as presentations. Then, they log into the institution's webinar platform (for example, Zoom, Teams, BigBlueButton, or even YouTube Live), and everyone can view it, comment, and save it for later in the archive.

If your students are very creative and would like to conduct their workshop collaborations and final presentations in a virtual world, they might want to use Facebook's Metaverse or record themselves interacting via avatars in Google Earth VR. For example, the workshop might be a field trip for geology to look at other locations using "street view" on Google Earth.

In the next section, we will look at when to incorporate group projects inside a workshop.

When are group project-based workshops best?

Although students might initially dread having to work in a group, bear in mind that their hesitation usually has to do with feeling uncomfortable about the mechanics and feeling shy. After they feel a sense of competence and confidence, working together to complete a project can be one of the most fruitful learning experiences of their education. Not only do they learn about a topic or skill, but they also practice interacting with each other and their "soft skills" while working in a distributed environment, much like the one we work in today in our cloud-based, global workplace.

However, to avoid frustration, it's important to carefully choose how and when you have students work in groups. If you know your students have widely varying schedules, live in different time zones, and have variable access to high-speed internet, you might need to give them certain guidelines so that they will be very supportive of each other.

Group projects work best in many different situations. What they all have in common is that people are truly learning from each other:

- The students need to show competency in the same thing (for example, how to build a tiny home).

- The students do not have a lot of time, and the outcome needs to be very concrete and focused (for example, a market study for building a day spa as a part of a casino expansion).

- The outcome is easily evaluated; for example, the products can include a written report, graphics, maps, a presentation, and a video, all of which are uploaded onto the cloud and a link is provided (to avoid the problem of file size limitations).

- Individuals are motivated, and they see a concrete value in the ultimate product of the workshop. For example, the workshop product can help individuals land a job, launch a consulting business, or develop social media presence.

The skills being developed require interaction and live demonstrations, followed by activities that require the application of the concepts. Additionally, knowledge transfer is most effective if the participants are asking questions, interacting with each other, and doing informal peer assessments.

Once you think about your course, your learning objectives, and the potential for topics for group projects, it is good to move on to develop specific strategies that align your students with their activities and outcomes.

The big questions

The fields in the workshop window give you many choices. No matter what you enter in each field, your many decisions can be summed up as follows:

- What will you have each student do? Create a file offline and upload it to the workshop? Write a journal entry? Participate in an online chat? Perform some offline activity and report on it via an email or wiki? While the workshop window enables a student to upload a file, you can also expect another activity from the student. What kinds of assignments will be expected, and where will they be uploaded? For example, if there are synchronous presentations in BigBlueButton (or Teams or Zoom), where will the recording be uploaded? Where will you put the link?

- Who will assess assignments? Will a teacher assess all assignments? Will students be expected to assess other students' assignments? Will each student self-assess their work?

- How will the assignments be assessed? Bear in mind that you can use a rubric to set out the criteria on which each assignment is assessed, the grading scale, and the type of grading. When will students be allowed to submit their assignments and assessments? A good resource is Moodle Docs, which can be viewed at `https://docs.moodle.org/dev/Moodle_4.0_release_notes`.

The assignment becomes available as soon as you show it. However, you can expect students to assess an example before being allowed to submit their own work; additionally, you can set a deadline to submit the assessment.

Let's take a look at an example to demonstrate how it works. Bear in mind that this example is from the Moodle.org Mount Orange School demo site, which you can access at `http://www.moodle.org`.

In this case, the workshop involves the following scenario:

Imagine that you are a screenwriter and have been asked to adapt the setting of La Haine for your own country. Your peers will assess you on how suitable your adaptation is.

Here is what the description looks like in Moodle 4.0:

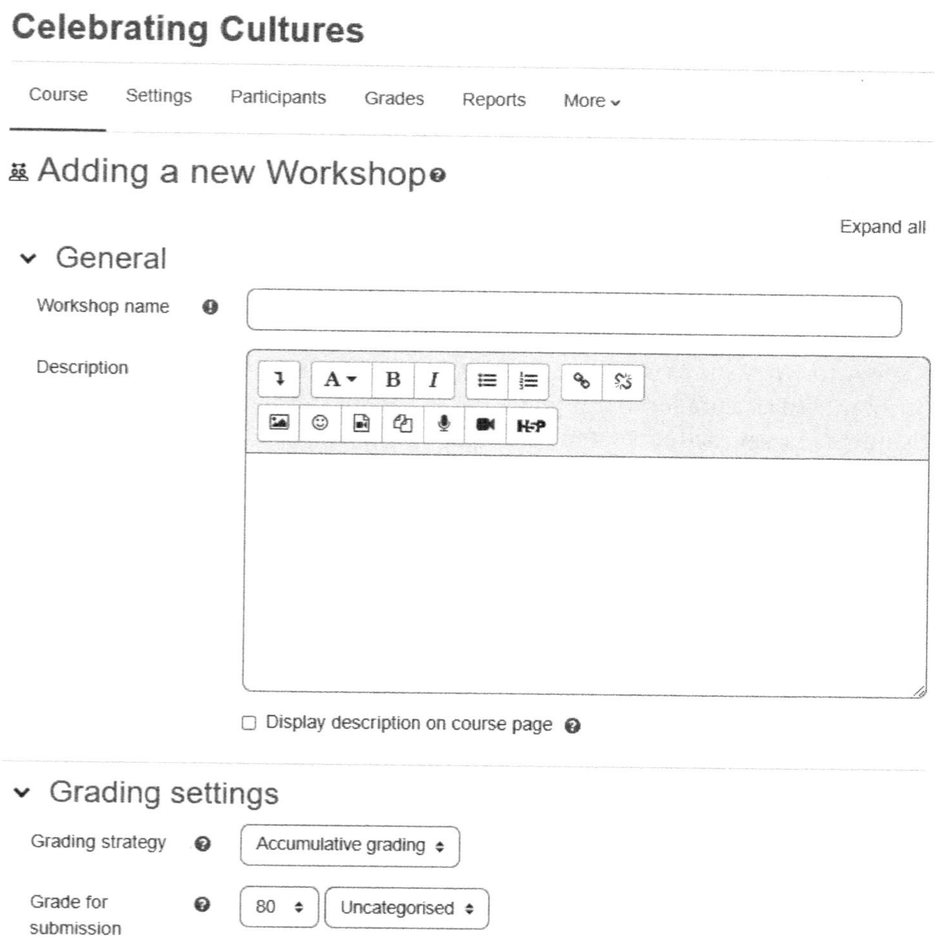

Figure 10.2 – An example of a workshop project

Next, let's take a look at the workshop strategies.

Workshop strategies

Workshops can be ungraded, peer-graded, instructor-graded, or a combination of peer- and instructor-graded. Workshops enable you to create very specific assessment criteria for graders to use. Also, workshops let you set due dates to submit grading work. You can use these and other features to build a strategy to make the best use of workshops within your courses:

Workshop				
Grading:	Ungraded	Peer-reviewed	Instructor-graded	Combination
Criteria:	No	Yes	Yes	Yes
Can set due dates:	Yes	Yes	Yes	Yes

Bear in mind that if you include peer assessments and required peer interactions, you'll be facilitating peer-to-peer learning. In other words, students will be learning from each other as they collaborate and create joint projects.

Peer assessment of submissions

One strategy for workshops is to have students assess each other's work before that same work is submitted as a graded assignment. For example, you can create a workshop in which students assess each other's subject matter, outlines, and hypotheses for their term papers, or they can assess each other's photos for specific technical and artistic criteria before they are submitted to the instructor for grading purposes. Additionally, you can ask students to assess their synchronous or recorded presentations with a special emphasis on real-world application.

The timing of submissions and assessments

Workshops enable you to set different due dates in order to submit work and assess other students' work. If you set both due dates at the same, many students might submit their work just before the submission deadline so that they cannot be assessed at all before the assessment deadline. Consider setting the submission deadline well before the assessment deadline. So, before opening up the assessment ability to students, examine the work submitted and ensure that it's close to what you expected or were trying to elicit from students. You might even want to use the time between the submission and assessment to refine your assessment criteria in response to the work submitted.

After you have developed your workshop strategies and set up the workshop in Moodle, you'll now enter into the actual functioning of the workshop. For convenience, it's useful to look at it as four phases or parts of the workshop. They consist of the setup, submission, assessment, and grading evaluation.

The four phases

When you run a workshop, you will go through four phases:

- **Phase 1**: The *setup* phase is when you create a workshop and choose settings for how it will work. You will learn more about the settings in the section entitled, *The setup phase - the edit settings page*.

- **Phase 2**: The *submission* phase is when students submit their work. Also, each student will be given assignments to assess the work of some other students. The assessments can be allocated automatically by a system, or a teacher can manually allocate assessments to students. Either way, at the end of the submission phase, each student will have submitted their work and been told to assess the work of one or several other students. Bear in mind that work is often submitted via a link to a cloud-hosted location for videos, audio, presentations, and more. This is important in order to avoid the file size limitations in Moodle.

- **Phase 3**: During the *assessment* phase, students will assess each other's work. The teacher will create assessment forms that students will use when conducting their assessments of each other's work. The forms will include prompts to encourage interaction and learning from each other. Their focus will be guided by the learning objectives.

- **Phase 4**: During the *grading evaluation* phase, students are given grades for how well they evaluated the work of their peers. This is the final phase of the workshop. Grading will tie to rubrics and also reinforce the corresponding levels of Bloom's taxonomy to make sure that you're achieving the learning objectives of the course.

In the next section, we will look at each phase of the workshop.

The setup phase – the edit settings page

The workshop activity is a powerful teaching tool that has many settings to consider. In the following description, we will just consider the important ones. Workshops are designed so that a student's work can be submitted and offered for peer review within a structured framework. There are several fields under a workshop, which will be explained in the following sections. They provide a place for students and teachers in the class to make the best use of Moodle:

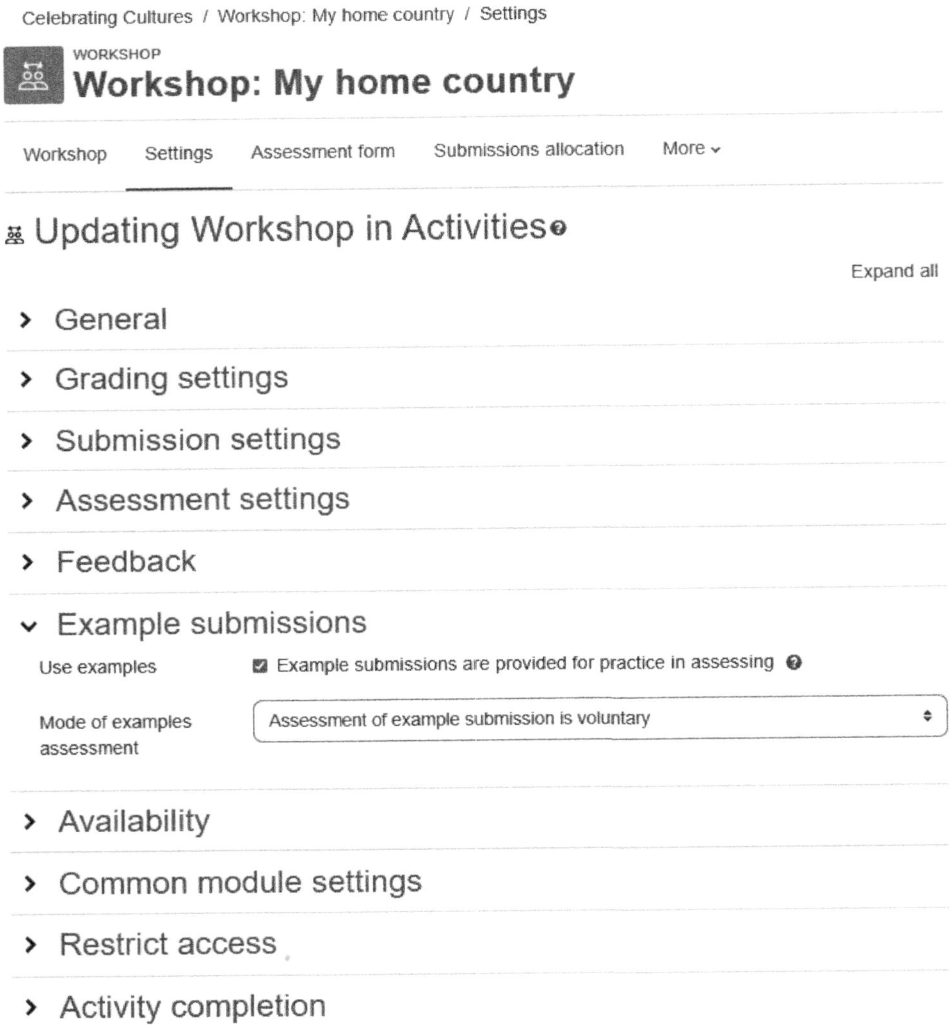

Celebrating Cultures / Workshop: My home country / Settings

WORKSHOP
Workshop: My home country

Workshop   Settings   Assessment form   Submissions allocation   More ⌄

⚖ Updating Workshop in Activities⊘

Expand all

> General

> Grading settings

> Submission settings

> Assessment settings

> Feedback

⌄ Example submissions

| Use examples | ☑ Example submissions are provided for practice in assessing ❷ |
| Mode of examples assessment | Assessment of example submission is voluntary   ⬍ |

> Availability

> Common module settings

> Restrict access

> Activity completion

Figure 10.3 – Customizable fields when setting up a workshop

Name and description

The settings under **General** partially answer the question, what will you have each student do? Be sure to describe the activity and to use the verbs that correspond to the level of Bloom's taxonomy. For example, if you have an entrepreneurship course and you're developing presentations for a *Shark Tank* pitch competition for start-ups, your description could be to create presentations for the pitches. You can use verbs such as design, assemble, construct, develop, or formulate (especially if you're asking them to incorporate a strategy):

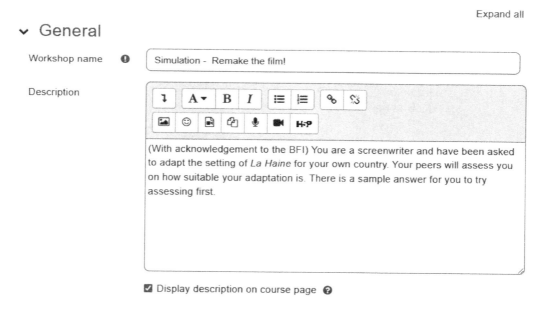

Figure 10.4 – Adding the name and description of the workshop

Your students will see and click on the **Workshop name** field. The **Description** field should give instructions on how to complete the workshop.

Grading settings

These fields determine the maximum points a student can earn for a workshop and how to calculate these points, as shown in the following screenshot:

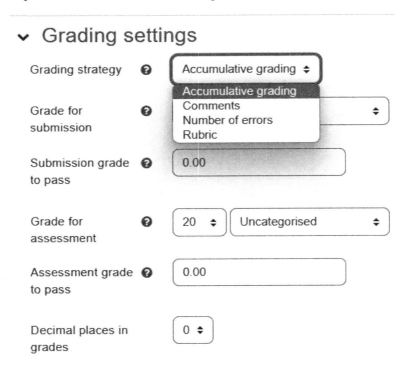

Figure 10.5 – Configuring the grading settings

The grading strategy

A workshop assignment is quite flexible in terms of the type of grading scheme used. This setting determines the overall scheme. This is a huge "plus" if your organization uses synchronous web conferencing as a primary strategy for student engagement and collaborative learning. You can set up your grading so that students receive points for their collaborative learning online (synchronous or asynchronous) and also for the final product.

In the **Accumulative grading** strategy, the grades are normalized so that they are out of 100 and then weighted. This style of grading enables you to present the reviewer with a numeric scale. Additionally, you can also present the reviewer with **Yes** or **No** questions. One of the questions is does this workshop meet the requirement? Alternatively, you can present the reviewer with a grading scale, such as **poor**, **fair**, **good**, and **excellent**. If you do use a **Yes** or **No** question, or a grading scale, you will assign a point value to each response. Consider informing the reviewer of the value of each response. For example, instead of just writing poor, fair, good, and excellent, consider writing poor (1 point), fair (2 points), good (3 points), and excellent (4 points).

When **Comments** is selected for **Grading strategy**, students can comment on each assessment element, but they cannot select a grade. However, teachers can grade students' comments. In this case, the workshop is transformed from where students grade each other to where the teacher grades each student's comments. The comments can be used for the collaborative "live" synchronous segments and asynchronous activities.

> **Tip**
> A workshop that uses **Comments** might be especially useful when you want to have a structured discussion on material that you present to students.

As a course creator, you can present your students with material that has been uploaded to the workshop or use the workshop's description to direct students to the material they must assess. After the students have viewed the material, they enter the workshop and leave comments according to the elements presented. As the workshop requires students to comment on clearly defined evaluation elements, the students' discussion is structured and kept on track.

When you choose the **Number of Errors** option, students evaluate a workshop with a series of **Yes** or **No** questions. Usually, you create questions to evaluate whether or not the submission met a requirement, such as `does the student have a variety of opinions?`

When writing one of these questions, ensure that it can be answered using only **Yes** or **No**. A sign that you need to revise your question is the presence of the word "or." For example, don't write "Did the student describe the plant well enough to distinguish it from others?" or "Is there still doubt as to which plant the student is describing?" Such a question cannot be answered with yes or no.

Sometimes, the answer to an evaluation question is very clear, and sometimes it is subjective. For example, the question "Did the student describe the plant well enough to distinguish it from others?" is subjective. One reviewer might think that the student did an adequate job of describing the plant, while another might think otherwise. These questions can be a good way to perform subjective peer evaluations of each student's work.

If the work requires a more objective evaluation (such as "Did the student include all five identifying features covered in this lesson?"), you might not need a workshop. This kind of objective evaluation can be easily performed by the teacher using an assignment.

For a rubric grading strategy, write several statements that apply to the project. Each statement has a grade assigned to it. The reviewers choose the one statement that best describes the project. This single choice completes the review.

You can create several such elements; the reviewers must select a statement for each of them.

Grade for submission is the maximum number of points a student can be given by a grader.

Grade for assessments is the grade that the student receives to grade other submissions. This grade is based on how close the assessment the student completes is to the average of all assessments for the same submission. For example, student A submits work, and students B, C, and, D assess the work and give scores of 10, 9, and 5. The average assessment is 8, so students B and C will receive higher marks for their assessments than student D. In essence, the grade for assessments is a grade given that evaluates how well a student assesses other students' work.

The Submission settings

The **Submission settings** page is where you enter instructions for your users. Additionally, you set limits on how many files students can upload to the workshop and how large those files can be. Often, it is best to include a link to the recording that they have uploaded to YouTube, Screencast-O-Matic, or even Slideshare if it is a presentation without a video. A team presentation might be the easiest to accomplish by having everyone log on and create a recording with Zoom or Teams, and then placing a link to it, rather than downloading the video file. In your instructions to the users, be sure to refer back to the assignment instructions.

The following screenshot is of the **Submission settings** page:

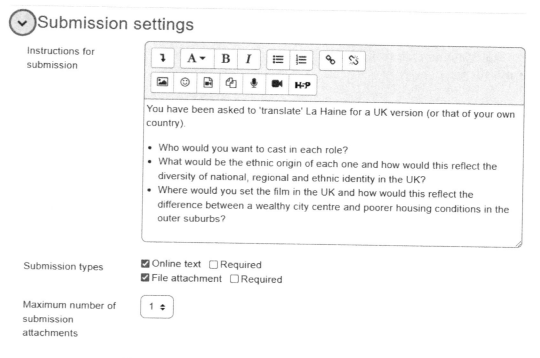

Figure 10.6 – Configuring the Submission settings page

The user will see the **Instructions for submission** label when they click on the workshop.

Both **Maximum number of submission attachments** and **Maximum submission attachment size** determine the size of a file and how many files the user can upload.

The **Late submissions** option allows users to submit their work after the deadline. The deadline can be set further down the page.

Functionality booster

You might ask your students to provide a narrated presentation or a video. These files can be quite large; however, in today's world, students will need to be able to create video content. It is a good idea to encourage students to upload their work to the cloud and then provide a link. For example, this can work with presentations in Screencast-O-Matic or a video on YouTube. You can upload videos to Teams, Google Drive, or other platforms, depending on the size. If you are recording on a platform such as Zoom, you will not have to upload it because it will already be there.

However, the downside is that access to the recording could expire. In that case, you might wish to download it too. This will help students avoid hitting the file size limit. You might wish to confine the apps to YouTube or Screencast-O-Matic and avoid TikTok, Facebook (Meta), Instagram, or other alternative platforms such as Rumble, Twitch, Odysee, BitChute, and more. It really depends on your institution and how stable the apps and platforms are.

Assessment settings

In this section, the settings are used to give the users instructions on how to perform their assessments and determine when to present the user with examples to assess.

The actual criteria used in the assessment are not created on this page. Instead, the criteria are created under **Administration | Workshop administration | Assessment form**.

We will cover the process of how to create the assessment form later. However, on this page, we will just give the user instructions for the assessment:

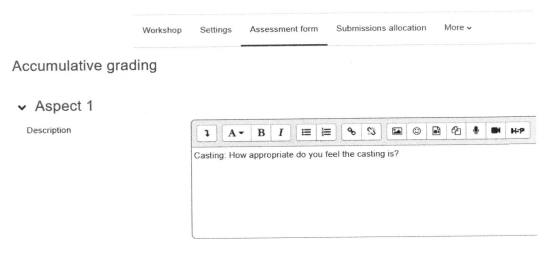

Figure 10.7 – Configuring the assessment settings

Feedback settings

If the **Overall feedback** mode is enabled, a textbox appears at the bottom of the assessment form. Students who will perform assessments can enter feedback into this textbox. You can make these comments optional or required.

The settings for feedback attachments determine whether the person who is assessing can upload a file(s) with their assessment. The student who submitted the work will see the attachment(s) with the assessment.

The **Conclusion** field gives the teacher a place to write a message that students can see after the workshop has finished. For example, you can instruct students to produce a new piece of work based on the feedback that they received during the workshop, instruct them to write a blog post reflecting on the activity, or just congratulate them on a job well done.

Example submissions settings

If the workshop uses examples, users can assess examples of work provided by the teacher. The user's assessment of the example is then compared to the assessment provided by the teacher. This enables users to practice assessing work before they assess each other's work:

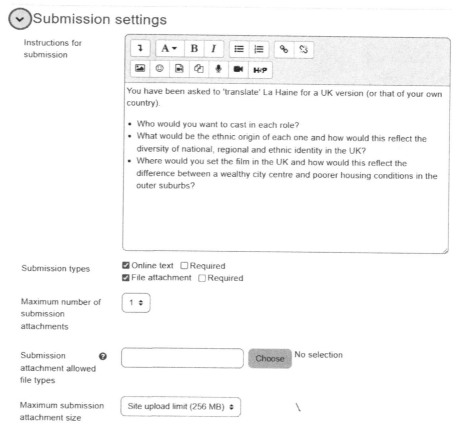

Figure 10.8 – The Submissions settings page

Users receive a grade for how well their assessment agrees with the assessment provided by the teacher. However, the grade is not counted in the grade book.

Availability settings

The settings in this section answer the following question: when will students be allowed to submit their assignments and assessments?

Note that the submissions and assessments can open on the same day. However, assessments cannot open before submissions (as there would be nothing to assess).

If you enable the **Switch to the next phase** setting after the submission deadline, then after the submission deadline, the workshop will automatically switch to the assessment phase. If you do not enable this setting, the teacher will have to manually advance the workshop to the assessment phase:

∨ Availability

Open for submissions from	15 ⇕	May ⇕	2022 ⇕	17 ⇕	36 ⇕	🗓 ☑ Enable
Submissions deadline	20 ⇕	June ⇕	2022 ⇕	17 ⇕	36 ⇕	🗓 ☑ Enable

☐ Switch to the next phase after the submissions deadline ❓

Open for assessment from	21 ⇕	June ⇕	2022 ⇕	17 ⇕	36 ⇕	🗓 ☑ Enable
Deadline for assessment	8 ⇕	July ⇕	2022 ⇕	17 ⇕	36 ⇕	🗓 ☑ Enable

Figure 10.9 – Availability

If you have the workshop automatically advanced to the assessment phase, you should also have the workshop automatically allocate assessments to the students. If the workshop doesn't automatically assign assessments to the students, it will advance to the assessment phase; there will be no assessments for students to perform. Setting up automatic allocations is performed under **Administration | Workshop administration | Submissions allocation | Scheduled allocation**:

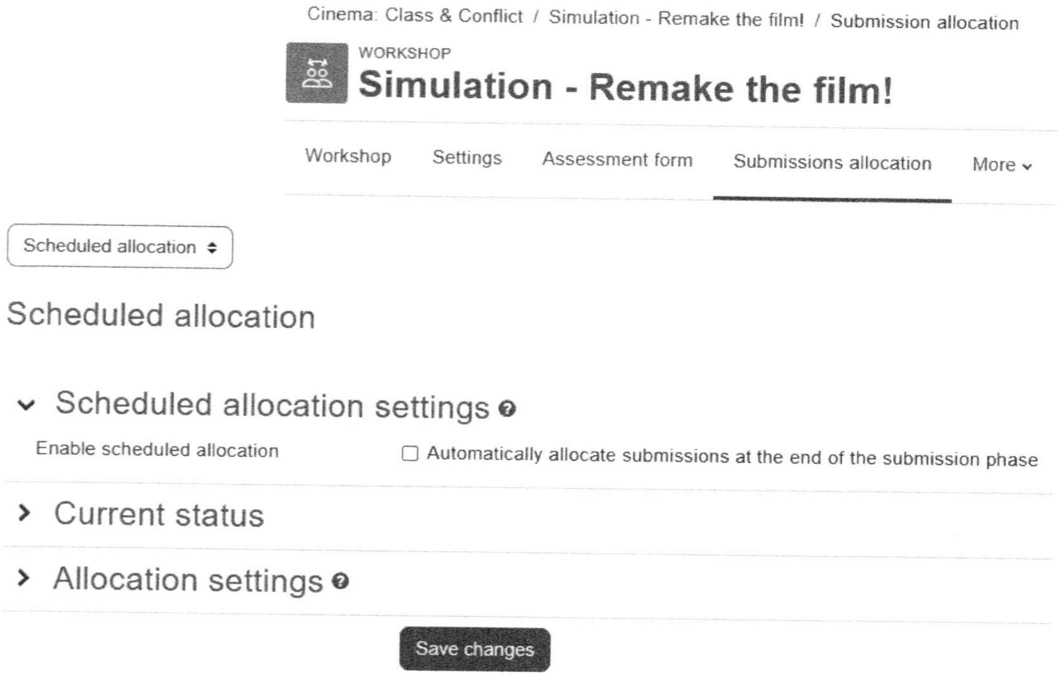

Figure 10.10 – The Scheduled allocation screen

The edit assessment form page

On this page, you enter the assessment criteria. The criteria should map to learning outcomes. So, you should refer to Bloom's taxonomy and use the verbs that correspond with the cognition levels. For example, if you are asking students to create a workshop that presents a pitch to attract investment to a start-up company, you might wish to use the verbs "design" or "develop" to indicate the higher-order act of creating. The exact contents of this page will change, depending on the type of assessment that you selected on the workshop settings page. In the following screenshot, the workshop grading strategy is set to **Accumulative grading**:

Figure 10.11 – Setting the aspects in the Accumulative grading screen

Making the maximum grade a multiple of the number of assessment elements enables students to more easily interpret their grades. For example, let's suppose a workshop is assessed for five elements. For each element, the assessor will choose from four statements:

- **A**: The workshop does not meet this requirement in any way (0 points).
- **B**: The workshop partially meets this requirement (1 point).
- **C**: The workshop meets this requirement (2 points).
- **D**: The workshop exceeds this requirement (3 points).

You can assign a point value of zero for each A selection, one point for each B selection, two points for each C selection, and three points for each D selection. Then, each element will be worth a maximum of three points. With five elements, the workshop will have a maximum grade of 15. This will make it easy for the student to interpret their grade.

When the student conducts an assessment, the assessment form looks similar to the following screenshot:

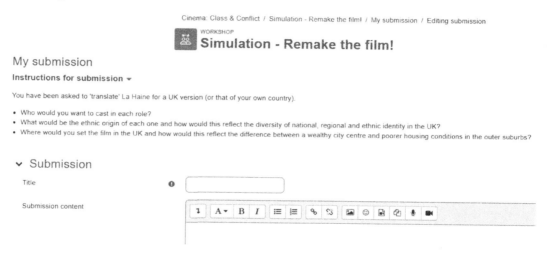

Figure 10.12 – The student view of the submission form

Note that for each assessment criteria, the student can enter comments.

Adding an example to the workshop

After you save the workshop settings and the assessment form, you can add an example to your workshop. Selecting a workshop will give you something similar to the following screenshot:

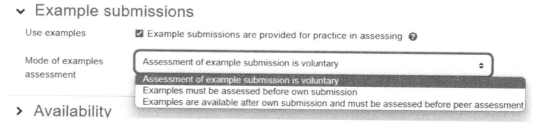

Figure 10.13 – Setting up an example for your workshop

To add an example submission, let's begin by clicking on the **Add example submission** button. In this case, it's the collaboratively created PowerPoint presentation that is the team's "pitch deck" for the *Shark Tank* workshop. This brings you to a page that displays the same assessment instructions that your users will see. This is where you can upload the example to be assessed:

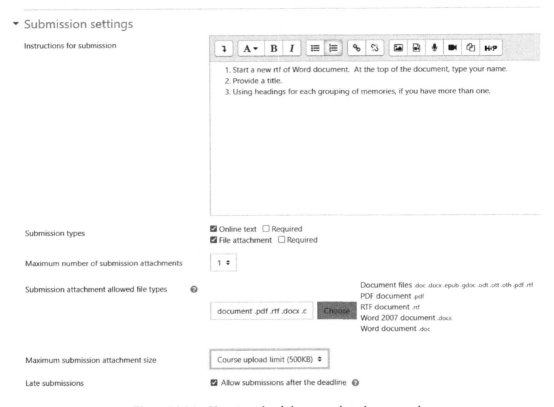

Figure 10.14 – How to upload the example to be assessed

To assess a submission, switch to the assessment phase and then scroll down to see the names of the people in the workshop and their submissions. Click on the submission to open it and begin to provide feedback:

First name ▲ ▼ / Surname ▼	Submission ▲ ▼ / Last modified ▲ ▼
Frances Banks	Wales modified on Saturday, 21 December 2013, 2:07 PM
Angela Bowman	Famous Belgians modified on Saturday, 21 December 2013, 3:28 PM
Lao Cai	My home modified on Friday, 20 December 2013, 10:45 AM

Figure 10.15 – Clicking on the name of the submission to assess it

After you assess the example, Moodle returns you to the workshop's home page. You will see the progress that you have made, which is indicated on this page:

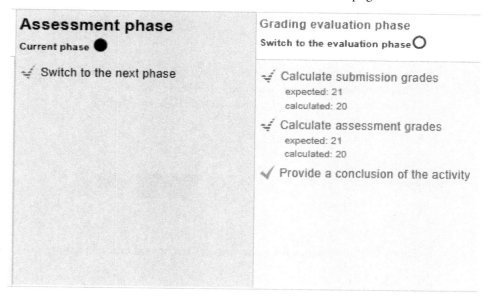

Assessment phase

Current phase ●

✔ Switch to the next phase

Grading evaluation phase

Switch to the evaluation phase ○

✔ Calculate submission grades
    expected: 21
    calculated: 20

✔ Calculate assessment grades
    expected: 21
    calculated: 20

✔ Provide a conclusion of the activity

Figure 10.16 – Switching to the evaluation phase; the current phase is gold

Note that the next step will be for the teacher to allocate the student submissions for assessment. However, no one has submitted anything yet. At this point, the teacher waits for students to submit their work.

The submission phase – students submit their work

Although the teacher has finished setting up the workshop and is ready for students to submit their work, students might still see this message: **The workshop is currently being set up. Wait until this is switched to the next phase.**

> **Tip**
> The teacher must manually switch the workshop from one phase to the next. Even if you're done with the setup and are ready to accept submissions, Moodle doesn't know that.

To switch to the next phase, the teacher must click on the light bulb before this phase. In our example, the teacher clicked on the light bulb before the submission phase and saw the following message:

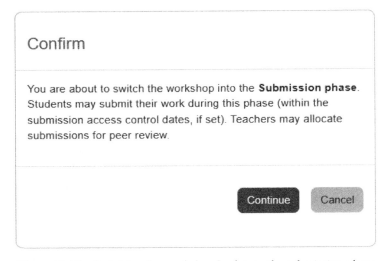

Figure 10.17 – Switching the workshop back into the submission phase

Now, when a student selects this workshop, they will see a prompt to submit their work:

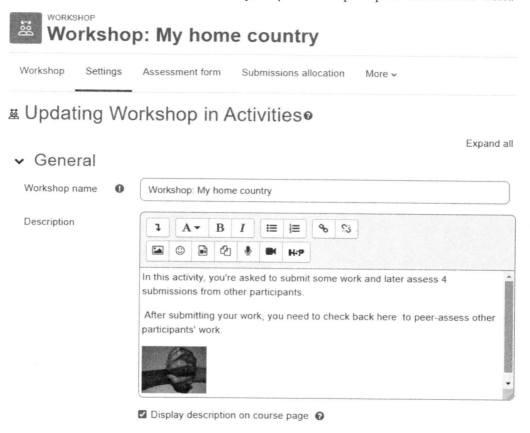

Figure 10.18 – The screen showing how to update the instructions for submissions

Note that the student can also assess the example at this point. In the settings page for **Mode of examples assessment** in this workshop, we selected **Voluntary**; therefore, this example is not required:

Figure 10.19 – The Mode of examples assessment option is set to voluntary

If we had made assessing the example mandatory, the student would receive a message indicating that they cannot submit work until the example has been assessed.

Allocating submissions

As soon as students begin submitting their work, you can start allocating these submissions to other students for assessment. Do this under **Workshop administration | Submissions allocation**. You can allocate submissions manually or randomly.

If you perform a random allocation, all the submissions that were sent up to that point in time will be allocated to other students for assessment. However, submissions sent after the random allocation will not be automatically allocated. You will need to perform another random allocation for the next submission, and so on until the workshop is complete.

The assessment phase

When you move the workshop to the assessment phase, the allocations that you made during the submission phase become available to students. In this phase, students will actually assess each other's work. All the work submitted for assessment appears on a single screen: the left-hand column includes the students' names, the middle columns are for the links to the file to submit, and the right-hand columns include the grades received and the grades given:

Figure 10.20 – The screen showing the work to be assessed and the assessments given

The grading evaluation phase

When you move the workshop to this phase, you can tell Moodle to automatically calculate the grades of students. Additionally, you can also override these grades and enter your own grades.

Note that, at this stage, students can no longer modify the submissions that they have sent in:

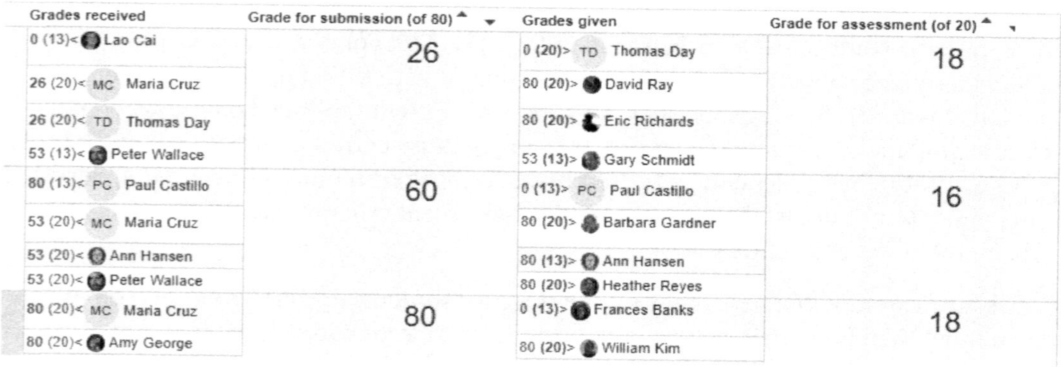

Grades received	Grade for submission (of 80) ▲ ▼	Grades given	Grade for assessment (of 20) ▲ ▼
0 (13)< Lao Cai		0 (20)> TD Thomas Day	
26 (20)< MC Maria Cruz	26	80 (20)> David Ray	18
26 (20)< TD Thomas Day		80 (20)> Eric Richards	
53 (13)< Peter Wallace		53 (13)> Gary Schmidt	
80 (13)< PC Paul Castillo		0 (13)> PC Paul Castillo	
53 (20)< MC Maria Cruz	60	80 (20)> Barbara Gardner	16
53 (20)< Ann Hansen		80 (13)> Ann Hansen	
53 (20)< Peter Wallace		80 (20)> Heather Reyes	
80 (20)< MC Maria Cruz		0 (13)> Frances Banks	
80 (20)< Amy George	80	80 (20)> William Kim	18

Figure 10.21 – Grade evaluation

The closed phase

When you close a workshop, the final grades are written in the course's grade book. These grades can be checked by students and administrators:

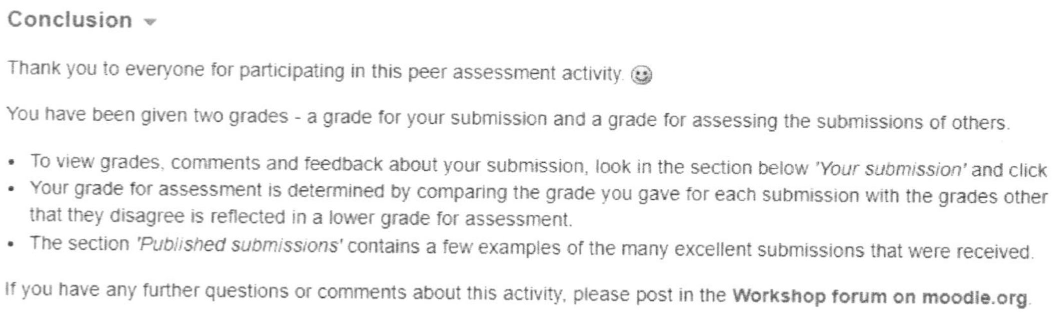

Conclusion ▼

Thank you to everyone for participating in this peer assessment activity. ☺

You have been given two grades - a grade for your submission and a grade for assessing the submissions of others.

- To view grades, comments and feedback about your submission, look in the section below 'Your submission' and click
- Your grade for assessment is determined by comparing the grade you gave for each submission with the grades other that they disagree is reflected in a lower grade for assessment.
- The section 'Published submissions' contains a few examples of the many excellent submissions that were received.

If you have any further questions or comments about this activity, please post in the **Workshop forum on moodle.org**.

Figure 10.22 – Message to students in the closed phase (an example)

Summary

Moodle offers several options for student-to-student and student-to-teacher interactions. When deciding which social activities to use, consider the level of structure and amount of student-to-student/student-to-teacher interaction that you want. For example, chats and wikis offer relatively unstructured environments with lots of opportunities for student-to-student interaction. They are good ways of relinquishing some control of the class to students. A forum offers more structure because entries are classified on the basis of topics. It can be moderated by the teacher, making it even more structured. A workshop offers the most structure, by virtue of the set assessment criteria that students must use when evaluating each other's work.

Workshops are collaborative. They set the stage for students to learn from each other. Even more than that, they include both formative and summative assessments, which is to say that students can check their progress toward achieving learning outcomes at multiple points along the way. Then, at the end, they have a chance to turn in a summative assessment – a project, presentation, portfolio, or something similar – in a supportive, nurturing setting, because they have been building each building block in a nurturing, supportive, encouraging environment.

In the next chapter, you will learn about groups and cohorts, and the differences between the two. You will see how to segregate students on a course into teams. Additionally, you will learn how to manage enrollments in a quick and efficient way using cohorts. In addition, you'll learn how to assess the individual students for their collaborative work.

11
Groups and Cohorts

People learn from each other. Moodle is designed for groups who work asynchronously as well as synchronously, in a blend of "on-demand" and "live" web conferencing. Being able to effectively coordinate activities so that groups and cohorts work well together will enable you to ensure that there are ideal conditions for learning, especially the collaborative learning that is so vital to online learning. Facilitating collaborative learning and communication between students is a straightforward process with groups and cohorts. Keep in mind that virtually all levels of learning can benefit from collaboration, from the lowest level of Bloom's taxonomy, Remember, which can include collaboratively defining terms, to the highest levels, Evaluate and Create, which can involve students working together to appraise, critique, design, and develop.

In this chapter, you will learn about the following topics:

- Using groups to build teams for collaboration and communication
- Differentiating between groups and cohorts
- How to mass-enroll students into courses
- How to manage students after they are enrolled

In the first section of this chapter, we will look at definitions of groups and cohorts in terms of how they relate to e-learners. We will then discuss when is the best time and way to organize students into groups and cohorts to achieve course learning objectives. By the end of the chapter, you will know how to create and manage groups and cohorts in Moodle.

Groups versus cohorts

Both groups and cohorts are collections of students. However, there are several differences between them. We can sum up these differences in one sentence, that is, cohorts are site-wide or course category-wide groups. Cohorts enable administrators to enroll and unenroll students en masse, whereas groups enable teachers to manage students during a class. So, you can think of a cohort as a collection of students who are staying together in order to complete an entire course or sequence of courses together. Groups are smaller sets of students within the course.

Here's another way to approach it: Think of a cohort as a group of students working together through the same academic curriculum; for example, a group of students all enrolled in the same degree program, and then they tend to have many courses together. For example, you may have a cohort (collection of students) who decide to pursue a Master's of Liberal Studies together. They will all be enrolled in the required sources together.

A group is different than a cohort. A group is at the course level rather than the degree program. Think of a group as a subset of students enrolled in a course. Groups are used to manage various activities within a course.

For example, members of a cohort may enter the degree program together, and they take the courses together in the same sequence. They have a lot in common because they have shared experiences, and over time, develop trust and long-term relationships.

The purpose of cohorts is to make it possible for all the members of a cohort to be enrolled in a course, with just a few clicks. We can do this with cohort sync, which synchronizes cohort membership with course enrollment.

There is a small amount of overlap between what you can do with a cohort and a group. However, the differences are large enough that you would not want to substitute one for the other.

We will start by looking closely at the primary characteristics of cohorts and examine how Moodle can be modified so that cohorts achieve the course and program learning objectives.

Cohorts

In this section, we'll look at how to create and use cohorts. You can perform many operations with cohorts in bulk, affecting many students at once. In general, cohorts consist of students who matriculate at the same time, and then take all their classes together, culminating in graduating together. For example, as in the case in the previous section, 20 students enter a master's degree program at the same time. They take three courses per term, and they do so at the same time. The students would interact with each other in each course, albeit in different ways. Over time, they would develop trust and they would learn from each other.

Creating a cohort

To create a cohort, perform the following steps:

1. From the main menu, select **Site administration | Users | Accounts | Cohorts**.

2. On the **Cohorts** page, click on the **Add** button. The **Add new cohort** page will be displayed:

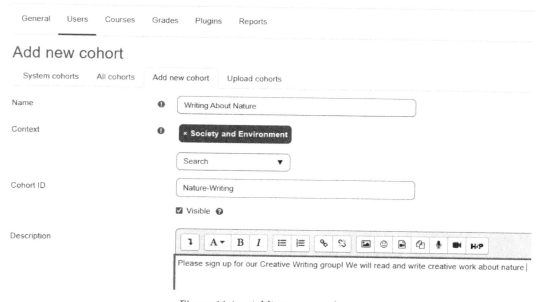

Figure 11.1 – Adding a new cohort

3. Enter a name for the cohort. This is the name that you will see when you work with the cohort. In this case, it is `Writing About Nature`.

4. Enter an ID for the cohort.

   If you upload students in bulk to this cohort, you will specify the cohort using this identifier. You can use any characters you want in the **Cohort ID** option; however, bear in mind that the file you upload to the cohort can come from a different computer system. To be safe, consider using only ASCII characters, such as letters, numbers, special characters, and no spaces in the **Cohort ID** option, for example, `Nature-Writing`.

5. Enter a description that will help you and other administrators remember the purpose of the cohort.

6.   Click on **Save changes**:

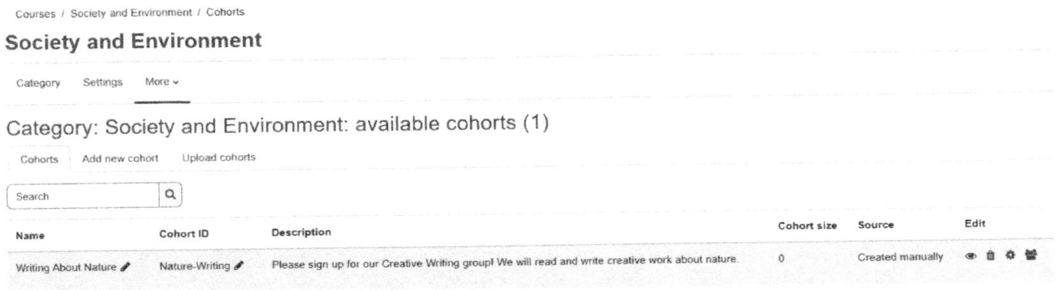

Courses / Society and Environment / Cohorts

Society and Environment

Category   Settings   More ⌄

Category: Society and Environment: available cohorts (1)

Cohorts   Add new cohort   Upload cohorts

| Search | 🔍 |

Name	Cohort ID	Description	Cohort size	Source	Edit
Writing About Nature ✏	Nature-Writing ✏	Please sign up for our Creative Writing group! We will read and write creative work about nature.	0	Created manually	👁 🗑 ⚙ 👥

Figure 11.2 – Describing the cohort within the category of Society and Environment

Now that the cohort has been created, you can begin adding users to this cohort.

Adding and removing students to and from a cohort

Students can be added or removed to a cohort manually by searching and selecting them. They can also be added in bulk by uploading a file to Moodle. Let's look at each of these methods in the next sections.

Manually adding and removing students from a cohort

We will look at how to manage cohorts and course enrollments in the *Cohort sync* section. For now, here are the steps on how to manually add and remove students:

1.   From the main menu, select **Site administration | Users | Accounts | Cohorts**.

2.   On the **Cohorts** page, for the cohort to which you want to add students, click on the **People** icon:

Edit

Figure 11.3 – The People icon

The **Cohort Assign** page will be displayed. The left-hand side panel displays users that are already in the cohort if any. The right-hand side panel displays users that can be added to the cohort:

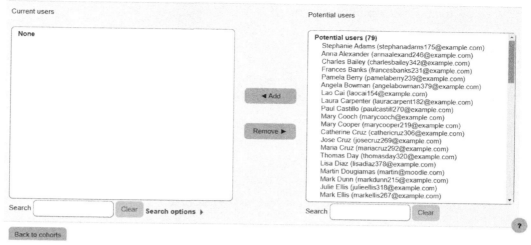

Figure 11.4 – The Cohort Assign page

Adding by uploading a file

In addition to manually adding individuals to the cohort, you can also upload cohorts by uploading a file:

Figure 11.5 – Uploading a cohort file

1. Use the **Search** field to search for users in each panel. You can search for text that is in the username and email address fields.

2. Use the **Add** and **Remove** buttons to move users from one panel to another.

Now that we have seen how to add or remove the students manually, in the next section, let's see how to add them in bulk to a cohort.

Cohort sync

By using the cohort sync enrolment method, you can enroll and unenroll large collections of students at once. The enrollment is automatic. Using cohort sync involves the following steps:

- Creating a cohort
- Enrolling students in the cohort
- Enabling the cohort sync enrollment method
- Adding the cohort sync enrollment method to a course

In the previous section, you saw the first two steps: how to create a cohort and how to enroll students in the cohort. In this section, we will cover the last two steps: enabling the cohort sync method and adding the cohort sync to a course.

Now we will focus on enabling a different type of enrollment. This one uses the cohort sync enrollment methods.

Enabling the cohort sync enrollment method

To enable the cohort sync enrollment method, you will need to log in as an administrator. Note that this cannot be done by someone who only has teacher rights:

1. Select **Site administration** | **Plugins** | **Enrolments** | **Manage enrol plugins**:

Enrolments

Manage enrol plugins
Cohort sync
Guest access
Manual enrolments
Self enrolment

Figure 11.6 – Managing enrollments

While you are on the **Plugins** page, you can click on **Manage enrol plugins** to open the screen to enable or disable the course enrolment plugins:

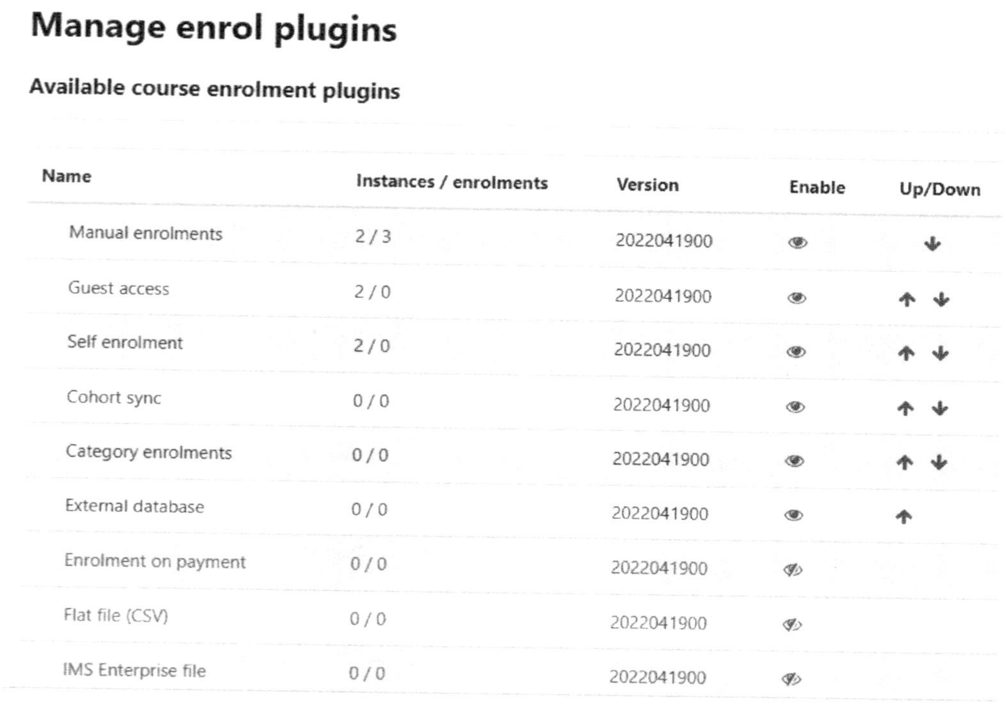

Manage enrol plugins

Available course enrolment plugins

Name	Instances / enrolments	Version	Enable	Up/Down
Manual enrolments	2 / 3	2022041900	👁	↓
Guest access	2 / 0	2022041900	👁	↑ ↓
Self enrolment	2 / 0	2022041900	👁	↑ ↓
Cohort sync	0 / 0	2022041900	👁	↑ ↓
Category enrolments	0 / 0	2022041900	👁	↑ ↓
External database	0 / 0	2022041900	👁	↑
Enrolment on payment	0 / 0	2022041900	👁	
Flat file (CSV)	0 / 0	2022041900	👁	
IMS Enterprise file	0 / 0	2022041900	👁	

Figure 11.7 – The types of course enrollment types that are available

2. Click on the **Enable** icon located next to **Cohort sync**.

3. Click on the **Settings** button located next to **Cohort sync**:

Cohort sync

Cohort enrolment plugin synchronises cohort members with course participants.

Default role enrol_cohort | roleid	Student ⇕	Default: Student
External unenrol action enrol_cohort | unenrolaction	Unenrol user from course ⇕	Default: Unenrol user from course

Select action to carry out when user enrolment disappears from external enrolment sc

Save changes

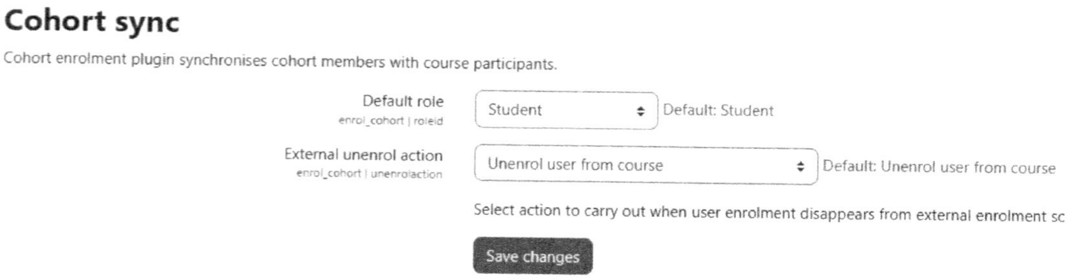

Figure 11.8 – The Cohort sync settings

4. From the **Settings** page, choose the default role for people when you enroll them in a course using **Cohort sync**. You can change this setting for each course.

5. You will also choose the **External unenrol action** option. This is what happens to a student when they are removed from the cohort.

6. If you choose **Unenrol user from course**, the user and all their grades are removed from the course. The user's grades are purged from Moodle. If you were to read this user to the cohort, all the user's activity in this course will be blank, as though the user was never in the course.

7. If you choose **Disable course enrolment** and remove the roles, the user and all their grades will be hidden. You will not see this user in the course's grade book. However, if you were to re-enroll this user to the cohort or the course, this user's course records will be restored.

After enabling the cohort sync method, it's time to actually add this method to a course.

Adding the cohort sync enrollment method to a course

To perform this, you will need to log in as an administrator or a teacher in the course. Perform the following steps:

1. Log in and enter the course to which you want to add the enrolment method.

2. Select **Course administration | Participants | Enrolment methods**:

Figure 11.9 – The enrollment methods from the drop-down menu

3. From the **Add method** drop-down menu, select **Cohort sync**:

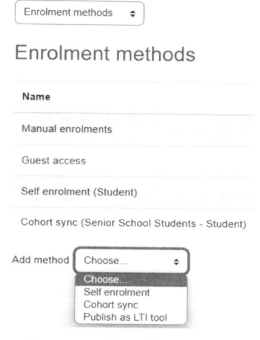

Figure 11.10 – The enrollment methods

4. In **Custom instance name**, enter a name for this enrollment method. This will enable you to recognize this method within a list of cohort syncs.

5. For **Active**, select **Yes**. This will enroll the users.

6.   Select the **Cohort** option:

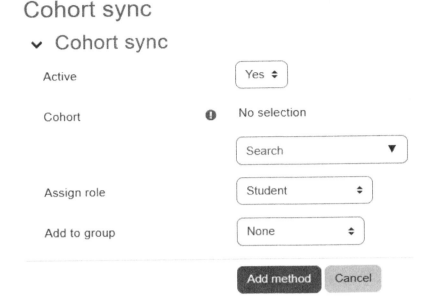

Figure 11.11 – Cohort sync activation

7.   Select the role that the members of the cohort will be given.

8.   Click on the **Save changes** button.

All the users in the cohort will be given a selected role on the course. Next, we will learn how to unenroll from a course.

Adding students to a cohort in bulk – uploading

When you upload students to Moodle, you can add them to a cohort.

Once you have all the students inside a cohort, you can quickly enroll and unenroll them to and from courses just by synchronizing the cohort to the course. If you wish to upload students in bulk, consider putting them in a cohort. This makes it easier to manipulate them later.

Here's an example of cohorts. Note that there are students enrolled in the cohort:

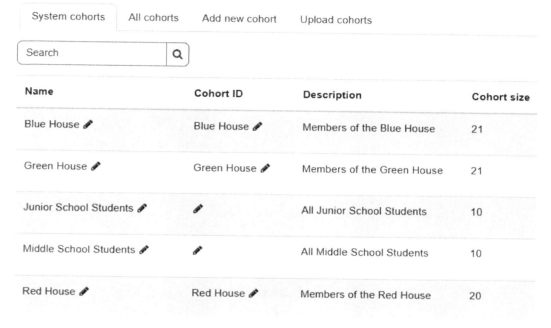

Figure 11.12 – Available cohorts

These students were uploaded to the cohort under **Site administration | Users | Accounts | Upload users**:

Figure 11.13 – Uploading users

After clicking on **Upload users**, the following opens:

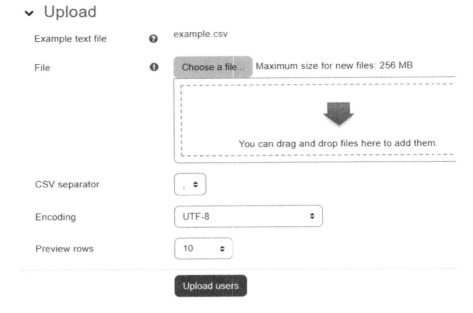

Figure 11.14 – Uploading students to the cohort under Site administration

The Excel file that was uploaded contained information about each student in the cohort. In a spreadsheet, this is what the file looks like. To make sure you keep track of the field names, you can place them in the first row to label each column. For more details on how to configure a file to upload to Moodle 4.0. Additionally, to test a file (such as the one displayed in the following screenshot), visit https://docs.moodle.org/400/en/Upload_cohorts#Valid_upload_file_for_testing:

username	password	firstname	lastname	email	sysrole1
efernandez		emilio	fernandez	efernandez@123.com	coursecreator
jbustillo		juan	bustillooro	jbustillo@123.com	coursecreator
bdipalma		brian	dipalma	bdipalma@123.com	coursecreator
kbigelow		kathryn	bigelow	kbigelow@123.com	manager
scoppola		sofia	coppola	scoppola@123.com	coursecreator

Figure 11.15 – Uploading an Excel file that contains cohort information

In this example, we have the minimum required information to create new students. They are listed as follows:

- The username
- The email address
- The first name
- The last name

Additionally, we have the cohort ID (the short name of the cohort) in which we want to place a student.

During the upload process, you can see a preview of the file that you will upload:

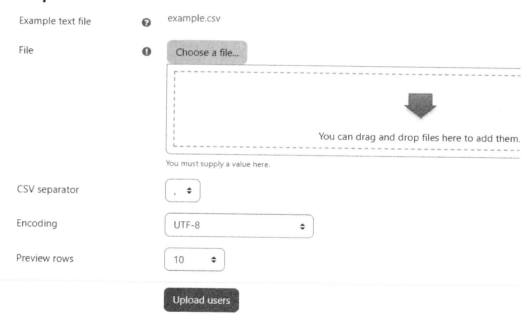

Figure 11.16 – A preview of the file that you will upload

Usually, when we upload users to Moodle, we create new users. However, we can also use the upload option to quickly enroll the existing users in the cohort.

> **Tip**
>
> In the *Manually adding and removing students from a cohort* section, you learned how to search for and then enroll users in a cohort.
>
> However, when you want to enroll hundreds of users in the cohort, it's often faster to create a text file and upload it than to search your existing users. This is because when you create a text file, you can use powerful tools, such as spreadsheets and databases, to quickly create this file. If you want to perform this, you will find the option to **Update existing users** under the **Upload type** field.

When you upload a user to a system, you can specify the city and country in the upload file or omit them from the upload file and assign the city and country to the system while the file is being uploaded. In addition, you can upload user pictures. This is performed under **Upload user pictures** on the **Users** page:

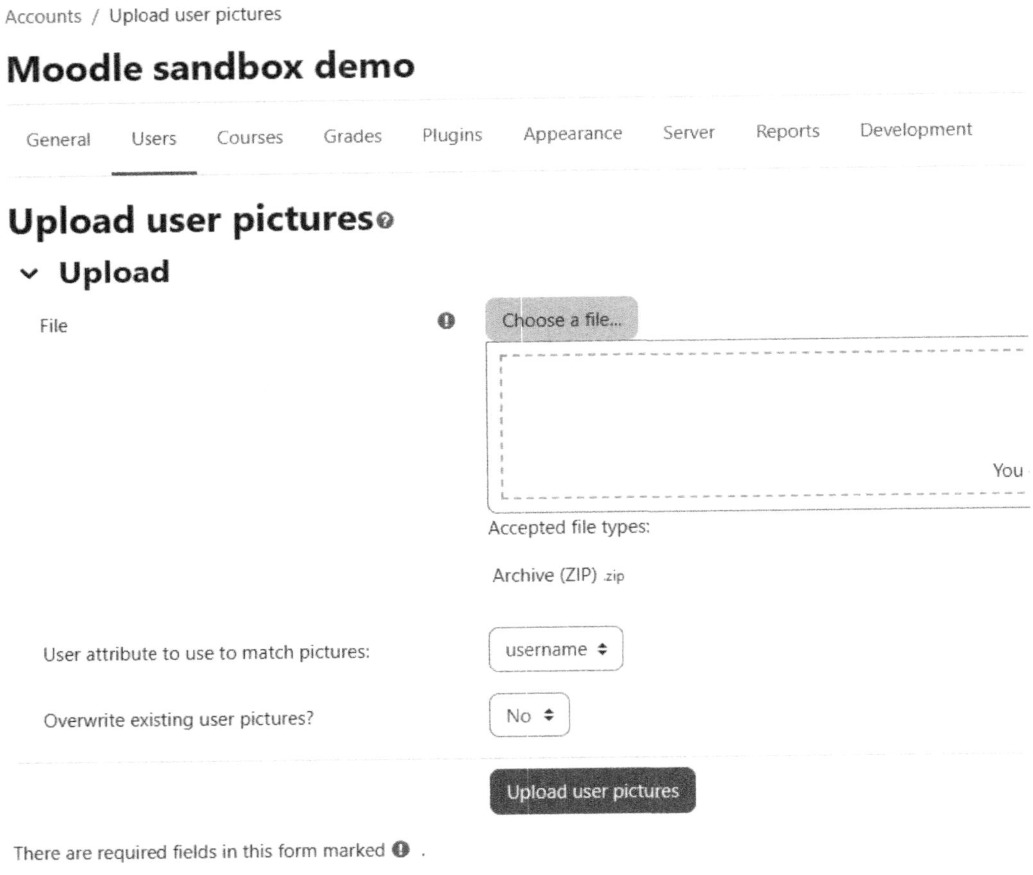

Accounts / Upload user pictures

Moodle sandbox demo

General   Users   Courses   Grades   Plugins   Appearance   Server   Reports   Development

Upload user pictures⊘

⌄ Upload

File   ❶   [Choose a file...]

                                          ┌ - ┐
                                          ¦   ¦
                                          ¦   ¦
                                          ¦   ¦
                                          ¦   You ¦
                                          └ - ┘

                                          Accepted file types:

                                          Archive (ZIP) .zip

User attribute to use to match pictures: [username ↕]

Overwrite existing user pictures?   [No ↕]

                                          [Upload user pictures]

There are required fields in this form marked ❶ .

Figure 11.17 – The Upload user pictures screen

Now that we have examined some of the capabilities and limitations of this process, let's list the steps to upload a cohort to Moodle.

Follow these steps to upload a cohort to Moodle:

1. Under **Administration | Site administration | Users | Upload users**, select the text file that you wish to upload:

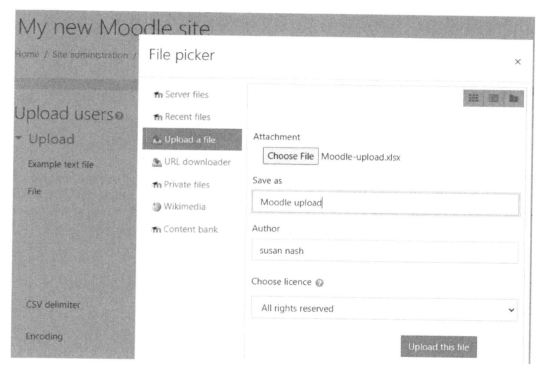

Figure 11.18 – Uploading a file to upload users

2. On this page, choose **Settings** to describe the text file, such as delimiter (separator) and encoding.

3. Click on the **Upload users** button.

   You will see the first few rows of the text file displayed. Also, additional settings become available on this page.

4. In the **Settings** section, there are settings that affect what happens when you upload information about the existing users. You can choose to have the system overwrite information for the existing users, ignore information that conflicts with the existing users, create passwords, and more.

5. In the **Default values** section, you can enter values to be entered onto the user profiles. For example, you can select a city, country, and department for all the users.

6. Click on the **Upload users** button to begin the upload.

Now that we have uploaded the cohort on Moodle, we will focus on how to use the cohort sync enrolment method in order to enroll and unenroll large numbers of students at the same time.

Unenrolling a cohort from a course

There are two ways to unenroll a cohort from a course. First, you can go to the course's enrollment methods page and delete the enrollment method. Just click on the **X** button located next to the cohort sync field that you added to the course. However, this will not just remove users from the course, but it will also delete all their course records.

The second method preserves the student records. Once again, go to the course's enrollment methods page located next to the **Cohort sync** method that you added and click on **Settings**. On the **Settings** page, select **No** for **Active**. This will remove the role that the cohort was given. However, the members of the cohort will still be listed as course participants. So, as the members of the cohort do not have a role in the course, they can no longer access this course. However, their grades and activity reports are preserved.

> **Tip – Cohort Sync Is Everyone or No One**
> When a person is added to or removed from the cohort, the person is added to or removed from all the courses that the cohort is synced to.

An alternative to cohort sync is to enroll a cohort, that is, you can select all the members of a cohort and enroll them in a course all at once. However, this is a one-way journey. You cannot unenroll them all at once; you will need to unenroll them one at a time.

If you enroll a cohort all at once, after enrollment, users are independent entities. You can unenroll them and change their role (for example, from a student to a teacher) whenever you wish.

To enroll a cohort in a course, perform the following steps:

1. Enter the course as an administrator or teacher.

2. Select **Administration** | **Course administration** | **Users** | **Enrolled users**.

3. Click on the **Enroll cohort** button. A pop-up window appears. This window lists the cohorts on the site.

4. Click on **Enroll users** next to the cohort that you want to enroll. The system will display a confirmation message.

5. Now, click on the **OK** button. You will be taken back to the **Enrolled users** page.

> **Important Note**
> Although you can enroll all users in a cohort (all at once), there is no button to unenroll them all at once. You will need to remove them one at a time from your course.

Now that we have enrolled students, we can start managing groups. In the next section, we will learn how best to group them so that their interactions and collaborations are focused on common course goals.

Managing students within groups

In this section, we will learn how to manage students within groups. A group is a collection of students on a course. Outside of a course, a group has no meaning.

Groups are useful when you want to separate students who are studying the same course. For example, if your organization is using the same course for several different classes or groups, you can use the group feature to separate students so that each group can only see their peers on the course. For example, each month, you can create a new group for employees hired that month. Then, you can monitor and mentor them together.

Groups are excellent for course projects and for conducting peer reviews, too.

After you have run a group of people through a course, you might want to reuse this course for another group. You can use the group feature to separate groups so that the current group doesn't see the work that was done by the previous group. This will be like a new course for the current group.

Additionally, you might want an activity or resource to be open to just one group of people. In that case, you don't want others in the class to be able to use that activity or resource.

Courses versus activities

Additionally, you can apply the group setting to an entire course. If you do this, every activity and resource on the course will be segregated into groups.

You can also apply the group setting to an individual activity or resource. If you do this, it will override the group setting for the course.

The three group modes

For a course or activity, there are several ways to apply groups. Here is a list of the three group modes:

- **No groups**: There are no groups for a course or activity. If students have been placed into groups, ignore it. Also, give everyone the same access to the course or activity.

- **Separate groups**: If students have been placed in groups, allow them to see other students and only the work of other students from their own group. Students and work from other groups are invisible.

- **Visible groups**: If students have been placed into groups, allow them to see other students and the work of other students from all groups. However, the work from other groups is read-only.

You can use the **No groups** setting on any activity on your course. Here, you want every student who ever took the course to be able to interact with each other. For example, you might use the **No groups** setting in the news forum so that all students who have ever taken the course can see the latest news:

Cinema: Class & Conflict Overview

Filter groups by:Grouping [No grouping ‡] Group [No group ‡]

Not in a group

Groups (1)	Group members	User count
No group	Joshua Knight (joshuaknight196@example.com), Donna Taylor (donnataylor203@example.com), Amanda Hamilton (amandahamilto205@example.com), Brian Franklin (brianfrankli228@example.com), Frances Banks (francesbanks231@example.com), Mark Ellis (markellis267@example.com), George Lopez (georgelopez271@example.com), Brenda Vasquez (brendavasquez355@example.com), Anthony Ramirez (anthonyramirez359@example.com), Gary Vasquez (garyvasquez366@example.com), Jeffrey Sanders (jeffreysanders199@example.com), Barbara Gardner (barbaragardner249@example.com)	12

Figure 11.19 – Using the No groups setting to enable access

Also, you can use the **Separate groups** setting for a course. Here, you will be able to run different groups at different times. For each group that runs through the course, it will be like a brand-new course.

You can use the **Visible groups** setting for a course. Here, students are part of a large, in-person class, so you want them to collaborate in small groups online.

Also, be aware that some things will not be affected by the group setting. For example, no matter what the group setting is, students will never see each other's assignment submissions.

Creating a group

There are three ways to create groups for a particular course. You can do any of the following:

- Manually create and populate each group.
- Automatically create and populate groups based on the characteristics of students.
- Import groups using a text file.

We'll cover these methods in the following subsections.

Manually creating and populating a group

Don't be discouraged by the idea of manually populating a group with students. It only takes a few clicks to place a student into a group. To create and populate a group manually, perform the following steps:

1. Select **Course administration | Users | Groups**. This will take you to the **Groups** page:

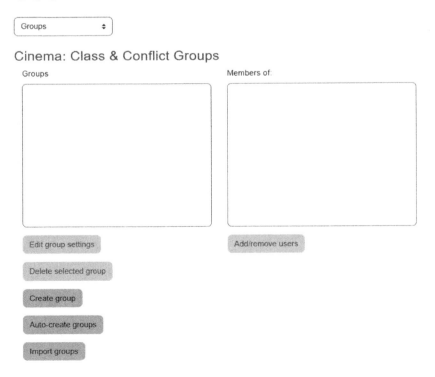

Figure 11.20 – Creating groups

2. Click on the **Create group** button. The **Create group** page is displayed:

Add/remove users: Films based on work by Edith Wharton

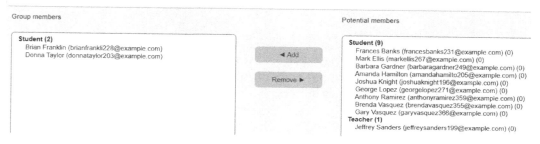

Figure 11.21 – Adding and removing users

3. You must enter a name for the group. This will be the name that the teachers and administrators see when they manage a group:

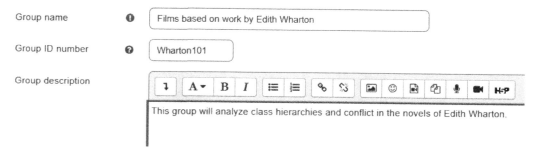

Figure 11.22 – Naming the group

4. The **Group ID** number is used to match up this group with a group identifier on another system. If your organization uses a system outside Moodle to manage students, and that system categorizes students in groups, you can enter the group ID from the other system into this field. It does not need to be a number. This field is optional.

5. The **Group description** field is optional. It's good practice to use this to explain the purpose and criteria for belonging to a group.

6. The **Enrolment key** setting is a code that you can give to students who self-enroll in a course. When the student enrolls, they are prompted to enter their enrollment key. On entering this key, the student is enrolled in the course and made a member of the group. Note that this is different from the `master` course enrolment key:

Figure 11.23 – Enrolment key

7. If you add a picture to this group, when members are listed (such as in a forum), the member will have the group picture shown next to them. You can change the photo by editing the user profile, as follows:

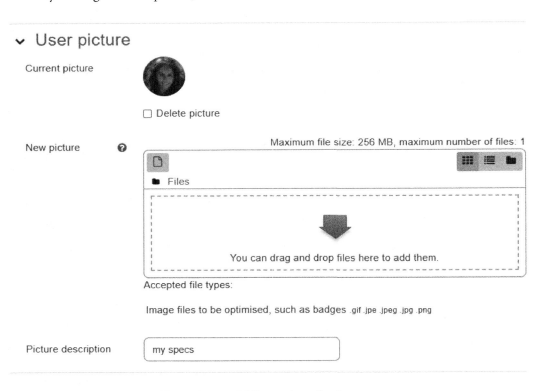

Figure 11.24 – Adding a photo for the group

8. Click on the **Save changes** button to save the group.

9. On the **Groups** page, the group appears in the left-hand column. Select this group.

10. In the right-hand column, search for and select the students that you want to add to this group:

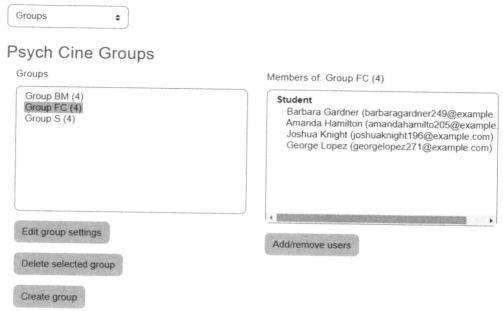

Figure 11.25 – Adding students to specific groups

Note the **Search** fields. These enable you to search for students that meet specific criteria. You can search for a first name, last name, and email address. The other part of the user's profile information is not available in this search box.

Now that we have learned how to create a group manually, we will move on to the next method where we will learn how to automatically create and populate groups.

Automatically creating and populating a group

When you automatically create groups, Moodle creates a number of groups that you specify and then takes all the students enrolled in the course and allocates them to these groups. Moodle will put the currently enrolled students into these groups even if they already belong to another group on the course.

To automatically create a group, perform the following steps:

1. Click on the **Auto-create groups** button. The **Auto-create groups** page will be displayed:

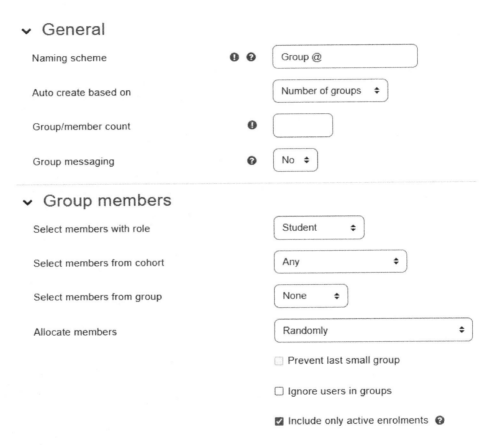

Figure 11.26 – Auto-creating groups

2. In the **Naming scheme** field, enter a name for all the groups that will be created.

   You can enter any character. If you enter @, it will be converted into sequential letters. If you enter #, it will be converted into sequential numbers. For example, if you enter Group @, Moodle will create **Group A**, **Group B**, **Group C**, and more.

3. In the **Auto-create based on** field, you will tell the system to choose either of the following options:

    A. Create a specific number of groups and then fill each group with as many students as needed (**Number of groups**).

    B. Create as many groups as needed so that each group has a specific number of students (**Members per group**).

4. In the **Group/member count** field, you will tell the system to choose either of the following options:

    A. How many groups to create (if you choose the preceding **Number of groups** option)

    B. How many members to put into each group (if you choose the preceding **Members per group** option):

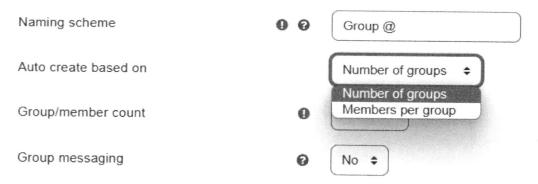

Figure 11.27 – Adding students to specific groups

5. Under **Group members**, select who will be put into these groups. You can select everyone with a specific role or everyone in a specific cohort.

The setting for **Prevent last small group** is available if you choose **Members per group**. This setting prevents Moodle from creating a group with fewer than the number of students that you specify. For example, if your class has 12 students and you choose to create groups with 5 members per group, Moodle will normally create 2 groups of 5. Then, it will create another group for the last two members. However, with **Prevent last small group** selected, it will distribute the remaining two members between the first two groups.

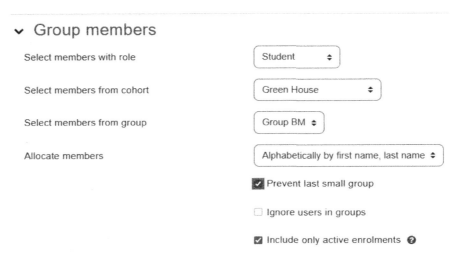

Figure 11.28 – The Prevent last small group setting

6. Click on the **Preview** button to preview the results. The preview will not show you the names of the members in the groups, but it will show you how many groups and members will be in each group.

Summary

Cohorts and groups give you powerful tools to manage your students. Cohorts are a useful tool to quickly enroll and unenroll large numbers of students. Groups enable you to separate students who are on the same course and give teachers the ability to quickly see only the students they are responsible for. Additionally, you can divide students by whether or not they are participating "on-demand" (asynchronously) or "live" (synchronously).

In the previous chapters, you saw how to add content and activities to your course. In this chapter, you learned how to use some tools to manage the students in your course. In the next chapter, you will see how to extend your course using the functionality of blocks.

Part 3:
Power Tools for Teachers and Administrators

In this part you will learn about the powerful tools for teachers and administrators that that help you assess student progress, performance, and the achievement of institutional goals. Upon completion, you will be able to identify the best tools for your purposes, install, and implement them.

In this part, we will cover the following chapter:

Chapter 12, Extending your Course by Adding Blocks

Chapter 13, Features for Teachers: Logs, Reports, Guides

12
Extending Your Course by Adding Blocks

Blocks add functionality to your site or course and they can be placed in many different locations on the page to help focus attention on content and provide useful information, such as assignment due dates on a calendar, course completion status, course overview, and more. Blocks are very flexible and have a wide array of uses. They are often used to build the student's self-confidence by helping them keep on track and manage their time effectively. This chapter will describe many of Moodle's blocks, help you decide which ones will meet your goals, and tell you how to implement them.

After completing this chapter, you will be able to do the following:

- Describe blocks.
- Explain their functionality.
- Configure blocks for your Moodle pages.
- Customize blocks for your courses in Moodle.

We will begin this chapter by describing what a block is and discussing how they are used. Afer that, we will look at some of the commonly used blocks and examples of them. Once we have seen these common blocks and examples, we will learn how to configure a block depending on where we want to place it. Finally, we will look at some of the most commonly used blocks that Moodle has to offer. Throughout this chapter, you will be asked to consider how best to align blocks with course objectives.

Defining a block

Blocks are great tools because they help you cluster content for easy use, and they can be organized around learning goals. Blocks are plugins that arrange chunks of text and links. They can be added to the side of a page in Moodle and can remind you of what a sidebar breakout looks like in a printed textbook. A block usually displays information in a small area in one of the side columns. For example, a block can display a calendar, the latest news, or the students enrolled in a course.

You can administer plugins from the **Site administration** site by going to **Plugins**:

Site administration

Figure 12.1 – Where Plugins appears in the Site administration menu

Blocks help keep students on task. They can also include links to parts of the course and thus act as navigation bars. It is important to keep in mind that not all instructional designers or course designers like using blocks, and some even consider them a bit anchored in the past. Those who do not like blocks often point to the Dashboard as a better alternative.

That said, for people who like blocks, they can be useful for maintaining engagement. For example, blocks can help keep students engaged by being a place to put **Check Your Knowledge** or **Did You Know?** engagers:

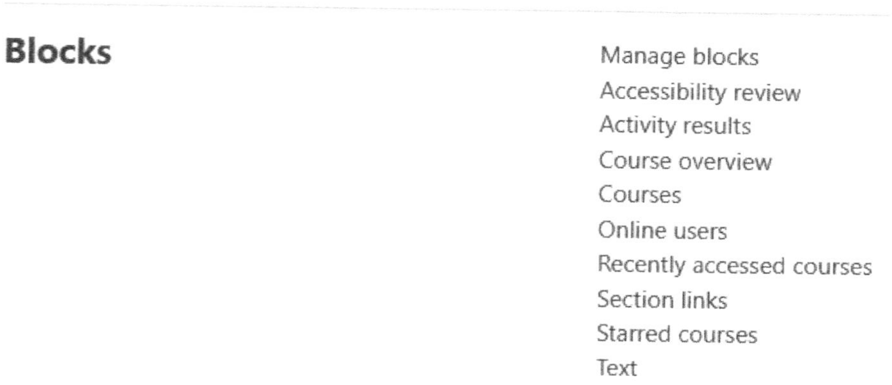

Blocks

Manage blocks
Accessibility review
Activity results
Course overview
Courses
Online users
Recently accessed courses
Section links
Starred courses
Text

Figure 12.2 – The Blocks menu on the Plugins page

Uses of blocks

When configuring the site, you can choose to display, hide, and position blocks on the site's front page. When configuring a course, you can also show/hide/position blocks on the course's home page. The procedure is the same as working on the site's front page or a course's home page. The site's front page is essentially a course. You can also permit students to add blocks to their **Dashboard** page and **My profile** page. Please keep in mind that some Moodle themes have pre-established blocks, so you may not be able to add blocks or reposition them.

Many blocks are available to you in a standard Moodle installation. The following screenshot shows the standard blocks in Moodle 4.0:

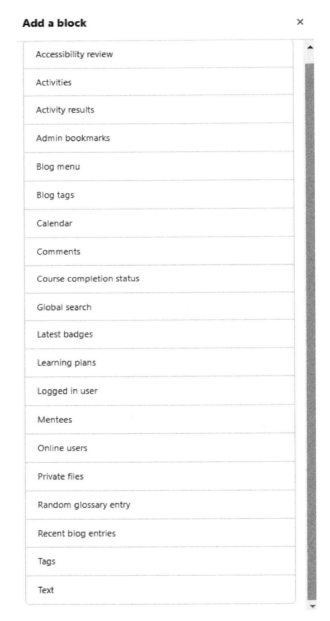

Figure 12.3 – Menu of standard blocks when adding a block

You can also install additional blocks, by going to `http://moodle.org/plugins`.

Examples of blocks in action

Many blocks are available in a standard Moodle installation. You can add the block by clicking **Add a block** in the top right-hand corner:

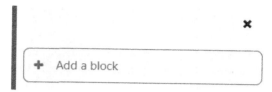

Figure 12.4 – The appearance of the Add a block option in the top right-hand corner

Be sure to select your blocks with care as you can easily create redundancy. For example, you can add an activity to the block, which would mean that it would appear in the right-hand column rather than in the center part of the page. Is that really what you want to do? Most of the time, the activities are best in the middle of the page. One notable exception could be **Glossaries** and **Wikis**, which can be conveniently placed "at one's fingertips" while in the course:

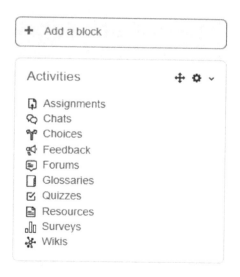

Figure 12.5 – Activities that can be added to a block

Perhaps the most popular option is the **Calendar** block, which you can position on either side so that it appears prominently on either side. The **Calendar** block is an excellent tool because it allows you to remind students of deadlines and key milestones.

The **Comments** block can help you organize comments and quickly allow you to communicate without having to go through several clicks or screens.

The **Course completion status** block is extremely useful as an engager and motivator because you can both remind students where they are in the course and reward them for progressing well through the course.

Blocks such as **Course overview** can help you create a nicely organized page. The **Course description** block has a similar function.

Other blocks are very useful as shortcuts to important pages within Moodle. These blocks include **Activities, Main menu, Courses, Section links**, and **Upcoming Events**.

Like any tool or app, blocks can be overused. They can be distracting and create clutter. To decide which blocks to use, think about your use of the blocks and prioritize what you'd like your students to do and see. Keep in mind that Moodle Mobile may display blocks at the bottom of the page instead of on the sides.

Now that you know what a block is, its uses, and the different types of blocks that Moodle has to offer, let's move on to the next section, where we will learn how to configure the blocks so that you can control where they appear.

Configuring where a block appears

You can configure a block to appear on the course's home page and all the resource and activity pages in the course. You can also configure a block to appear on all your courses. Additionally, you can create a block that contains categories of courses and lists the individual courses within those categories.

To configure where a block appears, click on the gear icon. In this case, we are configuring where to put the **Calendar** block:

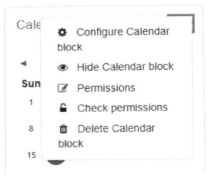

Figure 12.6 – Dropdown menu for managing a block

To move the blocks to the right-hand side of the screen and rearrange them, click on the crossed terminating arrows, hold down with your mouse, and move the selection around:

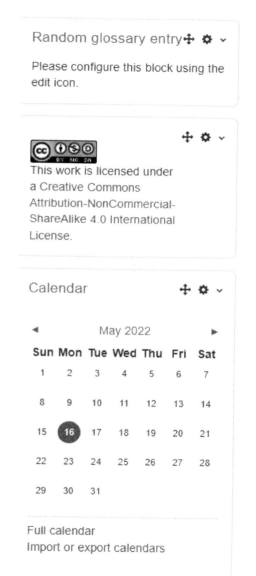

Figure 12.7 – To move the blocks, click on the cross, hold, and move

For example, in the following screenshot, the user is configuring the **Upcoming events** block in the **The Impressionists** course:

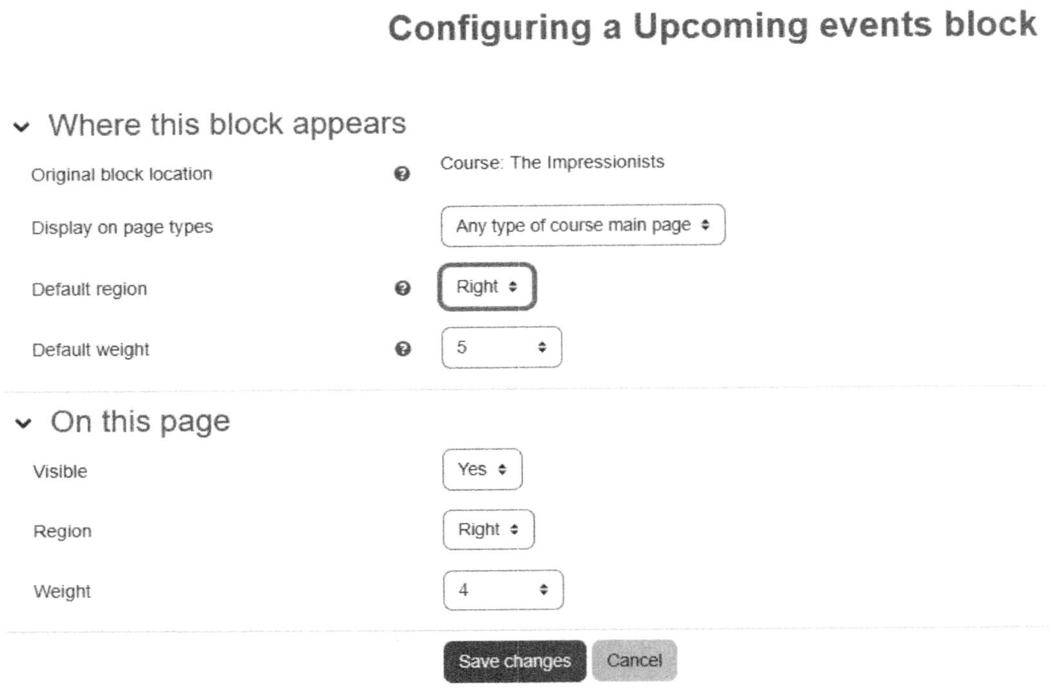

Configuring a Upcoming events block

∨ Where this block appears

Original block location	❓	Course: The Impressionists
Display on page types		Any type of course main page ⬍
Default region	❓	Right ⬍
Default weight	❓	5 ⬍

∨ On this page

Visible	Yes ⬍
Region	Right ⬍
Weight	4 ⬍

Save changes   Cancel

Figure 12.8 – How to configure an Upcoming events block

These settings work in combination to determine where a block appears. In some places, some of these settings have no effect. You can set the region on the page where the block will appear, and also which page types will feature the blocks. Notice that you must specify the block's weight. This is how you fine-tune where it appears on the page. **0** puts the block at the bottom, while **10** puts it at the top. Be sure to experiment with different settings to see how the block's position changes when you adjust the values.

When you add a block to a page, any display settings that you choose will affect the block from that page on, down through the hierarchy of pages. For example, suppose you add a block to the main page of a course, as the user is doing in the preceding screenshot. Any display settings will affect the block on that page and other pages inside that course.

As this block is being added to a course page, the block will not be displayed on any other pages outside of that course.

If you want a block to appear on every page of your site, or every occurrence of a specific page type, add the block to the front page of your site. From the **Site administration** screen, turn on **Edit mode** and click on **Add a block** in the right-hand corner:

Figure 12.9 – Adding a block to your site's home screen

Once you've done that, under **Block settings**, you will see choices for **Display on page types**. We will use the **Recent activity** block as an example:

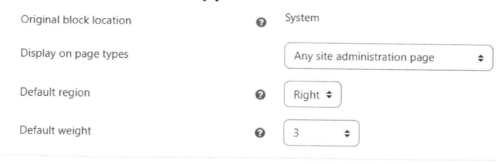

Figure 12.10 – Configuring the block so it will appear on any site administration page

Further down the page, you will see a setting that determines whether the block is displayed on this page (that is, on the front page):

Figure 12.11 – Determining whether the block is displayed on the front page

These settings can work together to produce the result that you want. For example, if you are an administrator and want a block to appear on every page of your site except for the front page, choose **Any site administration page**, and then for just the front page, set **Visible** to **No**.

You can also add a block to all the courses in a category. From the **Site administration** menu, select **Courses | Manage courses and categories**. Then, select the category:

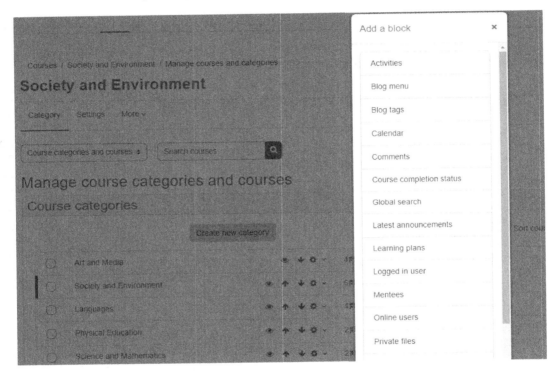

Figure 12.12 – Selecting the block to add from the pop-up menu

Add the block to the category page. Then, under the settings for **Where this block appears**, choose which pages in the category will display the block:

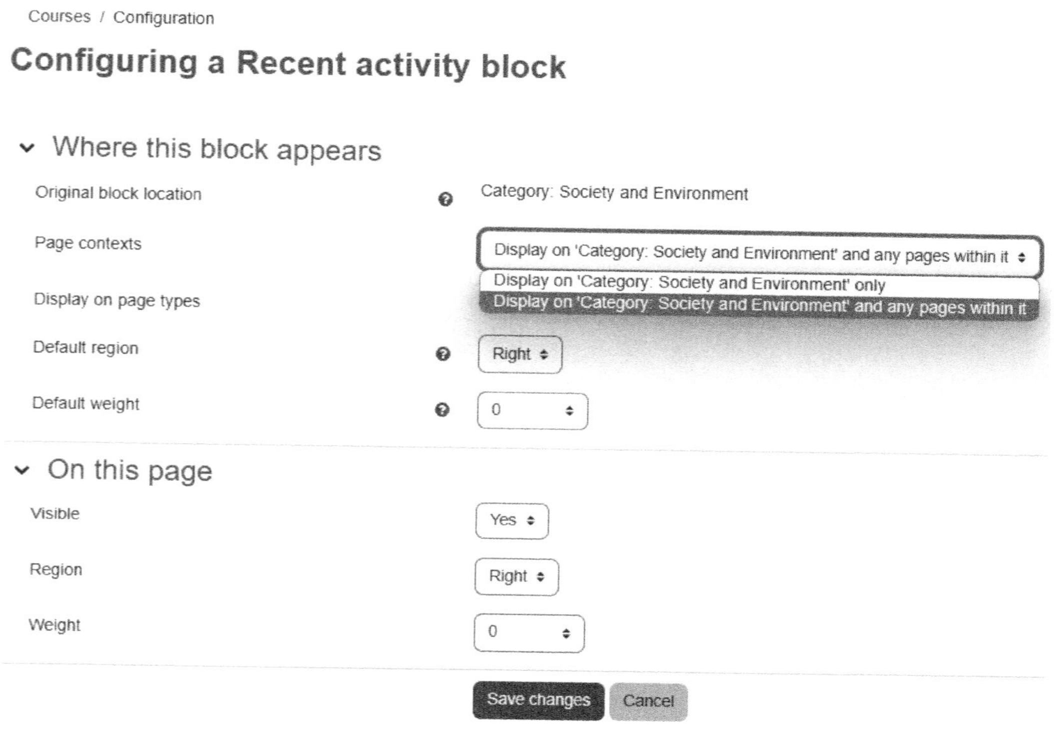

Courses / Configuration

Configuring a Recent activity block

∨ Where this block appears

Original block location	❷	Category: Society and Environment
Page contexts		Display on 'Category: Society and Environment' and any pages within it ⇕
Display on page types		Display on 'Category: Society and Environment' only
		Display on 'Category: Society and Environment' and any pages within it
Default region	❷	Right ⇕
Default weight	❷	0 ⇕

∨ On this page

Visible	Yes ⇕
Region	Right ⇕
Weight	0 ⇕

Save changes   Cancel

Figure 12.13 – Enabling the block on course category pages

Keep in mind that docked blocks will be displayed at the bottom of the page if you select a responsive theme for mobile devices such as phones and tablets. You now know how to configure where your blocks appear. In the next section, you will learn how to select and configure some of the blocks available to you.

Standard blocks

Moodle gives you many standard blocks that you can add to your courses. Some of the most useful ones will be discussed in this section. We will review **Activities**, **Blogs**, **Calendar**, **Comments**, **Course completion**, and many others, such as **Users** and **Badges**.

The Activities block

The **Activities** block lists all types of activities that are used in the course:

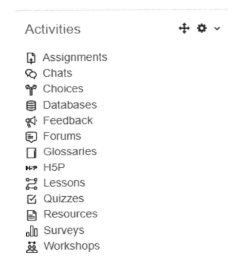

Figure 12.14 – Select the Activities block to list the activities used in the course

The activity type is only shown if your course contains at least one instance of that type. When a user clicks on the type of activity, all those kinds of activities for the course are listed.

In the following screenshot, the user clicked on **Forums** in the **Activities** block. By doing this, a list of the resources in the course is presented:

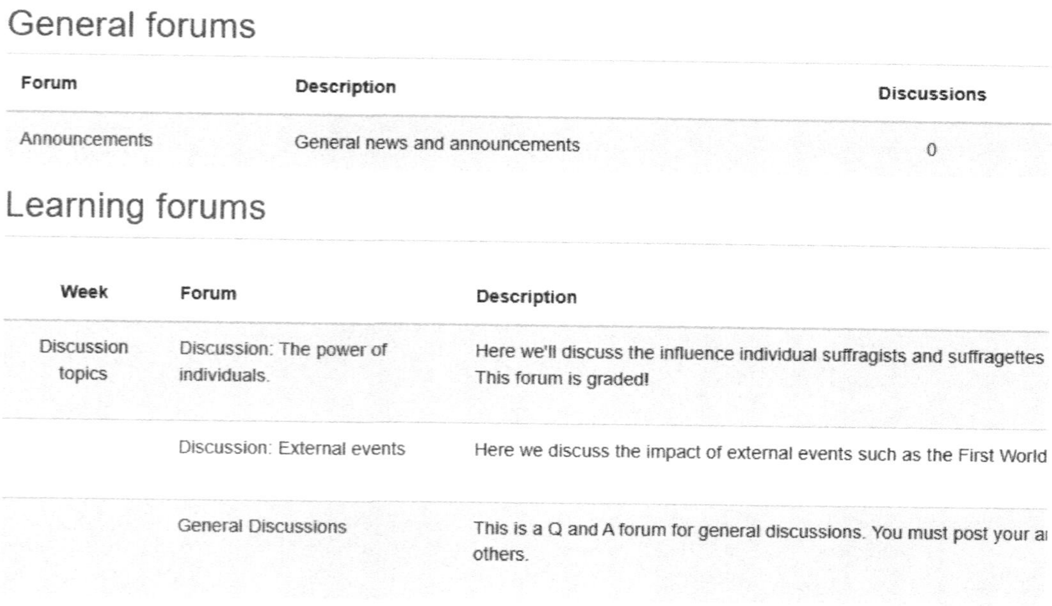

General forums

Forum	Description	Discussions
Announcements	General news and announcements	0

Learning forums

Week	Forum	Description
Discussion topics	Discussion: The power of individuals.	Here we'll discuss the influence individual suffragists and suffragettes This forum is graded!
	Discussion: External events	Here we discuss the impact of external events such as the First World
	General Discussions	This is a Q and A forum for general discussions. You must post your a others.

Figure 12.15 – You can use blocks to organize forums

> **Important Note**
> If this block is on the site's front page, clicking on a type of activity gives a list of the activities on the front page (not for the entire site).

The Text block

The **Text** block (formerly known as the **HTML** block before Moodle 4.0) creates a block in the sidebar that can hold any HTML (or any web content) that you can put on a web page. Most experienced web users are accustomed to the content in the sidebars being an addition to the main content of a page. For example, we can put menus and interesting links in the sidebars in most blogging software. I suggest that you keep with that standard. Use the **Text** block to hold content that is an interesting addition to the course, but not essential. For example, you can put an annotated link to another site of interest.

When you edit a **Text** block, Moodle provides the same full-featured web page editor that you get when adding a web page to a course.

Think of a **Text** block as a miniature web page that you can put into the sidebar of your course:

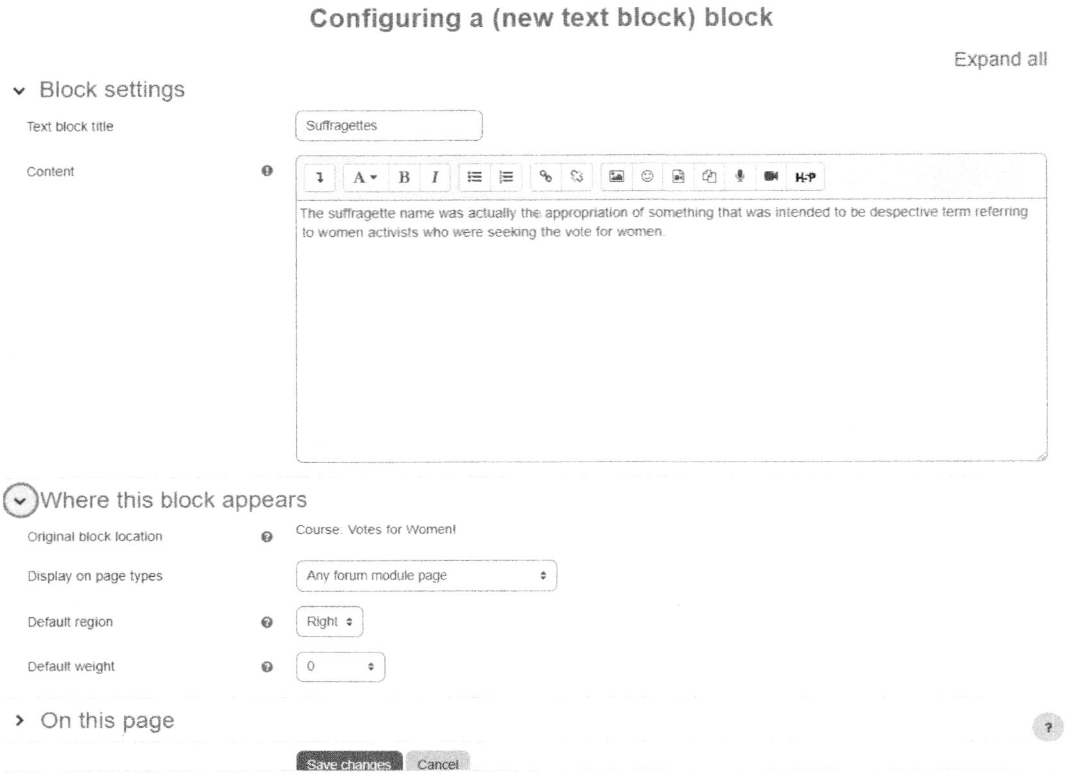

Configuring a (new text block) block

Expand all

Block settings

Text block title	Suffragettes
Content	The suffragette name was actually the appropriation of something that was intended to be despective term referring to women activists who were seeking the vote for women.

Where this block appears

Original block location	Course: Votes for Women!
Display on page types	Any forum module page
Default region	Right
Default weight	0

> On this page

Save changes   Cancel

Figure 12.16 – Configuring a Text block (formerly an HTML block)

After configuring the **Text** block, it will appear in the right-hand column, with a consistent appearance:

Suffragettes

The suffragette name was actually the appropriation of something that was intended to be despective term referring to women activists who were seeking the vote for women.

Figure 12.17 – How a configured Text box appears

The Blog menu block

By default, every Moodle user has a personal blog on the site. For more information, check out Moodle docs (`https://docs.moodle.org/400/en/Blogs`). Selecting this block, as shown in the following screenshot, puts the menu into the sidebar of the course:

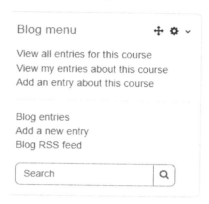

Figure 12.18 – The Blog menu block is positioned as a sidebar

The **Blog menu** block helps people have access to the blog posts that a student may have created. It allows you to incorporate blogs and develop custom content for the course that can be changed from term to term, which ensures it is up to date.

Note that this block provides shortcuts to blog entries about the course. If blogging will be a part of the course, include this block on the main page of the course.

The Blog tags block

This block displays a list of the blog tags used site-wide. The tags are listed in alphabetical order. The more blog entries that use a tag, the larger that tag is:

Figure 12.19 – The Blog tags block helps identify the topics

The Calendar block

The **Calendar** block is very useful because it helps students stay on track. Workshops, assignments, quizzes, and events appear on the **Calendar** block. Be sure to remind users that their timezone is correct. Otherwise, the times will not be adjusted to their timezone:

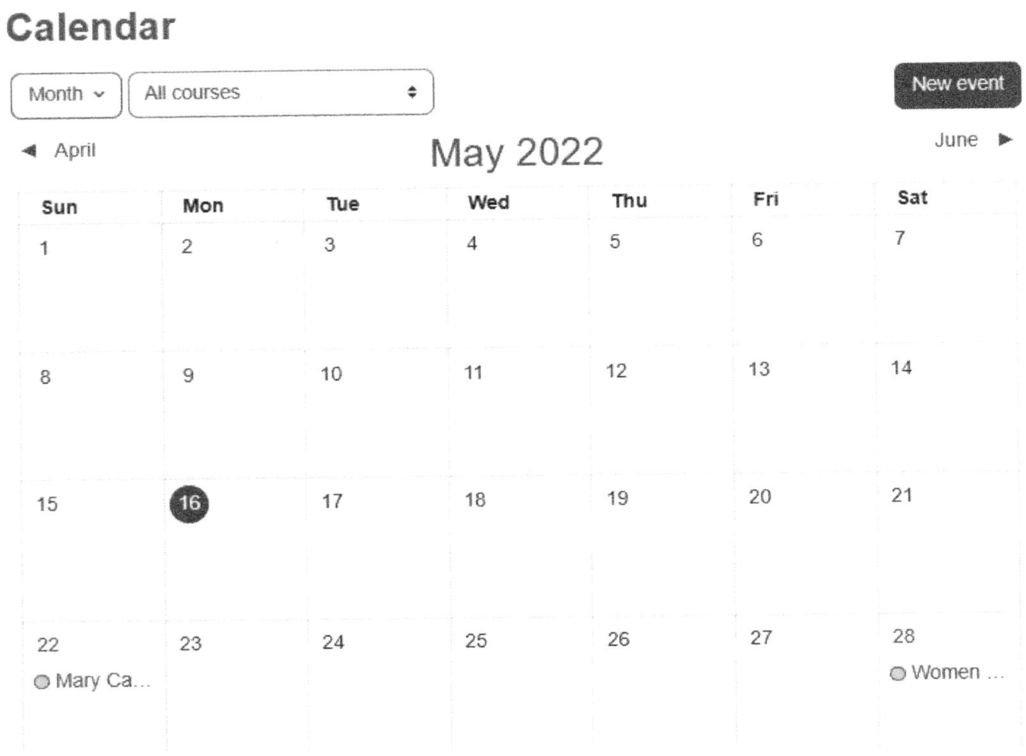

Calendar

Month ˅	All courses ⬍					New event

◄ April   **May 2022**   June ►

Sun	Mon	Tue	Wed	Thu	Fri	Sat
1	2	3	4	5	6	7
8	9	10	11	12	13	14
15	(16)	17	18	19	20	21
22 ○ Mary Ca...	23	24	25	26	27	28 ○ Women ...

Figure 12.20 – The Calendar block displays the scheduled activities by month

A pop-up window will appear and show the name of the event. This event was added to this course, so it is a course-wide event.

When the user clicks on one of the four links at the bottom of the **Calendar** block, it disables the display of that type of event.

When a deadline is added to an activity in the course, it will automatically be added to the calendar.

The Comments block

The **Comments** block enables anyone with access to it to leave and read comments. The comments are all saved, so you can accumulate quite a long list of comments.

In the following screenshot, the **Student1** user is logged in and has added a comment:

Figure 12.21 – The Comments block allows you to see comments in one place

> **Important Note**
> **Student1** can delete their comment but not the comment left by the course administrator.

Of course, the teacher, manager, and site administrator can delete anyone's comments.

As all comments are saved, and the list can get long, you probably want to limit the **Comment** block to a single course – that is, you don't want to add a comment site-wide, or to all the courses in a category. If you do, the block can become crowded with comments (unless this is the effect that you want). The site administrator can decide how many comments are displayed in comments blocks by going to **Site administration | Site home | Site home settings**:

Figure 12.22 – Determining how many comments can appear on a page

Consider adding a **Comments** block to an activity or a resource and using the first comment to encourage students to leave feedback, as follows:

Figure 12.23 – Adding the first comment to encourage students to leave feedback

The Course completion status block

This block works with course completion tracking. For this block to function, you must first set the criteria for completing the course, and completion tracking must be enabled at the site level. This can be done by going to **Settings | Completion tracking**:

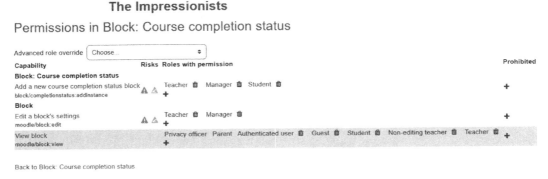

Figure 12.24 – The Course completion status block

When a student views this block, they see the conditions for course completion and the status of each condition. When a teacher views this block, they see a report of the completion status for each student in the course.

Course/site summary

If you add this block to the front page of your site, it will display the front page summary, which can be found by going to **Site administration | Site home settings | Edit settings**:

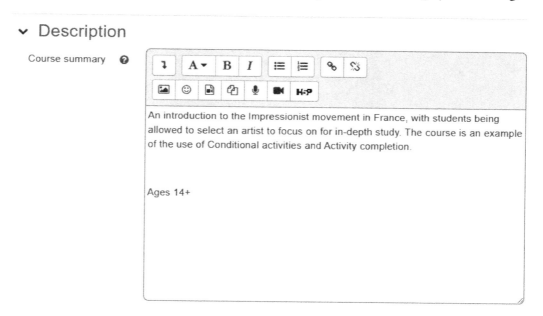

Figure 12.25 – The course description can appear in a block in the course

If you add it to a course page, it will display the course's description, which can be found by going to **Settings | Edit course settings | Course summary**.

The Learning plans block

The **Learning plans** block displays the competencies that the student needs to master. For useful references on learning plans, please visit Moodle docs (`https://moodle.org/plugins/block_learning_plan`):

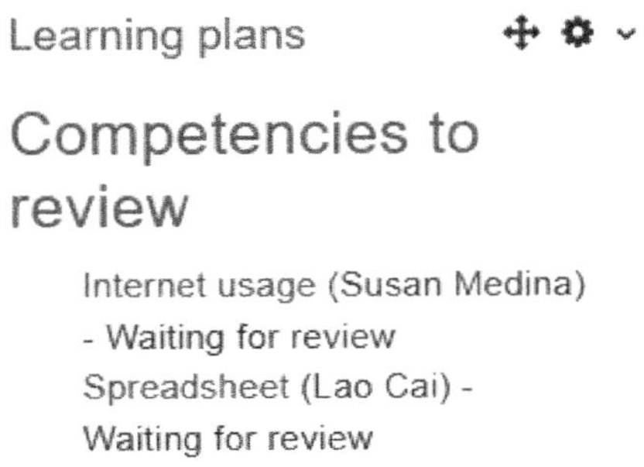

Learning plans

Competencies to review

Internet usage (Susan Medina)
- Waiting for review
Spreadsheet (Lao Cai) -
Waiting for review

Figure 12.26 – The appearance of the Learning plans block

The Online users block

The **Online users** block shows who is in the current course at present. If it is on the site's front page, it shows who is on the site. When it is added to a course, it can be a good way to lessen the isolation of e-learning. The block is updated every few minutes.

The Recent activity block

When the **Recent activity** block is added to the home page of a course, it lists all the student and teacher activity in that course since the user last logged in. The activity report filter and generator may be accessed via the **Full report of recent activity** link.

When added to the site's front page, it lists all the student and teacher activity on the front page, but not in the individual courses since the user last logged in. If someone is logged in as a guest user, this block displays any activity since the last time that guest logged in. If guest users are constantly coming to your site, this block may be of limited use to them. One strategy is to omit this block from the site's front page so that anonymous users don't see it and add it only to courses that require users to authenticate.

The Remote RSS feeds block

When the **Remote RSS feeds** block is added to a course, the course creator chooses or creates the RSS feeds to display in that block. When RSS feeds were first developed, they tended to be used in conjunction with subscribing to a person's blog. Now, they are in the backend and used for subscribing to podcasts, which have become more popular than ever. Podcast hosting services such as Podbean, Resonate, Captivate, and Buzzsprout automatically list their hosted podcasts on players and distribution platforms such as SoundCloud, Apple Podcasts, Google Podcasts, Spotify, TuneIn, and Overcast.

A feed can be added by the site administrator and then selected by the course creator for use in an RSS block. Alternatively, when the teacher adds the **Remote RSS feeds** block, they can add a feed at that time. If **Share feed** is set to **Yes**, the new feed becomes available to all other teachers, for use in all other courses.

The Search Forums block

The **Search Forums** block provides a search function for forums. It does not search for other types of activities or resources.

When it's added to the main page of a course, it only searches the forums in that course. It searches post titles and content.

This block is different than the **Search courses** field, which automatically appears on the site's front page. The **Search courses** field searches for course names and descriptions, not forums.

The Topics block

The **Topics** block displays links to the numbered topics or weeks in a course. Clicking on a link advances the page to that topic.

The Upcoming events block

The **Upcoming events** block is an extension of the **Calendar** block. It gets event information from your calendar. By default, the **Upcoming events** block displays 10 events; the maximum is 20. It looks ahead a default of 21 days; the maximum is 200. If there are more upcoming events than the maximum chosen for this block, the most distant events will not be shown. In the following screenshot, you can see how the events are listed, with short titles along with the date and time. The title is linked so that the learner can click and go to the site:

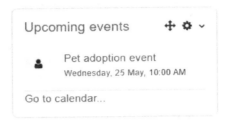

Figure 12.27 – The Upcoming events block

This block is helpful for reminding students of the tasks they need to complete in the course. Remember that if you want the upcoming events block to appear on all your pages, you'll need to add it to your site home page and select **Any page**:

Figure 12.28 – Configuring the Upcoming events block so that it appears on all pages

Summary

In this chapter, we looked at many of the blocks that are available in Moodle 4.0. Keep in mind that with 4.0, blocks appear on the Dashboard, and you can set them to appear on course pages to help remind your students of upcoming events, display important information, and keep them engaged. When deciding which blocks to use, resist the temptation to add too many. Blocks are helpful, but they can be a distraction and also confuse priorities. Use blocks strategically to make sure students stay on track, and also to flag important information. You can also use them as consistent motivators, where reminders of their positive achievements appear. Remember that you can turn blocks off and on as needed. The key is to use blocks to enable students to succeed. You can use blocks as signposts and guides. However, avoid overusing blocks since they can be distracting.

In the next chapter, you will learn how to optimize your course for teachers, including how to view course logs and activity reports to determine what students have done, how to view and categorize grades, and how to grade.

13
Features for Teachers: Logs, Reports, and Guides

Some of the most useful new features of Moodle 4.0 have to do with automatically generating progress reports that help students as well as teachers. For example, there is a new activity completion indicator that tracks the student's progress on their assigned tasks in each course. Similarly, the Dashboard has an updated **Timeline** block and a highly functional **Calendar** block that bring all the course deadlines together on one page.

For administrators, there are performance reports that have to do with the functioning of Moodle. This new feature of Moodle can be found by accessing the Site Administration menu, and following this path: **Site administration** > **Reports** > **Report builder** > **Custom reports**. Thus, the administrator can build custom reports that are useful for different constituencies within the organization, ranging from students, teachers, managers, and administrators.

For teachers, tracking progress, generating activity logs, and determining levels of engagement are vital in assessing **satisfactory academic progress** (**SAP**) and Moodle offers several features that are of special interest. These focus on determining how well your students are progressing through a course. Reports and logs show you who has done what on your site, or in your course. They can be invaluable tools in letting you know how students are achieving learning goals, and they can serve as useful gap analyses that allow you to make adjustments to your content and assessment strategies.

You may need to generate student progress reports at different times during the term. First, you may need to report which students never attended so that you can drop them for non-attendance. Then, you may need to generate mid-term progress reports. Finally, you may need to provide metrics on students' time on task and completion rates. Moodle's logs and reports can help you.

In this chapter, you will learn how to do the following:

- Identify the types of reports and logs available in Moodle

- Determine the types of reports needed based on course outcomes

- Prepare logs and reports that are needed

In the next section, we identify and generate logs and reports that can be used for several student progress assessments, as well as compliance for accreditation.

Student views of performance and progress

As a student, Moodle 4.0 gives you a chance to see where you are in your courses, as well as see "at-a-glance" reports of how your performance stacks up against others in the course.

First, there is the streamlined new Course Index, which is a column on the left-hand side of the screen if you're using a tablet or laptop. So, on the left-hand side of the screen on your tablet/laptop, you'll see the **Course Index**, which contains various topics (modules) and activities. In the center, you will see the navigation bar, which provides course information, announcements, links to resources and activities, and more. On the right-hand side are blocks that track activity, display performance in your course, and give you a link to collaborative activities if your teacher or administrator has permitted you to see them:

Figure 13.1 – View of the Course Index on the left-hand column

The redesigned **Calendar** and **Timeline** blocks are available to all users. They are especially helpful to students because upcoming assignments appear in the order that they are due, and they also appear on the redesigned **Calendar** block, which appears directly below. On the right-hand side is a redesigned **Learning plans** block, along with **Recently accessed items**, which features the newly redesigned activity and resources icons:

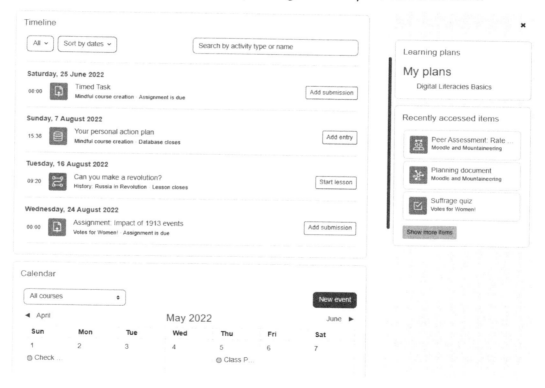

Figure 13.2 – View of the Timeline and Calendar blocks

The newly redesigned **Courses** page lets students know how many of their courses they have completed. For example, as shown in the following screenshot of the **My Courses** screen, the student has completed 42% of **Mindful Course Creation** but only 27% of **Celebrating Cultures**. Notice that the course category appears directly below the name of the course, which makes it easier to navigate:

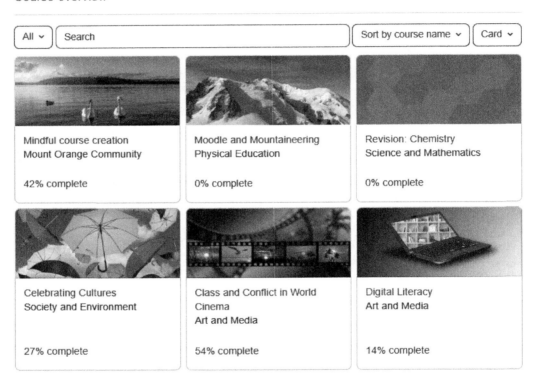

Figure 13.3 – Newly designed My courses page

So, while the progress reports for students are not technically found in the **Reports** section, they are reports and are extremely helpful in achieving satisfactory academic progress, and more.

Now, let's take a look at the logs and reports that you will need as a teacher, manager, or administrator.

Logs and reports

Moodle keeps detailed logs of all the activities that users perform on your site. You can use these logs to determine who has been active on your site, what they did, and when they did it.

> **Important Note**
>
> Some reports are available at the course level; teachers can access these reports. Other reports are available at the site level; you must be a site administrator to access these reports. Both are covered in this chapter.

Moodle has a modest report viewing system built into it, which has been enhanced in Moodle 4.0 as a report builder. The **Report builder** feature allows administrators to create and share custom reports. To build a custom report, go to **Site administration | Reports | Report builder | Custom reports**. Once you've created the reports, you can customize when they are released and where they are sent. You can also manage access to the reports. Keep in mind that when you are scheduling the reports, you can also automate when, where, and to whom they are sent.

However, for sophisticated log analysis, you need to look outside Moodle. It is a good idea to look at third-party plugins that are compatible with Moodle. A list can be found here: `https://docs.moodle.org/400/en/ad-hoc_contributed_reports`.

To view the logs and reports for a course, you must be logged in as a teacher or a manager. Then, select **My courses | Name of course | Reports**:

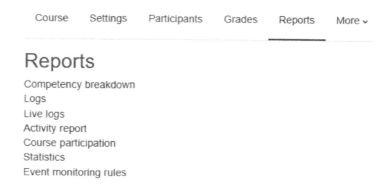

Figure 13.4 – View of the Reports screen

If you are a student, you will see your competency breakdown.

Competency breakdown

The competency breakdown keeps a log of which competencies are being fulfilled as course activities are completed. They appear in the student's learning plans. To activate automatic updating, it is necessary to tie the course activity completion logs to competencies or student learning plans.

Viewing course logs

Note that Moodle's display of the log files can be filtered by course, participant, day, activity, and action. You can select a single value for any of these filters, as shown in the following screenshot:

Figure 13.5 – How to view course logs

You cannot select multiple values for any of these filters – that is, you cannot look at the logs for two courses at the same time, four participants at the same time, or for a few days at the same time. If you want a more sophisticated view of the logs, you must use a tool other than Moodle's built-in log viewer.

Fortunately, you can download the logs as text files and import them into another tool, such as a spreadsheet. To download the logs, use the **Download table data as** drop-down menu at the bottom of the page, as shown in the following screenshot:

Figure 13.6 – Using the Download table data as drop-down menu to download logs

For example, you can use Excel's data menu to format, chart, and analyze the data. A complete discussion of Excel's data functions is beyond the scope of this book, but there are many sources of help for these functions. Here is Microsoft's support page: `https://support.microsoft.com/en-us/office/excel-functions-by-category-5f91f4e9-7b42-46d2-9b1-63f26a86c0eb`.

There are two ways to get information from several courses in the same place. First, you can run the report as an administrator, from the administrative interface. This enables you to run a report for all the courses on the site. Second, as a teacher, you can download the data from each course separately and combine it in one Excel sheet or workbook.

Functionality booster

In certain cases, you may be able to use live logs as proctoring tools. You can combine the live log with a streaming video (Zoom, BigBlueButton, or another web conferencing application) that shows the student at the computer as they work on their proctored assignment. These are best for courses that have directed readings or sections with few enrollments.

Viewing Live logs

Live logs shows what has happened in the current course, for the past hour:

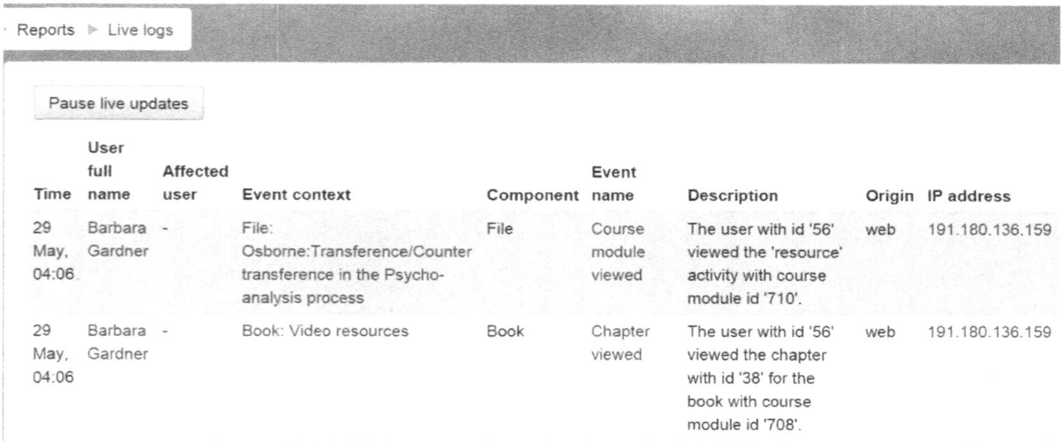

Time	User full name	Affected user	Event context	Component	Event name	Description	Origin	IP address
29 May, 04:06	Barbara Gardner	-	File: Osborne:Transference/Counter transference in the Psycho-analysis process	File	Course module viewed	The user with id '56' viewed the 'resource' activity with course module id '710'.	web	191.180.136.159
29 May, 04:06	Barbara Gardner	-	Book: Video resources	Book	Chapter viewed	The user with id '56' viewed the chapter with id '38' for the book with course module id '708'.	web	191.180.136.159

Figure 13.7 – Using Live logs to track activity

Use Live logs if you want to observe the students as they use the course. For example, you may monitor the course while students take a scheduled quiz.

In the next section, we will learn how to generate activity reports and analyze them.

Viewing activity reports

An activity report offers a user-friendly view of an activity in a single course. While the logs show complete information, an activity report just shows the course items, what was done in each item, and the time of the latest activity for that item. When you first select **Activity report** from the menu, you will be presented with a list of all the activities in the course, as shown in the following screenshot:

Figure 13.8 – View of the Activity report area

From this list, you can select the activity you want a report for, and you will be taken to that activity. In this example, the teacher selected **Assignment 1**, which opened that activity. Then, the teacher can select **View all submissions** to see how the students participated in this activity:

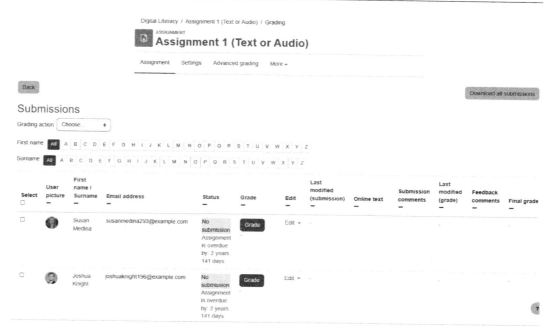

Figure 13.9 – Viewing the Submissions log/report

Note that an activity report only acts as a link to the activities in a course. Once you select an activity, you will use that activity's method for viewing a report.

Now, let's look at the participation reports that we can generate.

Participation reports – reports used for interventions to assure persistence

The **Course participation** report is especially useful for discovering which students need to complete an activity and sending them a reminder to complete it.

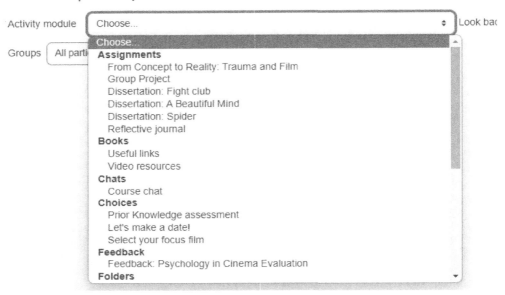

Figure. 13.10 – A menu showing the different types of Course participation reports

In the following example, the teacher is looking at the report for a feedback activity called **Psychology in Cinema Evaluation**. The teacher wants to see who submitted their feedback for the course:

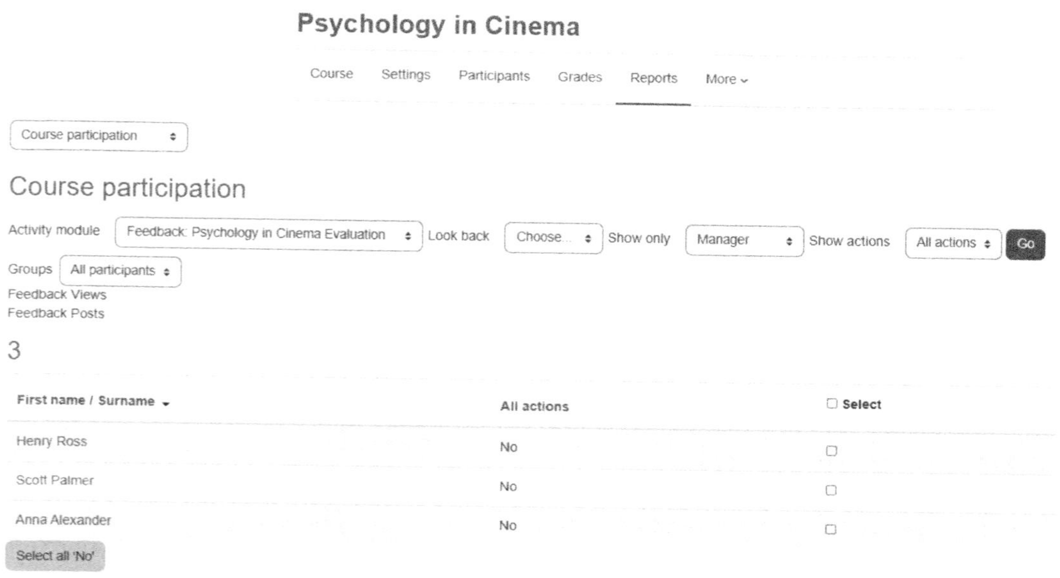

Psychology in Cinema

Course   Settings   Participants   Grades   Reports   More ⌄

Course participation   ⇕

Course participation

Activity module | Feedback: Psychology in Cinema Evaluation   ⇕ | Look back | Choose... ⇕ | Show only | Manager   ⇕ | Show actions | All actions ⇕ | Go

Groups | All participants ⇕

Feedback Views
Feedback Posts

3

First name / Surname ▾	All actions	☐ Select
Henry Ross	No	☐
Scott Palmer	No	☐
Anna Alexander	No	☐

Select all 'No'

Figure 13.11 – A Course participation report that shows who submitted feedback for a course

In this demonstration course, the teacher wants all the students to give their feedback. So, the teacher will send a message to the students who have not completed the activity. To do this, they can select the students and then, from the **With selected users...** drop-down list, select **Send a message**:

First name / Surname ▾	All actions	☑ Select
Henry Ross	No	☑
Scott Palmer	No	☑
Anna Alexander	No	☑

Deselect all 'No'

With selected users... | Choose... ⇕

Choose...
Send a message

Figure 13.12 – A method for requiring students to provide feedback

This takes the teacher to a page where they can create and send the message. The message will be sent to the students' email addresses and also stored in their Moodle messages.

Now, let's learn how to monitor at a more precise level.

Using activity completion

You can take monitoring to a more precise level. If the course has **activity completion** enabled, you can view a report showing the completion status of the activities in the course. Note that activity completion can be overridden with the right capability too. Activity completion allows you to modify and set completion criteria in each activity's settings. You can use it as a gateway for progress. For example, the student must achieve a certain score before progressing. This is common in mastery learning:

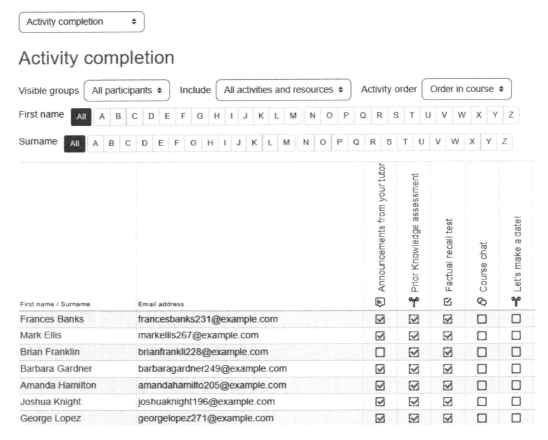

Figure 13.13 – Generating a report to show the completion status of activities

Note that you can show activities for just one group or all the students in the course. Also, this report only shows those activities whose completion status is being tracked.

Making sure that students achieve a mastery-level score (often 80 percent or higher) is a cornerstone of competency-based or proficiency-based learning. **Competency-based learning (CBE)** denotes a learning plan that sets out the categories of learning required for a certain skill or knowledge area. In CBE, the student will not receive a certificate or credit until completing the course with the designated score.

Now, let's learn how to review student achievement and grades.

Reports and accreditation

Keep in mind that these reports are often used in self-study for accreditation, particularly in relation to student progress, such as metrics for SAP, as well as for metrics to do with persistence.

Viewing grades

To access grades, select the course that you want to see the grades for and then select **Grade administration | Grader report**. This will display a summary of the grades for that course:

Figure 13.14 – Generating a Grader report with student grades in one place

Note that, in the preceding screenshot, some students have not completed the first assignment in this course – that is, **From Concept to Reality**.... Also, note the **Turn editing on** button in the top-right corner of the page; the teacher can use this button to override the grades being displayed by entering new ones. When the teacher clicks on that button, the grades on this page become editable.

In our example course, the teacher wants to investigate the lack of grades for the From Concept to Reality... assignment, so they must click on the name of the assignment, which will take them out of the **Grader report** area and into the assignment itself.

The Grader report area is the teacher's starting point for examining the grades in a course. It also enables the teacher to enter updated grades. From there, the teacher can click into individual activities and investigate or modify the grades.

Categorizing grades

Each of the graded activities can be put into a category. Note that you put activities into categories, not students. If you want to categorize students, put them into groups.

Viewing grade categories

Categorizing the graded activities in a course allows you to quickly see how your students are doing with various kinds of activities. If you do not assign an activity to a category, it will belong to the **Uncategorized** category by default.

In the **Quizzes** category, the grades are displayed for two quizzes. The page also displays the **Category** total value for Quizzes.

The **Non-quizzes** category only displays the Category total value. Grades for individual activities under Non-quizzes are not displayed. If the user clicks on the + sign located next to Non-quizzes, the individual grades in that category will be revealed.

In this example, the teacher can see that the scores of **Student1** in the quizzes are consistent with their scores in the non-quiz activities. Categorizing the activities made it easy to see the comparison.

Now, let's learn how to create grade categories.

Creating grade categories

Categories are created and items are moved into categories in the same window.

How to create a grade category

Follow these steps:

1. Select **Administration | Grades | Gradebook setup | Add category**:

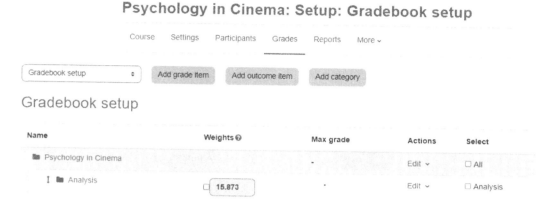

Figure 13.15 – View of the Gradebook setup area

2. At the bottom of the page, click on the **Add category** button. Then you can edit the category by clicking on the **Edit category** button. You can add the **Category name** and specify the method of calculating the grade (the kind of aggregation).

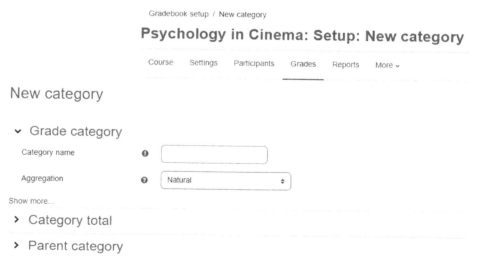

Figure 13.16 – View of the screen for setting up a new grade category

3. Fill out the page and save your changes.

How to assign an item to a grade category

Follow these steps:

1. Select **Settings | Graded | Grade category | New category**.

2. Select the item(s) that you want to assign to the category.

3. From the drop-down menu at the bottom of the page, select the category that you want to move the item(s) to:

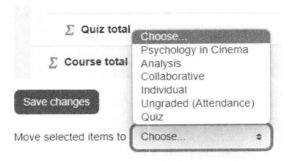

Figure 13.17 – Moving to a new grade category

4. Click the **Save changes** button.

The most important point here is to determine what kind of question you want to answer when you examine student grades and create categories that enable you to answer that question. You can categorize the grades around learning outcomes as well as topics or modules. For example, let's consider how students do on quizzes versus more interactive activities, such as workshops and forums. To answer that question, you can create a category just for quizzes, and then answer that question just by viewing the grades. Now, let's consider how students do on offline activities versus online activities. To answer that question, you can create online and offline grading categories.

> **Tip**
> Remember that these categories are not written in stone. If your needs change, you can always create and assign new grading categories as needed.

Summary

Moodle 4.0 has been updated with new functionalities to make it easier for students, teachers, and administrators to view performance and to see, at a glance, whether or not progress is being made, and where it might be necessary to intervene and motivate.

Whether in a classroom or online, managing a successful course requires two-way communication between the teacher and students. Constantly monitoring the course logs and grades gives you an early indication that a class may need a mid-course correction. You can use questions, surveys, and chats to discover specific problems and challenges that the students are facing. After bringing the course back on track, custom grading scales, extra credit, and curves can help you equalize the grades. When teaching online, make a habit of checking the logs and grades often.

You can use the reports and logs for administrative purposes as well, to comply with requirements to document when students first logged in and also their academic progress for student success. External accrediting institutions will often ask for course data. If you are a private training provider, you may wish to provide data to your students, who are paying customers.

Now that you have worked your way through this book, you have a basic toolkit for creating, delivering, and managing a successful online course in Moodle. However, you don't need to do it alone! When you need help with Moodle, there are many good resources.

Please keep in mind that this book is meant as a general introduction and focuses on instructional strategies that help you plan your course structure, resources, and activities to maximize your chances of success. Moodle is a robust learning management system with a complex structure, amazing flexibility and customizability, and reporting. It's easy to get overwhelmed. But, there's no need to worry. It is very easy to set up a basic shell or functional template, and you can add features as you go. The key is to keep your learning objectives and course goals in mind, and then to map out how you plan to teach by developing a template or storyboard.

First, the Moodle community at `http://moodle.org` is an excellent resource. The forums contain plenty of accumulated wisdom.

Second, you are welcome to visit my site at `http://www.beyondutopia.com` and click over to my blog at `http://www.elearningcorgi.com` for longer how-to articles about online learning. Leave comments and join the conversation. Also, feel free to contact me via LinkedIn at `https://www.linkedin.com/in/susannash/`.

Third, check out other Moodle books by Packt Publishing. They deal with specific topics in more detail, such as Moodle security, administration, and using Moodle in a corporate environment.

Thank you for taking a journey through Moodle with me. I look forward to seeing you online with the rest of the Moodle community.

Index

M

W

web pages
 composing, in HTML editor 125
 uploading, to Moodle 125, 126
wiki
 about 295
 collaborative projects, planning 298
 Default format setting 301, 302
 first-page name 300
 functionality booster 302
 using, for contributions and
    explanations of topic 296
 using, to create list of judging criteria
    for competition 296-298
wiki type and groups mode
 used, for determining wiki
    content editor 299
workshop
 about 305
 assessment phase 311, 328
 closed phase 329
 grading evaluation phase 311, 328
 need for 306, 307
 setup phase 311, 312
 submission phase 311, 326, 327
workshop strategies
 about 310
 peer assessment, of submissions 310
 timing, of submissions and
    assessments 310, 311

X

XAMPP Apache Friends packages
 reference link 25

Z

Zoom
 using, for synchronous online
    instruction 28

Other Books You May Enjoy

If you enjoyed this book, you may be interested in these other books by Packt:

Canvas LMS Course Design - Second Edition

Ryan John

ISBN: 978-1-80056-851-8

- Understand online learning as a powerful and unique tool for student growth
- Create, access, and personalize your user account and profile settings in Canvas
- Generate, upload, and import course content for students to engage with as participants in your courses
- Design and sequence the content of your course to present information and activities with clarity and simplicity
- Discover expert techniques for designing a curriculum and creating activities
- Explore Canvas features that meet your educational needs, such as online assessments and content delivery

Corporate Learning with Moodle Workplace

Alex Büchner

ISBN: 978-1-80020-534-5

- Understand the Moodle Workplace business model
- Support multiple business entities using multi-tenancy, organizations, positions, job assignments, and teams
- Explore best practices for organizing typical HR processes such as onboarding, compliance, and reporting
- Automate business workflows using dynamic rules and migrations
- Support blended and offline learning via seminar management and the Workplace app
- Incentivize skill development and learning through certificates, competencies, and badges
- Customize Moodle Workplace to reflect an organization's corporate identity
- Familiarize yourself with Moodle Workplace Web services

Packt is searching for authors like you

If you're interested in becoming an author for Packt, please visit authors. packtpub.com and apply today. We have worked with thousands of developers and tech professionals, just like you, to help them share their insight with the global tech community. You can make a general application, apply for a specific hot topic that we are recruiting an author for, or submit your own idea.

Hi!

I am Susan Smith Nash, author of *Moodle 4 E-Learning Course Development*. I really hope you enjoyed reading this book and found it useful for increasing your productivity and efficiency.

It would really help me (and other potential readers!) if you could leave a review on Amazon sharing your thoughts on this book.

Go to the link below or scan the QR code to leave your review:

https://packt.link/r/180107903X

Your review will help us to understand what's worked well in this book, and what could be improved upon for future editions, so it really is appreciated.

Best wishes,

Susan Smith Nash